Adam Smith's *The Theory of Moral Sentiments*

ALSO AVAILABLE FROM BLOOMSBURY

Hume's Natural Philosophy and Philosophy of Physical Science, Matias Slavov
The Bloomsbury Companion to Marx, ed. Andrew Pendakis, Imre Szeman, and Jeff Diamanti
The Tyranny of Opinion: Conformity and the Future of Liberalism, Russell Blackford

Adam Smith's *The Theory of Moral Sentiments*

A Critical Commentary

John McHugh

BLOOMSBURY ACADEMIC
LONDON • NEW YORK • OXFORD • NEW DELHI • SYDNEY

BLOOMSBURY ACADEMIC
Bloomsbury Publishing Plc
50 Bedford Square, London, WC1B 3DP, UK
1385 Broadway, New York, NY 10018, USA
29 Earlsfort Terrace, Dublin 2, Ireland

BLOOMSBURY, BLOOMSBURY ACADEMIC and the Diana logo are trademarks of Bloomsbury Publishing Plc

First published in Great Britain 2022

Cover design by Ben Anslow
Cover image: Charles I in three positions, 1635 (oil on canvas), Anthony van Dyck (1599-1641) / Flemish, (Royal Collection Trust © Her Majesty Queen Elizabeth II, 2021 / Bridgeman Images).

A catalogue record for this book is available from the British Library.

A catalog record for this book is available from the Library of Congress.

ISBN: HB: 978-1-3500-8857-3
ePDF: 978-1-3500-8856-6
eBook: 978-1-3500-8859-7

Typeset by Deanta Global Publishing Services, Chennai, India

For my parents, Ed and Mariane, and my brother, Eddie

Contents

Acknowledgments

The completion of this project has filled me with profound gratitude to the many people who helped make it possible. It would be arbitrary to limit these acknowledgments to those who made a direct impact on the actual writing of the book; this work also would not have been possible without, for example, the very close friend who long ago provided life-changing advice (Ed McCourt, who talked me into going to graduate school) or the very distant acquaintance who long ago provided work-changing advice (Eric Schliesser, who surely does not remember the brief but immensely impactful conversation I have in mind). However, I must restrict these acknowledgments in some such way, if only to prevent them from becoming longer than the book itself. Thus, the following list does not come close to covering all my debts.

Aaron Garrett, Charles Griswold, and Manfred Kuehn have guided and encouraged me from the moment I started working on Smith. Colleagues at Denison University—Sam Cowling, Barbara Fultner, Tony Lisska, Chris Lyons, Jonathan Maskit, Mark Moller, Ron Santoni, Kate Tull, Steve Vogel, Alexandra Bradner, Sergio Gallegos, Christa Johnson, John Ramsey, Amy Shuster, and Evan Woods—have provided the best possible atmosphere to do such work. Students at Denison have inspired and shaped much of my thinking; directed studies with Tristan Jefferies and Ryan Seibert were especially impactful. Colleagues and students at Colby College deserve recognition for the same reasons, even though I was only there for a short time. (Jim Behuniak, Dan Cohen, Jill Gordon, Lydia Moland, and Keith Peterson were all wonderfully supportive.) Several colleagues in the broader academic world have also been extremely helpful in a variety of ways; Ryan Hanley and Gordon Graham stand out for being particularly so.

Many organizations and institutions deserve recognition here. The book has benefited immensely from my attendance at conferences hosted by the American Philosophical Association, the American Political Science Association, the American Society for the Eighteenth Century Studies, the Canadian Philosophical Association, the Center for the Study of Scottish Philosophy, the Chicago Center for Teaching, the Hume Society, the International Adam Smith Society, the Institute for the Study of Scottish Philosophy, the Liberty Fund, the Ohio Philosophical Association, SUNY-Buffalo, and the Rousseau Association. The book has also benefited immensely from talks I have given at Kenyon College and Denison University. Additionally, I owe thanks to publishers of the following journals for granting permission to reuse here some previously printed material: the *British Journal for the History of Philosophy*, the *Journal of the History of Philosophy*, and *The Journal of Scottish Philosophy*. For the same reason, I also owe thanks to Routledge and the Edinburgh University Press. Oxford University Press deserves thanks for granting permission via PLS Clear to quote extensively from its 1976 edition of Adam Smith's *The Theory of Moral Sentiments*, which was edited by D. D. Raphael and A. L. Macfie and reprinted in 1982 for a Liberty Fund edition that I employ. Denison University deserves thanks for providing the professional development funds that were used for securing this permission.

Bloomsbury Press has been wonderful to work with. Liza Thompson, Lucy Russell, Mohammed Raffi and the production and design staff were all incredibly accommodating and helpful. Thanks also to the countless other people at Bloomsbury who were essential for seeing the book to the finish line and beyond. Craig Smith provided insightful and useful comments on an earlier version of the manuscript. Aaron Skubby deserves special thanks for his work on the index.

Finally, I owe thanks to my spouse, Melissa Feldner, the sine qua non of my whole life, of which this book is only a part.

Abbreviations

DP David Hume's "A Dissertation on the Passions"

EHU David Hume's *An Enquiry Concerning the Human Understanding*

EPM David Hume's *An Enquiry Concerning the Principles of Morals*

ES Adam Smith's "Of the External Senses"

HA Adam Smith's "History of Astronomy"

LJ Adam Smith's *Lectures on Jurisprudence*

LRBL Adam Smith's *Lectures on Rhetoric and Belles Lettres*

T David Hume's *A Treatise of Human Nature*

TMS Adam Smith's *The Theory of Moral Sentiments*

WN Adam Smith's *An Inquiry into the Nature and Causes of the Wealth of Nations*

1

Introduction

Adam Smith was born in 1723 to a well-off but not wealthy family in Kirkcaldy, a small port town just outside Edinburgh, Scotland. His father died before he was born, but his mother, Margaret (Douglas) Smith, remained in his life until six years before his own death. He eventually attended the University of Glasgow, where he studied under Francis Hutcheson, a central figure in what is now referred to as the "Scottish Enlightenment" and a formative influence on Smith and many other students. After Glasgow, Smith spent six years studying at Balliol College, Oxford. During this period, he began reading the work of David Hume, another formative influence who eventually became one of Smith's closest friends. Although a common next step for recipients of the fellowship that funded Smith's Oxford study was ordination in the Anglican church, Smith returned to Scotland a layman.[1] He quickly made a name for himself by giving a series of public lecture courses in Edinburgh on rhetoric and jurisprudence. The success of these lectures led to a position on the faculty of the University of Glasgow, where he remained from 1751 to 1763. While teaching at Glasgow, he developed his moral philosophy lectures into *The Theory of Moral Sentiments* (hereafter, TMS), which was published in 1759 to immediate acclaim. He left Glasgow to tutor the Duke of Buccleuch, a job which proved to be not only financially but also personally and philosophically lucrative. The Duke grew into another close friend,[2] and a few years travelling Europe with him gave Smith the opportunity to compare notes and debate with the French *économistes*; the result was *An Inquiry into the Nature and Causes of the Wealth of Nations* (hereafter, WN), which came out ten years after the Buccleuch period, in 1776. From 1778 to the end of his life in 1790, Smith held a position as Commissioner of Customs in Edinburgh.[3]

By all accounts, Smith was a unique person. Several comments and anecdotes from contemporaries portray him as an aloof, sometimes socially awkward intellectual, who "even in company . . . was apt to be ingrossed in his studies," often to the point of apparently muttering to himself.[4] Yet we also know that he was anything but useless in practical capacities. On the contrary, he was a generally competent, diligent person who thrived when he felt productive; thus, he described his time as a faculty member at the University of Glasgow, during which he composed the TMS and excelled in several administrative roles,[5] "as by far the most useful, and, therefore, as by far the happiest and most honourable period of my life" (Letter 274).[6] We also know that he fulfilled his duties in the Customs office admirably.[7] Moreover, he not only cultivated several deep friendships but also, while at Glasgow, became "something of a cult figure, a professor whose portrait bust could be bought by students at local bookshops."[8] While it is not impossible to imagine such a combination of traits in one personality, it is certainly difficult, if only because such a combination is rare.

Smith seemed to have thought of his philosophical work as constituting one massive project that Nicholas Philipson has argued is akin to Hume's "science of man."[9] The TMS offers a general theory of human sociability and morality (which, as we shall see, contains both descriptive and normative elements). When this theory gets to the topic of justice, however, Smith's project branches off into a discussion of law, which he divides into two subjects. The first provides a historical and normative account of "justice" proper, or "the general principles of law and government." The second provides a historical and normative account of "police, revenue, and arms, and whatever else is the object of the law" (VII.iv.37[10]).[11] The second project became the WN, and while the first project was never completed to Smith's satisfaction, some recently discovered student notes from his lectures give us some indication of what it would have looked like.[12]

In addition to these interests in the practical side of human life, Smith also had interests in the aesthetic and intellectual sides of human life.[13] Thus, he envisioned writing "a sort of Philosophical History of all the different branches of Literature, of Philosophy, Poetry and Eloquence" (Letter 248). He did not complete this project either, but we can catch glimpses of it both in more student notes on his lectures[14] and in a series of short essays on language, science, metaphysics, and perception.[15]

So despite his larger intellectual ambition, Smith's public philosophical reputation was and remains built upon the TMS and the WN. The latter went through five editions in Smith's lifetime. It obviously remains influential to this day. The former went through six editions in Smith's lifetime, and two of these include substantive revisions. The question of its influence today is not as open as it used to be. It has become so commonplace to hear or read comments about how Smith's moral theory is ignored by contemporary philosophers that these comments cannot but undercut themselves. Most people interested in such things are at this point well aware that the author of the *Wealth of Nations* also wrote an interesting and important book called *The Theory of Moral Sentiments*. Accordingly, there has been much excellent recent scholarship on the TMS, including several books. Most of these books, however, differ fundamentally from the present one. There have been books situating the TMS in the history of Western philosophy,[16] books situating the TMS in still-live but historically rooted debates,[17] books addressing the TMS' relationship either to another particular aspect of Smith's thought[18] or to his overall study of human life,[19] and books exploring the relationship between the TMS and the work of another philosopher.[20] There has even been a book commenting on the general philosophy of life that Smith articulates mainly in the TMS.[21] However, to my knowledge there has not been a recent book that simply treats the TMS as classic work of philosophy containing arguments to be explicated, interpreted, and assessed. The present book does just that.[22]

More specifically, the present book attempts to develop and reconstruct lines of thought that are not necessarily straightforward, reveal and resolve interpretive puzzles, and evaluate arguments and views when fruitful, all with an eye to being of use to newcomers and of interest to familiars.[23] In doing so, the book necessarily pays some attention to Smith's intellectual context. Since the TMS frequently demonstrates the influence of and even explicitly refers to other philosophers, there is no way to study it without also studying, at least to some extent, these philosophers. Furthermore, independently of the particular need to explain the TMS' own references to its context, there is a general one to situate *all* philosophical investigations in the debates that constitute their background. Thus, in discussing Smith's moral theory, the book will also discuss the work of other philosophers who are especially important to understanding it, especially Hume. And while the book is focused on the TMS, it will also refer, when helpful or important, to some of Smith's other writings.

At this point, some readers might legitimately demand a list of the principles I employ in balancing historical and contextual with ahistorical and acontextual interpretation and commentary. Or they might legitimately demand at least a general account of my overall methodology. These readers will be disappointed. I offer no such list or account because the task of providing them is itself a serious philosophical undertaking, one in which I am not presently engaged. Since this is neither a book on hermeneutics in general nor a book on the application of a particular kind of hermeneutics to Smith,[24] anything I say further about how I approach the relevant texts will necessarily amount to superficial handwaving. The most I will do in this regard is reiterate, all-too-vaguely, that I approach the texts as a philosopher. I leave it to others to determine what this means. Sometimes it's best just to think about the thing and leave thinking about what we are doing when we think about the thing for another occasion (especially when the thing in question is already itself to some extent "meta," as we shall soon see is the case here).

The book's treatment of the TMS is not structured exactly as the TMS itself is. Instead, the book starts with the last part of the TMS, in which Smith provides an overview of the major "systems of moral philosophy" that preceded his own. There are at least three good reasons for starting here. The first follows directly from the just-made comments about philosophical context. Even though the TMS engages with many other philosophers, Smith opens it abruptly, without providing a contextualizing introduction. Thus, we can benefit from treating TMS VII as a missing preface. This is especially true for readers approaching it without a feel for Smith's intellectual climate; these readers are at risk of being lost by the book, however clear its prose might be.[25] The second and a closely related reason for beginning with TMS VII follows from the fact that it not only provides context but does so in Smith's own voice. Thus, we can learn from it both something about the TMS' place in the history of Western moral philosophy and something about how Smith himself understands its place in the history of Western moral philosophy. In seeing what Smith himself thinks about the relationship between his own moral theory and those of his predecessors, we understand more fully what motivates his work and thus understand more fully the work itself.[26]

The third reason for beginning with TMS VII is that Smith explicitly organizes it in an especially helpful way. Just as the TMS' abrupt beginning fails to provide contemporary readers with an adequate sense of its context, it also fails to provide contemporary readers with an adequate sense of its content. Contrary to contemporary practice, Smith doesn't really provide a statement of purpose, let alone a plan of attack. He just dives right in. Thus, we should pay careful attention when he introduces TMS VII by distinguishing between two questions that must be considered by any moral theory. The first question is about "the tone of temper, the tenour of conduct, which constitutes the excellent and praise-worthy character" (VII.i.2). In Smith's language, this is a question about the "nature of virtue" (VII.iii.intro.1). The second question is about the "power or faculty in the mind" that leads us to prefer "one tenour of conduct to another" that "denominates the one right and the other wrong" (VII.i.2). In Smith's language, this is a question about the "principle of approbation" (VII.iii.intro.1). We can also refer to it as a question about the psychological foundation of moral judgment. This is a question about how we make moral distinctions. What part of ourselves do we ultimately employ when we conclude that some feelings and conduct are morally good, while other feelings and conduct are morally bad?

Smith's way of dividing up the jobs of the moral philosopher is not all that different from our own. Contemporary philosophers tend to divide the activity of theorizing about morality into the categories of normative ethics and metaethics.[27] Normative ethics considers how we should live; thus, it has practical implications. Metaethics, as its name suggests, deals with morality at a higher level of abstraction. The metaethicist does not ask ethical questions so much as questions about the entire enterprise of asking, answering, and acting upon the answers to ethical questions. The metaethicist wants to understand what we are doing and what is happening when we engage in this enterprise. Since metaethics is not concerned with how we should live, it is a purely theoretical, non-normative subject with no practical implications. Smith's distinction between moral theory's two main questions draws a similar line between the normative/practical and the non-normative/nonpractical. He points out that while our answer to the nature of virtue question "necessarily has some influence upon our notions of right and wrong in many particular cases," the psychological foundation of moral judgment question "is a mere matter of philosophical curiosity," devoid of any practical import, at least in "particular cases" (VII.iii.intro.3). Of course, there remain differences of other kinds between the two distinctions, most of which having to do with breadth. Smith appears to frame normative moral questions narrowly in terms of virtue, which is not a move that all present-day practitioners of normative moral theory would make. And the supposedly non-normative curiosity about moral judgment that Smith expresses here might be, in one sense, narrower, while, in another sense, broader than the present-day metaethicist's—narrower in that present-day metaethicists are interested in more than just moral judgment and broader in that Smith's interest in moral judgment is potentially more empirically focused than that of the present-day metaethicist.[28] We return to these differences later in the book.[29] Despite them, the parallel between Smith's and our most basic ways of dividing up the field of moral philosophy is close enough to be useful for smoothing our initial approach to his work.

Since Smith's distinction provides us with the organizing framework absent from the outset of the TMS, I use it to structure this book. I begin with the psychological foundation of moral judgment question. Chapter 2 unfolds Smith's discussion of answers that other philosophers have provided to this question, while Chapter 3 deals with his own. Chapters 5 and 6 follow this same pattern with respect to the nature of virtue question. In dealing with the way Smith builds an account of *good* moral judgment upon the psychological foundations he identifies in answering the first question, Chapter 4 sits at the intersection of it and the second one. The subject matter of the chapter is non-normative in that it concerns Smith's explanation of how we arrive at our criteria for good moral judgment; however, the subject matter of the chapter is also normative in that it concerns moral judgment that Smith believes is, well, good. Chapter 7 deals with two questions that emerge for us from consideration of Smith's two main ones: (a) how should we situate Smith's work in some of the contemporary metaethical debates in which, as mentioned earlier, he does not directly engage? and (b) why does Smith think we should judge and act based on what he and, according to him, we think of as good moral judgment? Chapter 8 closes the book with some brief, broad reflections upon the whole core of Smith's moral theory but especially his call to abide by this kind of judgment.

2

Smith's Survey of Answers to the Psychological Foundation of Moral Judgment Question

Smith's psychological foundation of moral judgment question is about

> the power or faculty of the mind which renders certain characters agreeable or disagreeable, makes us prefer one tenour of conduct to another, denominate the one right and the other wrong, and consider the one as the object of approbation, honour, and reward; the other as that of blame, censure, and punishment. (VII.intro.1)

He considers three different kinds of answers. According to some philosophers—Smith mentions Thomas Hobbes and "his followers" Samuel Pufendorf and Bernard Mandeville (VII.iii.1.1)—we make moral distinctions "from self-love only" (VII.iii.intro.2). According to other philosophers—Smith mentions Ralph Cudworth (VII.iii.2.4)—we make moral distinctions via "reason, the same faculty by which we distinguish between truth and falsehood" (VII.iii.intro.2). And according to a third group of philosophers—Smith mentions himself and Francis Hutcheson (VII.iii.3.4) and implicitly refers to David Hume (VII.iii.3.17)—we make moral distinctions via "immediate sentiment and feeling" (VII.iii.intro.2).

This chapter investigates Smith's critical discussion of these various theories. But first, two preliminary observations are in order. One has to do with the difference in organization between Smith's critical discussion and this chapter's treatment thereof. Smith follows a chronological order rather than a purely conceptual one; the main egoists, rationalists, and sentimentalists he discusses wrote in the order in which he discusses them. However, we should note that while chronological, Smith's discussion is not merely chronological. Instead, he always explains the shift from one view to the next in dialectical terms, so as to capture what motivated the later philosophers to critique the earlier ones. Thus, in keeping with the text's origin in Smith's lecture notes, this stretch reads how a good history of philosophy course might go. However, our purposes in examining Smith's mini history of philosophy are not the same as Smith's were in presenting it. Our primary concern is to see how Smith's own view fits conceptually into a taxonomy of views he saw as on the table; thus, while issues of influence and chronology matter to us (and will be addressed when appropriate throughout the book), they are less important to us than is philosophical clarity about Smith's sentiment-based answer to the psychological foundation of moral judgment question. So with an eye to pursuing this goal with minimal distraction from some background issues (which are important in their own right, though not worth pressing here), I adopt an alternative order. Since self-love is a sentiment, I arrange Smith's discussion in terms of a distinction between rationalism, which I handle first, and two forms of sentimentalism, one egoistic and the other not, which I handle second and third.[1]

The other preliminary observation has to do with the relatively limited nature of Smith's history of answers to the psychological foundation of moral judgment question. While the overview Smith provides of answers to the other main question of moral philosophy—that of the nature of virtue—goes back to the ancient Greeks, his overview of answers to this one only goes back a little more than a century before he himself was writing. His description of this recently proceeding period in history as "a time when the abstract science of human nature was but in its infancy" provides something of an explanation as to why (VII.iii.2.5). Smith seems to have taken engagement with the psychological foundation of moral judgment question to be part of new way of studying human beings. Thus, although we shall see that Smith's overall moral theory is in conversation with the entire history of Western philosophy, we should not lose sight of the fact that he takes at least part of what he is doing to be rather cutting edge.[2]

The first of these two features of this section of the TMS invites important questions about the comprehensiveness and accuracy of Smith's treatment of the history of Western philosophy. The second invites important questions about what Smith took to be the distinctive nature of this new "abstract science." Although we shall at least touch upon these issues throughout, grappling thoroughly with them is beyond the scope of the present chapter.[3] As implied by the first chapter's rationale for the overall structure of the book, its more limited goal is to use Smith's historical-philosophical story to set up our investigation into his own answer to the psychological foundation of moral judgment question. Hopefully, by the end of this chapter, we will understand why he defends a theory of moral sentiments in general, as well as part of why his particular theory of moral sentiments takes the form it does. We will also use Smith's story to expose some of his most foundational methodological and doctrinal commitments, as well as some of the questions with which his theory must eventually deal, both broad—such as that of the potential intersection between the psychological source of moral distinctions and the metaphysical status of morality—and narrow—such as that of whether his critique of Hutcheson's sentimentalism is consistent with his own positive view. Thus, the chapter will provide several previews and make several promises regarding what is to come.

Structurally, the chapter follows the aforementioned replacement of the order of Smith's text with one more conducive to our purposes; while he goes egoist-rationalist-sentimentalist, I go rationalist-sentimentalist 1 (egoist)-sentimentalist 2 (non-egoist). In each section, I first exposit Smith's thoughts and then react to them where fit.

Section 1: Rationalist Theories

According to Smith, the "systems which make reason the principle of approbation" arose in response to the perception that Hobbes made "the laws of the civil magistrate" into "the sole ultimate standards of what was just and unjust, of what was right and wrong." On Smith's telling, Hobbes arrives at this conclusion via the following chain of reasoning. The first claim is that "antecedent to the institution of civil government there could be no safe or peaceable society." The second is that the "existence of civil government depends upon the obedience that is paid to the supreme magistrate." From these claims, Hobbes concludes that "self-preservation," which requires "safe" and "peaceable" society, "ought to teach [us] to applaud upon all occasions obedience to the civil magistrate, and to blame all disobedience and rebellion." Thus, "the *very ideas* of laudable and blamable" end up being "the same with those of obedience and disobedience" to the government (VIII.iii.2.1; emphasis added).

Whether it is considered as an interpretation of Hobbes or on its own terms, there are gaps in this chain. One has to do with the assumption that self-preservation demands *absolute* obedience to the magistrate. Despite his justified reputation for defending absolutism, even Hobbes seemed to have thought that there can be a few instances in which disobedience is legitimate, namely those in which we have good reason to believe that the civil magistrate is endangering or not protecting us.[4] Another gap lies in the jump from praising obedience and blaming disobedience to *defining* both the praiseworthy and the blameworthy in terms of obedience and disobedience. A third lies in the undiscussed relationship between political and moral obligation; the argument runs them together without explanation.

We can ignore these gaps, however, because Smith is most interested in the reaction that rationalists like Cudworth had to the ultimate "supposition" behind the chain of reasoning that "there was no natural distinction between right and wrong, that these were mutable and changeable." Smith seems sympathetic to Hobbes's "avowed intention" of subjecting "the consciences of men immediately to the civil" instead of the "ecclesiastical powers, whose turbulence and ambition" his experience taught him "to regard as the principal source of disorders of society" (VII.iii.2.2). But Smith thinks the rationalists were correct to reject any denial of a natural distinction between right and wrong. The rationalists, especially Cudworth, responded by pointing out that it makes sense to ask about the moral status of the magistrate's laws themselves. If it is morally "indifferent" whether we obey these laws, then the laws cannot be a source of moral distinctions; morally neutral laws cannot give rise to laws with moral content. And if it is morally right (or wrong, for that matter) to obey these laws, then there must be "antecedent notions or ideas of right and wrong" that we can apply to them.[5] Thus, either way, there must be a "natural distinction between right and wrong" that "antecedent to all law or positive institution, the mind [is] naturally endowed with a faculty" of recognizing. This faculty, Cudworth concluded, is "reason, which pointed out the difference between right and wrong, in the same manner in which it did that between truth and falsehood" (VII.iii.2.3–5).

Smith's attitude toward the Cudworthian argument he presents is multifaceted. As I just mentioned, he agrees with its conclusion that moral distinctions are pre-legal and thus, in some sense, natural. He also agrees that reason plays an important role in "regulat[ing] the greater part of our moral judgments," as well as "our actions" (VII.iii.2.6). Yet he disagrees with the view that this role is foundational or "original" (VII.iii.2.5). For Smith, moral distinctions ultimately cannot "arise from reason"; rather, they must be "founded upon immediate sense and feeling" (VII.iii.2.9). How does Smith argue for this view? And what secondary role does he think reason plays in moral judgment and action?

Since Smith believes that "Dr Hutcheson" already established that moral distinctions must be "founded upon immediate sense and feeling," his own arguments for this claim are quick and derivative of Hutcheson's (VII.iii. 2.9).[6] Smith's first argument starts with the observation that approval and disapproval respectively involve the "perceptions" that "one tenor of conduct . . . pleases in a certain manner," while "another . . . displeases." But, Smith claims, "nothing can be agreeable or disagreeable for its own sake, which is not rendered such by immediate sense and feeling." Reason, when understood as the process by which we perceive "the difference . . . between truth and falsehood," can only "render" an object "agreeable or disagreeable" by showing that it is "the means of obtaining some other" object that "immediate sense and feeling" renders intrinsically pleasing (VII.iii.2.7). In other words, moral evaluation fundamentally involves a positively or negatively valenced affective response, but reasoning does not; thus, reason cannot be the psychological foundation of moral judgment.

Smith's second argument focuses on the relationship between moral evaluation and motivation. He observes that virtue is "desirable for its own sake" and vice an "object of aversion" for its own sake. This is the case, Smith implies, because the perception of virtue is pleasing and the perception of vice is painful; pleasure and pain, he writes, are "the great objects of desire and aversion." But pleasure and pain are "distinguished not by reason but by immediate sense and feeling." Thus, we cannot distinguish virtue and vice by reason alone. In other words, the perception of virtuousness or viciousness has an immediate motivational impact that the perception of truth and falsity cannot provide on its own. Again, we see Smith assign a purely instrumental role to reason. Reason can motivate action indirectly, by telling us what will provide pleasure or pain, but it can only do so on the basis of prior reports from "immediate sense and feeling" about what pleases and pains in the first place (VII.iii.2.8).

The positive but instrumental roles that Smith ascribes to reasoning in moral evaluation and action are easy to sniff out. He does not say so explicitly here, but his view clearly implies that reason can assist our sentiment-based moral faculties render verdicts by providing them with relevant factual information. As he does explicitly tell us here, reason can also help us form "general maxims of morality" via "induction" from "particular cases." The division of labor in this process is clear: "immediate sense and feeling" point out the distinction between virtue and vice in particular cases, and reason generates rules based on commonalities between these cases. These rules can then help us "regulate" our moral judgments and actions thereupon, despite the "many variations of immediate sentiment and feeling, which the different states of health and humour are capable of altering so essentially" (VII.iii.2.6). Smith's expression of this worry implies that his own full-blown account of moral judgment will privilege the experience of a certain kind of feeling, one from which these mood-based alterations deviate. The nature of this experience is not obvious (Chapters 3 and 4 will deal with this issue), but it is obvious that in helping us maintain evaluative and motivational stability in the face of our flightiness, reason is not exerting its own evaluative and motivational force but maintaining that of an affect, presumably also at the demand of an affect.[7]

Smith's attack on rationalism and presentation of his own view of reason's positive role in moral evaluation and motivation invites reflection on at least four different issues. First, in connecting the motivational force of moral evaluation to pleasure and pain, is Smith committing himself to a hedonistic theory of moral motivation, if not motivation in general? The evidence we have seen so far points in opposite directions. The claim that "pleasure and pain are the great objects of desire and aversion" suggests that he is a motivational hedonist in general. But the claim that virtue is "desirable for its own sake"—and thus not for the sake of pleasure—suggests otherwise. To grapple with this seemingly conflicting evidence, we must first get a handle on how Smith thinks moral evaluation works. Thus, I postpone the task for after I have finished laying out Smith's account of the foundation of moral judgment in Chapter 3; I turn to it in Section 1 of Chapter 4.

For a similar reason, I put off dealing with the second issue until we get to Section 4 of Chapter 4. Since Smith does not think that reasoning can generate evaluation or motivation on its own, he owes us more explanation of how the "general maxims of morality" to which it gives rise can "regulate" our evaluations and actions. Further complicating the picture is the fact in at least one other passage in the TMS, he explicitly appeals to the motivational power of reason to explain the motivational power of moral evaluation. Again, such puzzles can only be solved after we are comfortable with certain details of Smith's overall theory of moral evaluation.

Third is the question of whether Smith believes that affects always *accompany* moral evaluations or that affects *constitute* moral evaluations. At first glance, this question is easily translatable into contemporary philosophical parlance as one about whether Smith is a "cognitivist"—i.e., someone who believes that moral judgments report facts and thus are capable of being true or false—who just so happens to believe that affects are crucial for moral evaluation or a "non-cognitivist"—i.e., someone who believes that moral judgments express affects and thus do not report facts and stand capable of being true or false. However, before we make such a translation, we must determine whether Smith believes that the affects in question are mere feelings or themselves involve judgments capable of being true or false. If the latter is true, then Smith could believe that affects constitute moral judgments and still be a kind of cognitivist. Smith generally does not make the fine-grained distinctions necessary to address this line of questioning, but after getting more of his own views on the table, we will, in Section 1 of Chapter 7, try to do this work for him.

The fourth issue has as much to do with something Smith does not say as it does with interpreting something he does. One might expect Smith's discussion of rationalism to address the question of what is today called "moral realism." In contemporary philosophy, this phrase is often used to pick out the position that specifically moral facts exist in the world, independent from the human mind. This view is often associated with the kind of moral rationalism Smith discusses. Historical connections aside, one can see why.[8] The rationalists in Smith's sights believe that there is a "natural distinction between right and wrong" (VII.iii.2.2) that we know by the same faculty that points out the difference between "truth and falsehood" (VI.iii.2.5). It is but a short step from here to the view that the truths this faculty allows us to perceive are about moral facts. But if this is what the rationalists in Smith's sights believe, then to what does he commit himself when he rejects their claim about the faculty of moral evaluation but accepts their claim about the "natural distinction between right and wrong" (VII.iii.2.2), a distinction he elsewhere suggestively labels a "real and essential" one (VII.ii.4.1)? One possibility is that Smith is a moral realist who believes that "immediate sense and affection" rather than reason inform us about moral facts. Another possibility, however, is that Smith means by "natural" and "real and essential" something different from both what the early modern moral rationalist[9] and the contemporary moral realist means" to "some contemporary moral realists mean. In both the present and the just-mentioned context, Smith contrasts the position of which he approves with one that makes moral distinctions artificial, in the sense of depending "upon the mere arbitrary will of the civil magistrate" (VII.iii.2.2) or some "cheat and imposition upon mankind" (VII.ii.4.7). Smith could still maintain this anti-artificiality commitment if he believed that, for example, moral judgments are the product of our natural reactions to real things in the world but do not necessarily track moral properties that exist independently from these reactions; thus, it is possible that Smith holds a view like this or some other one that fits with his anti-artificiality.[10] Since we cannot settle these matters solely on the basis of the text at which we've looked so far, the safest interpretive option is to treat Smith's discussion of rationalism as concerned solely with the fundamental psychological sources of moral judgment, not moral metaphysics. Smith's discussion only concerns itself with the latter to the extent that he expresses agreement with the view that moral distinctions are not made up. What, metaphysically, grounds these non-artificial distinctions is a question that cannot be fully addressed without incorporating more of Smith's moral philosophy. As with the previous issue, we will take a crack at this one in Section 1 of Chapter 7.

Section 2: Self-Love Theories

If we agree that the psychological foundation of moral judgment is not reason but "immediate sense and feeling," our next job is to identify the relevant "sense" and/or "feeling." One possibility is the feeling of concern we have for ourselves, which Smith calls "self-love." Although Smith observes that "those who account for the principle of approbation from self-love, do not all account for it in the same manner," he is comfortable treating the account defended by "Mr. Hobbes and many of his followers" as an archetype. His immediate audience would have been comfortable with this decision too, as it was standard then to treat Hobbes as the main representative of this kind of view or as the guiding light for subsequent thinkers who held something like it (as mentioned earlier, Smith lists Pufendorf and Mandeville as examples).[11] Of course, one could ask whether this practice, both in general and as undertaken here by Smith, involved accurate or fair readings of Hobbes and "his followers," such is the case with all "standard" practices in the history of philosophy. But for our purposes, we can bracket these sorts of worries and treat Smith's discussion of the "self-love" answer to the psychological foundation of moral judgment question as one about a view that was in the air as a possible alternative to rationalism, regardless of who held it.[12] According to this answer, we approve of virtue and disapprove of vice because we realize that one is "the great support" and the other is "the great disturber of human society." However, since we care about "human society" in the first place not out of "any natural love" we feel for humanity but out of our realization that the "assistance of others" is necessary for our own "ease or safety," these moral judgments are ultimately rooted in our concern for ourselves or, in Smith's language, "self-love" (VII.iii.1.1).[13]

So on this view, whenever we make moral judgments, we are thinking about how the people we are judging impact us, either directly or indirectly, through their impact on our "society." But what about our moral reactions to people who are far away or long dead (or fictional, for that matter)? It seems implausible that these reactions rest upon thoughts about how our interests are impacted, even if only indirectly. According to Smith, the egoist explains these reactions by invoking thoughts about what "might have redounded to us" or what "might still redound to us, if in our own times should we meet with characters of the same kind" as the people we judge (VII.iii.1.3). In other words, the egoist claims that we make moral judgments in such cases by imagining how our interests *would be* impacted if we were in close enough proximity to the person we are judging.

Smith makes two arguments against the egoistic account of moral evaluation. The first is that it misrepresents the perspective from which moral judgment takes place. Smith concedes that egoist philosophers are correct to emphasize the benefits of social living and the importance of morality thereto. But they are incorrect, he argues, to conclude that moral appraisal requires consciously grasping the social utility of virtue and disutility of vice. He claims that we only notice "the tendency of virtue to promote, and of vice to disturb the order of society, when we consider it coolly and philosophically . . . in a certain abstract and philosophical light." Sure, from *that* perspective society "appears like a great, an immense machine, whose regular and harmonious movements" are rendered "more smooth and easy" by virtue and are "[obstructed]" by vice. But we can make moral judgments without ever adopting this bird's-eye, "political" perspective that reveals how society works. Thus, this point of "view . . . cannot possibly be the ground of the approbation and disapprobation" we feel toward virtue and vice, regardless of whether one thinks it triggers self-love or some other sentiment (VII.iii.1.2). (As we shall see in Section 5 of the next chapter, Smith also levels this kind of objection against Hume, whose answer to the psychological foundation of moral judgment question focuses upon utility but is not egoistic.)

Egoists could respond to this critique by downplaying the level of abstract reflection their account requires of moral judges. They would only need to provide a plausible explanation of how social and psychological forces render unreflectively habitual the extension of our evaluations from cases that do directly involve our self-interest to cases that do not. (As we shall also see in Section 5 of the next chapter, Hume could—and perhaps does—tell a story like this too.) But instead of trying to reconstruct this hypothetical exchange, let's consider what Smith's critique reveals about his own overall thought. Smith implies here—and, as we shall see throughout the book, in several other places—that one should theorize about morality from within a perspective that is as immanent as possible to moral life. He thinks that it is a major mistake to confuse the theoretical, reflective perspective of the philosopher with the practical, first-order perspective that the philosopher is trying to explain. In thus limiting the extent to which we can do moral philosophy from outside moral life, Smith might just be making an obvious point about the conditions for accurate observation and depiction of moral life as lived. But insofar as Smith seems to be drawing a line between the perspective of the philosopher and the perspective of the everyday moral judge and agent, he might be doing something more interesting,[14] if not problematic. Consider what happens when we apply this point to normative matters. Smith might, for example, be introducing restrictions on our ability to engage in fundamental critique of our own ideologies and practices.[15] We will return to such issues in Sections 2 and 6 of Chapter 4.

Smith's next attack on the egoistic account of moral evaluation focuses on its egoism. As we saw earlier, the egoist tries to explain our evaluations of agents who do not even indirectly impact our interests by invoking our ability to imagine "what we might gain or suffer if we were to act in society with such associates"; thus, we approve of characters that we think would benefit us and disapprove of characters that we think would harm us. Here we see Smith pressure this explanation's assumption that our evaluations *must* bottom out in self-love. He implies that a better explanation of these evaluations will involve sincerely unselfish concern for beneficiaries and victims. More specifically, he claims that the egoist is actually "groping" and "indistinctly pointing at" the phenomenon of "indirect sympathy which we feel with the gratitude or resentment of those who received the benefit or suffered the damage resulting from such opposite characters" (VII.iii.1.4). This sympathy—we'll see why he thinks it must be "indirect" in Section 5 of the next chapter—"cannot, in any sense, be regarded as a selfish principle," for "the imaginary change [it involves] is not supposed to happen to me in my own person and character, but in that of the person with whom I sympathize." Such an act cannot give rise to a "selfish passion" because it is not an act of imagining how one would feel in another person's circumstances but an act of imagining how these circumstances do feel for that other person; this is why, Smith claims, "a man may sympathize with a woman in child-bed; though it is impossible that he should conceive himself as suffering her pains in his own proper person and character." Thus, Smith concludes, a "confused misapprehension of the system of sympathy" is the ultimate source of egoistic "account of human nature . . . which has made so much noise in the world" (VII.iii.1.4).

The fact that Smith not only shades toward the past tense here—although, to say something "has made" noise is ambiguous as to whether one thinks it continues to do so—but also does not bother to argue at all against the egoist assumption that sincerely unselfish concern for others is not a real thing suggests that he takes the reality issue to be settled.[16] The question for him is not whether we are genuinely social but what psychological mechanisms are involved in our genuine sociality. As the passage just discussed hints, he believes the most central mechanism is what he calls "sympathy," which, as the next section reveals, is also his own answer to the psychological foundation of moral judgment question.

Section 3: Sentimentalist Theories

We have seen Smith argue that the psychological foundation of moral judgment is not reason but "immediate sense and feeling" or, in the language of the section to which we are about to turn, "sentiment." We have also seen Smith argue that "self-love" cannot be the psychological foundation of moral judgment; our reconstruction of the relationship between these positions has interpreted this argument as showing that self-love cannot be the relevant "sentiment." Now we must consider some other candidates. Smith observes that sentiment-based answers to the psychological foundation of moral judgment question "may be divided into two different classes" (VI.iii.3.1). The first class contains within it two varieties of views. One view grounds moral evaluation in a "particular power of perception," called a "moral sense," that gives rise to "sentiment of a peculiar nature distinct from every other" when we observe "certain actions and affections" (VII.iii.3.2). The other, similar view drops the "power of perception that is . . . analogous to the external senses" but keeps the "peculiar sentiment which answers [the] one particular purpose" of moral evaluation and "no other" (VII.iii.3.11). Smith uses Hutcheson as an example of a defender of the first variation in this class; it is unclear if Smith thinks of the second variation as a possible interpretation of Hutcheson's view or as possible response on Hutcheson's behalf to worries about his view.[17]

Defenders of views in the second class see "no occasion for supposing any new power of perception" or, presumably, new sentiment for explaining moral evaluation. Appealing to the "strictest oeconomy" with which "Nature acts," they explain moral evaluation by appealing to "sympathy, a power which has always been taken notice of, and with which the mind is manifestly endowed" (VI.iii.3.3). Smith's own view is of this kind, as is, he implies, Hume's.

Before we get to Smith's discussion of these options, I would like to make three sets of comments about the distinctions he makes between them. First, one might be surprised to see Smith classify the moral sense view alongside what we could call the "special moral sentiment" view and the sympathy view as "systems which make sentiment the principle of approbation" (VI.iii.4). Senses are not sentiments; in fact, as we shall see in more detail in Section 1 of the next chapter, sympathy, as understood by Smith, is as much a psychological process as it is a resulting sentiment. However, we can make some headway in understanding why Smith lumps these mechanisms together under the same general heading by distinguishing them both from reasoning. As we saw earlier, Smith believes that rationalism fails because it cannot account for the fact that the experience of moral evaluation is always positively or negatively valenced. We also saw that Smith believes that rationalism fails because it makes moral evaluation practically inert. Thus, he must think that all the views he sees as rooting moral evaluation in "immediate sense and feeling" or "sentiment" can provide accurate accounts of the experience of moral evaluation and straightforward explanations of how moral evaluation can motivate (VII.iii

.2.7). Additionally, his use of the word "immediate" to describe both "sense and feeling" is telling. This language conveys that on both the moral sense and the sentiments proper accounts, moral evaluation is rooted in an aspect of human nature that is basic and involuntary; in other words, on these views, moral evaluation is fundamentally an automatic response that would not be inaccurately described as "instinctual."

Second, puzzlement about why Smith lumps moral sense views, sentiments proper views, and sympathy views together in one category might rest upon an overly hasty assumption regarding what Smith even means by "sentiment." He does not spell out how he understands the differences between affects like passions, emotions, sentiments, and desires, let alone the differences between any of these and senses.[18] (This ambiguity was behind the complication introduced earlier to the question of whether Smith is a non-cognitivist about moral judgment.) However, as we will see across Chapters 3 and 4, as well as in Section 1 of Chapter 7, even if we cannot work out a full Smithian account of the distinctions between the various kinds of affects, we can say some substantive, general things about the ones he takes to be most important to his moral psychology.

Third, notice that Smith presents the sympathy account as motivated in part by concerns about conceptual economy. He tells us that instead of positing the existence of something new and sui generis, whether it be a sense or a special sentiment, defenders of the sympathy view try to explain moral judgment by employing already recognized features of human psychology. That Smith demonstrates this commitment to economical explanation is interesting on its own. But in doing so, he also at least *suggests* that he is committed to providing as naturalistic and as secular as possible an account of moral evaluation. I say "suggests" rather than "implies" because the connection is only rhetorical. One could coherently believe that a sui generis moral sense or sentiment is a natural feature of human psychology that some scientists of human nature have simply overlooked (cf. VII.iii.2.5). One could also coherently believe that the already recognized features of human nature underlying moral judgment are divinely implanted components of it. But it is hard to deny that the more reductionist route that Smith takes at least *feels* friendlier to a secular, naturalistic approach to the study of morality. In keeping with this reaction, Smith points out that

Hutcheson tries to "support" the moral sense theory that Smith rejects in part "by shewing that it was agreeable to the analogy of nature," i.e., to the idea that nature is ordered by a divine mind (VII.iii.3.7).[19] As we shall see especially in Section 2 of Chapter 7, Smith's assigns an important, positive role in moral life to the belief that the world was designed by a benevolent god. But he never ties the truth of any aspect of his moral theory to the truth of this view, despite the fact that he seems to hold it. So it is worth remarking here that Smith's account of moral judgment does not positively point toward it, even if only as a matter of rhetorical association.[20]

Let's turn now to Smith's discussion of the views in the first class. He tells us that Hutcheson's moral sense theory was a response to both the rationalistic and the egoistic accounts of moral evaluation. After arguing that neither reasoning nor consideration of one's own interest could ground moral evaluation, Hutcheson concluded that it must derive from the working of a faculty analogous to the "external senses." Just as the external senses make it appear that the "bodies around us . . . possess the different qualities of sound, taste, odour, colour," the moral sense makes it appear that the "various affections of the human mind . . . possess the different qualities of amiable and odious, of virtuous and vicious, of right and wrong" (VII.iii.3.5). We might wonder why anyone would take Hutcheson seriously, especially when we consider that, as Smith points out, he also recognized a "sense of beauty and deformity," a "public sense," a "sense of shame and honour," and a "sense of ridicule."[21] But despite all its talk of new senses, Hutcheson's theory of mind is not as bizarre as it might sound. He used the term "sense" for "every determination of our minds to receive ideas independently on our will, and to have perceptions of pleasure and pain."[22] Thus, Hutcheson invokes a new sense whenever he thinks he has hit upon an ability to receive information or undergo an evaluative response that is totally basic. The most important feature of this strategy for the present context is that it helps him push back against the egoist attempt to reduce all of our concerns to self-love. To put the contrast bluntly: while the egoist thinks that we like everything we do because we like ourselves, Hutcheson thinks that we like most of things that we do irreducibly.

The mechanics of moral judgment on Hutcheson's view are based on John Locke's general conception of knowledge. As Locke does, Hutcheson believes that sensation is the source of all simple ideas of the external world and that reflection (or inner sensation) is the source of all simple ideas of the human mind itself (VII.iii.3.7). Insofar as it attends to the "passions and emotions of the human mind" (whether another's or one's own), rather than to the external world, the moral sense operates via a form of Lockean reflection. And insofar as its operation presupposes an "antecedent perception" of these passions and emotions to which it reacts, the moral sense is not a "direct internal sense" but a "reflex, internal sense." Just as one must first directly "perceive the sound or the colour" before one can perceive the former's harmony and the latter's beauty, one must first directly perceive the "different passions and emotions" before one can perceive their "virtue or vice" (VII.iii.3.6).[23] The most important passions and emotions perceived by the moral sense are benevolence and malice, the respective roots of all virtue and vice. (We will consider this last aspect of Hutcheson's theory more thoroughly in Section 4 of Chapter 5.)

Smith levels at least two distinct arguments against this view and two against the aforementioned, hard-to-classify variation of it. One occurs in a different section of the TMS, but it warrants mentioning here. Smith argues that if we had a moral sense, we "would judge with more accuracy concerning" ourselves than "other men" because "our own passions . . . [are] immediately exposed to the view of this faculty," while those of "other men" are a "more distant prospect" (III.4.5). But it is an undeniable fact that we make mistakes in evaluating ourselves as or more often than we do in evaluating others. Thus, we cannot have a moral sense.

This argument is not very strong. Even if we grant the (plausible) assumption about how often we get things wrong in evaluating ourselves and overlook the crudely spatial way in which Smith seems to be thinking about the operation of the moral sense, we can still demand an explanation for why he thinks we would not get self-evaluation wrong with a moral sense as often as we would without one. Smith himself believes we have a strong propensity to rationalize our own conduct because "it is so disagreeable to think ill of ourselves"; thus, we often avoid accurate self-evaluation by "endeavor[ing] to exasperate anew those unjust passions which had formerly misled us" (III.4.5) so they can "discolour our views of things" again (III.4.3). Why can't this kind of self-deception cloud the lens of the moral sense as easily as it can interfere with any other psychological source of moral judgment? Hutcheson himself warns against the formation of false, "rashly form'd opinions of mankind" as malicious and evil that we can use to justify treating others poorly.[24] It seems obvious that we can interfere with the workings of the moral sense by tricking ourselves into holding such opinions.

A second, more interesting argument is that the moral sense theory fails because it is unable to account for our ability to pass moral judgment on moral judgment. If the moral sense is analogous to the other senses, then it, like them, cannot possess the qualities that it ascribes to its objects. The sense of sight cannot itself be "black or white," the sense of hearing cannot itself be "loud or low," the sense of taste cannot itself be "sweet or bitter," and the sense of morals cannot itself be "virtuous or vicious, morally good or evil" (VII.iii .3.8). But if this is true, then the moral sense theory cannot account for the obvious fact that "if we saw any man shouting with admiration and applause at a barbarous and unmerited execution," we would "consider it as the very last and most dreadful stage of moral depravity" (VII.iii.3.9). Nor can the theory account for the obvious fact that "correct moral sentiments . . . naturally appear in some degree laudable and morally good" (VII.iii.3.10).

Smith seems to be focused on a specific kind of moral judgment that he thinks a theory of moral judgment must be able to explain. But there might be more at stake here. Some philosophers have assigned deep significance to our ability to endorse our moral faculties with our moral faculties, not just in particular cases but also in general.[25] So in critiquing Hutcheson for being unable to explain how the moral sense can approve of itself, is Smith doing more than just making an isolated objection? We revisit this possibility in Section 2 of Chapter 7.

Smith's third argument aims at either an interpretation of Hutcheson's theory or a possible response on its behalf (again, Smith is not clear on which he has in mind). Smith considers what follows if we take "the name of a sense of right and wrong, or of a moral sense" to signify a "peculiar sentiment which answers [the] one particular purpose" of moral evaluation and "no other" (VII.iii.3.11). He concedes that this view "may not be liable to the same objections with the foregoing" (VII.iii.3.12). (Though he goes on to argue that it also fails to explain on its own the moral judgment of moral judgment; we'll leave this argument aside, as it rests upon the positive view that we have yet to see Smith develop (VII.iii.3.14).) But he argues that it simply misrepresents the experiences of moral approval and disapproval. In general, he claims, it is much easier to perceive similarities between different "variations" of emotions of the same kind than it is the variations themselves; thus, everyone can pick out "anger" as a kind but it takes "a very delicate attention" to distinguish the different "modifications" of anger (he cites the differences between "anger against a man," "anger against a woman," and "anger against a child" as examples). So if there are common "general features" of approval and disapproval, they should be easier to see than the "variations." But, in fact, the opposite is true. Rather strikingly, Smith claims that "if we attend to what we really feel when upon different occasions we either approve or disapprove, we shall find that our emotion in one case is often totally different from that in another, and that no common features can possibly discovered between them." The feeling of approval for "a tender, delicate, and humane sentiment, is quite different from that [of] . . . one that appears great, daring, and magnanimous"; similarly, "our horror for cruelty has no sort of resemblance to our contempt for mean-spiritedness" (VII.iii.3.13). Thus, it cannot be the case that there is *one* feeling of approval and *one* feeling of disapproval.

There are several interesting features of this argument. The first is the phenomenology of moral evaluation it assumes. Is it really the case that "there is *no sort of resemblance* between the emotions" excited in us by various kinds of morally praiseworthy conduct or various kinds of morally blameworthy conduct? Even if, as seems likely, the approval of bravery feels overall different from the approval of compassion, these experiences could be complex enough to include some commonality amid this difference; at the very least, these experiences are both positive in a way that disapproval is not. Second, in arguing that there is not a sui generis experience of moral approval or disapproval, Smith introduces for himself a difficult version of the problem common to all sentimentalist theories of moral judgment of explaining which sentimental experiences are the moral ones.[26] He would have an easy answer to this question if he thought there were irreducible moral sentiments that felt a distinctive way in all cases of moral evaluation. Since he apparently does not believe this, he faces the task of explaining what unites these sentiments into a class distinct from that of the nonmoral ones while maintaining his view that they differ dramatically among themselves. Thirdly and relatedly, as we shall see in Section 2 of the next chapter, Smith's claim that there are no "peculiar" moral sentiments seems to fly directly in the face of his own positive account.[27]

I return to these sorts of issues in Section 2 of the next chapter, in the introduction to Chapter 4, and in Section 6 of Chapter 4. The fourth Smithian objection to Hutcheson's moral sense theory, whether understood as positing a sixth sense or as simply describing special moral sentiments with sensory metaphors, is a bit of a callback to Smith's initial point about conceptual economy. Here, Smith makes the related argument that Hutcheson-style views are too innovative. If there really were a distinctively moral sense or sentiment, "which Providence [would have] undoubtedly intended to be the governing principle of human nature," there would be a long track record of common names for it. Yet "the word moral sense" is both new and uncommon; "the word approbation" is most standardly used not to signify a distinctive moral feeling but to cover the positive attitude we take toward "whatever is entirely to our satisfaction," including "the form of a building . . . the contrivance of a machine . . . [and] the flavor of a dish of meat"; and "the word conscience" does not pick out a "moral faculty" but "signifies our consciousness of having acted agreeably or contrary" to the "directions" of our moral faculties, whatever they be (VIII.iii.3.15).[28] Once again, we see the authority Smith ascribes to common moral life when formulating theory. (We also see again the complexity of his attitude toward things godly; nothing he says here is inconsistent with his believing that whatever he thinks really is psychologically responsible for moral evaluation was intended by a deity "to be the governing principle of human nature.") He simply does not think it plausible that philosophers could have discovered something about human nature that had previously gone so unobserved by everyone else as to have not even been given a name.

While this assumption is by no means unquestionable and the etymology he provides in applying it is limited, there is something appealing about the notion that we should at least *try* to explain moral evaluation with the conceptual and terminological resources with which we are already familiar before we start inventing a new sense or sentiments. And this is exactly what Smith thinks he is successful in doing. After summing up his own view, he thus expresses the burden upon the Hutcheson-style innovator: "I should be glad to know what remains [unexplained by my view], and I shall freely allow this overplus to be ascribed to a moral sense, or to any other peculiar faculty, provided any body will ascertain precisely what this overplus is" (VII.iii.3.15).

This brings us to the Humean alternative. Rather than positing the existence of a new faculty or sentiment, this view grounds moral evaluation in sympathy. Smith briefly points out here that this view cannot account for certain features of moral evaluation, but these comments cannot be understood fully without first going through his own view. Thus, we will save discussion of Smith's attitude toward Hume's account of the psychological foundation of moral judgment for the next chapter, which lays out the details of Smith's own account. Since it is difficult to disentangle Smith's presentation of his own positive theory from his engagement with Hume's, we will start by doing some comparative work.

3

Smith's Own Answer to the Psychological Foundation of Moral Judgment Question

As we saw in the previous chapter, both Smith and his predecessor Hume answer the psychological foundation of moral judgment question with "sympathy." However, they conceive of sympathy in different ways and apply these conceptions of sympathy to differing conceptions of moral judgment. This mixture of similarity and difference makes it difficult to discuss Smith's answer to the psychological foundation of moral judgment question without commenting on its relationship to Hume's. Thus, this chapter will be in large part concerned with that relationship. The first section focuses on each thinker's view on sympathy alone. I pay special attention to Hume's criticism of Smith's theory and Smith's response thereto, as this exchange concerns the heart of Smith's sympathy-based answer to the psychological foundation of moral judgment question. The second section develops this answer, which requires sympathy not to enable approval but to *be* approval. This section also touches upon Smith's general conception of "sentiment." Additionally, this section grapples with the apparent contradiction between Smith's answer to the psychological foundation of moral judgment question and the claim we saw in the last chapter that "no common features can possibly be discovered between" the approval of different kinds of sentiments (VII.iii.3.13). The third and fourth sections complete Smith's answer by laying out the conception of moral judgment that is bound up with his conception of sympathy; each section covers one half of his distinction between judgments of propriety and judgments of merit. Since Smith's distinction between these two categories constitutes a fundamental disagreement with the conception of moral judgment bound up with Hume's conception of sympathy, we must also return to Hume in the fifth section.

Section 1: Sympathy[1]

Given his dedication to theorizing about everyday life from within everyday life, it is not out of character for Smith to open the presentation of his sympathy theory by almost apologizing for its innovativeness. He expects at least some of his readers to understand "sympathy" as synonymous with "pity and compassion," which "signify our fellow-feeling with the sorrow of others." But, he hopes, "sympathy . . . may now . . . without much impropriety be made use of to denote our fellow-feeling with any passion whatever," including positive ones like "joy" and "gratitude" (I.i.1.4–5). Thus, Smith sees himself as using a term in a way that has recently come into philosophical vogue, though has not necessarily trickled into common usage.

While many other intellectuals in Smith's context were using the term in his way,[2] the most important other theorizer of sympathy he would have had in mind was Hume. Both philosophers were clearly fascinated by our natural tendency to feel what each other feels, a tendency that today often gets labelled "empathy" rather than sympathy.[3] In Hume's words, "no quality of human nature is more remarkable, both in itself and in its consequences, than that propensity we have to sympathize with others, and to receive by communication their inclinations and sentiments, however different from or even contrary to our own" (T 2.1.11.2/SBN 316).[4] And, as we have seen Smith point out, both philosophers answer the psychological foundation of moral judgment question by invoking sympathy. But their accounts of sympathy seem to differ in significant ways.

Smith's account begins by pointing to two features of sympathy that any theory thereof must explain. One is epistemic and the other is affective. Since "we have no immediate experience of what other men feel . . . our senses [alone] will never inform us" of what another is feeling, let alone make us "even feel something" like what another is feeling; in recognizably Humean language, Smith observes that our "own senses" can never provide us with direct experience of another person's "impressions" (I.i.1.2). Sure, "upon some occasions," we immediately observe what another is feeling and then feel the same way. For instance, when we come across "a smiling face" or "a sorrowful countenance," we immediately know that someone is feeling "joy" or "grief," and we immediately feel "cheerful" or "melancholy" ourselves; in cases like these, "sympathy may seem to arise merely from the view of a certain emotion in another person." But even in such cases, both our knowledge of what the other person is feeling and our subsequent fellow-feeling with the other person are "extremely imperfect." Immediate observation only gives us a "general" sense or "vague idea" of what the other person is feeling. Consequently, the sympathetic feelings we feel only match up with what the other person feels in the most superficial way. And in some cases, immediate observation does not even generate a superficial correspondence of feeling. It might be obvious that another person is feeling anger, but our immediate affective response to this observation is usually "disgust" and a disposition to oppose any actions that follow from the angry person's feelings (I.i.1.6–9).

But of course we often do both understand and feel what others are feeling, even when they are feeling passions like anger. Smith's point is that when this happens, we have done more than just observe something. He claims that if we are to form "any conception" of another person's feelings and "feel something" like what this other person feels, we must employ our "imagination [to] place ourselves in his situation" (I.i.1.2). Thus, for Smith, "sympathy . . . does not arise so much from the view of [another person's] passion, as from that of the situation which excites it" (I.i.1.10). Since our conception of this "situation" can include both external, environmental factors and internal, personality-based ones, Smith believes that in imagining ourselves into it, we "become in some measure the same person with" the person with whom we sympathize (I.i.1.2; cf. VII.iii.1.4).

This theory accounts for what is missing in cases of "imperfect," immediate-observation-based sympathy. When we superficially sympathize with immediately observed joy or grief, we feel more of a combination of "curiosity to inquire into [the other person's] situation" and "some disposition to sympathize" than we do "any actual sympathy." Actual sympathy, in which we fully understand and feel what others are feeling, requires a thorough conception of a situation into which we can imagine ourselves. This is especially the case with respect to passions like anger. Sympathy with such passions is not merely incomplete until "we are acquainted with what gave occasion to them." Sympathy with such passions is always fighting an uphill battle against our natural aversion to them, a battle that can only be won with background information that—as we shall see across the next three sections—justifies them in our eyes.

Thus, by requiring the act of imagining oneself into another's situation, which itself requires information about a person's situation, Smith's theory captures the fact that sympathy with others' sentiments is not always automatic; rather, we usually have to think about what gave rise to their sentiments before we too can feel them (I.i.1.7–9). (Again, as we shall see soon, this feature of Smith's theory of sympathy is a crucial part of what allows it to double as a theory of moral evaluation.) Smith also notes a second advantage of his theory. By requiring the act of imagination it does, the account easily explains our tendency "sometimes [to] feel for another, a passion of which he himself seems to be altogether incapable," as when we vicariously "blush" for a clueless other's "impudence and rudeness," pity a person suffering unawares from a "loss of reason," commiserate with a sick infant, or sympathize with the dead. In all these cases, "a passion arises in our breast from the imagination, though it does not in [the other's] from the reality" (I.i.1.10–13).

Like Smith, Hume begins his account by addressing the problem of how we figure out what another person is feeling, given that "no passion of another discovers itself immediately to the mind." However, Hume deals with this problem at a more fundamental level than Smith does. Recall that Smith seems to believe that we can read simple joy and grief directly off of another's facial expressions. His view might be that in these cases, we are making an inference from external expression to inner feeling, but one that is so simple it would not be misleading to describe the form of sympathy that follows from it as arising "merely from the view of a certain emotion"; as we shall see in Section 3, his frequent references to the "expressions" of passions point in this direction (I.i.1.6–7). Nevertheless, Smith does not articulate a definitive position on how we acquire the knowledge involved in "imperfect" sympathy; we only know that for him, however this kind of sympathy works, a more perfect understanding of and fellow-feeling with other people requires the cognitively complicated act of imagining oneself into their situations (I.i.1.9). Hume, on the other hand, provides an explanation for how we go about attributing feelings to others even in extremely basic ways, such as when we immediately label a "countenance," "sorrowful" (I.i.1.6). The process begins with an inference from the externally observable "causes or effects" of another's passion (T 3.3.1.7/SBN 576). Of course, because we cannot directly observe others' passions, we also cannot directly observe constant conjunctions between these passions and either their causes or "external signs" (T 2.1.11.3, 206/SBN 317).[5] Thus, we must infer others' passions ultimately via analogy between their causes and external signs and the causes and external signs of our own. These analogies appear to rest upon what Hume intriguingly refers to as a "kind of *presensation*; which tells us what will operate in others, by what we feel immediately in ourselves" (T 2.2.1.9/SBN 332).

Unlike Smith, Hume also explicitly provides an explanation for how merely thinking about what others are feeling generates an actual feeling. Smith assumes, plausibly, that the act of imagining what it is like to be in a situation can trigger a real affective response. And by suggestively observing that "our imaginations copy . . . the impressions of our own senses" when we sympathize and that we experience stronger sympathetic feelings the more "vivacity" with which we "conceive or . . . imagine that we are in" another's situation, Smith provides some resources to work out an explanation for how a thought about a feeling turns into a feeling (I.i.1.2).[6] But Hume goes a step further in actually explaining how an inferred idea of another's passion gets "converted into an impression, and acquires such a degree of force and vivacity, as to become the very passion itself" (T 2.1.11.3/SBN 317). The engine that provides the enlivening force necessary for this conversion is the lively "idea, or rather impression of ourselves," which "is always intimately present to us" (T 2.1.11.4/

SBN 317).[7] Depending on the extent to which we perceive the other person to be related to us via "resemblance," "contiguity," "causation," or "acquaintance," the imagination carries the force of the idea/impression of the self to the idea of the other person's passion (T 2.1.11.5–6/SBN 318). The closer the perceived relation between self and other, the easier the imagination's transition between the perception of self and the perception of the other's passion, and the more "force and vivacity" it carries from one to the other.[8] Thus, a mere thought about a feeling transforms into an actual feeling.

Thus far, other than some relative lack of detail both in Smith's account of the knowledge involved in cases of "imperfect sympathy" and in his account of how imagining a feeling can generate a feeling, the most glaring difference between the two theories seems to be that Smith's involves a more cognitively robust act of imagination. On Hume's view, the process by which we come to feel what others feel seems automatic and unconscious; thus, he observes that "the affections readily pass from one person to another" in the same way that "motion" passes between "strings equally wound up" in a musical instrument (T 3.3.1.7/SBN 576). Taking their hint from this imagery and language Hume uses elsewhere (e.g., T 3.3.3.5/SBN 605), scholars today sometimes refer to Hume's account of sympathy as a "contagion" theory, according to which we "catch" others' emotions the way we catch their colds.[9] Smith's view, on the other hand, is sometimes described as a "simulation" theory, according to which we feel what others feel after using our imaginations to simulate what it is like to be in their shoes.[10]

Smith might have had this difference in mind when he pointed to the two previously mentioned explanatory benefits of his own theory. On one straightforward understanding of Humean sympathy, it can only give rise to one-to-one correspondences between original and sympathetically received "inclinations and sentiments." It is not obvious that Hume's sympathy theory can account for either the fact that we do not automatically sympathize with every affect in our vicinity or the fact that we do sometimes sympathize with affects that are not felt by the people with whom we sympathize (T 2.1.11.2–3/SBN 316–17).

However, closer attention to the details of Hume's theory reveals that it does account for both phenomena. The role Hume's theory assigns to perceived associations between self and other allows it to account for the first. Hume's theory implies both that we are most disposed to sympathize with people we take to be like us and/or related to us, and that we are least disposed to sympathize with people we take to be unlike us and/or unrelated to us. Insofar as a person demonstrates feelings that we would not feel (or, better, that we do not see ourselves as ever feeling), that person falls into the latter category; thus, Hume observes, "the praises of others never give us much pleasure [via sympathy], unless they concur with our own opinion" (T 2.1.11.13/SBN 322).

The role Hume's account assigns to experience-based habitual tendencies in determining what another person is feeling allows his theory to deal with cases of sympathy with "affections, which have no existence." "When a person of merit falls into what is vulgarly esteem'd a great misfortune," these tendencies lead us to carry "our fancy from the cause to the usual effect" and thus overlook "that greatness of mind, which [actually] elevates him above such emotions" (T 2.2.7.5/SBN 370). We take on the pain that we *imagine* is being experienced and not the personal strength that actually is; this is why we can still end up feeling compassion in such cases. We similarly sympathize with fools who "shew no sense of shame" and with sleeping, totally unhurt murder victims (T 2.2.7.5–6/SBN 371).

Thus, Hume's sympathy theory involves more complicated acts of cognition and accounts for more complicated phenomena than both some of his metaphors and the "contagion" label suggest.[11] But there does seem to be something significant about the fact that Hume's account does not involve the kind of imaginative act that Smith's does. Some commentators have emphasized the epistemic import of Smith's insistence that sympathy requires imaginatively projecting oneself into another's situation. Writing in response to David Raynor's argument that Smith's writings on sympathy must not have Hume in their sights,[12] Samuel Fleischacker[13] interprets Smith as arguing that Hume cannot account for how we get an idea of what another is feeling. On Fleischacker's reading, Smith prefers his imagining-oneself-into-another's-shoes account of the first stage of ("actual," not "imperfect") sympathy to Hume's inference-from-external-to-internal account because the latter ultimately does require that we experience constant conjunctions of others' external behavior and expressions with their internal mental states, which, as pointed out, is impossible by Hume's own lights.[14]

In order to evaluate Fleischacker's interpretation, we would have to settle the issue raised earlier regarding what Smith thinks is going on in cases of "imperfect" sympathy; if Fleischacker is correct, it would be hard for Smith to believe that these cases of sympathy involved an inference from external to internal. Furthermore, we would have to deal with Hume's previously referenced claim about a "kind of *presensation*; which tells us what will operate in others, by what we feel immediately in ourselves" (T 2.2.1.9/SBN 332). And we would have to think hard about why Smith would think his own account of how we come to know what another is feeling is satisfactory; *how* does imagining myself in another's shoes convey information about what that person is feeling? But even without doing all this, we can still conclude that Fleischacker is right at least with respect to the general point that Smith both saw his sympathy theory as having important epistemic features.[15] As we've seen in part, Smith's presentation of his very first example of sympathy, a case involving an apparently simple act of sympathizing with "our brother on the rack," is littered with epistemic and cognitive language. Smith tells us that "by changing places in fancy with the sufferer," we get an "idea," we get "inform[ed]," and we get a "conception" of what the sufferer feels (I.i.1.3). As we've also seen, epistemic concerns are evident in Smith's criticism of the view that all sympathetic feelings "arise merely from the view of a certain emotion in another person"; the sympathy that arises from such an immediate "view" is "imperfect" in part because it involves a "vague" and "general idea of good or bad fortune" (I.i.1.6–9). It seems hard to deny that with all this epistemic language, Smith is saying, at least in part, that sympathy involves a form of understanding that requires more than just the ability to classify an agent's emotion in purely propositional terms[16] that pick out things like its object and affective character. As Fleischacker points out elsewhere, Smithian sympathy "consists not simply in feeling *what* another might feel, but in being aware that that is how things feel *for*" this other person, from their distinctive point of view (2019: 24–5; cf. 31–4).[17] For Smith, this kind of understanding requires imaginatively entering into someone's perspective.

We can leave open the questions of whether Smith intends this point to be a criticism of Hume and of whether Humean inferences and analogies can generate the same kind of knowledge Smithian acts of imaginative projection can. I am not sure the former is fully answerable, and I am sure that we cannot sufficiently grapple with the latter without wading into a currently live debate in philosophy of mind between proponents of "theory-theory," proponents of "simulation-theory," and proponents of hybrid accounts of how we read each other's minds.[18] (The first argue that we normally interpret, understand, and predict others' behavior, feelings, and thoughts by employing a primitive, "folk" psychological theory of how human minds operate; the second argue that we normally interpret, understand, and predict others' behavior, feelings, and thoughts by using our imaginations to simulate their situation; and the third, obviously, argue that we do both.[19]) Fleischacker seems to be right when he acknowledges that Hume and Smith themselves "care far more about the fact that your feelings interest me than whether or not I properly know what you feel." So if there are major differences between the two theories, the interpretively most important ones must have something to do with how sympathy relates to our "interest" in others' feelings. Thus, for now, let's shift our attention away from the epistemic and toward the affective elements of sympathy. How, for Hume and Smith, does sympathy factor into human sociability or serve as an "emotional glue that hold[s] social relationships together" (Fleischacker 2012: 274; cf. 299)?[20]

Most scholars agree that sympathy functions in both Hume and Smith in part as a non-benevolence-based response to the egoistic account of human sociability of which we caught a glimpse in the previous chapter.[21] Keeping in mind the risk of oversimplification that haunts any claim made from as broad a perspective as that which considers the very nature of human sociability, one can say that their responses to the egoist make our tendency to feel others' feelings more basic to and pervasive in human sociability than our comparatively limited other-directed concern. Remy Debes argues that Smithian sympathy plays this role in part by better grounding concern for others than does any contagion-style view; he asks, "how much more likely will you be to sympathize with a friend's grief, and to what a greater degree of sensitivity and depth, and, in a word, accuracy, if your own sorrowful response to her grief involves your *imagining* her life and her loss as *she* sees it—that is, as opposed to reacting to the mere countenance of sadness she wears on her face" (2016: 202; cf. 198-99)? Of course, as we've seen, Hume himself likely does not hold the latter, contagion-y view, which requires only a glance at a "mere countenance."[22] But regardless of what Hume thinks, there are gaps to fill in moving from Smithian sympathy to sincere concern for another person.

On some descriptions of the act of imagination involved in sympathy, Smith says that a spectator's sympathetic feelings "arise altogether from the consideration of what he himself would feel if he was [in] the same . . . situation" as the agent (I.i.1.11). On this description, Smithian sympathy requires an imaginative projection of self into another's shoes. Unsurprisingly, many of Smith's readers have taken this account of sympathy to be oddly egoistic. Manfred Holler comments that Smithian sympathy seems to yield "feeling for oneself, and not for the other" (2007: 172).[23] With a similar concern in mind, M. Jamie Ferreira describes Smith's theory pejoratively as a "substitution" theory (1994: notes 29, 30, 45).[24] Gerald Postema prefers the term "introjection" (2005: 293, note 36).[25] This reaction goes all the way back to Thomas Reid, who wrote Lord Kames that Smith's moral theory is "indeed only a Refinement of the selfish System" (1997: 66),[26] an accusation Reid does not even level at "Mr Hume," whose system, Reid thought, nevertheless included some "things which border upon licentiousness" (1997: 72, 69–70).[27] And though he does not criticize this aspect of Smith's sympathy theory directly, Hume himself faults the ancient Greek historian Polybius for holding a Smithian-style view, which, Hume claims, assigns a "selfish origin to all our sentiments of virtue" (EPM 5.6/E 215).[28]

In the previous chapter, we saw Smith respond directly to this worry by arguing that sympathy does not involve an imaginative projection of oneself in another's shoes. Rather, he explains that in sympathizing, an "imaginary change is not supposed to happen to me in my person and character, but in that of the person with whom I sympathize"; when I sympathize with you, he continues, "I consider what I should suffer if I was really you, and I not only change circumstances with you, but I change persons and characters. My grief, therefore, is entirely upon your account, and not in the least upon my own. It is not, therefore, in the least selfish" (VII.iii.1.4). Here Smith describes what Robert Gordon calls an "imaginative shift in the references of indexicals" that occurs when we imagine ourselves not just in another person's situation but *as* this other person (1995: 734). Note that Smith is not modifying his sympathy theory here so much as he is unfolding it; we've seen him comment on the very first page of the TMS that when we sympathize we "become in some measure the same person" as the other (I.i.1.2). The act of imagining oneself as another person is simply a more thorough act of imagining what it is like to be in this person's situation. If I imagine myself in your external "circumstances," I have not fully imagined myself in your situation, for your situation is defined as much by the point of view dictated by your "person and character" as it is by these circumstances. Since it thus requires that we ultimately remove ourselves from the content of the acts of imagination that give rise to sympathy, Smith argues, his sympathy theory is not egoistic.

However, it is not obvious that, on its own, the act of identifying with another can generate sincerely other-directed feelings. Identification alone does not explain how my feeling bad as a result of my imaginative experience of your situation *as you* becomes my feeling bad *for you* once I have "returned" to my real self. My act of imagining *being* you does not in and of itself generate any feeling for or toward *you*. It might generate temporary concern about the same thing you are concerned about. And it might generate a temporary *self*-directed feeling—I feel bad for myself, though for myself as you. But it seems that something else must happen for these feelings to stick around, let alone get directed *toward you* in any meaningful way after I have returned to being my normal, different self. Unfortunately, Smith does not complete this story.[29]

Yet this problem is one only on the assumption that sympathy's primary job in Smith's account of natural sociability is to explain at a more fundamental level the features that involve other-directed concern. Smith's response to the egoistic answer to the psychological foundation of moral judgments certainly suggests something like this, as do comments he makes elsewhere basing "pity or compassion" on "sympathy" (I.i.1.1) and identifying "affection" with "habitual sympathy" (VI.ii.1.7). However, when we focus on the role that Smithian sympathy plays in Smith's answer to the psychological foundation of moral judgment question, we quickly see that this is not the case. This is where we start to see the most significant differences between Smith and Hume.

For Hume, we morally approve of character traits because they are useful to their possessors or other people or because they are intrinsically agreeable to their possessors or other people (e.g., T 3.3.1.24–9/SBN 587–90). We do so because we care, at least to some extent, about the fact that other people are positively impacted in these ways by the traits. This baseline concern for others also explains our disapproval of damaging and intrinsically disagreeable traits. But since, in the *Treatise* anyways,[30] Hume denies the existence of "the love of mankind, merely as such," he needs a way to explain this concern (T 3.2.1.12/ SBN 481). Thus, one of the main jobs of his sympathy theory is to explain how we come to sincerely care about others' feelings. The theory seems up to the task in part because Hume never describes the process by which our ideas of what others feel generate feelings in us in terms of an act of imaginative projection. In this regard, his account does not face the problems with potential egoism that Smith's does. Furthermore, even if one thinks that, similarly to what we just saw regarding Smith's identification-based response to egoism, Hume's theory leaves gaps between feeling what another feels and feeling concern for another, Hume fills these by telling a complicated story about the interplay between sympathy and basic other-directed emotions like pity, love, and benevolence that explain how sympathy can trigger such concern.[31]

In contrast, since Smith does not believe that moral approval involves recognizing that character traits are useful to their possessors or other people or simply agreeable to their possessors or other people, the primary job of Smith's sympathy theory in his account of moral judgment is not to explain other-directed concern, at least not in the same sense that Hume's theory must.[32] The next three sections will spell out Smith's alternative account of what moral evaluation targets. But for now, we can identify and focus on the un-Humean feature of Smithian sympathy that allows it to play the role Smith believes it does in moral evaluation. Smith claims that "*nothing pleases us more* than to observe in other men a fellow-feeling with all the emotions of our own breast; *nor are we ever so much shocked* as by the appearance of the contrary"; thus, for him, the experience of sympathy is inherently pleasing and the experience of its absence—Smith's examples imply that the bar for a relevant social experience to be negative does not start as high as that of mutual antipathy—is inherently painful (I.i.2.1; emphases added). What Smith calls "mutual sympathy" provides a distinct "source of satisfaction," an "agreeable sensation" or "auxiliary pleasure" of its own; it is not just a transfer mechanism for other affects, as it appears to be for Hume (I.i.2.2; I.i.2.5). Since Smith goes on to argue that mutual sympathy is something we pursue, it makes sense to attribute to him belief in a *desire* for mutual sympathy; the existence of this desire is the centerpiece of his account of human sociability. And since, as we'll see in the next section, he argues that the pleasure of mutual sympathy constitutes approval, it also grounds his account of moral evaluation. While Hume employs his sympathy theory to explain moral approval by explaining how it comes to matter to us when other people are impacted by useful and agreeable character traits, Smith employs his sympathy theory *as* his theory of approval by making the positive feeling of sympathy and the negative feeling of its absence double as feelings of approbation and disapprobation.[33]

Smith assumes more than he argues that we desire and take pleasure in mutual sympathy and are averse to and take pain in its absence. However, he does argue against attempts to reduce these features of human psychology to other ones. He first argues against the egoist claim that they, like all our other "sentiments," depend upon "certain refinements of self-love" (I.i.2.1). He has in mind the rather crude view that we enjoy mutual sympathy and dislike its absence only because we see it as a guarantee of future "assistance" from those with whom we share it. Smith responds that since we often feel the pleasure of mutual sympathy and pain of its absence "instantaneously" and on "frivolous occasions"—his example involves the joy and disappointment one feels when one's "jest" cause laughter or not—neither feeling can require the kind of reflection upon long-term self-interest that the crude egoist has in mind (I.i.2.1).

Smith next takes on the view that mutual sympathy pleases "altogether from the additional vivacity" our "mirth" gets when it is seconded by another person's sentiments, perhaps via a mechanism similar to that involved in contagion-style sympathy (I.i.2.2). Smith does not indicate whether he takes this view to be egoistic. Nor does he indicate whether he takes it to be Hume's. (As we have seen, Hume's sympathy theory is more complicated than a pure contagion one. But as we shall see, Hume does recognize a pleasure in mutual sympathy, and he accounts for it in a way that resembles the view Smith has in mind here, though it is ultimately different.) Smith responds to this view by pointing out that it cannot explain why sympathy makes us feel better when we are in pain; if others' sympathy only "[seconded]" our sorrow in the way that the proponent of this view thinks it does our joy, it would only make us feel worse (I.i.2.4). Thus, Smith concludes that mutual sympathy must provide an "agreeable sensation" distinct from any "enlivening" effect it has on our preexistent feelings (I.i.2.2). Of course, the enlivening view could still account for the sympathetic joy we feel when we do things such as—to use Smith's example—introduce someone to a "book or poem" that we once enjoyed but that "we can no longer find any amusement in reading" alone. This possibility becomes especially easy to see if we understand the state we are in before the sympathetic boost as one of dull or stale pleasure instead of pure indifference. But Smith apparently thinks that since cases in which sympathy "alleviates" grief must involve an "agreeable sensation" distinct from any enlivening effect, there is no reason not to conclude that cases in which sympathy "enlivens" joy also involve this "additional source of satisfaction" (I.i.2.2).

Although these are different arguments against different positions, they draw the same conclusion: mutual sympathy pleases and attracts us intrinsically, not solely because we think it will help us attain or experience some other pleasing thing, like "assistance" from others or a boost in our "mirth." It is not clear whether Smith aims his first argument at a particular egoist or is thinking very generally, as when he takes on "Hobbes and his followers."[34] It is also not clear whether Smith aims his second argument at anyone in particular. Again, he *might* have Hume in mind; the language of "enlivening" certainly *sounds* Humean, despite the fact that the view Smith presents is, for reasons we have seen, an oversimplification.[35] But regardless of whether Smith was attacking Hume with this argument, Hume certainly attacked Smith's position on the pleasure of mutual sympathy. Smith's response to this attack is important for clarifying his own view.

In a July 1759 letter, Hume explicitly criticizes Smith for claiming that sympathy is always intrinsically pleasing. Hume demands that Smith prove "more particularly and fully" in the second edition of the TMS that "all kinds of sympathy are necessarily agreeable." Hume levels what appear to be three different kinds of objections to this position:

1) An appeal to the very nature of sympathy:

   As the sympathetic passion is a reflex image of the principal, it must partake of its qualities, and be painful where that is so.

2) A *reductio ad absurdum*:

   It is always thought a difficult problem to account for the pleasure, receivd from the tears and grief and sympathy of tragedy; which woud not be the case, if all sympathy was agreeable. An hospital would be a more entertaining place than a ball.

3) An appeal to experience:

   Indeed, *when we converse with a man with whom we can entirely sympathize*, that is, where there is a warm and intimate friendship, the cordial openness of such a commerce overpowers the pain of a disagreeable sympathy, and renders the whole movement agreeable. But in ordinary cases, this cannot have place. An ill-humord fellow; a man tir'd and disgusted with every thing, always *ennuie*; sickly, complaining, embarass'd; such a one throws an evident damp on company, which I suppose wou'd be accounted for by sympathy; and yet is disagreeable. (Letter 36)

In sum, Hume claims: (a) given what sympathy is, sympathy with a painful passion cannot be agreeable; (b) if all sympathy were agreeable, the problem of tragedy would not be a problem—this is not only implausible in its own right but also implies that we would enjoy hanging out at hospitals as much as or more than we do attending parties; and (c) an experience involving sympathy with a painful passion can only be agreeable under preexistent conditions of "warm and intimate friendship."

A footnote Smith added to the second edition of the TMS responds directly to Hume's first criticism. Smith agrees that the "sympathetic passion of the spectator . . . may either be agreeable or disagreeable, according to the nature of the original passion, whose features it must always in some measure, retain." However, he claims that "the emotion which arises from his observing the perfect coincidence between this sympathetic passion in himself, and the original passion in the person principally concerned . . . is always agreeable and delightful" (I.iii.1.9, note). Thus, Smith reiterates that the *observation* of sympathy between oneself and another is always pleasing, even when the passion with which one is sympathizing is not.[36]

Insofar as it mirrors Hume's own solution to the paradox of tragedy, this distinction also goes some way toward responding to his second criticism, the *reductio*.[37] For Hume, "a well-written tragedy" is pleasing even though it generates "disagreeable and uneasy" sympathetic passions in spectators because aesthetic pleasures like those felt in response to "eloquence" and "imitation" are "predominant" in the spectators' experience (Tragedy 216–26).[38] It is possible that the pleasure we take in observing our sympathy with others functions in the same way for Smith as this aesthetic pleasure does for Hume. If true, this could also explain why there might be cases in which we do enjoy hospitals more than parties.[39]

However, by turning to Hume's third objection, the appeal to experience, we see that Smith's distinction goes only part of the way toward responding to what is bothering Hume both in the second objection and in general. In levelling the third objection, Hume concedes that "where there is a warm and intimate friendship," sympathy itself, or "the cordial openness of such a commerce," *does* provide pleasure. Furthermore, this pleasure in sympathy itself can "[*overpower*] the pain of a disagreeable sympathy" with a painful passion (Letter 36; emphasis added). Thus, Hume appears to grant something like the distinction Smith himself makes in response to the first objection. This means that Hume's worries cannot really be about whether mutual sympathy is itself ever pleasing. Rather, they are about the extent to which this pleasure can "overpower" a sympathetically derived pain and about the frequency with which this pleasure even occurs.

Sensitivity to the former worry, the one about the power of the pleasure of mutual sympathy, can clarify our understanding of the second objection. According to Hume's theory of mind, passions that are simultaneously "present in the mind . . . readily mingle and unite" and "are naturally transfused into each other" (T 2.3.4.2–4/SBN 420–21; cf. DP 163–4).[40] But when one "predominates," it totally "swallows up the inferior" (T 2.3.4.2/SBN 420; cf. DP 163). This is what Hume thinks happens with respect to well-written tragedy. The spectator's awareness of the tragedy's fictitiousness "softens" the painful sympathetic passions, thereby rendering them "inferior" and prepping them to serve as fuel for enhancing the now-predominant aesthetic pleasures (Tragedy 221). "Being the predominant emotion[s]," these aesthetic pleasures "seize the whole mind, and convert [the spectator's painful sympathetic passions] into themselves" (Tragedy 220).[41] Thus, Hume's second criticism of Smith becomes that he fails to explain how the pleasure of observing sympathy can avoid being "swallowed up" entirely in most cases of painful sympathy. More precisely, since "the thought that [in sympathy, we ourselves] are not *really* the sufferers" serves as an obvious analog to awareness of the fictitiousness of a tragedy and thus explains the inferiority of painful sympathetic feelings, Hume's second criticism must be that the intrinsic pleasure of mutual sympathy is usually not positively predominant enough to "overpower" those feelings (I.i.4.7; emphasis added). If this pleasure were not predominant, Hume would argue, the sympathizer would at most undergo two more or less equally strong feelings that just cancel each other out.

Obviously, worries about the power of the pleasure of mutual sympathy are only relevant to cases in which that pleasure exists. As we have seen, Hume concedes that sympathy sometimes does generate its own pleasure; that it does not always do so is the other main point of the third criticism. He provides a detailed account of when it does in the section entitled "Of the love of relations," in Book II of the *Treatise*. There, Hume explains how sympathy can generate exceptions to the rule that we love others because we associate them with an independently pleasing thing, such as a personal quality. In some cases, he observes, sympathy alone leads us to give someone a "share of our love . . . without enquiring into his other qualities" by providing its own agreeable experience (T 2.2.4.2/SBN 352). Why do we love our "blood [relations] . . . our countrymen, our neighbors, those of the same trade, profession, and even name with ourselves," as well as acquaintances with whom "we have contracted a habitude and intimacy . . . tho' in frequenting [their] company we have not been able to discover any very valuable quality" (T 2.2.4.2–3/SBN 352)? According to Hume, "a rational and thinking being like ourselves, who communicates to us all the actions of his mind," presents us with "the liveliest of all objects" of perception and thus pleasingly "agitate[s]" our otherwise potentially "languid . . . spirits" (T 2.2.4.4/SBN 352–3). This agreeable stimulation we experience just from being around other people is especially "durable" when we happen to be related to them in some way, such as by family or mere acquaintance. In these cases, the mental transition from our "lively" conception of ourselves to our conception of them and their passions is particularly smooth and thus generates particularly stable, "peculiarly agreeable" instances of the pleasingly lively thought of another human being (T 2.2.4.5/SBN 353). Of course, this is the same mechanism by which we sympathize with other people; in each case, our idea of another person or another person's passion inherits "liveliness" from our conception of ourselves. Thus, in claiming that the experience of a lively conception of another person or another person's passion can itself be pleasing, Hume is claiming that sympathy can itself be pleasing. Furthermore, since the mental transition from self to other or other's passion goes especially smoothly when we perceive resemblance between us, the intrinsic pleasure of sympathizing builds on itself, as the more we sympathize with others, the more we come to resemble them; thus, the more we sympathize with particular people, the more "peculiarly agreeable" pleasure we feel in sympathizing with them (T 2.2.4.7/SBN 354).

This explanation is similar to the increased vivacity account of the pleasure of mutual sympathy that we saw Smith attack. In both accounts, an increase in mental "liveliness" is a source of pleasure. But while the increased vivacity account that Smith has in mind derives this pleasure from an increase in underlying joy, Hume's account derives this pleasure from the increased mental liveliness or vivacity itself. With this account, Hume can claim that the sympathy we experience with people we easily associate with ourselves, such as friends, family members, and those with similar "tempers and dispositions" to us, is itself notably pleasing because it provides an especially strong degree of mental stimulation (T 2.2.4.6/SBN 354). As his response to Smith shows, he also believes that sometimes, in cases like these, this pleasure *is* strong enough to overpower the pain of the affect with which we sympathize, thereby rendering an entire experience of sympathy with pain agreeable. Smith's mistake, Hume argues, is in thinking that both the pleasure of mutual sympathy and its predominance occur in all "ordinary cases."[42]

Hume's critique is not without problems. One, which arises with respect to the worry about overpowering and predominance, is that it assumes that Smith is trying to describe experiences that are always wholly pleasant, rather than often of a more ambivalent character. For Smith, sympathy with grief involves two feelings, namely, the pain of sympathetic grief and the pleasure of observing fellow-feeling. These could be, in Humean language, contrary passions with different objects—the source of the shared pain in the first case and the sharedness itself in the second—that could stay unmixed and out-of-contact, like "two opposite liquors in different bottles" (DP 201). Thus, however much he tends to emphasize the positive aspects of the experience of sympathy with pain, there is no need for Smith to defend the view that "the whole movement" of a sympathetic experience is "agreeable."

Another problem for Hume's criticism, which arises with respect to the worry about frequency, is that Smith does not think that we automatically sympathize with everyone. As Hume does, Smith thinks that we only sympathize with people we see as similar to us, that is, people who feel the same way that we do or would feel. And, as Hume does, Smith thinks that only this kind of sympathy is a source of intrinsic enjoyment. For both, the pleasure of mutual sympathy depends upon a perception of similarity. The difference between them on this issue seems to be that in imagining interaction "*with a man with whom we can entirely sympathize*," Hume sets a higher bar for pleasure-causing similarity (Letter 36). For Smith, the intrinsic pleasure of sympathy can be triggered by particular, hyper-localized agreements in sentiment. For Hume, it seems to depend upon more "entire" correspondences, such as those between people who share "particular tempers and dispositions" (T 2.2.4.6-7/SBN 354). But there is nothing in the detail of Hume's moral psychology that forces this conclusion upon him. He even admits that "the company of *strangers* is agreeable to us" because even it "[inlivens] our thought" in the way described previously; however, since relations like familial ties, acquaintance, and resemblance are not present, it only does so "*for a short time*" (T 2.2.4.5/SBN 353; former emphasis added).

Thus, Hume and Smith's disagreement about the intrinsic pleasure of mutual sympathy is fundamentally one of emphasis. Smith stresses the possibility that other human beings are all like us enough to be partners in pleasing mutual sympathy, so much so that he treats the desire for mutual sympathy as a fundamental human motive. Again, there is no principled reason why Hume cannot treat sympathy itself as this pervasive a goal.[43] Officially, however, he simply does not think that the pursuit of mutual sympathy is a central component of human social life.

The philosophical import of this difference of emphasis lies in what Smith builds upon his side of it. One such thing is a unique general conception of human sociability that will come into greater focus for us in Sections 1, 2, and 4 of the next chapter. Another is a unique answer to the psychological foundation of moral judgment question. We turn to this answer in the next three sections of this chapter.

Section 2: Sympathy and Approbation

I mentioned earlier that for Smith, the pleasure of mutual sympathy and pain of its absence respectively constitute approval and disapproval; this is the way in which Smith's sympathy theory answers the psychological foundation of moral judgment question. In this section, we consider in more detail how Smith thinks about the relationship between mutual sympathy and approval. In the two following sections, we turn to the two-pronged conception of moral evaluation bound up with his conception of this relationship.

We have seen that we feel the pleasure of mutual sympathy when we "observe" concord between our "sympathetic emotions" and another person's non-sympathy-based ones (I.i.3.1). In other words, if I imagine myself into another person's position, feel the same way that I believe she does, and notice this agreement in feeling, then I feel a certain kind of pleasure. Several clarifications are in order. First, as Robert Shaver points out, the pleasure of mutual sympathy seems fundamentally to depend upon my ability to drum up an *actual feeling*, not just a *belief* about a feeling I would have in the other person's circumstances[44] (although, as we will see in Section 2 of the next chapter, the qualifier "fundamentally" is very important). Second, kind and degree of feeling both matter in determining the existence of concord; the point about kind is obvious, and Smith is explicit that degree matters as well (I.i.3.1).[45] Third, since concord can be a matter of degree, the pleasure of mutual sympathy can be a matter of degree. (This follows not just in principle but also from Smith's frequent examples of degrees of approval and disapproval; we'll see some of these in the next section.) Fourth, notice that the pleasure of mutual sympathy requires comparing our own sympathetic feelings with another person's non-sympathetic ones. We must get our idea of the latter either with or without a prior imaginative act of the same kind as that involved in sympathizing. Smith does not spell out how this first stage in the process works. What we have seen him say or at least insinuate about the epistemic aspects of sympathy suggests that this first stage must involve an act of imagining oneself into another's position (or even *as* another). However, if it does, then the process by which we feel the pleasure of mutual sympathy becomes much more complicated and—if this process is to be the same as that by which we make moral judgments—problematic than it first appeared; we return to this issue at the end of the next section.

To get from the pleasure of mutual sympathy to the pleasure of approval, Smith adds the claim that having sentiments is inseparable from approving of them as "just and proper, and suitable to their objects" (I.i.3.1); the same goes for "opinions" (I.i.3.2). From this claim, it is a short step to one about how our approval of others' beliefs and feelings work: noticing that we feel the same way or believe the same thing as another person is inseparable from approving of this other person's feelings or beliefs. Smith's choice of words indicates that he sees this connection as both a psychological and a conceptual one.[46] If I notice that you admire a work of art in the same way as I do, I "must surely allow" that your admiration is warranted; if I notice that you do not laugh at something I find funny, I "cannot avoid" concluding that you've made a mistake. If I notice "perfect concord" between us, I "necessarily" approve of your beliefs or sentiments. This approval is the "same thing" as noticing the concord; "neither can I possibly conceive that I should do the one without the other." In fact, it is "acknowledged, by every body," that "to approve or disapprove" of others' "opinions" or "sentiments or passions" can "*mean no more* than to observe their agreement or disagreement with our own" (I.i.3.1–2; emphasis added). After all, "I neither have, nor can have, any other way of judging about" things like "your sight," "your ear," "your reason," "your resentment," and "your love" than by consulting my own like faculties; there is no "other rule or canon" or "standards and measures" for me to use (I.i.3.9–10; I.i.3.1).

Regardless of whether he saw the connection between feeling and approving as psychological, conceptual, or both, Smith's observation of it demonstrates agreement with a version of Nicolas Malebranche's famous dictum that the passions justify themselves. Malebranche says that "all passions seek their own justification" by causing us to make judgments that justify and thus maintain them.[47] In his essay on the history of astronomy, Smith expresses agreement with this point when he explicitly reminds us that "our passions, as Father Malbranche observes, all justify themselves; that is, suggest to us opinions which justify them" (HA III.1.48).[48] Smith also expresses agreement with this point in the TMS but with slightly different language: "the passions . . . as father Malebranche says, all justify themselves, and *seem reasonable and proportioned to their objects as long as we continue to feel them*" (III.4.3; emphasis added). If the passions "suggest" distinct "judgments" and "opinions" that support them, then they will also certainly appear "reasonable and proportioned to their objects." Thus, in emphasizing the outcome of this process of self-justification in the second expression, Smith is not distorting Malebranche's meaning; this becomes especially evident when we consider the context of Smith's citation, which is a chapter on the ways in which "violent emotions" can "discolour our views of things" (III.4.3).[49] However, it remains notable that Smith's second expression of agreement with Malebranche's dictum that the passions justify themselves makes the relationship between feeling a passion and approving of it seem especially close, such that the approval is either built into the passion or at least more closely connected to it than the other version of the dictum might suggest.

That we automatically see our passions as justified in this way suggests that the affects in which Smith is interested are not mere feelings. As I mentioned in Section 1 in the previous chapter, Smith provides no taxonomy of the differences and relationships between various affect concepts. He has no problem running them together, as he does in this single sentence: "In every *passion* of which the mind of man is susceptible, the *emotions* of the by-stander always correspond to what, by bringing the case home to himself, he imagines should be the *sentiments* of the sufferer" (I.i.1.4; emphases added). But regardless of whether he refers to them as passions, emotions, sentiments, or something else, the affects Smith sees as involved in sympathy-based approval are much more complicated than, for example, the sensation of warmth. Rather, these affects not only have objects—such that we are, for example, always afraid *of* something or angry *at* someone—but also dispose us to call to mind considerations that act for us as reasons for feeling them—such that we can always say, for example, that we are afraid of that thing *because* it is dangerous or angry at that person *because* he insulted us.[50] Of these two apparently cognitive components or close accompaniments of the affect, the second one is what justifies it in our eyes and thereby makes it the case that we approve of feeling it.[51]

As we'll see in Section 3 of the next chapter, Smith believes that social interaction is either causally or logically necessary to trigger the disposition to call to consciousness considerations that justify our passions. But this detail aside, it seems clear now that the pleasure we take in noticing mutual sympathy constitutes approval of others and the displeasure we take in noticing its absence constitutes disapproval of others because of this disposition toward approval of our own sentiments. And it does so regardless of which sentiments we find to be in or out of sympathy. As Smith puts the point in his explicit response to Hume: "in the sentiment of approbation, there are two things to be taken notice of; first, the sympathetic passion of the spectator; and secondly, the emotion which arises from his observing the perfect coincidence between this sympathetic passion in himself, and the original passion in the principle principally concerned"; the sentiment of approbation "properly consists" in the latter, "always agreeable and delightful" emotion (I.iii.1.9).[52]

Though this distinction between our sympathetic passion and our reaction to noticing mutual sympathy provides Smith with a response to Hume, it generates problems for his own criticism of Hutcheson-style accounts of approbation. Recall from Section 3 of the previous chapter Smith's emphatic claim that "no common features can possibly be discovered between" the respective approval and disapproval of different kinds of sentiments; it simply feels different, he believes, to approve of a "tender, delicate, and humane sentiment" from how it feels to approve of a "great, daring, and magnanimous" sentiment. Smith continues that his own account of moral evaluation can account for this difference because the role it assigns to sympathy gives the feeling of approbation something "in common with the sentiments we [approve] of"; thus, approbation of a humane sentiment feels differently from approbation of a magnanimous one because sympathy with a humane sentiment feels differently from sympathy with a magnanimous one (VII

.iii.3.13). This claim, however, contradicts Smith's distinction between "the sympathetic passion of the spectator," which does take on the character of the agent's "original passion," and the sentiment of approbation that the spectator feels upon noticing sentimental concord with the agent, which does not.

Perhaps Smith just made a mistake on one side of this contradiction. Since the distinction between the pleasure of mutual sympathy and the sympathetic passion is crucial to his response to Hume, who rightly perceived the former to be the "Hinge of [Smith's] system," it would be better for him if the mistake was in denying there is a "peculiar sentiment" of approbation (Letter 36; VI.iii.3.11).[53] As we saw in the last chapter, the phenomenology to which he appeals in making this denial is not obvious. Furthermore, there does not seem to be any major problem in identifying the pleasure of mutual sympathy as such a "peculiar sentiment." We might worry that this amounts to the kind of philosophical innovation that he wished to avoid. But Hume, while also championing methodological closeness to common life (e.g., EHU 12.25/E 162),[54] identifies moral approval and disapproval with "a pleasure or uneasiness of a particular kind" that is also caused by sympathy (T 3.1.2.3/SBN 471). Thus, there would be generally friendly precedent for Smith to follow in taking this road.[55] Moreover, doing so would only involve pointing to a sentiment that manifests itself in common life but has been philosophically overlooked, not inventing a totally new one; thus, Smith can still maintain that his view is less innovative than the Hutchesonian or Hutcheson-inspired one.

But perhaps we can resolve the contradiction on Smith's behalf by reinterpreting one of the two positions involved in it. One way to avoid the contradiction is by emphasizing Smith's initial reference to the "sentiment of approbation" as involving "two things to be taken notice of," the "sympathetic passion of the spectator" and the observation of the "perfect coincidence" between this passion and the "original" one. If the sentiment of approbation consists of this *combination*, the former component could account for the variety in our experiences of approval and disapproval. Maybe this is exactly what Smith has in mind in the argument against the special moral sentiment view. The trouble, though, is that he claims that the sentiment of approbation "properly consists" only in the latter; by implication, the former is something only "to be taken notice of" in the overall experience leading up to the approbation.[56]

So maybe we can reinterpret the other side of the contradiction. In making the argument against the special moral sentiment view, Smith could mean that there is "quite a different species" of concord and discord present in different instances of moral approval and disapproval. Maybe his idea is that the pleasure of approbation and pain of disapprobation that we feel upon noticing concord and discord is always *inflected* by the sentiments between which the concord and discord occur, such that the pleasure we take in concord with humane feelings differs from the pleasure we take in concord with magnanimous ones and the pain we take in discord with "cruelty" differs from the pain we take in discord with "mean-spiritedness" (VII.iii.3.13). Such a reading would be consistent with his example of how an "emotion of a particular kind" can undergo several "variations." He tells us that "anger against a man is, no doubt, somewhat different from anger against a woman, and that again from anger against a child." Here he distinguishes between three "modification[s]" of the same passion by distinguishing between the "particular character of [their] object[s]." Similarly, the pleasure of observing concord could be modified by the "particular character of its object," with "object" taken to signify the kind of passions that are in concord. Of course, Smith's overall point in this passage is that while it is easy to identify anger as a "species" and difficult to make fine distinctions regarding its particular "variations," it is easy to distinguish between the many different instances of approval and disapproval but difficult to see what unites them into general classes. So on the present interpretive strategy, Smith would need the different "variations" of the pleasure of concord and pain of discord to have less in common with each other than the different variations of anger, but enough in common in absolute terms to remain consistent with his response to Hume (VII.iii.3.13). The former requirement seems especially meetable when the pleasure of concord and pain of discord are inflected by different kinds of passions. It might not be when the pleasure of concord and pain of discord are inflected by different instances of the same kind of passion; however, Smith's choice of examples suggests that he is not committed to the view that such experiences even are all that different.

In any case, an important point has become clear: for Smith, the psychological foundation of moral judgment is sympathy because sympathizing *is* evaluating.[57] The next two sections complete Smith's answer to the psychological foundation of moral judgment question by respectively laying out the two different forms he believes that moral judgments take. However, before we turn to each form, we should unpack some of the interesting language Smith uses in making the distinction between them. He begins by claiming that all moral evaluations target a "sentiment or affection of the heart." The first kind of evaluation considers a "sentiment or affection . . . in relation to *the cause which excites it*, or *the motive which gives occasion to it*" (I.i.3.5; emphases added). Smith calls these evaluations "judgments of propriety." He continues: "In the suitableness or unsuitableness, in the proportion or disproportion which the affection seems to bear to the cause or *object which excites it* consists the propriety or impropriety, the decency or ungracefulness of the consequent action" (I.i.3.6; emphasis added). The language of "cause which excites" from both quotations is pretty straightforward. With it, Smith is saying that we judge each other's emotional reactions to the things that happen us. These reactions can be, in his language, proper or improper, or, in what is perhaps ours, warranted or unwarranted. (To the extent that judgments of this kind presume control over our sentimental reactions, Smith's recognition of them provides more evidence of his complex, cognitively laden conception of sentiment; after all, affects with such components or accompaniments seem more controllable than pure feelings do.) However, the language of "motive which gives occasion" to our feelings is less clear. Is Smith talking about judgments that consider whether we are, from identifiable motives, deliberately generating "sentiments or affections" in ourselves for the right reasons? I think the language in the second quoted description indicates that he has a wider class of evaluations in mind than this idiosyncratic one. There, he supplements "cause which excites" with "object which excites" (he does the same at II.i.intro.2). If this combination mirrors the previous one, as it likely does, then Smith seems to be making a distinction between responsive *sentiments*, *feelings*, *passions*, *etc.*, and responsive *desires*. A personal tragedy, for example, might *cause* us to overreact, underreact, or react appropriately, and a desirable *object* might cause or "motivate" appropriate or inappropriate kinds and degrees of desires in us to attain it. It makes sense to talk about warranted and unwarranted reactions in both cases. And given the maximally inclusive way in which Smith talks about affects, it is unsurprising to see him lump these kinds of cases together.

The next category considers a "sentiment or affection . . . in relation to *the end which it proposes*, or *the effect which it tends to produce*" (I.i.3.5; emphases added). Smith calls these evaluations "judgments of merit." He continues: "In the beneficial or hurtful nature of the effects which the affection *aims at*, or *tends to produce*, consists the merit or demerit of the action, the qualities by which it is entitled to reward, or is deserving of punishment" (I.i.3.7; emphases added). Again, we see a combination of straightforward and ambiguous language. The phrases "end which it proposes" and "aims at" belong in the former category; clearly, Smith is saying that we judge people based on whether they *intentionally* attempt to produce "beneficial or hurtful" things. But the phrase "tends to produce" suggests that a feeling can also be evaluated just for *causing* good or bad consequences, potentially regardless of intent. We will soon see that Smith does thinks that we make evaluations of this latter kind, but his own attitude toward at least some of them is complicated. Also note the blurriness of the line between the former kind of judgment and what I just identified as a desire-focused propriety judgment. As we will also soon see, this blurriness is indicative of the fact that judgments of merit are really just special kinds of judgments of propriety.

Smith believes that philosophers commonly recognize the second category of moral evaluation but not the first.[58] Thus, he sees his distinction between the two as a necessary corrective:

> Philosophers have, of late years, considered chiefly the tendency of affections, and have given little attention to the relation which they stand in to the cause which excites them. In common life, however, when we judge of any person's conduct, and of the sentiments which directed it, we constantly consider them under both these aspects. When we blame in another man the excesses of love, of grief, of resentment, we not only consider the ruinous effects which they tend to produce, but the little occasion which was given for them. The merit of his favourite, we say, is not so great, his misfortune is not so dreadful, his provocation is not so extraordinary, as to

> justify so violent a passion. We should have indulged, we say; perhaps, have approved of the violence of his emotion, had the cause been in any respect proportioned to it. (I.i.3.8)

In trademark fashion, Smith again takes philosophers to task for overlooking a feature of common moral life. Obviously, he believes the mistake they have made is an important one, as it led them to overlook an entire category of moral judgment, which, as I just mentioned, ends up being the more fundamental of the two.

So how does each kind of judgment work? It will help us throughout our discussion of them if we familiarize ourselves now with the simple model of social interaction that Smith employs to explain them. This model always contains at least two positions but sometimes three. The first position is inhabited by the "spectator," who is the person making a moral evaluation by attempting to sympathize with an "agent," the person who inhabits the second position. If the agent is doing anything that impacts or could impact a third person, the "patient"—this is my term, not Smith's—enters the mix; importantly, the spectator attempts to sympathize with and thus evaluates this person too.

Section 3: Judgments of Propriety

Let's start with propriety judgments. We make these judgments by comparing how and what we think the agent feels with how and what we feel upon imagining ourselves into the agent's situation. The nearer our sympathetic feelings approach how and what we think the agent feels, the more pleasure of mutual sympathy we feel and the more we approve of the agent's feelings as "just[ified] and proper and suitable to their objects." The further our sympathetic feelings remain from how and what we think the agent feels, the more pain we feel in the absence of mutual sympathy and the more we disapprove of the agent's feelings as "unjust[ified] and improper, and unsuitable to the causes which excite them."[59] (Since the presence and absence of mutual sympathy are correlative, it seems in principle possible to hit a point of perfect neutrality between them. Smith does not discuss this possibility, but the fact that it is one is unproblematic; after all, we do sometimes find ourselves caught between approbation and disapprobation.) When the match or mismatch between the spectator's and the agent's feelings is one of degree rather than kind, Smith conceptualizes the relation between the two feelings in terms of "proportion" (I.i.3.1).[60] And he often expresses his conception of these proportions with music-related language; for example, he tells us that passions can be in "concord" or not (I.i.3.1), can "beat time" to each other or not, and can match in "pitch" or "sharpness of . . . tone" or not (I.i.4.8).

He distinguishes between propriety judgments regarding "sentiments" having "objects" with no "peculiar relation" to agent or spectator and propriety judgments regarding sentiments having objects "considered as peculiarly affecting one or the other of us" (I.i.4.1; cf. I.i.4.5; I.ii.intro.1). The former involve attribution of "the qualities of taste and good judgment" regarding matters like

> the beauty of a plain, the greatness of a mountain, the ornaments of a building, the expression of a picture, the composition of a discourse, the conduct of a third [presumably unrelated, random] person, the proportions of different quantities and numbers, the various appearances which the great machine of the universe is perpetually exhibiting, with the secret wheels and springs which produce them. (I.i.4.2)

The latter involve not these "matters of speculation" or "taste" but more emotionally charged, personal ones, such as how I react to "the misfortune that has befallen me, or the injury that has been done me" (I.i.4.5). It is tempting to classify the former judgments as nonmoral and the latter judgments as moral, especially in light of the standing challenge mentioned in Section 3 of the previous chapter for all moral sentimentalists to identify which sentiments are indeed the moral ones and in light of the fact that Smith explicitly classifies positive evaluations of the former kind as evidence that their objects possess potentially nonmoral "intellectual virtues" (I.i.4.3). However, we should note that Smith does not explicitly make this distinction. Furthermore, the attack we saw Smith make on Hutcheson for being unable to explain how we morally evaluate moral evaluations flies in the face of classifying the here-mentioned ability to evaluate properly "the conduct of a third person," even a totally random one, as a nonmoral, intellectual virtue. And while we might be tempted to interpret the more robust act of imagining oneself in another's situation required by the latter kinds of judgments than the former to be a mark of the moral, we shall see in Section 6 that Smith classifies as moral, albeit in a secondary sense, a kind of judgment that does not require this sort of act. As we shall also see, Smith does invoke the secondary status of this kind of judgment in an attempt to limit the focus of specifically moral evaluation to human beings. But he still never explicitly says that this kind of judgment is nonmoral when applied to human beings. Thus, for the sake of being careful, let's just proceed only sure that the TMS seems way more interested in the latter class of propriety judgments identified here than it is the former.[61]

While we will give full attention in Chapter 6 to Smith's propriety-based, first-order account of how we should live, it is worth going over some of the more detailed explanatory but partly normative comments he makes regarding the kind of propriety judgment in which he is most interested. That these comments are partly normative is clear from the language he employs in the title of the section in which he makes them, "Of the Degrees of the different Passions which are consistent with Propriety" (I.ii). This language indicates that he is not just describing and explaining judgments we tend to make but also endorsing them as correct. However, given our present focus, as we proceed, we should think of these observations mainly as examples that help illuminate how propriety judgments work, rather than expressions of first-order moral commitments.

Smith's account of how propriety judgments work for different kinds of passions can be organized via three distinctions. The first overarching one is between "Passions which take their origin from the body" (I.i.1) and "passions which take their origin from the imagination" (I.i.1.6). The second distinction sits underneath the latter heading, between "Passions which take their origin from a *particular turn or habit* of the Imagination" (I.i.2; emphasis added) and those that do not. And the third distinction, which falls under each of these last two prongs, is between "unsocial Passions" (I.ii.3), "social Passions" (I.ii.4), and "selfish Passions" (I.ii.5). Collectively, Smith's treatment of these categories reveals four general patterns in our propriety judgments. The first and most basic one is that we tend to make negative propriety judgments of sentiments that too heavily tax the sympathetic imaginations of spectators. This should be unsurprising. Since what we take to be the point of propriety for any sentiment is determined by our ability to sympathize with it, what we take to be the point of propriety must be sensitive to features of our ability to sympathize. For Smith, the sympathetic imagination is powerful enough to drum up real feelings in a spectator, but it has limits. Thus, we should expect to see patterns in propriety judgments that are linked to these limits. The second pattern involves the impact of sympathy with the person who is the object of the agent's sentiments—the earlier-named patient—which can either counteract or enhance the spectator's sympathy with an agent. A third pattern is that we tend to make positive propriety judgments of sentiments that are pleasing and negative propriety judgments of sentiments that are painful because spectators are respectively prone and averse to sympathizing with the former and the latter. A fourth pattern involves judgment-impacting, sympathy-conducive, and sympathy-inhibitive feelings that reliably arise under certain circumstances.

The first pattern undergirds the first distinction, that between bodily passions and imagination-based passions. Smith claims that the imagination simply cannot cause us to feel bodily passions such as "violent hunger" (I.ii.1.1), "the passion by which Nature unites the two sexes" (I.ii.1.2), or "bodily pain" (I.ii.1.5). It is important to stress that Smith is thinking about purely bodily versions of these affects. A bodily passion can also function "as a situation that gives occasion to other passions" (I.ii.2.2). Our imaginations can lead us to feel versions of these other passions, "which take their origin from the imagination" of the agent (I.ii.1.5.6). Smith provides several examples to make this point: when we read a "journal of a siege, or of a sea voyage" in which people are starving, we feel, for example, vicarious fear, but we don't get hungry (I.ii.1.1); we sympathize more with suffering from "dangerous diseases" than we do with comparatively more painful but less dangerous ones, like "the gout or the tooth-ach" because the former involves imagination-based "anxiety" about the future (I.ii.1.9); when "Greek tragedies" represent "the agonies of bodily pain," they only successfully trigger sympathy in spectators when this pain involves an imagination-based passion like the dread of death (I.ii.1.11); and even though some of us might "faint and grow sick at the sight of a chirurgical operation," the fact that surgeons do not reveals that this has more to do with the "novelty" of them than with sympathy with bodily pain (I.ii.1.10). As a result of the spectator's relative inability to sympathize with purely bodily passions and ability to sympathize with imagination-based ones, the level of feeling and expression of the latter that is consistent with propriety is much higher than that of the former. We are generally willing to listen when others are fearful about the prognosis of a painful illness, but we would also generally rather they stop moaning.

However, the level of acceptability is not equally high for all imagination-based passions. Some are almost as little likely to win sympathy from a spectator as bodily passions are. These sentiments are rooted in a "peculiar turn or habit of imagination." In principle, they are more accessible to the imagination of the spectator than are bodily ones, but since they are rooted in repeated experience of an imagination "having run in the same channel," they are idiosyncratic enough to be rather closed off. Romantic love for a particular person is Smith's prime example here.[62] If a friend is in love, we might be able to sympathize with his concomitant "high hopes of happiness" or "exquisite distress" when these hopes fail. But as was the case with bodily passions like hunger and physical pain, we are not sympathizing with his romantic love "as a passion, but as a situation that gives occasion to other passions which interest us," passions that are rooted in neither the body nor a particularly conditioned imagination; this same mechanism, Smith observes, also best explains our sympathetic reactions to characters in fictional "tragedies and romances" (I.ii.2.2–3). Thus, due to the spectator's inability to sympathize with passions rooted in a "peculiar turn or habit of imagination," we are expected to practice a "certain reserve" when we talk not only of our romantic attachments but also of any other potentially idiosyncratic affection or interest, such as those tied to "our own friends, our own studies, our own professions" (I.ii.2.6).

The next three patterns appear in Smith's discussion of his third distinction. Among the passions that "take their origin from the imagination," whether a "peculiar turn or habit" of it or not, are "unsocial," "social," and "selfish" passions. "Hatred and resentment" are the most fundamental unsocial passions, though they are both subject to "different modifications." These passions have an even harder time winning the spectator's sympathy than bodily or essentially idiosyncratic ones do. Sure, "violent hunger" and romantic love might not win much sympathy from a spectator. But if we are ourselves "in health," we sympathize with hunger at least to the extent that it is "agreeable to see our companions eat with a good appetite," even if watching them "eat voraciously is universally regarded as a piece of ill manners"; moreover, when someone is ill-mannered in this way, we are at most annoyed (I.ii.1.1). Similarly, spectators cannot really sympathize with romantic love, but it is at worst "ridiculous" to them; it also often includes a "strong mixture" of passions with which we have "the greatest propensity to sympathize," which renders it even "less disagreeable" in itself (I.ii.2.5). But passions like hatred, resentment, anger, etc. tend to "divide" our sympathy in opposing directions, "between the person who feels them, and the person who is the object of them"; other things being equal, any sympathy we feel for the angry agent gets cut by sympathy we feel for the object of the anger, the patient who presumably also disapproves of the anger. One might think that the standard result Smith has in mind is something like neutrality, as sympathy with the resenter and sympathy with the resented cancel each other out. But Smith believes that the unsocial passions "are the only [ones] of which the expressions . . . do not dispose and prepare us to sympathize with them." Thus, other things being equal, the conflict between the resenter and the resented is not an equal one. The sight of hatred and resentment just seems to turn us off: "both these passions are by nature the objects of our aversion" (I.ii.3.5). Smith also points out that we are naturally averse to sympathizing with the unsocial passions because they are intrinsically "disagreeable" to feel (I.ii.3.7). So since passions like hatred and resentment are always fighting an uphill battle to win a spectator's sympathy, our default response is to disapprove of them.

These same two patterns—one having to do with the role of sympathy with the patient and one having to do with the intrinsic agreeableness or disagreeableness of the agent's passions—explain why the default response to "social and benevolent affections" like "generosity, humanity, kindness, compassion, [and] mutual friendship and esteem" is sympathy and approval (I.ii.4.1). When faced with instances of these passions, we tend to experience "a redoubled sympathy" with "the person who feels them" and "the person who is the object of them," whose feelings complement rather than oppose each other.

In trying to sympathize with the agent, the spectator immediately thinks about the patient who is object of the agent's "social" feelings, who, in contrast with the patient who is the object of "unsocial" feelings, tends to approve of them. Thus, the attempt to sympathize with a benevolent agent and the attempt to sympathize with the patient who is object of this agent's benevolence pull the spectator in the same direction. Furthermore, both the fact that the agent and the patient who is object of her social feelings are in pleasing mutual sympathy with each other and the fact that social feelings are themselves intrinsically "agreeable" to feel enhance the spectator's natural proneness to sympathize with and approve of them. Smith concludes, "we have always, therefore, the strongest disposition to sympathize with the benevolent affections" (I.ii.4.2).

Smith does believe that there are cases in which spectators approve of unsocial passions and disapprove of social ones. Thus far, we have only seen him describe the spectator's default settings. In the case of the unsocial passions, the spectator will sometimes stray from these settings once she gets more information about the "cause which excited," for example, resentment (I.ii.3.5). The spectator will sympathize and approve if she sees that the resentment is a response to a prior "injury," but not a sign of knee-jerky hot-headedness or, in Smith's words, "insolence" or "petulance and low scurrility" (I.ii.3.8). In fact, Smith believes that the spectator can sometimes expect resentment strongly enough to disapprove of its absence: "a person becomes contemptible who tamely sits still, and submits to insults" without response (I.ii.3.3). Similarly, Smith believes that there are circumstances in which more information about the "cause which excited" a social passion will prevent the spectator from sympathizing with it. This seems to be so in the cases of "the too tender mother, the too indulgent father, the too generous and affectionate friend." In all these instances, the spectator simply cannot sympathize with the "excessive" strength of the agent's social feeling. However, since we are so disposed to sympathize with social feelings, the disapproval we feel in such cases involves "a species of pity, in which, however, there is a mixture of love" but never "hatred and aversion" (I.ii.4.3).

The spectator's default stance toward selfish passions, such as "grief and joy, when conceived upon account of our own private good or bad fortune," tends to be neutral. When these passions are excessive, we never disapprove of them as strongly as we do excessive unsocial passions because "no opposite sympathy" is involved. And when these passions are proper, we never approve of them as strongly as we do proper social passions because there is no "double sympathy" involved. However, there is one caveat to this general neutrality, which has to do with the fourth pattern. Smith claims we tend to sympathize more with "small joys" felt either in isolation or in "gradual succession" than we do a "sudden revolution of fortune" in a positive direction. He also claims we tend to sympathize more with "great sorrow" (I.ii.5.1) and "deep distress" than we do "small vexations" (I.ii.5.3–4). His explanation for the former tendency is that though we are naturally prone to sympathize with joy because it is agreeable, the observation of sudden, massive success can trigger the sympathy-inhibiting "sentiment of envy" (I.ii.5.1). His explanation for the latter tendency is that though we are naturally averse to sympathizing with grief because it is disagreeable, the observation of "deep affliction" proves impossible to resist; the observation of "small vexations . . . from frivolous causes," on the other hand, not only faces our general aversion to sympathizing with grief but also triggers a certain sympathy-inhibiting "malice in mankind" that "renders . . . [such] little uneasinesses . . . in some measure diverting" (I.ii.5.3).[63] Thus, we tend to disapprove of the "extravagant joy" of the upstart (I.ii.5.1) but sympathize with and approve of a "habitual cheerfulness" in response to "all those frivolous nothings which fill up the void of human life" (I.ii.5.2). And we tend to disapprove when someone is made "uneasy by every little disagreeable incident" (I.ii.5.3) but sympathize and approve to the extent of "weep[ing] even at the *feigned* representation of a [real] tragedy" (I.ii.5.4; emphasis added).[64]

Barring a massive amount of targeted psychological research, the best we can do toward assessing this litany of empirical claims about our psychological tendencies is to register some preliminary intuition-based reactions. Some of Smith's claims seem implausible. Take the one that we cannot imagine ourselves into arousal or hunger. If this is true, then how do pornography and food advertising work? Or take the claim that we cannot imagine ourselves into physical pain. What about psychosomatic conditions? But then again, all Smith needs to establish is that it is *more* difficult to imagine ourselves into these feelings than into a feeling like fear, for example. This claim does not seem as implausible as the non-relative one. Also consider Smith's claim that we are averse to sympathizing with unsocial passions like anger and resentment. If so, how do we explain the attraction to political talk radio and a large portion of social media? Perhaps Smith could say that the resentment to which sympathizers are attracted always involves the kind of background beliefs about injury that is involved in his own discussion of approval-winning resentment. Such an account strikes me as spot on.

There are also at least three interpretive questions that demand our attention. The first is that of whether Smith believes that judgments of propriety concern the *expressions* of feelings or the *feelings themselves*. The answer seems to be that some categories deal with the expressions, while others deal with the feelings. As we have to some extent already seen, his discussion of bodily passions focuses explicitly on their expression (I.ii.1.1; I.ii.1.15), as does his discussion of passions rooted in specific imaginings (I.ii.2.1; I.ii.2.6). This restriction of attention to expression seems to follow from Smith's view about the imagination's inability to drum up these kinds of passion in a spectator. If propriety judgments about them were about the passions themselves, not their expressions, then they would never be deemed proper. But surely, we don't think it improper to feel really hungry or interested in some particular thing, whether it be a person or subject. What we seem to want regarding these matters is for people to shut up about them. However, we do seem to want more from agents regarding the other passions. It seems that when we deem resentment or anger inappropriate or deem humanity and kindness appropriate, we really do not want agents to feel the former and really do want agents to feel the latter.[65] It also seems that when we think an agent has overreacted to a small annoyance, we really do want the agent actually not to feel so bothered. Relevantly, in his discussion of virtue, Smith makes a distinction between restraint of one's passions from "the sense of propriety," after which they are "all in some degree moderated and subdued," and restraint of one's passions from "prudential considerations" alone, after which they remain "lurking in the breast with all their original fury" (VI.concl.3–4). Bracketing the thorny matter of how to apply these comments from the clearly normative context of Smith's virtue theory to the current one, which we are treating as mainly descriptive, they seem to provide clear evidence that Smith takes at least some propriety judgments to be concerned with what we actually feel.[66]

But before we rest contented in carving things up this way, we must recognize that expressions also factor prominently in Smith's discussions of unsocial (I.ii.3.5), social (I.ii.4.1), and selfish passions (I.ii.5.1–3). Furthermore, Smith frames the whole section by apparently prioritizing expression over actual feeling:

> There are some passions which it is indecent to express very strongly, even upon those occasions, in which it is acknowledged that we cannot avoid feeling them in the highest degree. And there are others of which the strongest expressions are upon many occasions extremely graceful, even though the passions themselves do not, perhaps, arise so necessarily. (I.ii .intro.2)

Thus, Smith seems to think that expressions do matter even with respect to the class of propriety judgments in which they appear to matter least.

So in what sense do expressions matter in this class of propriety judgment? It seems that Smith's expression talk should be read epistemically, such that the expression of a passion matters because it indicates what an agent actually feels, which is what really interests the spectator in the class of cases in question. This seems to be what is going on when Smith talks about "passions of which the expressions" do or "do not dispose and prepare us to sympathize with them" (I.ii.3.5). If an agent expresses benevolence or resentment, the spectator then knows that the agent is feeling benevolence or resentment, and the spectator is disposed to sympathize or not to sympathize accordingly. Furthermore, as Shaver observes, expressions can indicate not just what an agent is feeling but how strongly the agent is feeling it; in keeping with this point, Smith describes an example of resentment that wins sympathy and approval as occurring "when no word, no gesture, escapes [the agent] that *denotes* an emotion more violent than what we can keep to" (II.i.5.8; emphasis added). Thus, when Smith says that "the expression of a passion has propriety or impropriety," he means that it does so "according to whether I feel that passion to a degree that would produce that expression, after imagining myself in the relevant situation" (2006: 192–3).

The second interpretive puzzle concerns the question of what, within the category of propriety judgments that fundamentally concern passions, Smith believes is the role of the connection between passion and action. At the end of the previous section, we saw Smith refer to "the propriety or impropriety, the decency or ungracefulness of the *consequent action*" that follows from a sentiment (I.i.3.6; emphasis added). Elsewhere, he describes propriety and impropriety as "qualities ascribed to the *actions and conduct* of mankind" (II.i .intro.1; emphasis added). This language suggests that even though judgments of propriety target sentiments, they do so only insofar as the sentiments issue in *action*, even if only potentially. But directly after the passage from which the first quotation is taken, he distinguishes judgments of propriety in the following way:

> When we blame in another man the excess of love, of grief, of resentment, we not only consider the ruinous effects which they tend to produce, but the little occasion which was given of them. The merit of his favourite, we say, is not so great, his misfortune is not so dreadful, his provocation is not so extraordinary, as to justify so violent a passion. We should have indulged, we say; perhaps, have approved of the violence of his emotion, had the cause been in any respect proportioned to it. (I.i.3.8)

This characterization of judgments of propriety certainly seems focused on sentiments without any reference to action. Furthermore, it seems that Smith would want to maintain a distinction between the negative attitude we feel toward excessive anger per se and the negative attitude we feel toward excessive anger that issues in violent action; to jump ahead a little, this seems to be exactly what his distinction between judgments of propriety and judgments of merit is doing. So how should we understand his position on the role of action in propriety judgments?

I suggest that we treat these references to action similarly to how we treated the references to expressions. Actions, like expressions, can indicate what a person is feeling and how strongly. As Smith observes, "there is no other way of marking and distinguishing [passions] from one another, but by describing the effect which they produce without, the alterations which they occasion in the countenance, in the air and external behavior, the resolutions they suggest, the actions they prompt to" (VII.iv.5). Thus, we can evaluate actions in the way we evaluate expressions as signs of a passion.

Smith's overall position on the relationship between passion, expression, and action, then, seems to be as follows. In relevant cases—ones not involving bodily passions or idiosyncratic imagination-based passions—we make propriety judgments first and foremost about sentiments, even if they do not issue in expression or action. If they do issue in expression or action, our propriety judgments extend to these too. In these cases, we can think of the expression or action as indicative of the strength of the sentiment behind it. When we do this, we deem the expression or action proper or improper in a sense that is entirely secondary to and derivative from the propriety or impropriety of the sentiment. However, it might be better, even if only in some cases, to think of the expression or action as inseparable from the sentiment behind it. When we do this, we deem the expression or action as proper or improper in a sense that is bound up with the propriety or impropriety of the sentiment; the sentiment and the expression or action together constitute one object of evaluation. The most obvious example of a case like this, involving action anyways, would be when a sentiment involves an explicit intent to act. As Smith eventually observes, "the whole nature and circumstances of [an] action" include the "intention or affection" behind it (II.iii.intro.1).

When an action that factors into a propriety judgment (in whatever way) impacts or tends to impact the interests of another person, we are making what Smith classifies as a judgment of merit. The next section considers how these judgments work. However, before turning to them, I would like to point to a third puzzle regarding propriety judgments, though one that I will not attempt to solve until the next chapter. Recall from Section 1 of the previous chapter that Smith responds to the egoist answer to the psychological foundation of moral judgment question by stressing that sympathy involves not imagining oneself into the position of another person but imagining what it is like to *be* another person; in Smith's words, "I do not consider what I . . . should suffer" in your circumstances but "what I should suffer if I was really you" (VII.iii.1.4). In the first section of this chapter, we also saw that this claim just renders more explicit a feature of his own conception of sympathy (I.i.1.2). However, the sympathy-based answer to the psychological foundation of moral judgment question that we have seen come together in this and the previous section requires sympathizing spectators to maintain a gap in their imaginations between themselves and the agents with whom they attempt to sympathize. If I imaginatively *identify* with an agent, I cannot compare how I feel upon imagining myself into the agent's shoes with how I believe the agent feels. Yet this comparison is required for me to judge the agent according to my perception of sentimental concord or discord between us. It seems, then, that there is a tension within Smith's account of sympathy.[67]

Several ways to resolve this apparent problem are available. Some commentators have stressed that as a matter of fact, there will always be a gap between the spectator and the agent, which implies that space for critical evaluation will always remain open.[68] At least one commentator has implied that there is no real tension in Smith's view because disapproval ends up being what happens when our attempts to identify with an agent fail.[69] Fleischacker, however, provides the deepest relevant suggestion by doubting that Smith holds a "stable conception of the self by which we could definitively resolve . . . what counts as your perspective and what belongs instead to mine, when I try to imagine myself in your shoes."[70] If lines between selves are essentially blurry, there cannot be enough of a difference between imaginatively projecting myself into another's situation and imaginatively identifying myself with this person to render any tension between the two acts even articulable; I am always, to some degree, performing both.[71]

All three of these options are plausible (though the third at least complicates our basic understanding of Smith's answer to the psychological foundation of moral judgment question). But regardless of whether imaginative identification is possible or even coherently distinguishable at any fundamental level from imaginative projection, there seems to be a difference in intent between using one's imagination to sympathize for the sake of evaluating and using one's imagination to sympathize for the sake of identifying (even if we are, as I imagine a proponent of the third option would argue, always doing both). This difference also gets papered over by the suggestion that disapproval is just what happens when attempts at identification fail. Thus, I return to this issue in Section 6 of the next chapter.

Section 4: Judgments of Merit

As we saw at the end of the second section, judgments of merit consider a sentiment not "in relation to the cause or object which excites it," as judgments of propriety do, but "in relation to the end which it proposes, or to the effect which it tends to produce" (II.i.intro.2). The ends and effects Smith has in mind relate to the interests of the patient. In contrast with his account of propriety judgments, Smith's account of merit judgments involves a fair amount of what looks like conceptual analysis (though he does support the account with plenty of examples from both everyday life and history) (II.i.1.5–6; II.i.3.2; II.i.5.3–4). He establishes a logical chain from "merit" to deservedness of "reward" to being the "proper and approved object of that sentiment which most immediately and directly prompts us to reward, or to do good to another"; he does the same thing from "demerit" to deservedness of "punishment" to being the "proper and approved object of that sentiment which most immediately and directly prompts us to punish, or to inflict evil upon another" (II.i.1.1). Actions are meritorious when they deserve reward and demeritorious when they deserve punishment. And actions deserve reward when they are the proper object of the sentiment that motivates rewarding and deserve punishment when they are the proper object of the sentiment that motivates punishing. Therefore, determining what these sentiments are and when they are proper is the key to understanding how merit judgments work.

The sentiment that drives us to reward is gratitude, and the sentiment that drives us to punish is resentment. These sentiments have specific structures. Like all other sentiments, they involve an object and dispose us to refer to considerations that serve for us as reasons for them. But for these sentiments, such components or accompaniments can be highly specified in advance. First, these sentiments involve the belief that their objects "produced" or attempted to produce our pleasure or pain "from design" (II.iii.1.6). Second, they involve approval or disapproval of this design for reflecting an opinion about what we deserve, i.e., an opinion about "the worth of our own character, and the esteem that is due to us"; thus, the object of gratitude "values us as we value ourselves," while the object of resentment values us less than we value ourselves (II.iii.1.4–5). Third, they involve the desire not just to cause happiness or misery in their objects but to be "instrumental" in this process. Fourth, they involve the desire for their objects to see this happiness or misery as a reward or a punishment, such that they are made "conscious" that this happened "on account of [their] past conduct" (II.iii. 1.4). Thus, gratitude and resentment aim to make their objects rejoice *for* that particular benefit and grieve "*for* that particular wrong" they respectively caused or intended (III.i.1.5–6; emphasis added). Fifth, gratitude aims at reinforcing the "concord between [its object's] sentiments and our own," while resentment aims at making its object "sensible, that the person whom he injured did not deserve to be treated in that matter" and thus rectifying this discord in opinion (II.iii.1.4–5).[72]

We determine when an action is the proper object of gratitude or resentment in the same way in which we determine whether any other sentiment is the proper one to feel: we imagine ourselves into the position of the patient and see what it feels like. If we feel gratitude, then we conclude that the agent is the proper object of gratitude, and if we feel resentment, then we conclude that the agent is the proper object of resentment. These forms of sympathy are extensions of the sympathy we feel for the "joy" or the "sorrow" the patient suffers. Smith seems to think that, in standard cases, we first sympathize with these basic responses to the agent's action upon the patient and then sympathize with the patient's attitude toward the agent as their cause. In this regard, sympathy with joy or sorrow prepare us for sympathy with gratitude or resentment by disposing us positively or negatively toward whomever is responsible for the joy or sorrow; in Smith's language, the latter sympathy is "animated" by the former one, which "enhances and enlivens" it (II.i.2.4–5; II.i.5.2).

Thus, we see that a judgment of merit involves a prior judgment of propriety regarding gratitude and resentment. But this judgment of propriety itself requires yet another judgment of propriety. As we saw in the previous section, our propriety judgments about social passions like gratitude and unsocial passions like resentment are impacted by our consideration of the people who are the objects of these passions. We also saw that while spectators are naturally disposed to sympathize with and approve of gratitude and naturally disposed against sympathizing with and approving of resentment, more information about the "cause which excited" them can either feed into or push against these natural dispositions (I.ii.3.5). Since the causes that excite gratitude and resentment involve other people's sentiments, judgments about the propriety of gratitude and resentment amount to judgments about whether they are the proper responses to these other sentiments. As responses, gratitude and resentment are not just forms of joy or sorrow about something; they also involve agreement or disagreement with a view expressed by the sentiments that caused or intended the something. Therefore, sympathy with gratitude and resentment requires sympathy with a view held by grateful or resentful people about what they deserve. Grateful people hold that their benefactor is right in seeing them as deserved of the benefit, while resentful people hold that their malefactor is wrong in seeing them as deserved of the harm. But in order to determine whether we sympathize with these views, we must determine whether we sympathize with the benefactor or the malefactor. And this requires a second propriety judgment, one of *their* sentiments.

So no matter "how beneficial soever on the one hand, or how hurtful soever, the actions or intentions of the person who acts may have been," we do not sympathize with and approve of gratitude for actions performed from sentiments with which we do not sympathize and of which we do not approve, and we do not sympathize with and approve of resentment for actions performed from sentiment with which we do sympathize and of which we do approve (I.i.3.1). We do not sympathize with gratitude in response even to great benefits provided from "trivial motives," and we do not sympathize with resentment even to great harms caused by "motives and affections which we thoroughly enter into and approve of." In the former case, "our contempt for the folly of the agent" prevents us from sympathizing much with the gratitude of the man who benefits, no matter how much we might sympathize with his joy; thus, for example, we do not sympathize much with the gratitude of a man who was given an estate "merely because his name and sirname happen to be the same with those of the giver." In the latter case, our sympathy with the agent prevents us from sympathizing with the patient's resentment because this sympathy implies that the agent does "no more than what we ourselves should have wished," even if we do sympathize with the patent's misery; thus, for example, we can feel "compassion for [the] misery" of a criminal while feeling "no sort of fellow-feeling with his resentment" (II.i.3.2–3).

Notice that these are all cases in which we disapprove of gratitude or resentment because we either do not sympathize with an agent in the way required for sympathy with the patient's gratitude or we do sympathize with an agent in a way that goes against sympathizing with the patient's resentment. Thus, we do not deem the agent meritorious in the former or demeritorious in the latter. But importantly, we can also disapprove of how a patient reacts because we do sympathize with an agent's intentions even when they do not provoke a patient's gratitude or because we do not sympathize with an agent's intentions even when they do not provoke a patient's resentment. In this way, our merit judgments are not shaped by what patients actually feel but by what we think they should feel (II.i.5.11).

The extent to which merit judgments are based on propriety judgments is clear. In the very act of making a merit judgment, we are making not one but *two* interconnected propriety judgments: one of the patient's gratitude or resentment and one of the agent's motives. Thus, Smith describes our "sense of merit" as a "compounded sentiment." The agent-focused part of the compound requires an act of "direct sympathy," while the patient-focused part of the compound requires an act of "indirect sympathy," presumably because sympathy with gratitude and resentment must travel through sympathy or antipathy with an agent (II.i.5.1).

Thus far, we have dealt with judgments of merit regarding "the beneficial or hurtful effects which [an] affection proposes" (II.i.intro.2). Such judgments require sympathy with a patient's gratitude or resentment, which intrinsically attribute to the agent both a view about the patient's value and an intent or "design" that reflects this view. So when we approve of a patient's gratitude and thus approve of an agent's action as meritorious or approve of a patient's resentment and thus disapprove of an agent's action as demeritorious, we do so partly on the basis of what we take these agents to intend or "propose." But Smith also says that merit judgments consider "the beneficial or hurtful effects which [an] affection . . . tends to produce" (II.i.intro.2). This language suggests that we sometimes make merit judgments solely on the basis of an action's effect, with no regard to intention. If so, however, these merit judgments would not fit with Smith's explanation of merit judgments in terms of sympathy with gratitude and resentment; such cases seem not to involve an opinion and design to which the patient reacts.

However, for at least one sense of "tends to produce," this is not the case. Sentiments that relevantly "propose" ends are those that deliberately aim at benefiting or hurting. Clearly, these sentiments could be the standard objects of gratitude or resentment. But notice that we can feel grateful or resentful toward someone who ends up helping or hurting us, even if they lack an explicit intention to do so. This is easiest to see in the case of resentment. Smith writes:

> What chiefly enrages us against the man who injures or insults us, is the little account which he seems to make of us, the unreasonable preference which he gives to himself above us, that absurd self-love, by which he seems to imagine, that other people may be sacrificed at any time, to his conveniency or his humour. (II.iii.1.5)

The potential connotations of "sacrifice" notwithstanding, this observation describes resentment toward an action done from "self-love" rather than malice or some other form of direct ill-will toward us. Resentment of this kind could be felt toward a person who acts without thinking about us at all—and thus without "proposing" to harm us—but who harms us nonetheless, out of a total lack of concern for how we are impacted, even though it is clear that we will be impacted. Elsewhere, Smith explains the "proposes" versus "tends to produce" distinction as follows: "the only consequences for which [an agent] can be answerable . . . are those which were some way or other intended, or those which, at least, show some agreeable or disagreeable quality in the intention of the heart, from which he acted" (II.iii.intro.3). The first half of the disjunction captures the meaning of "proposed" and covers cases of actions in which an agent consciously intends to hurt someone. The second half of the disjunction captures the meaning of "tends to produce" and covers cases of actions in which an agent does not consciously intend to hurt anyone but who nevertheless acts on intentions with a "disagreeable quality." This disagreeable quality seems to be that of disregarding the well-being of other people. While perhaps less intuitively, we can offer a similar gloss for gratitude by making a distinction between actions consciously intended to help and actions that help or at least not harm in a way that demonstrates what is perhaps just above a minimally basic level of respect for others.

Thus, Smith thinks that we expect from people a high enough degree of sensitivity to others' interests that there can be actions we deem worthy of punishment and resentment that do not follow from straightforwardly malicious motives. (We'll return to this point when we get to Smith's theory of the virtue of justice in Section 3 of Chapter 6.) Again, less intuitively, Smith also seems to allow for actions worthy of reward and gratitude that do not follow from straightforwardly beneficent motives.

Another sense of "tends to produce," however, does point to kinds of merit judgments that do not fit with Smith's overall account. Smith eventually admits that under some conditions we *do* feel a "sort of . . . [in]complete and [im]perfect" gratitude and resentment in response to any kind of cause of benefit or harm; thus, he observes that we can feel versions of gratitude and resentment toward inanimate objects and animals who benefit or harm us, as well as toward people who do so totally accidentally. As a result, we *do* make forms of merit judgments that focus solely on consequences, without regard for intention or any otherwise agreeable or disagreeable quality in an agent (II.iii.1.1–4). Depending upon how we understand qualifiers like "sort of," "incomplete," and "imperfect," the forms of gratitude and resentment upon which these judgments are based might serve as counterexamples to my suggestion that Smith is undertaking conceptual analysis of these sentiments. And depending upon how we understand Smith's attitude toward the merit judgments based upon such an "irregularity of sentiment," his recognition of them might require rethinking our understanding of this category of judgment (II.iii.intro.6,2). I return to this "irregularity" in Section 6 of Chapter 5 and in Section 2 of Chapter 7.

Section 5: Completing Smith's Foundational Account of Moral Judgment

Here is what we have seen so far. For Smith, the psychological foundation of moral judgment is sympathy. More specifically, it is the pleasure we feel upon observing mutual sympathy between ourselves and another person, and the pain we feel upon observing the absence of mutual sympathy between ourselves and another person. When we imagine ourselves into an agent's situation and feel the same way that we believe that the agent does, we deem the agent's sentiments proper; when we imagine ourselves in an agent's situation and feel differently from how we believe that the agent does, we deem the agent's sentiments improper. When agents act in such a way that we deem them worthy of reward, we deem their actions and the sentiments behind them meritorious; when agents act in such a way that we deem them worthy of punishment, we deem their actions and the sentiments behind them demeritorious. We deem actions and the sentiments behind them worthy of reward when we believe they are the proper objects of gratitude; we deem actions and the sentiments behind them worthy of punishment when we believe they are the proper objects of resentment. We see actions and the sentiments behind them as the proper objects of gratitude when we feel gratitude upon imagining ourselves into the position of the patient, and we feel gratitude upon imagining ourselves into the position of the patient only if we also feel the sentiments that we believe motivated the agent upon imagining ourselves into the agent's position; we see actions and the sentiments behind them as the proper objects of resentment when we feel resentment upon imagining ourselves into the position of the patient, and we feel resentment upon imagining ourselves into the position of the patient only if we also do not feel the sentiments that we believe motivated the agent upon imagining ourselves into the agent's position. In this regard, judgments of merit involve two judgments of propriety.

We have not yet addressed two key aspects of Smith's full-blown account of moral judgment. The first has to do with the fact that our judgments of propriety and merit cannot be mere expressions or reports of our subjective feelings; the next chapter is dedicated to dealing with this issue. The second is that Smith recognizes "four sources" of moral approval, not just the two we've discussed:

> First, we sympathize with the motives of the agent; secondly, we enter into the gratitude of those who receive the benefit of his actions; thirdly, we observe that this conduct has been agreeable to the general rules by which

> those two sympathies generally act; and, last of all, when we consider such actions as making a part of a system of behavior which tends to promote the happiness either of the individual or the society, they appear to derive a beauty from this utility, not unlike that which we ascribe to any well-contrived machine. (VII.iii.3.16)

The first two categories respectively refer to judgments of propriety and merit. The third refers to the general rules that reason helps us inductively derive from individual judgments of propriety and merit; we were first introduced to these rules in Section 1 of the previous chapter, and we will return to them in Section 5 of the next chapter. The fourth category, however, is new. By listing it as the *last* consideration we employ in making a moral judgment, Smith is registering an explicit disagreement with Hume, to whom we now return.

In the first section of this chapter, we explored the disagreement between Smith and Hume regarding the nature of sympathy. Now we will see how this disagreement manifests itself with respect to the fundamental structure of moral judgment. In his overview of sentiment-based answers to the psychological foundation of moral judgment question, Smith describes Hume's view as one that "places virtue in utility, and accounts for the pleasure with which the spectator surveys the utility of any quality from sympathy with the happiness of those who are affected by it" (VII.iii.3.17). (The role of Humean sympathy in this account should be clear from the first section, where I mentioned that it must do the work of explaining how we come to care about the happiness of other people.) Although we should note that while he is more careful elsewhere (IV.2.3), Smith's reduction of Hume's view here to one that places all virtue in utility overlooks the difference between the category of the "useful" and the category of the "agreeable" in Hume's account of moral judgment. For Hume, we approve of traits not only because they are useful to their possessors or other people but also because they are simply agreeable to their possessors or other people (e.g., T 3.3.1.24–9/SBN 587–90). Nevertheless, Hume does say that "reflexions on the tendencies of actions have by far the greatest influence, and determine all the great lines of our duty" (T 3.3.1.27/SBN 590). Thus, even if Smith's attack is incomplete, it still covers a significant, if not the most significant, aspect of Hume's thinking about moral evaluation.

Most of Smith's attack against Hume on the role of utility in moral evaluation occurs in TMS IV.2. (TMS IV.1 provides some fascinating argument against Hume's account of what attracts us to useful things in the first place; we'll revisit this in Section 5 of Chapter 6, where I discuss Smith's account of prudence.) Some strains in Smith's attack appear to appeal directly to considerations that do not rest upon his own view regarding how moral judgment works; others do seem to appeal directly to this view; and at least one appears to do both. In the first category is Smith's claim that we approve and disapprove more directly and immediately than Hume's account, which requires reflection upon utility, suggests. Smith acknowledges that it is "universally the case" that virtue is "fitted . . . to promote . . . the happiness both of the individual and of the society," while vice is fitted to "disturb" it (IV.2.1). But, Smith argues, the "view of this utility or hurtfulness" is not "the first or principal source of our approbation and disapprobation"; at most, it is a secondary consideration by which our moral sentiments are "enhanced and enlivened" (IV.2.3; cf. VII.iii .3.16–17). We get this wrong when we consider the "actions and conduct of mankind" only in "an abstract and philosophical light." By considering virtue and vice from this perspective, we see only their "usefulness or inconveniency." But this perspective does not present us "in a very clear and distinct manner, the conception of any one particular action either of cruelty or humanity"; instead, we get only "the vague and indeterminate idea which the general names of [such] qualities suggest to [us]" (IV.2.2).

This is more or less the same methodological argument we saw Smith level against the egoist in Section 2 of the previous chapter. On this line of thought, both Hume and the egoist mistakenly end up focusing on the social utility of virtue and social disutility of vice because they both study our approval of virtue and disapproval of vice from a more abstract perspective than that which we inhabit when we actually feel approval and disapproval. (The difference between Hume and the egoist, of course, is that Hume does not think we care about the social utility of virtue and disutility of vice solely out of self-love.) But just as the egoist could, Hume could respond by trying to downplay the level of reflection involved in his account of moral evaluation. Such an account might demand that moral judgment *sometimes* involve reflection upon the utility of virtue and disutility of vice, but it need not demand that this always be the case. With enough experience and education, we could cultivate the unreflective habit of making utility-based moral judgments without thinking about utility at all. Arguably, this is precisely the kind of view Hume has in mind.[73] We only have reason to accept such a view, however, if we already accept the truth of the utility-based account of moral judgment. Thus, consideration of Smith's apparently methodological attack on Hume ultimately brings us back to comparing more directly his fundamental account of moral judgment with Smith's.

Something similar happens with one of Smith's other apparently independent attacks, though perhaps less immediately. Smith claims that Hume confuses "the approbation of virtue" with the sentiment "by which we approve of a convenient and well-contrived building" or "chest of drawers" (IV.2.4). Smith also levels this kind of objection in his overview of sentiment-based answers to the psychological foundation of moral judgment question; there, he argues that Humean sympathy is "the same principle with that by which we approve of a well-contrived machine" (VII.iii.3.17). Smith claims that the approbation of virtue and approbation of a useful machine simply cannot be sentiments "of the same kind" (IV.2.4). Hume agrees that "the sentiments, excited by utility are, in the two cases, very different" (EPM 5.1, note 17/SBN 213, note 1). But he concedes that he cannot account for this difference; it is, in his words, a "very inexplicable" brute fact (T 3.3.5.6/SBN 617; cf. T 3.1.2.4/SBN 471–2). The "original constitution of [human] nature" dictates that the observation of useful character traits prompts a special kind of approval that is directed exclusively at human beings (EPM 5.1, note 17/SBN 213, note 1; cf. T 3.3.1.3/SBN 575). This feeling of approval "is mixed with affection, esteem, approbation, etc.," while approval of machines is "not" (EPM 5.1, note 17/SBN 213, note 1). It is not obvious, however, that Smith provides any more than this. On the one hand, he also seems to identify approval with a feeling that, as a matter of brute fact, we do not feel in response to useful machines. But on the other hand, Smith does render this fact somewhat explicable. It is impossible to feel the pleasure of mutual sympathy with machines because they cannot be the objects of the imaginative acts upon which the pleasure of concord, and therefore judgments of propriety and merit, is based; one cannot imagine oneself into the situation of a machine and compare how one feels with how it feels.[74] Of course, this is yet another brute fact,[75] but at least Smith ends up at it a step further down the road than Hume does.[76] Notice, though, that even if we see the addition of this extra step as a mark in favor of Smith's sympathy-based account of moral judgment,[77] it seems like a small enough one that our decision to favor his account overall still requires that we measure its plausibility against Hume's on other grounds. Once again, then, we end up having to compare their sympathy-based accounts of moral judgment more directly.

Smith also makes some arguments that immediately and solely invoke his own substantive views. He claims that what we miss when we inhabit Hume's "abstract and general" perspective is precisely the "propriety or impropriety, the merit or demerit of actions" (IV.2.2). He also claims that when we attend more closely to our approval of "qualities most useful to ourselves," like "superior reason and understanding" and "self-command," as well as our approval of "qualities most useful to others," like "humanity, justice, generosity, and public spirit," we see that it "always involves in it a sense of propriety [and sometimes, by extension, a sense of merit] quite distinct from the perception of utility" (IV.2.5–11). Obviously, our attitude toward these arguments will depend upon our attitude toward Smith's positive account of moral judgment.

Smith's final argument seems to blend together independent considerations and his own account of moral judgment. He claims that any "sentiment of approbation [that] arises from the perception of [the] beauty of utility . . . has no reference of any kind to the sentiments of others" (IV.2.12). The thought seems to be that the structure of moral judgment is somehow social in a way that Hume's theory overlooks and Smith's theory captures. On the one hand, this argument seems to rest upon independent reason for favoring Smith's view. Either accounts of moral judgment are sufficiently social or they're not. But on the other hand, it is hard to understand what this claim about the sociality of moral judgment even means, especially when applied to a thinker as sensitive to human sociality as Hume is, in abstraction from Smith's own account.[78] In order to see what Smith has in mind, we must finish our overall account of his theory of moral judgment. Thus, we'll return to this issue in Section 3 of the next chapter.

4

Building upon the Foundation: Smith's Full-Blown Account of Moral Judgment and Its Impact on Moral Action

In the previous chapter, we saw Smith answer the psychological foundation of moral judgment question as follows: the pleasure we take in observing mutual sympathy between our own and another's sentiments constitutes approval, and the pain we take in observing the absence of mutual sympathy between our own and another's sentiments constitutes disapproval. But identifying the psychological foundation of moral judgment is not necessarily the same thing as providing a full-blown account of moral judgment. To provide such an account, Smith has at least three more tasks to complete. First, he must explain how we are capable of making moral judgments that do not line up with how we actually feel. Second, he must explain the fact that there is significant agreement within groups of people regarding what is proper or improper and meritorious or demeritorious, even though the feelings upon which this agreement is based are, in some sense, subjective. Third, he must explain the fact that we can distinguish between moral judgments we consider to be correct and moral judgments upon which our group agrees. This chapter concerns Smith's attempt to complete these three tasks.

We should note that at this point, the line between Smith's descriptive first and normative second main questions of moral philosophy begins to blur. On the one hand, this chapter concerns descriptive matters insofar as it attempts to complete Smith's explanation of how we make moral judgments. This becomes especially clear if we see the judgments of propriety and merit covered in the previous chapter as not yet specifically moral, as my language of "full-blown moral judgment" might suggest. But even if we see that chapter as covering moral though not very good moral judgments—again, Smith is not clear on such matters—we can see this chapter as covering Smith's explanation of the nature and causes of *our view* of good moral judgment. However, on the other hand, Smith clearly *endorses* this view of moral judgment. To that extent, then, his account of it is a normative enterprise.[1] While I offer no view of how to disentangle these strains in Smith's account of moral judgment (or of whether they even can be),[2] I try to complete this account first in a descriptive mode, before turning to its normative aspects toward the end of the chapter and beyond.

Some reconstructive work is necessary to expose Smith's explanations of the three previously mentioned features of moral judgment, but the TMS provides two easily identifiable starting points. I organize the chapter partly via a distinction between accounts of moral judgment starting from each of these two points. However, since each account centers on the desire for mutual sympathy, the first section of the chapter deals with that notion; in doing so, this section revisits the question of whether Smith is a motivational hedonist, either in general or with respect to mutual sympathy in particular. The second section turns to what I call the "perspective trading account," and the third section turns to what I call the "autonomy account." These accounts consider human morality from different perspectives. The former explains how moral judgment with certain features develops within a group, while the latter explains how moral judgment with certain features develops within an individual.[3] But these accounts are complementary in that the former is well suited to explain the first two features of moral judgment, while the latter is well suited to explain the third. They are also complementary in that the autonomy account zeroes in on a moment at which the perspective trades in the perspective trading account fail. And, as the fourth section shows, the two accounts are complementary in a third, perhaps deeper way. In this section, we see that the psychologies respectively underlying each account fit together more continuously than it might seem; we also see that these continuous psychologies are each more complicated than they might seem. In the fifth section, we turn to the account of moral motivation that follows from Smith's full-blown account of moral judgment. This section also tries to make sense of a passage in which Smith appears to contradict his official view on the role of reason in motivation. The sixth and final section considers the conception of "correct" at work in Smith's explanation of how we learn to "correct" the moral judgments of our neighbors. This section also covers Smith's TMS V discussion of the relationship between correct moral judgments and customary ones.

Section 1: The Desire for Mutual Sympathy

Smith seems most immediately interested in establishing the pleasure of experiencing mutual sympathy, not the desire for it (I.i.2). However, he does in at least one place say that the spectator "passionately desires" to be in mutual sympathy with the agent (I.i.4.7). Furthermore, as we shall see in the next two sections, he provides descriptions of social interactions that only make sense on the presumption that their participants desire mutual sympathy. And, obviously, pleasure can be an object of desire. Thus, there are good reasons to attribute to Smith belief in a desire for mutual sympathy, even though he explicitly introduces the concept of mutual sympathy by emphasizing the pleasure we take in experiencing it. However, this apparent prioritization of pleasure invites us to wonder if Smith thinks that we desire mutual sympathy solely for the pleasure it will bring. This is an interesting question both in its own right and insofar as it provides a test case for addressing the more general one of whether Smith is a motivational hedonist across the board. Maybe Smith believes that our desire for mutual sympathy boils down to a desire for pleasure because *all* our desires boil down to a desire for pleasure.

So there are two questions here. Is Smith a hedonist about motivation in general? And, even if not, does Smith believe the desire for mutual sympathy in particular reduces to a desire for pleasure? There is resistance to answering "yes" to each question.[4] But there are also reasons for taking them both seriously.[5] We have already seen the strongest reason for taking seriously the possibility of motivational hedonism in general: Smith's claim that "pleasure and pain are the great objects of desire and aversion" (VII.iii.2.8). While obviously providing the strongest reason for taking the second question seriously, Smith's initial characterization of mutual sympathy as a pleasing experience also provides a secondary reason to taking the first question seriously, insofar as it provides a good example of the kind of reduction that a motivational hedonist would make. We seem to see another example of this kind in the very first line of the TMS: "How selfish soever man may be supposed, there are evidently some principles in his nature, which interest him in the fortune of others, and render their happiness necessary to him, *though he derives nothing from it except the pleasure of seeing it*" (I.i.1.1; emphasis added). Even though Smith is not talking about motivation here, if he is saying that we take an "interest" in the "fortune of others" *only* because we derive pleasure from seeing their happiness and, by implication, pain from seeing their misery, then he is providing yet another reduction of the kind that the motivational hedonist would make.

With this last possible example especially in mind, one might object to reading Smith as a motivational hedonist in general on the grounds that doing so pushes him toward egoism. If we care about others' well-being—and about mutual sympathy with them, for that matter—only because of the pleasure or pain we feel in response, then we only care about and desire these things selfishly. However, the problem with this objection is that the kind of egoism it worries about attributing to Smith is not necessarily a kind of egoism he sought to avoid. We saw in Section 2 of Chapter 2 that he rejects a subtle form of egoism that he takes to rest upon a misunderstanding of sympathy. But as we also saw, this form of egoism, which presumes that sympathy always arises from imaginatively "putting myself in your situation" rather than changing "persons and characters" with you, is consistent with the claim that any concern and desire I feel as a result of the latter imaginative act ultimately targets my own pleasure or pain (VII.iii.1.4). As we saw in

Section 1 of Chapter 3, Smith also rejects a cruder form of egoism. There, we saw Smith argue against the view that we enjoy mutual sympathy not because we find it intrinsically pleasing but because we see it as a guarantee of future "assistance" from others (I.i.2.1). Similarly, a passage just quoted attacks the view that we take an "interest" in "the fortune of others" only because we "get" something "out of it," not because of the intrinsic pleasure or pain we feel upon "seeing" them benefited or harmed (I.i.1.1). Also similarly, Smith takes on the following views: we value friendship for the "frivolous good offices" friends provide us not because of the intrinsically pleasing "harmony of hearts" and "happy commerce" it involves (I.ii.4.1); and we look up to "the rich and the powerful" from "private expectations of benefit from their good-will" instead of from intrinsic "admiration for the advantages of their situation" (I.iii.2.3). The egoist Smith has in mind in all these cases believes that we value and desire everything with conscious reflection upon our own personal costs and benefits, apparently understood in the most superficial terms. Smith could reject this form of egoism while still believing that our concerns and desires are either all or mostly reducible to deep, potentially unconscious concerns about and desires for our own pleasure. In fact, Smith might not think that views of the latter kind even count as forms of egoism, let alone a form that troubles him. The main point of his discussion of Hutcheson's theory of virtue, which will get our full attention in Section 4 of the next chapter, is that Hutcheson misrepresents the "common judgments of mankind" when he concludes that "a regard to the pleasure of self-approbation . . . diminishe[s] the merit" of an otherwise virtuous action because it makes that action at least partly self-interested. In making this point, however, Smith demonstrates ambivalence about whether "a regard to the pleasure of self-approbation" really even is a self-interested motive. He writes, "this was a selfish motive, [Hutcheson] *thought*," perhaps wrongly (VII.ii.3.13; emphasis added).[6]

If Smith believes that the hedonistic reductions of the kind we are considering do not also meaningfully count as egoistic ones, his view would not be without at least close precedent. Hume, for example, did not seem to care that much about whether "general benevolence" to others "will resolve into some nice considerations of self-love," such as those that would be implied by a hedonistic reduction of it. It mattered more to him that general benevolence is "real," which he apparently took to be consistent with any view that resolves it into "nice considerations of self-love" in the way that the motivational hedonist does (EPM App2.5, note 60/SBN 298, note 1).[7] However, Hume ultimately disagreed with this kind of resolution, and it would be surprising if Smith did not as well. The most direct evidence we have that Smith disagreed with motivational hedonism in general occurs in a passage in which he makes the point that the "Author of nature has not entrusted" the "slow and uncertain demonstrations of our reason" to tell us which means to adopt in pursuit of some of the ends we need naturally pursue. On the contrary, Smith observes, we naturally desire the means to some of these ends directly and totally unreflectively. He continues that while we naturally pursue the ends of "self-preservation, and the propagation of the species," we also have "original and immediate instincts," such as "hunger, thirst, the passion which unites the two sexes, the love of pleasure, and the dread of pain," that "prompt us to apply [the] means for their own sakes" to those ends. The fact that he lists "the love of pleasure, and the dread of pain" as single components among several others implies that Smith did not take those other components to be reducible to them. Moreover, the fact that the list is of specific examples that help make a more general point suggests that he takes it to be incomplete. In that very same passage, he implies that an unreflective desire to inflict punishment on "unmerited and unprovoked malice" should also be on the list (II.i.5.10).

Thus, there is reason to conclude that Smith is not a motivational hedonist in general. But what about the possible particular examples of hedonistic reductions we have seen, that of the "pity or compassion" that might lead us to help others and that of the mutual sympathy we seek to be in with them (I.i.1.1)? We've just seen reason to believe that Smith was not that worried about the egoistic implications of such reductions. But maybe he should have been, especially regarding the latter, as he claims that sympathy "cannot, *in any sense*, be regarded as a selfish principle" (VII.iii.1.4; emphasis added). So there is reason to see if we can avoid reading Smith as providing hedonistic reductions of these desires.

Since we are presently interested in mutual sympathy, I am going to set aside "pity or compassion." (I believe some version of the reasoning we are about to apply to the case of mutual sympathy would work similarly in the case of "pity or compassion," but I leave it to the reader to see if this is so.) We saw that Smith introduces us to the concept of mutual sympathy by stressing the pleasure we experience when we notice that we are in it and the pain we experience when we notice that we are in its opposite. Only after making this point does he describe forms of social interaction that rest upon our desire to be in mutual sympathy and to avoid being in its opposite. The sheer order of presentation here suggests that the pleasure gets priority over the desire, in the sense that the former explains the latter. But what if the reverse were true? What if we could better capture Smith's generally non-hedonistic psychology by prioritizing the desire over the pleasure, such that we have a natural desire to be in mutual sympathy, which generates pleasure or pain when it is fulfilled or not?[8] Hume's argument against the aforementioned attempts to resolve sentiments like "general benevolence" into "nice considerations of self-love," such as those involved in hedonistic reductions, provides a model for the kind of view I have in mind. Echoing Hutcheson and Butler[9] and using examples that call to mind the position we just saw Smith adopt on our direct pursuit of some means to natural ends, Hume points out that "hunger and thirst have eating and drinking for their end," while "vanity," "ambition," and "[anger]" impel us to seek other "particular objects, such as fame or power, or vengeance." He continues that "when these objects are attained, a pleasing enjoyment ensues, as the consequence of our indulged affections" (EPM App2.12/SBN 301–2). Thus, one might think that these desires must ultimately be self-interested because they all ultimately aim at this pleasure we feel when they are satisfied. But, Hume argues, these desires must first have objects independent of themselves before we can even try to satisfy them out of a more reflective, self-interested desire for the pleasure of this satisfaction. "Where is the difficulty in conceiving," he asks, "that this may likewise be the case with benevolence and friendship, and that, from the original frame of our temper, we may feel a desire of another's happiness or good," especially when it is obvious that something like "vengeance, from the force alone of passion, may be so eagerly pursued, as to make us knowingly neglect every consideration of ease, interest, . . . safety," or, we might add, pleasure (EPM App2.13/SBN 302)? If we apply this line of thought to Smith, the desire for being in mutual sympathy aims at *being in mutual sympathy*, i.e., an object other than the pleasure we feel upon having the desire satisfied. Of course, upon reflection, we *can* pursue mutual sympathy, for the pleasure we feel once we attain it. But, the argument implies, this kind of pursuit is only possible because we first already desire being in mutual sympathy intrinsically, just as we do food, water, sex, vengeance, and pleasure itself.

On this interpretation, Smith begins by pointing to the pleasure we take in observing the fact that we are in mutual sympathy with others because he wants to stress that we in general care about being in mutual sympathy without thinking about how we are instrumentally benefited thereby. But by stressing this pleasure, Smith is not committed to thinking that it is the fundamental object of our desire when we desire being in mutual sympathy. However, an interpretive problem remains. One of the primary reasons for attributing this kind of view to Smith is that he did not seem to be a motivational hedonist in general and thus would not have had reason to provide a hedonistic reduction of the desire for being in mutual sympathy. But then what do we do with the claim we saw him make in Chapter 2, that "pleasure and pain are the great objects of desire and aversion" (VII.iii.2.8)? We can legitimately de-emphasize this hedonism-friendly comment because it conflicts both with Smith's anti-hedonistic comments and with a well-precedented anti-hedonistic view that it would be plausible to attribute to him. But even if we do, we still should try to interpret the hedonism-friendly claim in a way that minimizes inconsistency.

More specifically, the challenge is to interpret the claim in such a way that does not commit Smith to motivational hedonism while also allowing it to function properly in his argument against rationalism *and* does so in way that is consistent with how he thinks moral judgment and motivation work. Here is the relevant argument against rationalism in full:

> Pleasure and pain are the great objects of desire and aversion: but these are distinguished not by reason, but by immediate sense and feeling. If virtue, therefore, be desirable for its own sake, and if vice be, in the same manner, the object of aversion, it cannot be reason which originally distinguishes those different qualities, but immediate sense and feeling. (VII.iii.2.8)

The wording of the passage itself forces us to make an interpretive choice. It says that "pleasure and pain are the great objects of desire and aversion." It also says that virtue is "desirable for its own sake" and vice "the object of aversion" for its own sake. If we read the former statement as a claim to exclusivity, then the latter statement does not make sense; if we desire or avoid something for its own sake, then we do not desire or avoid that thing solely for the sake of experiencing pleasure or avoiding pain. We could see this potential inconsistency as a reason to reinterpret the latter statement in terms of the former's apparent commitment to motivational hedonism. But, again, given the other passage indicating that Smith is not a motivational hedonist, as well as the Humean precedent, we should focus our efforts on reinterpreting the former claim. Thus, we should take "the great" to mean something like "important," not "the only."

But while this move makes the passage both internally consistent and consistent with anti-motivational hedonism, it makes murky its overall meaning. If Smith thinks that virtue is intrinsically desirable and that vice is intrinsically undesirable, why does he mention pleasure and pain at all? Why not just argue that reason alone cannot distinguish between virtue and vice because virtue is intrinsically desirable and vice is intrinsically undesirable, and reason alone, without reference to "immediate sense and feeling," cannot distinguish between intrinsically desirable and undesirable things? Perhaps Smith believes that the pleasure of recognizing virtue is a necessary condition of the intrinsic desirability of virtue and the pain of recognizing vice a necessary condition of the intrinsic undesirability of vice, but not that the desires to achieve virtue and avoid vice are reducible to the desires to experience pleasure and avoid pain. Earlier, I posited a relationship like this one between the pleasure and intrinsic desirability of mutual sympathy. I suggested we read Smith as saying that it pleases us to notice that we are in mutual sympathy with others but that we can desire being in mutual sympathy with others for its own sake, not for the sake of pleasure; the same went for the pain of noticing and undesirability of being in the opposite of mutual sympathy. This reading applies directly here because Smith believes we recognize the distinction between virtue and vice via mutual sympathy; he also, as we will see beginning in Section 3, believes the main reason we pursue virtue and vice is to achieve some form of mutual sympathy. Thus, if we desire being in mutual sympathy intrinsically and take pleasure in the success of this desire, we also desire achieving virtue intrinsically and take pleasure in the success of this desire. But can we identify any rationale for thinking that the intrinsic desirability of mutual sympathy and virtue *requires* taking pleasure in recognizing the achievement of that desire? Maybe this is a brute fact about which there is nothing more to say. But maybe Smith believes that pleasure simply *is* part of the experience of a desire being satisfied, at least in the case of the desires for mutual sympathy and virtue. On a view like this one, the absence of pleasure in something counts as evidence against the claim that we desire it without implying that the desire must aim at this pleasure; similarly, the presence of pleasure in something counts as evidence in favor of the claim that we desire it without implying that the desire must aim at this pleasure.[10] Thus, it becomes relevant that reason alone cannot distinguish between pleasure and pain. If reason alone cannot indicate what is pleasing or painful, it cannot indicate what is virtuous or vicious, given that virtue is intrinsically desirable and thus pleasing and vice is intrinsically undesirable and thus painful.

This interpretive strategy is not flawless. Even if it identifies a reason why Smith talks at all about pleasure and pain here, it fails to provide one for why he talks specifically about the motivational importance of pleasure and pain. I am not sure what to do with that. Maybe he is just being sloppy. Or maybe he has rhetorical reasons for emphasizing pleasure and pain in the context of attacking rationalism. Regardless, it seems that, on the whole, the strongest interpretive reasons weigh against reading Smith as a motivational hedonist in general and against reading Smith as a motivational hedonist about the particular desire for being in mutual sympathy. The latter claim involves prioritizing the desire for being in mutual sympathy over the pleasure we take in noticing that we are in mutual sympathy and the aversion to being in the opposite of mutual sympathy over the pain we take in noticing that we are in the opposite of mutual sympathy. This view suggests that "nothing pleases us more than to observe in other men a fellow-feeling with all the emotions of our own breast" and nothing "[shocks]" or "[pains]" us more than "the appearance of the contrary" because we *desire* nothing more than to be in mutual sympathy with others (I.i.2.1).

By understanding mutual sympathy primarily as a goal we desire, Smith is able to provide a stronger, more direct account of moral motivation than can some of his sentimentalist counterparts. Smith is often lumped with Hutcheson and Hume into the category of philosophers who hold a fundamentally "spectatorial," as opposed to "agential," conception of morality. On views like these, the primary moral phenomena to be studied are the perceptions of a moral faculty or the reactions of a moral sentiment. These perceptions and reactions ground moral judgment, but they only generate moral action indirectly, by generating goals for totally independent desires; the perceptions and reactions deliver a moral verdict, and we act on this verdict from some desire for the approval of the perceptions and reactions.[11] Thus, on these views, moral judgment and moral motivation come apart, with the latter getting explanatory priority over the former. But on Smith's view, moral judgment and moral motivation are bound up with each other.[12] The fact that mutual sympathy has a two-sided, symmetrical nature[13] allows it *both* to constitute moral approval *and* to serve as a motive. No matter what side it is observed from, concord is still concord; thus, Smith's use of the phrase "sense of propriety" can univocally refer to something possessed and enacted by the spectator, by the agent, or by both (cf. IV.2.8).[14] Furthermore, the fact that this sentiment is a desire means that if either of the two is explanatorily prior, it is motivation over judgment. Mutual sympathy is something that both moral agents and moral judges seek. Moral agents are obviously motivated by their desire for mutual sympathy. But so are moral judges. They *want* to be in mutual sympathy with the agents they judge, and they approve or disapprove when this desire is fulfilled or unfulfilled. Thus, Smith depicts moral life not as akin to an art gallery, in which we walk around passively appraising each other's conduct and sometimes do things in the hope of winning these positive appraisals, but as an arena of constant action, in which even judging spectators are doing something out of desire, even if only imaginatively projecting themselves into the agent's situation.[15] So it should come as no surprise to see the desire for mutual sympathy factor prominently in our attempt in the next three sections to complete Smith's full-blown account of moral judgment.

Section 2: The Perspective Trading Account

As we have seen, Smith identifies the "sentiment of approbation" with the pleasure one feels upon observing concord between one's own "sympathetic emotions" and "the original passions" of the agent (I.i.3.3; I.i.3.1). However, as Smith notices, there are surely cases in which we approve without feeling a sympathetic emotion and thus without observing concord between our sympathetic emotion and the agent's original one (I.i.3.3). Smith explains these cases by introducing the notion of "conditional sympathy." Suppose we come across a "stranger" demonstrating "all the marks of the deepest affliction; and we are immediately told that he has just received the news of the death of this father." Smith thinks it obvious that we would approve of this person's grief. But if the man and his father "are entirely unknown to us, or we happen to be employed about other things, and do not take the time to picture out in our imagination the different circumstances of distress which must occur to him," we might not feel *any* of the man's grief, let alone the full "violence of his sorrow." But we approve of his grief because "we know that if we took time to consider his situation, fully and in all its parts," we would "sincerely sympathize with him." The same thing happens even in cases of "a very frivolous nature," such as when we "approve of a jest" at which we do not laugh because "we are in a grave humour, or happen to have our attention engaged with other objects"; since we know that "upon most occasions" we would laugh, we deem the jest funny. Thus, while approval is founded upon the observation of *actual* mutual sympathy, we often approve on the basis of sympathy we believe we *would* experience under different conditions (I.i.3.3–4).

Smith tells us that we base this belief on "general rules derived from our preceding experience of what our sentiments would commonly correspond with." Let's bracket until Section 5 this talk of general rules, which we also saw in our Chapter 1, Section 1, discussion of the role that Smith thinks reason plays in moral judgment and motivation. For now, let's focus on the nature of the perspective Smith believes we privilege and on our motivation to privilege it. Some of his language implies that this perspective is simply the one that we find ourselves inhabiting most often. For example, he describes the feelings we experience from this perspective as those we feel "upon most occasions" or most "commonly" (I.i.3.4). In this way, Smith explains our first unexplained feature of moral judgment, that of intrasubjective stability.

Obviously, our evaluations are intrasubjectively stable if they rest upon our most commonly felt sentiments. But why do we privilege these sentiments?

Presumably, we have purely internal psychological incentives to do so, such as a desire for some sense of personal equilibrium. Habit also likely plays a role. However, essentially social causes of this intrasubjective stability are more important for Smith (and probably in general). In fact, it is better to think of his explanation of this feature of moral judgment as a by-product of his explanation of the second one, i.e., intersubjective stability. In the very same paragraph explaining conditional sympathy in the grieving son case, Smith uses language implying that the perspective that we privilege in conditional sympathy is best understood not as one that we as individuals inhabit most often but as a shared one that we and others inhabit most often. He says that our experience tells us that "such a misfortune" as the loss of a father "naturally excites" a certain degree of sorrow and thus a certain degree of sympathy (I.i.3.4). This language, which refers not to what we as individuals feel most often but to what *people in general* feel most often, points not only to intra- but also to intersubjective stability in our evaluations.

We might expect Smith's account of intersubjective stability to stop here. Such stability seems built into the very notion of "natural" sentimental reactions; since we all experience them, we all approve when others experience them. But Smith seems to believe that intersubjective stability in our sentimental reactions makes possible intersubjective stability in moral judgment without fully explaining its existence. One obvious reason for this is that even if we all naturally feel more or less the same way in the same situations, we do not naturally find ourselves in the same situations at the same time. Thus, we need to explain what motivates us to adopt as a standard how we would feel under different circumstances from the ones in which we actually are.

Smith's main resource for explaining what leads us to adopt this intersubjective standard is the desirability of mutual sympathy and undesirability of its absence. Smith draws a broad distinction between two classes of interactions—or, more specifically, "conver[sations]"—in which we attempt to achieve sentimental harmony (I.i.4.5). When our sentiments concern "objects" that have no "peculiar relation, either to ourselves or to the person whose sentiments we judge of," such as "the beauty of a plain, the greatness of a mountain, the ornaments of a building, the expression of a picture, the composition of a discourse, the conduct of a third person, the proportions of different quantities and numbers, the various appearances which the great machine of the universe is perpetually exhibiting, with the secret wheels and springs which produce them"—in short, "all the general subjects of science and taste"—the "most perfect harmony of affections" is relatively easy to achieve. Disagreement in such cases arises from "different degrees of attention, which our different habits of life allow us to give easily to several parts of those complex objects" or from "different degrees of natural acuteness in the faculty of the mind to which they are addressed." Thus, we can resolve it by calling attention to things our interlocutor might have missed or by walking our interlocutor through the thought process we employed. Neither of these or similar procedures requires an "imaginary change of situations" (I.i.4.1–2).

Smith must mean something very specific here by "situation"; the same goes for his claim that we tend to consider such matters "from the same point of view." There is a certainly a sense in which aesthetic disagreement, for example, can rest upon a difference in "point of view." Moreover, it seems obvious that resolving such disagreements even in the ways just listed involves *some* kind of "imaginary change of situations." How could I not be said to change my "situation" or "point of view" when I attempt to reexperience an artwork with an eye to attending to certain things I might have missed before? Smith must mean, then, that we inhabit the same points of view in these cases in the sense that we are all spectators with no relevant personal attachments.[16] Of course, one might downplay or even deny the existence of such a disinterested, objective perspective—maybe everything we care about is, to some degree, personal—but that would just mean that *all* cases in which we "judge of the propriety or impropriety of the sentiments of another person" belong in Smith's next category, not that he is wrong about how instances of this first would work, if they were real (I.i.3.1). Furthermore, his distinction between the two categories is maintained even if it ultimately amounts to one of degree.

The second category involves sentiments regarding objects "considered as peculiarly affecting one or the other of us" (I.i.3.1). These interactions involve not "judgments in matters of speculation" or "sentiments in matters of taste" but sentiments like "grief" in the face of "misfortune" or "resentment" in the face of "injury." As we've seen, disagreement about the former matters is easily resolvable. And when it is not resolved, it is easy to "overlook." But disagreement in the latter matters makes us "intolerable to one another." Thus, establishing "harmony and correspondence" in them is not only "more difficult" because it requires a psychologically taxing "imaginary change of situation" but also "vastly more important" (I.i.4.5). In such cases of disagreement, the spectator and the agent, or "person principally concerned," trade perspectives in order to satisfy their desires for at least "some correspondence of sentiment." Spectators try to heighten their feelings by imagining themselves into the positions of agents. But this effort can only go so far because the act of imagination upon which sympathy rests is "but momentary" and easily interrupted by thoughts about one's own actual situation; thus, sympathy can never generate "that degree of passion which naturally animates the person principally concerned." Since agents realize this but also "passionately [desire] a more complete sympathy," they try to lower the "pitch" of their feelings by imagining themselves into the position of the spectators. This effort too can only go so far; Smith does not say so explicitly, but there is no reason not to think that thoughts of one's own real circumstances intrude upon the mind of agents imagining themselves into spectators' shoes as easily as it does spectators imagining themselves into agents' shoes. But as a result of their combined efforts, the agent and the spectator end up feeling sentiments that, while different in "degree" and, "in some measure, kind," are in enough "correspondence" to render their interaction pleasing to both (I.i.4.6–7).

Smith claims that via our desire for mutual sympathy, "nature teaches" us to engage "constantly" in this process of perspective trading (I.i.4.8). While this process will never generate "unisons," it will generate "concords," which is "all that is wanted or required" for "the harmony of society" (I.i.4.7). With these expressions, he invites us to see the society-wide iteration of this process as the cause of our widespread adoption of shared standards of appropriate ways to feel that we invoke when making judgments based on conditional sympathy. So rather than judging on the basis of how I as an individual actually feel or on the basis of how I as an individual usually feel, I come to judge on the basis of how *we* usually feel.[17] Clearly, Smith's confidence in this outcome is at least partly based upon his confidence that we share a nature. It goes without saying that we are less than totally comfortable today with assumptions about what is natural to human beings, even when "natural" is understood purely descriptively, to pick out links in a chain of efficient causes.[18] (We will discuss the normative aspects of Smith's use of the concept in Section 2 of Chapter 7.) However, we should notice how thin Smith's most fundamental assumptions are. For a theory of human nature and accompanying explanation of the origin of certain features of morality to count as Smithian in spirit, they must recognize that we naturally care a lot about being in mutual sympathy with each other, that our sentiments are generally similar enough or flexible enough to render it persistently possible for us to be in mutual sympathy with each other, and that success or failure in this regard generates approval or disapproval.[19] Of course, he could be wrong about these and related claims, but it is at least less likely that he is wrong about these than that he is wrong about some of the more specific ones we saw him make in Sections 3 and 4 of the previous chapter. And as we shall see in the final section of this chapter, the fact that Smith himself explicitly recognizes the possibility of a fairly diverse range of mutual-sympathy-based group norms of how to feel and act suggests that even he is not very committed to hyper-specific claims about our natural sentiments and sympathetic tendencies.

Regardless of how robust Smith's assumptions about human nature are, one might think that when combined with his explanation of the second feature of moral judgment, they also explain the third, the conception we have of correct moral judgment regardless of what our group thinks. It seems easy enough to distinguish between the shared feelings of a particular group and "natural" ones, and the shared feelings of *all* human beings. Another reason to think we might already have an explanation for the third feature is that Smith characterizes the evaluative perspective to which the perspective trading process commits us as that of a "candid and impartial" person (I.i.4.8). He then appeals to this perspective throughout his discussion of propriety and merit judgments as the one from which propriety and merit are determined, sometimes adding descriptors like "cool," "indifferent," "equitable," or "perfectly consistent" (I.i.5.4; I.i.5.8; I.ii.3.8; II.i.2.2; II.ii.1.3; II.ii.2.1; II.ii.2.4; II.iii.2.2; II.iii.2.4; II.iii.2.10; II.iii.3.6). These labels, especially that of "impartiality," seem to point to an evaluative perspective that is potentially distinct from a merely shared one. Since, as Smith recognizes, group perspectives are just as capable of partiality as individual ones (e.g., III.3.41–3—more on this in the Section 6), an impartial perspective will not always be identical with a group perspective, no matter how impartial that perspective might be to the individuals that make up the group. The problem with both of these suggestions, though, is that the move to a "natural" perspective that is potentially impartial with respect to one's group involves an additional step that requires explanation. It seems that the motivation to adopt the perspective of one's group simply differs from the motivation to adopt a perspective that transcends one's group and is potentially impartial with respect to it. Our desire for mutual sympathy with the people around us makes it easy to explain why we would adopt a perspective from which we will all feel the same way. But what motivates us to adopt a perspective from which it becomes possible to deem these shared sentiments inappropriate? The autonomy account, to which we turn in the next section, is more helpful for answering this question than is the perspective trading account.

Before we get to that account, we should consider what Smith's apparent belief that social life is pervaded by perspective swaps for the sake of mutual sympathy might reveal about his conception of the nature of human sociability. One might worry that, perhaps ironically, both Smith's sympathy theory and account of sympathy-driven perspective trading implies a fundamentally atomistic, asocial conception of human beings. Is Smith imagining us as essentially and exclusively discrete individuals who just so happen to want desperately to enter into each other's private worlds? If so, he would be depicting us as social to the extent that we want to achieve sentimental harmony with each other but asocial at some more basic level. However, as Charles Griswold has made clear, Smith is not offering a sympathy-focused genealogy of social interaction of the kind presumed by this worry. On the contrary, Smith's theorizing about social interaction is more analytical than genealogical, in that it unpacks components in a complicated compound that it treats as an essential feature of the human condition. Rather than provide an account of this compound's actual origins, it treats the compound as basic.[20] In this regard, Smith's project does not commit him to belief in an asocial state of nature from which we emerge to become social beings; in fact, Smith explicitly rejects the possibility of such a state.[21]

But one still might worry that Smith's insistence that we must use our imaginations to project ourselves into each other's shoes assumes that despite always living together, we are cut off from each other in some deep, implausible way. Griswold argues that Smith's faith in the power of our imagination to grant us this access to each other actually has the opposite implication. In Griswold's words, Smith believes the human condition is partly defined by a "ground-level sociability" that grants us, via the imagination, "access to each other's thoughts" and even an ability to "think the same thoughts" as each other.[22] There might be reasons not to buy Smith's imagination-based explanations for how we access each other cognitively and emotionally.[23] But even if we accept these reasons, we should realize that they are distinct from any reasons there might be to reject Smith's conception of human sociability on the grounds that it is not sufficiently social. Reasons of the latter kind are hard to find.

Section 3: The Autonomy Account

Thus far, most of our discussion of Smith's account of moral judgment has focused on Parts I and II of the TMS. Part I deals with judgments of propriety, and Part II deals with judgments of merit. In both cases, Smith is primarily concerned with explaining how we evaluate others. Part III deals with the ways in which we apply these judgments to ourselves. Here is where Smith provides what I've labelled the "autonomy account" of moral judgment. While this account is explicitly focused on self-directed evaluation, it can easily be extended to cover other-directed evaluation, especially the features of it that follow from self-correction. Thus, whatever the account explains applies generally to all Smithian moral judgment.

We should note at the outset the interpretive challenges presented by the passages most relevant to the autonomy account and to what presently most interests us about it—i.e., its ability to explain the development of our conception of correct moral judgment, independent of what our neighbors think. Since Smith heavily revised this stretch of text twice, once for the second edition and once for the sixth, there might be three different versions of the account. My position, however, is that there is really only one. I contend that the revisions most relevant to the autonomy account are, on the whole, not philosophically substantive; rather, they mainly reorganize, clarify, emphasize, or render explicit that which is implicit.[24] While I do not provide anything like a systematic defense of this claim, I do provide, at least piecemeal, some reasons for holding it. As I have throughout the book, I use in this section the sixth edition of the TMS as my textual baseline. But I also occasionally cite text from earlier editions, and when I do so, I call attention to and attempt to defuse reasons for thinking that the earlier text says something substantively different from its later analogue.[25]

Smith's explanation of self-directed moral evaluation can be understood as an attempt to resolve a tension between two positions. On the one hand, Smith believes that self-directed moral evaluation must be structurally symmetrical to other-directed moral evaluation; in a letter to his friend Gilbert Elliot, which includes a draft of revisions to the second edition version of TMS III, Smith observes that "it would seem very odd if we judged of our own conduct by one principle and of that of other men by another" (Letter 40; cf. III.1.2). Thus, since we "either approve or disapprove of the conduct of another man according as we feel that, when we bring his case home to ourselves, we either can or cannot entirely sympathize with the sentiments or motives which directed it," we must "either approve or disapprove of our own conduct according as we feel that, when we place ourselves in the situation of another man . . . we either can or cannot entirely enter into and sympathize with the sentiments and motives which influence it." As a result, our self-directed moral sentiments "must always bear some secret reference" to the sentiments of some other person who we imagine is trying to sympathize with us (III.1.2). In that same Elliot letter, Smith refers to this result as his "Doctrine" (Letter 40).

The theoretical elegance of making other- and self-directed moral judgment symmetrical is certainly appealing. But does Smith's commitment to this doctrine have any other roots in his thinking? The attack on Hume's utility-focused account of moral judgment with which I ended the last chapter invokes this doctrine. Smith argues that the doctrine follows from a view he holds about the nature and strength of self-evaluative sentiments like "the triumph of self-applause" and "the shame of self-condemnation." "All such sentiments," he writes, "suppose the idea of some other being, who is the natural judge of the person that feels them" and with whom we sympathize or not. If we try to account for these sentiments without incorporating such an idea into the account, as Smith claims that Hume does when he grounds the "sentiment of approbation" in "perception of [the] beauty of utility," we end up making self-directed moral sentiments "merely a matter of taste" with "all the feebleness and delicacy of that species of perception" (IV.2.12).

I am not sure what to make of this argument. If there is a sense in which Smith is correct that Hume's account of self-directed moral sentiments has "no reference of any kind to the sentiments of others" and is thus too weak for this very reason, it must only be so with precisely articulable qualifications (IV.2.12). Since Hume clearly believes that all our sentiments, including the ones we feel upon perceiving the utility of our own character, have *some* reference to others, Smith owes us more explanation regarding why this "reference" is not deep enough to account for the phenomena of sociality and strength he has in mind (see, e.g., T 2.2.6.21, 236/SBN 365; and EHU 8.17/SBN 89).[26] More importantly, regardless of what Hume thinks and of whether Smith is right about what Hume thinks, Smith seems to owe us some independent reason for thinking in the first place that pride and shame must involve "the idea of some other being" evaluating us. In Section 2 of the previous chapter, I suggested that the connection Smith sees between approval and the observation of mutual sympathy grows out of his view that our sentiments justify themselves in the sense of either containing or always causing thoughts about considerations that provide reasons for them. But Smith must think that interaction with others is in some way required for this propensity to generate robust self-directed moral sentiments, especially negative ones.

We can see Smith's view on this matter by turning to his social account of self-evaluation:

> Were it possible that a human creature could grow up to manhood in some solitary place, without any communication with his own species, he could no more think of his own character, of the propriety or demerit of his own sentiments and conduct, of the beauty or deformity of his own mind, than of the beauty or deformity of his own face. All these are objects which he cannot easily see, which naturally he does not look at, and with regard to which he is provided with no mirror which can present them to his view. Bring him into society, and he is immediately provided with the mirror he

> wanted before. It is placed in the countenance and behavior of those he lives with, which always mark when they enter into, and they disapprove of his sentiments; and it is here that he first views the propriety or impropriety of his own passions, the beauty and deformity of his own mind. To a man who from his birth was a stranger to society, the objects of his passions, the external bodies which either pleased or hurt him, would occupy his whole attention. The passions themselves, the desires or aversions, the joys or sorrows, which those objects excited, though of all things the most immediately present to him, could scarce ever be the objects of his thoughts. The idea of them could never interest him so much as to call upon his attentive consideration. The consideration of his joy could in him excite no new joy, nor that of his sorrow any new sorrow, though the consideration of the causes of those passions might often excite both. Bring him into society, and all his own passions will immediately become the causes of new passions. He will observe that mankind approve of some of them, and are disgusted by others. He will be elevated in one case, and cast down in the other; his desires and aversions, his joys and sorrows, will now often become the causes of new desires and new aversions, new joys and new sorrows: they will now, therefore, interest him deeply, and often call upon his most attentive consideration. (III.1.3)

The gist of the passage is that since others provide us with a mirror in which to see ourselves and a new reason to care about the quality of what we see, they trigger the self-justifying tendencies we saw in Section 2 of the previous chapter. Thus, social interaction is a necessary condition for the kinds of self-conception and self-evaluation that Smith has in mind in his argument against Hume. Smith's doctrine follows from this claim only if we take it to imply that these kinds of self-conception and self-evaluation are both *initially* and *thereafter* fundamentally conducted with the perspective of others in mind. The first implication seems more obvious than the second. But the second would follow if it were also the case that the initial instances of other-referring self-conception and self-evaluation gave rise to a stable psychological habit of always having others in mind when one thinks of and judges oneself. The second implication would also follow if the connection between social interaction and both self-conception and self-evaluation was not merely a psychological, causal one but a logical, conceptual one. In a subsequent passage, Smith says something that suggests he believes just this. He observes that since it is "as impossible . . . that the cause should, in every respect, be the same with the effect" as it would be that "the judge should, in every respect, be the same with the person judged of," the perspective we consult in self-evaluation must, seemingly as a logical or conceptual matter, be that of some other person (III.1.6).[27]

Whether he thinks of this connection as a psychological or a logical one, Smith's conception of the structure of self-evaluation is undeniably deeply social.[28] However, this conception has potentially troubling implications both for the content of self-evaluation and for what motivates the self-evaluating agent. These possible implications constitute the other half of the tension at the heart of TMS III. If our self-directed moral sentiments "always bear some secret reference" to some other person, does self-evaluation become a matter of figuring out how best to win the approval of our neighbors? The letter to Elliot reveals that many of Smith's revisions for the second edition of the TMS aimed at responding to Elliot's concern that the first edition did not provide a clear enough negative answer to this question. In Smith's language, these revisions emphasize that "real magnanimity and conscious virtue can support itselfe under the disapprobation of all mankind" (Letter 40). (In support of the "no real change" thesis about Smith's revisions, he also in this letter asks Elliot to assuage his worries by rereading some passages from edition one: "I would likewise beg you to read what I say upon Mandeville's system and then consider whether upon the whole I do not make Virtue sufficiently independent of popular opinion" (Letter 40). We will get to Smith's discussion of "Mandeville's system" in Section 2 of the next chapter.) But how is it possible to pursue virtue in the face of disapprobation from others if conscious self-evaluation always involves considering what someone else thinks of us?

Smith's answer has two main components. The first is a distinction he emphasizes most strongly in edition six. He claims that we care not just about being praised or blamed but also about being worthy of praise or blame. These concerns, he stresses, are "distinct and independent" from each other (III.2.2). One might think that we care about being worthy of praise only because being worthy of praise is a good way to secure it. But Smith insists not only that these concerns are distinct but also that if there were a foundational dependence relation between them, it would work the other way, as we most often pursue praise for the sake of confirming that we are worthy of it (III.2.3). Thus, Smith also believes that praiseworthiness is more important to us than actual praise is. (Some of the best evidence that Smith's revisions to TMS III include philosophically substantive changes of opinion is that, unlike the sixth, the first five editions seem to make the love of praiseworthiness dependent upon and less important to us than the love of praise. But in my opinion, the most relevant text from editions one through five is too ambiguous to be read as obviously saying this (see, e.g., III.1.2, note e).)

Smith argues for both the independence and importance claims by inviting us to reflect upon the experiences of receiving praise that we do not think we deserve (III.2.3) and of knowing that we deserve praise even when we do not get it (III.2.5). The former experience, he claims, brings "no solid joy," while the latter brings "real comfort" (III.2.5). Thus, he concludes, we care about being worthy of praise both distinctly from and even more than we care about receiving praise. He also argues that apparent counterexamples only further prove this point. Those who pursue praise they do not deserve do so under an "illusion of the imagination" that convinces them that they do (III.2.4). And those who are not comforted much by knowledge of their own praiseworthiness without receiving actual praise are simply "uncertain" about their own praiseworthiness and thus stand in need of the confirmation that actual praise brings (III.2.16).

Interestingly, the relationship between the hatred of blame and the hatred of blameworthiness is not perfectly isomorphic to that between the love of praise and the love of praiseworthiness. The fact that people sometimes expose themselves to actual blame by confessing to crimes implies that the "horror of blame-worthiness" will often "conquer the dread of blame" in the same way that the love of praiseworthiness often conquers the love of praise (III.2.9–10). But to be blamed when we know we do not deserve it is often "mortifying" to a degree that does not mirror the impoverishment of the pleasure we receive from unmerited praise (III.2.11). Smith provides several explanations for this difference: in general, pain is "a more pungent sensation than the opposite and correspondent pleasure" and thus cannot be disregarded without difficulty (III.2.15); unmerited blame causes us to feel painful "just indignation" and "violent resentment" that often "cannot be gratified"; and blame not only indicates, painfully, that others "think . . . meanly" of us (III.2.11), but also can invite us, painfully, to doubt our own merit (III.2.15). Nevertheless, the hatred of blame is just as distinct from the hatred of blameworthiness as the love of praise is from the love of praiseworthiness. And even though we care more about avoiding blame than we do winning praise, the relationship between the respective importance of our hatred of blame and hatred of blameworthiness still parallels that between the respective importance of our love of praise and love of praiseworthiness.

By recognizing a distinct, strong concern about whether we deserve praise or blame, Smith prevents self-evaluation from reducing to mere anticipation of what others will think – hence my label "autonomy account." But how can Smith recognize this concern while continuing to maintain his doctrine that self-directed moral sentiments must have some reference to another person? The answer to this question is the second main component of his account of self-evaluation. According to Smith, when we check to see if our own characters are worthy of praise or blame, we think not about how actual others do or would feel about us but about how they would feel about us if they were "impartial" and "better informed" (III.2.6). Thus, it turns out that the "secret reference" that self-evaluation bears to the sentiments of others is not to their actual sentiments but to what their sentiments "ought to be," i.e., what they "would be" under conditions like those listed in the previous section: candidness, coolness, indifference, equitability, consistency, and impartiality (III.1.3). Smith famously unifies his conception of this corrected audience under the heading of "the supposed impartial and well-informed spectator" (hereafter, WIS[29]). So, for Smith, consulting our "consciences" amounts to consulting the judgment of this imaginary figure, not the judgment of the actual people who happen to be around us (III.2.32).

The mechanics of this consultation are complex and open to interpretation. One possibility is that in evaluating myself via the sentiments of the WIS, I first imagine myself into the position of the WIS and then attempt to sympathize with my actual self from this position. Another possibility is that I first imagine a WIS who is trying to sympathize with me and then attempt to sympathize with this WIS, specifically with regard to this WIS' attempt to sympathize with me. Which interpretation we prefer will depend upon which we think better captures Smith's "Doctrine," and which we think better captures Smith's "Doctrine" will depend upon whether we think that imagining myself directly into the position of a WIS trying to sympathize with me differs from imagining a distinct figure trying to sympathize with me. Additional mechanical complications pop up when we extend this account of self-directed moral judgment to moral judgment in general. Perhaps I invoke the WIS to correct my evaluations of others as a part of my more general self-correction. On this view, when I evaluate others well, I directly employ my own sentiments, though after they have been corrected in self-reflection. Or perhaps I invoke the WIS directly as a third party whenever I evaluate another person, such that I sympathize with the WIS who is attempting to sympathize with this other person.[30] While I favor the former account because I believe it to be more consistent with the location of the WIS theory in Smith's discussion of self-evaluation,[31] these kinds of details do not matter as much to understanding the aspects of Smith's thought with which we are presently concerned[32] as it does that we see the fundamental authority his full-blown account of moral judgment attributes to the sentiments of an imaginary WIS. And once we see this, we see how he attempts to account for the third feature of moral judgment, the ability to make evaluations that we take to be correct independent of what the people around us think.

This attempt gives rise to at least three interpretative questions. The first has to do with the love of praiseworthiness itself. How does it relate to the desire for mutual sympathy that drives the perspective swapping process? The second has to do with how the love of praiseworthiness leads us to turn to a WIS. What is Smith's account of the process by which we start doing this? The third has to do with the way in which we take the judgments of the WIS to "correct" the judgments of our neighbors. How might this correction work? The next section deals with the first two questions (in doing so, this section also brings together the perspective swapping account and the autonomy account). Since this discussion will set us up perfectly to address Smith's account of moral motivation, that will be the subject of the subsequent section. We return to the third question in the final section, in which I also cover Smith's views on cultural differences in morality.

Section 4: A Closer Look at the Driving Forces in the Two Accounts[33]

In this section, I first identify two different spectra of ways of pursuing mutual sympathy, each based on a different way of understanding the relation between mutual sympathy and the self-justifying tendency of our sentiments (in "A" and "B"). Then, I ground the love of praiseworthiness in one way of pursuing mutual sympathy from each spectra (in "C"). Thus, I respond to the first question in two ways. Next, I employ the two mutual-sympathy-based interpretations of the love of praiseworthiness to complete the previous section's presentation of the autonomy account by developing two Smithian explanations of the turn to the WIS. Thus, I respond to the second question in two ways. Additionally, by establishing links between the love of mutual sympathy, which grounds the perspective trading account, and the love of praiseworthiness, which grounds the autonomy account, and by completing the autonomy account in ways that are informed by these links, I better connect the perspective and autonomy accounts; in doing so, I also highlight Smith's interesting way of conceptualizing humanity's natural orientation toward morality (all in "D"). Since this section provides two strategies for understanding the pursuit of mutual sympathy, the relation between this pursuit and that of praiseworthiness, and the turn to the WIS, I close the section by sketching an account of the relationship between them (in "E").

(A) The First Spectrum of Ways of Desiring Mutual Sympathy

On one way of reading Smith, we are unsatisfied with the self-justifications built into or accompanying our sentiments because we have a deeply social need for mutual sympathy per se. Within this reading, there are several ways of interpreting this need. We might think that there is only one, especially cheery way to interpret what motivates us to engage in the sympathy-driven perspective swaps discussed in the second section. If we emphasize the "mutual" in the mutual sympathy each party is after, we might conclude that the desire for mutual sympathy is a desire for sentimental harmony of a kind that obtains when all participants see each other as equals. With a notion like this one in mind, some scholars have argued that the perspective trading driven by the desire for mutual sympathy commits its participants to norms of equal respect and dignity. In Stephen Darwall's words, "the implied framework" behind these swaps and the judgments they involve "is a moral community among equal persons." The idea seems to be that by taking on another person's perspective, one recognizes it as independent from one's own and thereby just as worthy of respect as one's own.[34] As Debes shows, if we accept an idea like this one, we must be sure to distinguish between the explanation it offers for our psychological tendency to respect and attribute dignity to others and any justification it might offer for the claim that human beings actually have dignity and are thus worthy of a special kind of respect. But while the second task might seem much more difficult than the first, we should not underestimate the first's complexity.[35] Sure, we *can* pursue mutual sympathy in a way that involves an attitude for respect for our partner as an individual. But it also seems possible to engage in perspective trading for mutual sympathy without respecting our partner as an equal.

Consider again Smith's initial claim about how much we like mutual sympathy: "nothing pleases us more than to observe in other men a fellow-feeling with all the emotions of our own breast" (I.i.2.1). When read with the right inflection and emphasis, this description of our enjoyment of mutual sympathy can make it easy to interpret our interest in it as essentially self-centered in a way that is inconsistent with respect for others as equals. Keep this possibility in mind while thinking again about Smith's very first example:

> A man is mortified when, after having endeavoured to divert the company, he looks round and sees that nobody laughs at his jests but himself. On the contrary, the mirth of the company is highly agreeable to him, and he regards this correspondence of their sentiments with his own as the greatest applause. (I.i.2.1)

There are several ways to understand the attitude we adopt when we try to make others laugh. If I desire that others laugh *with me*, my desire for mutual sympathy with them amounts to a desire that they synch up their sentiments *to mine*, not a desire for our sentiments to agree simply per se; when I desire mutual sympathy in the former way, I want to be the cause or the center of this agreement, not just a participant in it. Several of Smith's most fundamental observations regarding human nature suggest that he acknowledges something like a desire for mutual sympathy with this quality. For example, he observes that human beings have a naturally "tyrannic disposition" and a "love of domination and authority" (LJ.b.134; LJ.a.iii.114; cf. WN III.ii.10).[36] Of course, it matters that he calls attention to these traits in the context of discussing slavery, not joke-telling. But if these are natural human traits, they will manifest themselves throughout human life. More directly relevant to the form of self-centeredness potentially manifest in the joke-telling case, Smith also observes that "the desire of being believed, the desire of persuading, of leading and directing other people, seems to be one of the strongest of all our natural desires" (VII.iv.25). Smith even makes a direct connection between this natural desire to "lead and direct" others' sentiments and the desire for mutual sympathy when he classifies the desire for wealth as an ambition "to be observed, to be attended to, to be taken notice of with sympathy" (I.iii.2.1).

These are cases in which we pursue mutual sympathy without much respect for the other's independent perspective. There also seem to be cases in which we pursue mutual sympathy without much respect for our own independent perspective. Smith recognizes that human beings are naturally just as much capable of being excessively impressionable or submissive as they are of being excessively domineering. He observes that our "natural disposition is always to believe" others, some of whom consequently become our "leader[s] and director[s]" (VII.iv.23–5). He also identifies a natural psychological disposition "to admire, and almost to worship, the rich and the powerful" that mirrors a disposition "to despise, or at least, to neglect persons of poor and mean condition" (I.iii.3.1); these dispositions allow "the rich and the great . . . to set, or to lead what is called the fashion," such that "even their vices and follies are fashionable" (I.iii.3.7).

But as suggested at the outset, in contrast with both the way of desiring mutual sympathy that aims at sentimental agreement that we dominate and the way of desiring mutual sympathy that aims at sentimental agreement that some other person dominates,[37] there seems to be a way of desiring mutual sympathy that aims at sentimental agreement in which we and another person just so happen to be members of the agreeing parties.[38] Since this way of desiring mutual sympathy privileges neither of us, it seems to respect us both equally.

(B) The Second Spectrum of Ways of Desiring Mutual Sympathy

On another way of reading Smith, we are unsatisfied with the self-justifications built into or accompanying our sentiments because we feel a need to ensure that these justifications are legitimate and see mutual sympathy as evidence that they are. Two comments are in order regarding my suggestion of this reading. First, I intend this reading to highlight the merely phenomenological difference between pursuing sentimental harmony to avoid feeling alone and pursuing sentimental harmony to shore up one's self-justification; I bracket any relevant metaethical matters until Section 1 of Chapter 7. Second, the textual basis of this reading is worth reiterating. Again, as we saw in Section 2 of the previous chapter, Smith adopts Malebranche's point that feeling a sentiment implies approving of feeling that sentiment. Smith's identification of sympathy with approval follows from this connection; since my sentiments "necessarily appear" to me "just and proper, and suitable to their objects," your sentiments will "necessarily appear" to me "just and proper, and suitable to their objects" when they coincide with mine (I.i.3.1). It is in this way that our own sentiments serve as our "standards and measures," our "rule or canon" of evaluation (I.i.3.1; I.i.3.9). All this language suggests that in approving of our own sentiments, we do not see them as mere subjective preferences; rather, we see them as involving or causing evaluative judgments that we take to be correct. It is with this aspect of Smithian sentiments in mind that I suggest that the experience of seeking mutual sympathy with others can present itself to us as seeking their endorsement of our self-justification.[39]

Within this reading, there are several ways to interpret the need for others' mutual sympathy. More specifically, it seems that we can seek mutual sympathy as a form of endorsement of our sentiments in ways that mirror the three ways of seeking mutual sympathy identified earlier (in both cases, I have in mind a spectrum with much space between identifiable poles, not an exclusive list of options). We certainly can pursue mutual sympathy without prejudice in favor or against any particular perspective, from a sincere commitment to getting things right by respectfully entertaining as many different perspectives as possible. But it seems we can also seek mutual sympathy to confirm our unwavering confidence in the rectitude of our own sentiments. It also seems that we can seek mutual sympathy to confirm our unwavering confidence in the rectitude of some other person's sentiments.

The two spectra present us with two different interpretations of mutual-sympathy-based social interaction. On one interpretation, the desire for mutual sympathy reflects a need to share feelings with others. On the other interpretation, the desire for mutual sympathy reflects a need for others to endorse our approval of our own sentiments as accurate. As we have seen, both needs can be experienced more or less egocentrically (whether the "ego" in question is oneself or some other particular person from whom one takes one's bearings). The least egocentric versions of each, the desire of sentimental agreement per se and the unprejudiced desire to get things right seem able to capture what motivates us to seek sympathy with the perspective of the WIS; I have not said much about what this perspective is like, but we can be sure that it is impersonal to the extent that it is not that of any particular person. But since Smith tells us that the love of praiseworthiness is what leads us to adopt the perspective of the WIS, we should try to see how it interacts with these two ways of desiring mutual sympathy.[40]

(C) The Two Spectra and the Love of Praiseworthiness

Smith classifies the desire to be worthy of praise as "natural" (III.2.1; III.2.6–7). Intriguingly though, he describes the desire for praise or "approbation" as not only "natural" but also "original" (III.2.6).[41] This language suggests that despite what we saw him say in the previous section, Smith sees the desire to be worthy of praise as in some sense less basic than that of praise. He does the same when he follows a reference to the desire to be worthy of praise with the appositive phrase, "the desire of possessing those qualities, and performing those actions which we love and admire in other people" (III.2.33). And in another place, he explains the love of praiseworthiness by pointing out that "the love and admiration which we naturally conceive for those whose character and conduct we approve of, necessarily dispose us to desire to become ourselves the objects of the like agreeable sentiments, and to be as amiable and as admirable as those whom we love and admire" (III.2.3). We might take these explanations to reduce the desire to be worthy of praise to a desire to win our own praise. But Smith cannot mean that in desiring praiseworthiness, we desire our own praise in the same way that we can desire others' praise per se, or without qualification. In saying that we want "*to be* as amiable and as admirable" as the objects of our approval are, Smith is saying that we want to possess the qualities and perform the actions they do. The idea here seems to be that we want to be the objects of our own approval not just because we want to be approved of but because we take our own approval to pick out what is worthy of approval and we care about being worthy of approval. This characterization seems necessary to prevent the love of praiseworthiness from collapsing into the love of praise, albeit the love of one's own praise. This characterization also seems to follow from what approval and praise even are. We approve of and praise what appears worthy of approval and praise, not what appears, nonsensically, to possess the qualities of being approved of and praised by us.[42] But of course, if this characterization of what Smith is saying is correct, it provides just another way of saying that we want to be worthy of praise. Thus, the love of praiseworthiness must be just as basic to Smith's moral psychology as the love of praise per se is.[43]

Of course, these two loves could be equally basic while both being reducible to or at least presupposing forms of the love of mutual sympathy. Recall that for Smith, to approve of others is to take pleasure in observing mutual sympathy between one's own sentiments and theirs. Although praise is not the same thing as approval, it certainly presupposes approval (it might even just *be* strong approval). To this extent, then, it too must at least depend on the pleasure of mutual sympathy. And since, as we saw at the end of the first section, *mutual* sympathy is a relation with two sides, the enjoyment of the approval we receive from others must just be pleasure taken in observing this same mutual sympathy from our side of it. Thus, via its relationship with the love of approval, the love of praise must at least depend on some form of the love of mutual sympathy. The same goes for the love of praiseworthiness, insofar as, via Smith's "Doctrine," it refers to the sentiments that others *would* feel with more information, less partiality, and so on; this built-in reference to others gives the two loves an "affinity" to each other (VII.ii.4.9).[44]

It seems obvious that on the first spectrum, the love of mutual sympathy involved in the love of praiseworthiness is the least egocentric kind, that of a desire for sentimental agreement per se. It also seems obvious that on the second spectrum, the love of mutual sympathy involved in the love of praiseworthiness is the least egocentric kind, that of an unprejudiced desire for others' endorsement. (On account of the connection we have just seen Smith make between the love of praiseworthiness and respect for one's own approval, we might think that on both spectra, the love of mutual sympathy involved in the love of praiseworthiness is the first egocentric kind, that of a desire for sympathy *with me* or a desire to confirm our unwavering confidence in the rectitude of our own sentiments. However, both the general moral import Smith obviously sees in the love of praiseworthiness and, as we'll see in the next subsection, its role in his account of our turn to the WIS make it more plausible that neither is the case.) The most obvious candidate for the kind of love of mutual sympathy involved in the love of praise per se is that which involves taking our bearings from the sentiments of other actual people, whether understood in terms of a desire to be in harmony *with them* or in terms of a desire to confirm our unwavering confidence in the rectitude of their sentiments. We can also think of the other kind of egocentric way of desiring mutual sympathy, that of wanting others to be in harmony *with us* or of wanting confirmation of our unwavering confidence in the rectitude of our own sentiments, as capturing a more dominant way of desiring praise per se. Smith's distinction between the proud and the vain man is helpful for illustrating the distinction I have in mind here. Neither man is as concerned with being worthy of praise as he is with being praised. But they have different attitudes toward praise. The former expects others to recognize and accommodate themselves to his "superiority," while the latter measures himself solely on the basis of others' judgments (VI.iii.34–47). The proud man is "sincere, and, in the bottom of his heart, is convinced of his own superiority'; thus, he "seldom visits his superiors" because they might disagree (VI.iii.35, 39). The vain man, on the other hand, doubting his own self-estimation, desperately "courts the company of his superiors" so that their "splendor" will "[reflect]" upon him (VI .iii.40). One man seeks mutual sympathy that he dominates, while the other seeks mutual sympathy dominated by others. Neither desires sentimental agreement per se or to get his sentiments right without prejudice.

(D) The Turn to the WIS

Bracketing for a moment the issue of how to understand the relationship between these two spectra, we should note here that by linking the love of praiseworthiness with the love of mutual sympathy, however understood, we better link the perspective trading and autonomy accounts. This becomes clear when we turn to Smith's completion of the autonomy account with an explanation of our turn to the WIS. As we saw in the previous section, the love of praiseworthiness motivates this turn. Our natural loves of both praise and praiseworthiness subject us to two different "tribunals." The "jurisdiction" of "the man without" is "founded altogether in the desire of actual praise, and in the aversion of actual blame," while the "jurisdiction" of the "higher tribunal" of the WIS, "the man within," is "founded altogether in the desire of praise-worthiness, and in the aversion to blame-worthiness" (III.2.33). However, in passages that Smith added to the second edition of the TMS, he also describes the turn to the WIS as a response to a failure to achieve mutual sympathy with "the man without":

> When we first come into the world, from the natural desire to please we accustom ourselves to every person we converse with, to our parents, to our masters, to our companions. We address ourselves to individuals, and for some time fondly pursue the impossible and absurd project of gaining the good-will and approbation of every body. We are soon taught by experience, however, that this universal approbation is altogether unattainable. As soon as we come to have more important interests to

> manage, we find, that by pleasing one man, we almost certainly disobliged another, that by humouring an individual, we may often irritate a whole people. The fairest and most equitable conduct must frequently obstruct the interests, or thwart the inclinations of particular persons, who will seldom have candour enough to enter into the propriety of our motives, or to see that this conduct, how disagreeable soever to them, is perfectly suitable to our situation. In order to defend ourselves from such partial judgments, we soon learn to set up in our minds a judge between ourselves and those we live with. We conceive ourselves as acting in the presence of a person quite candid and equitable, of one who has no particular elation either to ourselves, or to those whose interests are affected by our conduct, who is neither father, nor brother, nor friend either to them or to us, but is merely a man in general, an impartial spectator who considers our conduct with the same indifference which we regard to that of other people. (III.2.31, note r; cf. III.3.22)[45]

The scenario Smith is imagining is one in which we find ourselves unable to sympathize with the sentiments that other people are feeling toward us; presumably, we have tried to imagine ourselves into their perspectives and simply cannot feel as they do. Since this is a scenario in which the perspective trading process breaks down, the perspective trading and autonomy accounts get linked in one way here. They get linked in another way in that it makes sense to describe our failure to sympathize with others' sentiments toward us as caused by our love of praiseworthiness.

But if this breakdown is caused by our maintaining self-approval in the face of public disapproval, why doesn't it always lead us to turn to an imaginary spectator that is poorly informed or biased in our favor? (For reasons we saw in the previous section, Smith assumes that our need to be in mutual sympathy with some figure takes turning totally inwards off the table.) Smith is not naïve. He thinks a tendency to do just this kind of thing is common enough to be "the source of half the disorders of human life" (III.4.6). But this tendency is recognizable as a moral problem only on the assumption that we recognize the sentiments of a truly WIS as authoritative. So why do we turn to the WIS in the first place? Here the distinction between two spectra of desiring mutual sympathy and their respective connections with the love of praiseworthiness opens up two helpful possibilities.

Applying the first to Smith's account of the turn to the WIS, we get the following picture. Though we initially take our bearings from the sentiments of others, we eventually find ourselves unable to sympathize with the sentiments they hold toward us. Then, perhaps a from newfound sense of personal strength that catalyzes our more self-oriented (as opposed to other-oriented) egocentric love of sympathy, we might turn to an imaginary spectator who always shares our sentiments. Eventually, however, from a love of mutual sympathy understood as agreement per se, we turn to the WIS. As shown earlier, this way of loving mutual sympathy can be understood as underlying the love of praiseworthiness. What needs to be shown more fully here, though, is the connection between loving mutual sympathy in this way and loving mutual sympathy specifically with the WIS. The key lies in the fact that loving mutual sympathy in this way amounts to loving intersubjective sentimental agreement for its own sake, independent of who participates in it; the fact that we usually or always do participate in it is merely a by-product of the fact that our pursuit of mutual sympathy in this way usually or always is *our* pursuit and thus involves *our* own sentiments. Our general attraction to intersubjective sentimental agreement for its own sake manifests itself specifically in attraction to intersubjective sentimental agreement based upon well-informed, true—Smith does not mention "truth," but I am taking it to be implied—beliefs; sentiments based upon well-informed, true beliefs make maximal sentimental agreement possible. Similarly, our general attraction to intersubjective sentimental agreement for its own sake manifests itself specifically in attraction to the intersubjective sentimental agreement that obtains when people inhabit an impartial perspective; sentiments felt from this perspective also make maximal sentimental agreement possible.[46]

Applying the second spectrum to Smith's account of the turn to the WIS, we get the following picture. Though we initially might have unwavering confidence in the rectitude of the sentiments of those around us, we eventually find ourselves unable to agree with them. Then, perhaps from newfound confidence in our own views, we might turn to an imaginary spectator who always endorses them. Eventually, however, from an unprejudiced desire to get our sentiments right, we turn to the WIS. As shown earlier, this way of loving mutual sympathy can also be understood as underlying the love of praiseworthiness. Now the question becomes that of why we see qualities like well-informedness and impartiality as correctness-conferring. Since the former is a good candidate for the most fundamental feature of our conception of a correctness-conferring perspective, its inclusion seems easy to explain. We might also naturally see impartiality as correctness-conferring; perhaps it is simply part of what it is for us to see our own or any other sentiments as correct that we see them as endorsable from an impartial perspective.

In explaining the turn to the WIS not just via the love of praiseworthiness but also via versions of the love of mutual sympathy, these two pictures deepen the link between the perspective trading account and autonomy account by basing them upon a continuous psychology. Each picture, however, contains an explanatory gap flagged by their uses of "eventually." What leads us to start valuing mutual sympathy understood as agreement per se or as getting our sentiments right in a way that is not mixed up with our desire that we or any other individuals *be* the ones who drive the agreement or deliver the right verdict? Here is where we see the importance of Smith's insistence that the love of praiseworthiness is as naturally basic as the love of praise. If I am right that each of the just-mentioned ways of valuing mutual sympathy are involved in the love of praiseworthiness, then they must be naturally basic too. In other words, Smith must just believe that it is part of human nature to care about such things.[47] Assuredly, this concern requires cultivation via education and experience, but it is not for that reason reducible to some other, unmistakably nonmoral concern. Thus, Smith builds into his conception of human nature an orientation toward what we take to be a stable, nonsubjective moral point of view. Our sincere commitment to this point of view seems to emerge in some way from social interaction. To this extent, then, this point of view is the product of human making. But it is not "made" simply for the sake of helping us satisfy any old nonmoral desires; rather, it is made to satisfy what we could describe as a natural desire to make a moral point of view. In this respect, while the distinction between nature and artifice in general is inherently muddy and especially so with respect to certain features of moral life, Smith's account of how moral life emerges from some combination of human nature and human interaction is interesting for muddying the distinction in a unique way.[48]

(E) The Relationship between the Two Pictures

What is the relationship between the two pictures I have proposed? On the first, our natural orientation toward the point of view of the WIS is a natural orientation toward maximal social solidarity. On the second, our natural orientation toward the point of view of the WIS is a natural orientation toward rectitude of sentiment, understood as having sentiments that are endorsed from a correctness-conferring point of view. These two kinds of orientation seem to generate commitment to the same evaluative sentiments: the sentiments that express maximal social solidarity are the sentiments that would be endorsed from the correctness-conferring point of view, and the sentiments that are endorsed from the correctness-conferring point of view are the sentiments that would express maximal social solidarity. Moreover, the orientations are not mutually exclusive; Smith can coherently think that we are oriented in both ways. Thus, we might wonder whether there is any interpretive reason to emphasize one over the other, let alone choose between them, given that both present plausible readings of the text. In fact, the two pictures complement each other in each capturing, even if only rhetorically, a deep feature of Smith's moral thought. The first has the advantage of stressing the fundamental sociality that Smith sees in human beings, expressed perhaps most strongly in his "doctrine" regarding self-evaluation. The second has the advantage of stressing Smith's anciently pedigreed conception of human nature as naturally directed toward the development of virtue. (We'll see this conception across the next two chapters and in Section 2 of Chapter 7.) For these reasons, then, I propose letting them both stand as complements to each other.

Section 5: Smith's Account of Moral Motivation[49]

Given what we saw at the end of the first section regarding the connection between moral judgment and moral motivation in Smith's moral psychology, we should expect the desire that leads us to make moral judgments by consulting the sentiments of the WIS also to be what motivates us to act on these judgments. Thus, since we evaluate ourselves and others out of our desire to be in mutual sympathy with the WIS, we must bring our conduct in line with the WIS out of our desire to be in mutual sympathy with the WIS. Phenomenologically speaking, this tight connection between moral judgment and moral motivation in Smith's moral psychology puts him closer to the moral rationalists than either Hutcheson or Hume. Insofar as it identifies the sentiment that grounds moral approval with the sentiment that grounds moral motivation, Smith's view echoes the rationalistic one that moral obligations are intrinsically compelling as soon as they are recognized. Again, this kind of symmetry between approval and motivation is not present in either Hutcheson or Hume, who both tend to think of moral approval in sensory, aesthetic terms and who both thereby conceptually and phenomenologically separate approval from motivation in the way described at the end of the first section.[50] But before we read this rationalistic echo as anything more than phenomenological, we must remember that Smith agrees with Hutcheson and Hume in thinking that moral approval must not be rooted in reason *because* moral approval is capable of motivating; unlike his predecessors, Smith just thinks that the sentiment-based approval/motivation connection works in such a way that is reminiscent of rationalistic phenomenology. Thus, we should be puzzled when we see Smith claim that the "strongest impulses of self-love" can only be counteracted by "reason, principle, conscience, the inhabitant of the breast, the man within, the great judge and arbiter of our conduct" (III.3.4). What could Smith even mean when he claims that "reason" provides a "more forcible motive" than self-love (III.3.4)?

This rationalistic-sounding claim becomes even more provocative when considered in relation to the context in which it occurs. Smith makes the claim in the context of a thought experiment he uses to explain how we overcome selfishness in cases where "the happiness or misery of others depends in any respect upon our conduct" (III.3.5). He asks us to "suppose that the great empire of China, with all its myriads of inhabitants, was suddenly swallowed up by an earthquake." Then, he asks us to "consider how a man of humanity in

Europe" would feel upon hearing the news of this "dreadful calamity." Smith's description of this man's reaction is worth quoting in full:

> He would, I imagine, first of all, express very strongly his sorry for the misfortune of that unhappy people, he would make many melancholy reflections upon the precariousness of human life, and the vanity of all the labours of man, which could thus be annihilated in a moment. He would too, perhaps, if he was a man of speculation, enter into many reasonings concerning the effects which this disaster might produce upon the commerce of Europe, and the trade and business of the world in general. And when all this fine philosophy was over, when all these humane sentiments had been once fairly expressed, he would pursue his business or his pleasure, take his repose or his diversion, with the same ease and tranquility, as if no such accident had happened.

In other words, while the "man of humanity" would "express" sorrow in words, he would not really care about the victims of the earthquake. As Smith puts it:

> if he was to lose his little finger to-morrow, he would not sleep to-night; but, provided he never saw them, he will snore with the most profound security over the ruin of a hundred millions of his brethren, and the destruction of that immense multitude seems plainly an object less interesting to him, than this paltry misfortune of his own.

However, the man's reaction would change if he were asked whether he would "be willing to sacrifice the lives of a hundred millions of his brethren" in order to prevent "this paltry misfortune to himself." With striking conviction, Smith states that "human nature startles with horror at the thought, and the world, in its greatest depravity and corruption, never produced such a villain as could be capable of entertaining it." This observation leads to him to ask: "What makes this difference? When our passive feelings are so sordid and so selfish, how comes it that our active principles should often be so generous and so noble?" The crucial line quoted earlier constitutes Smith's answer: "reason, principle, conscience, the inhabitant of the breast, the man within, the great judge and arbiter of our conduct" (III.3.4).

Smith's point seems to be that truly other-preferring, self-sacrificial moral action is not motivated by other-directed care, such as that exemplified by the "feeble spark of benevolence" or the "soft power of humanity" (III.3.4). As the TMS' editors point out, by using these phrases, Smith is likely attacking Hutcheson and Hume (III.3.4, note 7). The first phrase probably refers to Hutcheson, who, as we saw in Chapter 2, argued that we have an innate moral sense that approves only of benevolence. Thus, one of Smith's goals in this passage must be to show that Hutcheson's moral psychology cannot fully explain self-sacrificial, other-preferring moral action because it must *either* claim, implausibly, that benevolence alone generates such action *or* identify an additional motive for it and thereby claim, also implausibly, that this motive would win no moral approval. The second phrase probably refers to Hume who, in *An Enquiry Concerning the Principles of Morals*, declared that the sentiment of "humanity" is "originally the same" with the "sentiment of morals" (EPM 6.5/SBN 235–6).

Any criticism Smith is levelling at Hume here is too complex for the concise summation that sufficed regarding the probable criticism of Hutcheson.[51] In denying that the sentiment of humanity is behind our "active principles," Smith seems to agree with at least one possible reading of Hume. This sentiment, Hume argued, grounds our general other-things-being-equal preference for seeing people helped and pleased instead of harmed and pained; this preference then grounds our positive evaluations of character traits that help and please their bearers or the people around them. Hume was willing to admit, however, that despite being the source of moral judgment, the general feeling of humane concern for others might not actually do much in the way of motivating action (e.g., EPM 9.4/SBN 271; cf. T 3.3.1.23/SBN 586).[52] Thus, Smith appears to be endorsing a Humean position. Yet Smith's tone is rather non-Humean. As I read the passage, he uses the term "humanity" and its cognate, "humane," almost sarcastically to describe the European man's superficial but "fairly expressed" concern for his distant "brethren" (IV.3.4). The mild vitriol in this description of the eloquent "man of humanity" seems foreign to Hume's moral theory, which—again, on one possible reading—explicitly limits itself to explaining the moral "discourse" we use to serve "all our purposes in company, in the pulpit, on the theatre, and in the schools" (EPM 5.42/SBN 229; cf. T 3.3.1.23/

SBN 586–7). Thus, unlike Smith, on this reading, Hume seems to have doubted that moral sentiments have much direct impact on our practice. So while Smith agrees with Hume's observations regarding humanity's general inability to motivate, he also, *for this very reason*, criticizes Hume's willingness to ground moral sentiment in it.[53]

The trouble with the reading of Hume upon which this reading of Smith is based is that it overlooks the fact that Hume actually *can* provide a relatively robust conception of moral motivation, albeit one grounded not in humanity but in moral self-love and self-hatred; we see this in Hume's ultimate answer to the sensible knaves who want to know why they should not pursue a policy of disguised vice and dishonesty: even if you are successful, you will hate yourselves (EPM 9.22–5/SBN 282–4; cf. T 3.2.1.8/SBN 479).[54] In claiming that the "sentiment of morals and that of humanity . . . are originally the same," Hume means that the sentiment of humanity makes the sentiment of morals *possible*, not that the two are synonyms (EPM 6.4–5/SBN 235–6). Thus, Humean moral motivation is derived more directly from humanity-based, self-directed moral evaluation than from humanity itself.

It is certainly possible that Smith's criticism of Hume's conception of moral motivation is simply off the mark. There are two reasons, however, why we should not be so quick to draw this conclusion. The first is that Smith could just be making the point that regardless of whether Hume's moral psychology allows for a conception of moral motivation, it does so clumsily or only as a secondary aim.[55] A second, more philosophically substantive reason is that Smith might mean that the moral self-evaluation involved in Hume's account of moral motivation is *problematically reducible* to the sentiment of humanity. After all, since Humean moral approval is ultimately rooted in the sentiment of humanity, Humean agents seeking their own moral approval must do so in some sense *because* of the sentiment of humanity. Of course, if this is what Smith has in mind, he must indicate the sense of "because" involved in Hume's account and show exactly why this sense causes philosophical trouble.

In any case, putting aside the question of whether Smith's criticisms of Hume and, for that matter, Hutcheson are any good, we now must consider what Smith offers as an alternative to the positions he criticizes. If neither benevolence nor humanity nor humanity-influenced love of self-approval generates other-preferring, self-sacrificial moral action, what does? In other words, what does Smith mean by "reason, principle, conscience, the inhabitant of the breast, the man within, the great judge and arbiter of our conduct" (III.3.4)?

At least the last four components of the list must refer to Smith's WIS theory of conscience. Thus, similarly to Hume, Smith here is at least *in some sense* grounding moral motivation in love of one's own moral approval, as delivered by one's conscience; in keeping with this parallel, as we saw in the first section, Smith explicitly criticizes Hutcheson but not Hume for denying that "a regard to the pleasure of self-approbation, to the comfortable applause of our own consciences" is a morally legitimate motive (VII.ii.3.13).[56] Given this similarity to Hume, if Smith's criticism of Hume is even to identify a position that is non-Humean, it must offer a non-Humean account of the sentimental roots of the love of self-approval.

Another question obviously arises about the first two components of the list, "reason" and "principle." By employing these terms in the context of criticizing the two most significant sentimentalists of the day, Smith must be doing something that is more than just rhetorically significant. Maybe he really is saying that reason takes over as a motive when sentiment fails, perhaps as a boost to the love of self-approval. The editors of the TMS call our attention to an even more specific reason to take this possibility seriously: it is hard not to see the thought experiment Smith employs as an explicit contradiction of Hume's famous summary statement of sentimentalism, "'Tis not contrary to reason to prefer the destruction of the whole world to the scratching of my finger" (T 2.3.3–6/SBN 416; III.3.4, note 6).

Let's tackle the second question first. As we saw in Chapter 2, Smith's attack on rationalists like Cudworth allows for a positive role for reason to play in moral judgment and motivation. Our ability to make and act upon moral distinctions cannot ultimately "*arise from* reason"; rather, it must be "founded upon immediate sense and feeling" (VII.iii.2.9; emphasis added). But reason does help us form inductive "general maxims" on the basis of what "pleases or displeases" our nonrational "moral faculties" (VII.iii.2.6). So maybe the puzzling language in the earthquake passage simply points to these reason-based general rules.[57] This reading seems plausible. Later in TMS III, Smith tells us that the practical function of these rules is to combat "the violence and injustice of [the] selfish passions" that often arise in the heat of a moment lead us "to induce the man within the breast to make a report very different from what the real circumstances of the case are capable of authorising"; we can understand this form of self-deceit in terms of a decision to turn to a partial, poorly informed spectator instead of the WIS (III.4.1). Smith has in mind the kinds of general moral policies we might employ against performing certain actions because we know that any context-sensitive deliberation in which we engage regarding them will most likely just rationalize our desire to do something we know is wrong.[58] We use these rules so often as "standards of judgment in debating concerning the degree of praise or blame that is due to certain actions of a complicated and dubious nature" that we might be misled, as "several very eminent authors" have been, into thinking that they form the basis of "the original judgments of mankind with regard to right and wrong" (III.4.11). But as Smith's discussion of moral rationalism makes clear, the rules are "founded upon experience of . . . particular instances" of sentiment-based approval and disapproval (III.4.8). To the extent that these rules inherit their motivational power from the sentiments upon which they are based, Smith can say that respect for such rules is what allows a man to refuse to sacrifice the lives of a hundred million strangers about whom he does not really care in order to save a little finger about which he cares deeply, without going back on his view that reason alone does not motivate. (In further support of this rule-focused reading of the passage, the fact that the man in the example refuses to harm others or allow them to be harmed for his own benefit[59] makes his choice derive specifically from a consideration of *justice*; in this regard, it serves as a paradigmatic example of a case in which, according to Smith, we *should* act out of respect for general moral rules (III.6.8–11). In Section 3 of Chapter 6, we will discuss at length both what Smith means by "justice" and why he thinks rules should motivate adherence to it.)

Smith owes us an account of exactly how these rules inherit motivational force from the sentiments upon which they are based. He calls the practical "regard" to these rules the "sense of duty," but, beyond a reference to the "reverence" for them that we develop when we are "virtuously educated," he does not provide any more detail about how they motivate (III.5.1). However, it seems that it would be easy enough for him to work out these details, particularly by invoking, perhaps in Humean fashion, the power of the "habit and experience" of acting upon the sentiments upon which the rules are based (III.3.2). (I will also say more about this issue in Section 3 of Chapter 6.) But regardless of whether Smith can explain how the habit and experience of acting from the sentiments that ground the general rules can generate motivational respect for them, the earthquake passage ultimately does not concern this kind of inherited motivation. Throughout the thought experiment, it is "the man within" who reminds our "man of humanity" that "he is no better than his neighbor," even though the man within does so by reminding our man of humanity that he is about to "violate one of those sacred rules, upon which the tolerable observation of which depend the whole security and peace of human society" (III.3.6). As we have seen, Smith brings up general moral rules to explain how we deal with cases in which our conception of the man within becomes untrustworthy. Cases such as these occur when "furious resentment" deceives us into thinking that the targets of our wrath deserve punishment or when selfishness deceives us into thinking that others are not really harmed by our actions (III.4.12; cf. III.6.10). This specific problem does not come up in the little finger example, which Smith appears to be using only to explain how conscience works in the first place; the example occurs at the beginning of a chapter titled, "Of the Influence and Authority of Conscience" (III.3).

Surprisingly, we can move toward figuring out what Smith means by "reason" and "principle" in the little finger passage by noticing that this language is puzzling not only with respect to how it relates to the rest of Smith's moral psychology but also with respect to other features of the passage itself. Right after he uses this language, Smith restates his point as follows:

> It is not the love of our neighbour, it is not the love of mankind [that accounts for the choice in question]. It is a stronger *love*, a more powerful *affection*, which generally takes place upon such occasions; the *love* of what is honourable and noble, of the grandeur, and dignity, and superiority of our own characters. (III.3.4; emphases added).

This language makes it quite clear that there must be an *affection* ultimately motivating our "man of humanity." Thus, even the passage itself indicates that Smith's references to "reason" and "principle" must ultimately be to a sentiment. But which one?

An answer presents itself when we shift our attention back to his reference to "conscience, the inhabitant of the breast, the man within, the great judge and arbiter of our conduct" (III.3.4). As mentioned earlier, this language suggests that the love of self-approval, in some sense, motivates the "man of humanity," a suggestion furthered by the immediately subsequent reference to "the love of . . . the grandeur, and dignity, and superiority of our own characters." If both Smith's overall moral psychology and the little finger passage itself suggest that the references to "reason" and "principle" be understood in terms of a sentiment, and the predominant sentiment in the passage is some kind of love of self-approval, then it seems that these references should be understood in terms of this kind of love of self-approval. Thus, I turn now to what Smith must mean by it. This account still must be distinguished from Hume's in order to reveal the positive position Smith is even defending in this passage. As we shall see, doing so will also help us make better sense of his reference to reason's ability to motivate.

Even before we completed Smith's full-blown account of moral judgment by incorporating the WIS, it would have been easy to distinguish how Smith thinks of self-approval from how Hume does. As we saw in Sections 1 and 6 of the previous chapter, Hume rejects Smith's view that sympathy is constitutive of approval in general, whether of self or other. Thus, Smith must be claiming, at least in part, that insofar as it must be rooted in his mutual-sympathy-based conception of the love of approval in general, his account of the love of self-approval can explain moral self-sacrifice without making any implausible claims about our ability to care more about others' interests than our own (though, of course, Smith's argument demands that we find plausible the position that we care more about mutual sympathy than about the interest we take in things like our little fingers).[60] And we can conclude that even if he is misreading Hume, Smith thinks that his mutual-sympathy-based conception of the love of self-approval somehow does a better job at this than does Hume's conception of the love of self-approval.

After the previous two sections of this chapter, we know that Smith thinks of the love of self-approval specifically in terms of the love of mutual sympathy with the WIS, understood in either of the two ways identified in the previous section.[61] The role of the WIS in this account reveals a substantive rationale for Smith's references to "reason" and "principle." If moral motivation amounts to desire for mutual sympathy with the WIS, then it amounts to desire for mutual sympathy with what is felt from a perspective that anyone can adopt; recall Smith's description of the WIS as a "man in general" (III.2.31, note r). Since it filters out subjective idiosyncrasies that inhibit sympathy, leaving only what human feeling per se would dictate, this perspective can be plausibly described as "objective"; thus, in the previous section, I was able to describe our attraction to it in terms of either a desire for maximal social solidarity or a desire for rectitude of sentiment. And in being objective in this way, this perspective is also one from which evaluations are maximally coherent and consistent; the man who values the lives of millions of strangers about whom he cares little over a little finger about which he cares much demonstrates a desire to render his sentiments consistent and coherent with those of pretty much anyone who is not him. When we act from a desire for mutual sympathy with the WIS, then, we act from a desire to bring ourselves in line with evaluations that can be described as objective, consistent, and coherent, qualities that are traditionally identified with rationality but here given an affective basis.[62] Therefore, there is reason to read the language of "reason" and "principle" in the earthquake passage as pointing to a similarity between the experience of acting from desire for mutual sympathy with the WIS and the experience of acting from purely rational considerations.[63] In this respect, the aforementioned general resemblance between Smith's and a rationalist phenomenology is actually much sharper than it might have first appeared.

Section 6: Correction and Cultural Differences

In the introduction to this chapter, I characterized the third recognizable feature of moral evaluation that Smith must explain as the distinction we make between moral judgments we consider to be correct and moral judgments upon which our group agrees. This description is potentially ambiguous. Does the distinction only concern moral judgments our group makes in applying our shared standards, or does it also concern the standards themselves? It seems that the turn to the WIS both enables us to make moral judgments that we see as based upon better information and less partiality than those made by members of our group in applying our shared standards and enables us to make moral judgments that we see as employing standards based upon better information and less partiality than those applied by the members of our group. In this section, I spell out in more detail how the first kind of correction works for Smith, spell out in more detail how the second kind of correction *would* work for Smith, suggest that Smith has the resources to recognize this kind of correction, and make the case that Smith actually does recognize this kind of correction.[64]

There seem to be at least three kinds of correction of the first kind. The first two have to do with the "W" criterion. Many of the examples Smith uses to establish the distinctions between the love of praiseworthiness and the love of praise and the hatred of blameworthiness and the hatred of blame involve cases in which we are either praised or blamed "either for actions which we have not performed, or for motives which had no influence upon us" (III.2.32; cf. III.2.4–5; III.2.11). In these cases, the turn to the WIS corrects for false factual beliefs about what an agent did or why the agent did it. Secondly, it is also easy to imagine ways in which the WIS could correct for ignorance. For example, while a regular, non-well-informed spectator might disapprove of an agent's resentment, the WIS approves because of better information regarding what prompted it. The WIS could also correct for false or incomplete information in the harder to define, not-necessarily-factual sense of "understanding" mentioned in Section 1 of the previous chapter.[65] One way to resolve the tension we saw there between Smith's occasional claims that sympathy involves an act of imaginatively becoming another person (I.i.1.2; VII.iii.1.4) and his view that sympathy is evaluative and thus requires that we maintain a gap between what we would feel in an agent's situation and what the agent does is by treating the former claims as pointing to nonevaluative, perspective-grasping acts of imagination. According to this resolution, "well-informed" in the sense of "understanding" spectators first nonevaluatively imagine themselves as agents and then evaluatively project into the agents' situations with this understanding in mind.[66] Thirdly, the WIS obviously corrects for partiality. The WIS might not agree, for example, with what your mom thinks of you. Notably, partiality corrections can pave the way for either factual or understanding-focused information corrections. For example, partiality can prevent someone whose interests are adversely impacted by something an agent did from looking into the agent's motives or from sincerely trying to see things from the agent's perspective; thus, this person does not sympathize with the agent's motives and see that the agent's action was justified.[67]

In these ways, our turn to the WIS explains how we can make moral judgments that we take to be correct independent of what our neighbors happen to think; after all, these neighbors might be judging in ways that we think are biased and/or based on bad information. Notice that on this view, it is in principle possible for us to employ the WIS to judge in a way that disagrees with what *everyone* in our society thinks. Perhaps they *all* hold false beliefs about what a person they are condemning did and/or *all* lack information or understanding about this person's circumstances and/or are *all* biased against this person. But even in a case like this one, we might appeal to the WIS only because we think that the people around us are misapplying the standards of propriety and merit at which we have collectively arrived via the perspective swapping process outlined in the second section. So there is reason to consider what it might look like when we turn to the WIS in disagreement not with an evaluation our society makes in light of its own standards but with the standards themselves.[68]

It seems that corrections of this kind would mirror corrections of the first kind. The only difference would be that they apply directly to standards instead of to the application thereof. It is not hard to see how a group's standards can be based upon false factual beliefs or factual ignorance. Imagine, for example, standards tied to some kind of superstition. It is also not hard to see how a group's standards can be based upon false or incomplete understanding. Imagine, for example, standards tied to a systematic misrepresentation of the perspectives and experiences of either another group of people or a subgroup of people within the group who holds the standards.[69] Nor is it hard to see how a group's standards can be too partial. They might, for example, favor the interests or perspectives of the members of either the group itself or a subgroup within it.[70]

The question, though, is whether Smith either does or has the resources to recognize these kinds of WIS-based corrections. Although the question of resources is a big one, we should observe that the plausibility of the quick examples in the previous paragraph generate at least prima facie reason for believing that the WIS can explain these kinds of corrections. Furthermore, I deeply suspect that while intrinsically legitimate, a hard distinction between the two classes of corrections is not built into the everyday experience that Smith is trying to capture. It is just not obvious to me that everyday appeals to conscience in the face of moral disagreement operate with a clear sense of this distinction. The experience of disagreeing with someone's moral judgment regarding factors relevant to the application of a norm does not seem immediately different from the experience of disagreeing with someone's moral judgment regarding the norm itself; in each case, we are just saying that the person in front of us is incorrect. One might think that disagreements of the latter kind are had only in a hyper-reflective, philosophical mode. But consider how often we disagree about the relevant weight of certain norms we all accept. Such disagreements certainly can be about how accurately we are each representing our shared society's ranking system. Yet it seems more plausible to me to see them as about how the norms in question should be weighed against each other in principle, independent of what we think our groups says (this interpretation seems especially plausible given how unclear it often is *how* our group weighs norms). In short, there must be a reason why one has to teach to students something like the distinction between the two classes—even if to lead them to consider whether criticisms of the second kind are untenable; there also must be a reason why one sometimes has to remind people about it when, for example, they get upset in a certain kind of way about a judge's legal ruling. If the experience of making criticisms of both kinds is thus continuous, then there is reason to believe that an account of the second seems to fall right out of an account of the first, which Smith obviously provides. Moreover, I suspect that any defense of an account of the first that does not also defend an account of the second would misrepresent everyday life in a way that Smith wants to avoid. And if this is right, then Smith's commitment to remain close to everyday life does not cut off the possibility of ideological critique in the way mentioned in Section 1 of Chapter 2.[71]

Of course, a suspicion, however deep, is not an argument. So let's leave my hunches about resources to one side and turn to the question of whether Smith recognizes the second class of WIS-based correction. One piece of evidence that he does derives from his observation that our moral sentiments are "never so apt to be corrupted as when the indulgent and partial spectator is at hand, while the indifferent and impartial one is at great distance" (III.3.41). These "indulgent and partial" spectators that crowd the WIS out of our thinking might be people whose bias in our favor is most relevant to the first class of corrections; consider, for example, grounding one's self-evaluation in the sentiments of one's loving parents (cf. III.3.22). But Smith also seems to think that these people can be biased in our favor in a sense most relevant to the second class of corrections. He writes that "the real revered, and impartial spectator . . . is upon no occasion, at a greater distance than amidst the violence and rage of contending parties" (III.3.43). We see such "violence and rage" when "factions, whether civil or ecclesiastical," are "hostile" to each other; we also see it, to a lesser degree, when one nation is at "variance" with another one. In such situations, members of opposing groups see each other as undeserving of "the plainest and most obvious" just treatment, as "public enemies," as "rebels," or as "heretics" (III.3.42–3). In doing so, they see each other through partial rather than impartial eyes. If this form of partiality can be understood as cultural, then in ignoring the WIS, people in these situations are being culturally biased. It follows, then, that Smith believes the return of the WIS to their thinking would solve this problem.[72]

More relevant evidence derives from Smith's explicit treatment in TMS V of the relationship between customary and natural moral sentiments. There, he argues that custom generally coincides with the sentiments of the WIS. To the extent that this argument implies that customary sentiments and the WIS' sentiments are not the same thing, it supports the view that Smith recognizes the second class of WIS-based correction. Tellingly, Smith frames the question of how much what he calls "custom and fashion" influences moral judgment in a way that does not even acknowledge the possibility that it does so all the way down. Instead, he interprets this question as one about *how much* custom—as we shall see in the following, fashion is a species of custom—can "pervert" our natural moral sentiments and thereby cause us to have "irregular and discordant [moral] opinions" (V.2.1; V.1.4). In doing so, Smith reminds us that he is straightforwardly not a relativist in that he believes that the moral sentiments are rooted in human nature and thus are fundamentally the same for everyone. Since Smith does not offer an argument for this claim, there is little to say about his reasons for holding it.[73] However, there is a lot to say about the fact that in answering his question, "not much," and thereby bringing custom and the WIS together, Smith appears to demonstrate ambivalence about whether his full-blown account of moral judgment includes in it a significant practical role for the second class of correction, no matter how possible in principle it might be. As we shall see, Smith ultimately concludes that despite the general correspondence between custom and the WIS, we should not make moral judgments on the basis of custom alone.

Smith sets up the answer to his question of the influence of custom on moral judgment by first explaining the psychological mechanisms that give custom and fashion their influence. The account is unmistakably Humean:

> When two objects have frequently been seen together, the imagination acquires a habit of passing easily from the one to the other. If the first appear, we lay our account that the second is to follow. Of their own accord they put us in mind of one another, and the attention glides easily along them. Though, independent of custom, there should be no real beauty in their union, yet when custom has thus connected them together, we feel an impropriety in their separation. The one we think is awkward when it appears without its usual companion. We miss something which we expected to find, and the habitual arrangement of our ideas is disturbed by the disappointment.

This is a recognizable phenomenon. The sheer fact that we are used to seeing things a certain way disposes us to approve of things being that way, independent of our seeing any intrinsic merit in it; similarly, the sheer fact that we are used to seeing things a certain way disposes us to disapprove of things being an alternative way, independent of our seeing any intrinsic demerit in it. As a result, "when there is any natural propriety" in the way we usually experience things, "custom increases our sense of it, and makes a different arrangement appear still more disagreeable than it otherwise would seem to be." And when there is any natural impropriety in the way we usually experience things, "custom either diminishes, or takes away altogether, our sense of the impropriety" (V.1.2). Thus, Smith recognizes custom as a new, additional factor in our evaluations, distinct from what the WIS dictates. Smith also gives special attention to the influence of "fashion," which is a "particular species of custom." The influence of fashion involves a third factor. Fashion influences our evaluations when the mechanism behind the influence of custom is enhanced by the mechanism behind the influence of esteem for the rich and the great. The result of this combination is that an otherwise "indifferent" way of appearing or doing things gets "connected in our imagination with the idea of something that is genteel and magnificent" and thus "seems, on account of this relation, to have something about it that is genteel and magnificent too" (V.1.3).

Since the influence of fashion assumes the influence of custom and since the psychological root of the distinction between the two is best left until the discussion of prudence in Section 5 of Chapter 6, I will follow Smith in focusing mainly on custom. Before getting to morality, Smith explains how custom impacts our aesthetic evaluations in a variety of domains. His first example involves "dress": "a suit of clothes, for example, seems to want something if they are without the most insignificant ornament which usually accompanies them, and we find a meanness or awkwardness in the absence of even a haunch button" (V.1.3). Smith expects us to recognize the impact of custom on styles of dress. He also expects us to recognize the impact of custom on styles of "furniture." Since clothing and furniture wear out relatively quickly, we see their styles frequently change in our lifetimes. The case is otherwise in arts like architecture, poetry, and music, which produce more durable objects. Since buildings, poems, and compositions last a long time, we become accustomed to certain forms in these domains; we also infrequently see changes in them. Thus, we often make the mistake of believing that "all the rules" which we are used to seeing observed in them, "are founded upon reason and nature, not upon habit and prejudice" (V.1.4). However, reflection should reveal that it is "a little difficult to conceive" that the forms upon which our culture has hit are the only good ones (V.1.5).

Once we realize the power of custom in aesthetic evaluation, we might be tempted to adopt "the system of [the] learned and ingenious Father," Claude

Buffier, which explains "the whole charm" of beauty as arising "from its falling in with the habits which custom had impressed upon the imagination, with regard to things of each particular kind." Smith cites Buffier's custom-based account of the beauty of natural objects as an instance of this kind of explanation. On Smith's telling, Buffier argues that we judge the beauty of natural objects first by referring them to the "class" or "species" of things to which they belong and then by determining the extent to which they approximate "that form and colour, which is most usual among things of that particular sort":

> Thus, in the human form, the beauty of each feature lies in a certain middle equally removed from a variety of other forms that are ugly. A beautiful nose, for example, is one that is neither very long, nor very short, nor very straight, nor very crooked, but a sort of middle among all these extremes, and less different from any one of them, than all of them are from one another. It is the form which Nature seems to have aimed at in them all, which, however, she deviates from in a great variety of ways, and very seldom hits exactly; but to which all those deviations still bear a very strong resemblance.

Perhaps surprisingly, the appeal to the goodness of what nature "aims at" does no real explanatory work here; if anything, on Smith's reading of Buffier, the psychological power of custom explains the appeal of nature's aims, not the other way around. The example Smith uses involves human beings, but he notes that the account also explains how we judge the beauty of "flowers, or horses, or any other species of things." In our experience with different instances of a kind, we become accustomed to what is present in all of them, the ways in which they resemble. From these points of resemblance, we develop the idea of a "pattern" that they all approximate, which becomes for us the standard of beauty (V.1.8). Since the idea of this pattern depends upon experience, it takes experience to develop expertise in both seeing and applying it. Also since the idea of this pattern depends upon experience, different groups of people have different standards of beauty, depending upon how the things around them, human beings included, happen to look.

Although Smith acknowledges the explanatory power of this account, he comments, "I cannot, however, be induced to believe that our sense even of external beauty is founded altogether on custom." One aesthetic criterion that seems objective to him is "the utility of any form, its fitness for the useful purposes for which it was intended" (V.1.9). In architecture, for example, many forms can be "agreeable" but they all must be conducive to structural integrity; forms that do not keep a building upright seem "absolutely unreasonable," independent of culture (V.1.5). Smith also claims that "certain colours are more agreeable than others," "a smooth surface is more agreeable than a rough one," "variety is more pleasing than a tedious undiversified uniformity," and "connected variety, in which each new appearance seems to be introduced by what went before it, and in which all the adjoining parts seem to have some natural relation to one another, is more agreeable" than is variety per se (V.1.9). Since Smith provides no argument for most of these examples of objective aesthetic criteria—the sole exception is utility, which we revisit in Section 5 of Chapter 6—one gets the sense that he cares much less about establishing them than about registering his belief that *some* such criteria exist, whatever they may be.

Despite believing that such criteria exist, however, Smith ultimately concedes that responsiveness to them is a less important factor in our aesthetic evaluations than custom is. Custom is such a powerful force in these evaluations that "there is scarce any one external form so beautiful as to please, if quite contrary to custom . . . or so deformed as not to be agreeable, if custom uniformly supports" (V.1.9). In other words, custom is so influential that *some* agreement with it is necessary for positive aesthetic evaluation even of independently beautiful things and *enough* agreement with it can be sufficient for positive aesthetic evaluation even of independently ugly things. Thus, custom can "pervert" our aesthetic evaluations by leading us to deem ugly an objectively beautiful form or deem beautiful an objectively ugly one.

This is not the case, Smith goes on to argue, "concerning the beauty of conduct" (V.2.1). Custom and its subspecies, fashion, influence our moral sentiments via the same psychological mechanisms that they influence our aesthetic ones. Our being used to seeing certain conduct positively disposes us toward it and negatively disposes us to its opposite, both all the more so when the conduct is demonstrated by the wealthy and powerful—hence the positive impact of "good company," the negative impact of being "brought up amidst violence, licentiousness, falsehood, and injustice," and the powerful impact either way of good or bad conduct in the rich and great. (Smith reveals his general opinion of the wealthy and powerful by only explaining how fashion can "give reputation to a certain degree of disorder, and, on the contrary, discountenance qualities which deserve esteem." But the psychological mechanisms he employs would also allow for fashion to have a positive impact (V.2.2–3).) However, the influence of custom—again, I'll leave fashion aside—upon the moral sentiments is generally weaker than the influence upon the aesthetic ones. The ultimate cause of this difference, Smith claims, is that

> the principles of the imagination, upon which our sense of beauty depends, are of a very nice and delicate nature, and may easily be altered by habit and education: but the sentiments of moral approbation and disapprobation, are founded on the strongest and most vigorous passions of human nature; and though they may be somewhat warpt, cannot be entirely perverted. (V.2.1)

This distinction demands further explication both for the sake of developing Smith's psychology of aesthetic evaluation on its own and for the sake of more clearly distinguishing it from that of moral evaluation than Smith himself does. (In the opening sentence of the very paragraph from which the quotation is taken, Smith muddies this distinction by treating sentiment regarding morals as a "kind" of sentiment regarding "beauty."[74]) I leave these tasks unfinished here. However, we should note that given its parameters, Smith's acceptance of this distinction should make it generally obvious why he also believes that custom can have little impact upon our moral sentiments: if the moral sentiments are as strong and vigorous as he says they are, then conduct that flies in the face of them will never happen consistently enough to become customary (cf. V.2.16).

Smith supports the claim that custom has less influence on the moral sentiments than the aesthetic ones with three sets of examples of the interaction between custom and propriety. The most important set for the present purposes is that which involves the "general style of character and behavior" customary not just to different societies but to different *kinds* of societies (V.2.12). Smith divides societies here into two kinds, "savage" ones, like those of North America, Africa, pre-ancient Greece, and pre-ancient Rome, and "civilized" ones, like those of Europe, ancient Greece, and ancient Rome (V.2.8–10; V.2.10; V.2.15). At least partly due to custom, the former societies emphasize the virtues "which are founded upon self-denial and the command of the passions," while the latter emphasize "the virtues which are founded upon humanity" (V.2.8). As a result, members of the former interact "with the reserve of strangers" compared to members of the latter societies, who "converse together with the openness of friends" (V.2.10–11).

Obviously, Smith's use of this dichotomy between the civilized and the savage is both factually and morally embarrassing. However, for the sake of at least complicating how we understand what Smith was thinking, we should observe both the positivity in his attitude toward what he takes to be savage cultures and the negativity in his attitude toward the way the members of what he takes to be savage cultures have been treated by members of what he takes to be civilized ones.[75] It is difficult not to hear admiration in Smith's claims that members of savage societies often possess "magnanimity and self-command" to a degree "almost beyond the conception of Europeans" when they, for example, demonstrate "contempt of death and torture" upon being captured by enemies. In a remarkable passage worth quoting in full, Smith observes,

> There is not a negro from the coast of Africa who does not, in this respect, possess a degree of magnanimity which the soul of his sordid master is too often scarce capable of conceiving. Fortune never exerted more cruelly her empire over mankind, than when she subjected those nations of heroes to the refuse of the jails of Europe, to wretches who possess the virtues neither of the countries which they came from, nor of those which they go to, and whose levity, brutality, and baseness, so justly expose them to the contempt of the vanquished. (V.2.9)[76]

Even though Smith describes the slave owners as lacking the virtues of their own countries, irony remains in the fact that he immediately follows this passage with a discussion of how civilized societies emphasize humane, social virtues. However, perhaps because he is aware of this irony, Smith focuses more on the civilized de-emphasis of self-denial and self-command than directly on the civilized emphasis on humanity. His depiction of the civilized character has much more to do with tolerance for strongly felt and expressed passions than with kindness. This tolerance, Smith worries, "sometimes destroys the masculine firmness of the character" (V.2.13).[77]

As one would expect, Smith is also critical of what he takes to be the savage character. The "hardiness" and emotional closed-offedness typical in savage societies not only tends to diminish "humanity" (V.2.13) but also "necessarily [fosters] the habits of falsehood and dissimulation." In contrast, the emotional openness typical in civilized ones tends to make people more "frank, open, and sincere." Furthermore, the savage habit of masking "furious and violent" passions often makes them more so, while the civilized habit of expressing passions in ways that are "often clamorous and noisy" makes them neither "so furious or so desperate" (V.2.11). (Smith does not mention here how each society compares with respect to the truly transformational WIS-motivated form of self-command we shall discuss in Section 6 of Chapter 6.) So while it is not the case that Smith employs his dichotomy between savage and civilized simply to celebrate the latter, it is also not the case that he does so simply to celebrate the former. Each society, he concludes, tends to emphasize the "duties of one virtue . . . so as to encroach a little upon the precincts of some other" (V.2.13).

Nevertheless, Smith does argue that these customary characters are generally "suitable to the circumstances" that give rise to them (V.2.13). The circumstantial factors Smith has in mind are the difficulty attaining basic "wants and necessities" and the expectation of sympathy from others. The two factors are related because "we must in some measure be at ease ourselves . . . before we can feel much for others." Thus, when it is difficult for everyone to attain basic wants and necessities, we can expect little sympathy, and when it is easy for everyone to attain basic wants and necessities, we can expect a lot of sympathy. Since their members find themselves in the former situation, savage societies emphasize the virtues of self-command; since their members find themselves in the latter situation, civilized societies emphasize virtues of humanity. In concluding that these emphases are "suitable," Smith must mean that WIS approves of them. In approving of the savage emphasis on self-command, the WIS must sympathize with it upon imagining how he would feel if he were both struggling to survive and surrounded by others who, because they are also struggling, do not sympathize much with him. In approving of the civilized emphasis on humanity, the WIS must sympathize with it upon imagining how he would feel if he were both surviving with little difficulty and surrounded by others who, because they are also surviving with little difficulty, sympathize quite a bit with him. However, since both the savage and the civilized societies tend to overemphasize their characteristic virtues, these instances of WIS-sympathy must not be totally perfect. This minor imperfection is the product of custom, which leads the savage and civilized societies to push things just a little too far in one direction.

The conclusion Smith draws from these examples is that "in general, the style of manners which takes place in any nation may commonly upon the whole be said to be that which is most suitable to its situation" (V.2.13). We might expect him to conclude, then, that there is no serious moral need for readiness to make the second kind of WIS-based correction of what is customary to the kind of society in which we find ourselves. However, he points out that "with regard to particular usages" and "particular actions," the "influence" of custom can be "destructive of good morals" (V.2.14).[78] Smith's most important example of how custom can corrupt the moral sentiments with respect to a particular practice is the ancient Greek licensing of "the exposition, that is the murder of new-born infants . . . whenever the circumstances of the parent rendered it inconvenient to bring up the child." Smith hypothesizes that this practice began when terrible poverty might have rendered it necessary:

> The extreme indigence of the savage is often such that he himself is frequently exposed to the greatest extremity of hunger, he often dies of pure want, and it is frequently impossible for him to support both himself and his child. We cannot wonder, therefore, that in this case he should abandon it. One who, in flying from an enemy, whom it was impossible to resist, should throw down his infant, because it retarded his flight, would surely be excusable; since, by attempting to save it, he could only hope for the consolation of dying with it. That in this state of society, therefore, a parent should be allowed to judge whether he can bring up his child, ought not to surprise us so greatly.

We might quibble over whether Smith is claiming here that infanticide is justified or merely unsurprising under conditions of extreme poverty. To my ear, which gets caught on the word "excusable," he is saying the former. Everything hangs on how tight of an analogy he sees between horrible poverty and being pursued by a murderous enemy. But even if Smith believes that infanticide is unjustified even under conditions of extreme poverty, he clearly believes that it is even more unjustified—or, to alter a phrase he uses here, "[*less*] pardonable"—under the conditions that obtained "in the latter ages of Greece." In those far less indigent ages, the practice was supported "from views of remote interest or conveniency" and "far-fetched considerations of public utility." There can be no analogy between these justifications and that of sacrificing one life to save another when the only alternative is losing both. Yet, Smith argues, these kinds of justifications held sway even with philosophers like Plato and Aristotle because "the uniform continuance of the custom had hindered them afterwards from perceiving its enormity." Thus, the ancient Greek licensing of infanticide provides an example of how the fact that something is "commonly done" can blind us to its immorality (V.2.15). It also provides us with an example of both the importance and functioning of the second class of WIS-based correction. We can see such a "horrible" mistake only by stepping outside of what is customary and questioning both our society's assumptions about what is necessary for overall utility and the partialities that might underlie these assumptions (V.2.16).

Smith also provides examples of custom-based mistakes that occur at the more general level of character type. These mistakes concern the "manners which custom teaches us to approve of in the different professions and states of life," presumably within civilized societies. These differences "do not concern things of the greatest importance," as "an old man as well as . . . a young, . . . a clergyman as well as . . . an officer" are expected to abide by broader social norms regarding things like "truth and justice" (V.2.13). Nevertheless, these differences are interesting in that, according to Smith, they can still coincide with propriety or not.

Frequent experience with old people leads us to expect and approve in them "that gravity and sedateness which [old age's] infirmities, its long experience, and its worn-out sensibility seem to render both natural and respectable."

Frequent experience with young people leads us to expect and approve in them "that sensibility, that gaiety and sprightly vivacity which experience teaches us to expect from the lively impressions that all interesting objects are apt to make upon the tender and unpracticed sense of that early period of life" (V.2.4). Frequent experience with clergymen leads us to expect and approve in them a certain "grave" and "austere and abstracted severity" (V.2.5). Frequent experience with those in the "military profession" leads us to expect and approve in them "the character of gaiety, levity, and sprightly freedom, as well as some degree of dissipation" (V.2.6). All these judgments follow the aforementioned rule Smith attributes to Buffier that "in each species of things, we are particularly pleased with the middle confirmation," approximations of which we are accustomed to seeing in every instance of the kind. So in the age case, old and young alike "may easily have too much of the peculiarities which belong to" their age. And in the profession case, while we expect "a man . . . [to] look like his trade and profession," we find "the pedantry of every profession disagreeable" (V.2.4).

According to Smith, many of these custom-based evaluations obviously coincide with propriety. The character we expect the clergyman to have is "suitable" to a person whose profession requires him "to be continually occupied with what is too grand and solemn, to leave any room for the impressions of those frivolous objects, which fill up the attention of the dissipated and the gay." "These reflections" about the propriety of the clergyman's customary character, Smith claims, "are so very obvious, that there is scarce any man so inconsiderate as not, at some time, to have made them, and to have accounted to himself in this manner for his approbation of the usual character of this order" (V.2.5). But custom-based evaluations also often coincide with propriety even when conscious consideration of propriety does not accompany them at all. In fact, this can happen even in cases in which it appears that custom and propriety conflict. A little reflection, especially if done with our judgment of the clergyman in mind, might make it appear that "the most serious and thoughtful turn of mind" would be most appropriate to those in the "military profession," whose lives are "continually exposed to uncommon danger" and who thus must be "more constantly occupied with the thoughts of death and its consequences than other men." However, a little more reflection reveals that since the military man, unlike the clergyman, is frequently exposed to the possibility of his own actual death and thus is frequently required to overcome the fear of it, he must, for the sake of coping, choose whenever possible "to lose in continual pleasures and amusements all anxiety about [his] situation" (V.2.6). Thus, even in this case, custom tracks propriety. So for all the cases Smith mentions—he does not tell us here what he thinks about customary judgments relevant to age but comments he makes elsewhere suggest that they also track propriety (see III.3.19)—he must believe that our customary expectations are matched by the sentiments of the WIS, who takes circumstances like age and profession into account when attempting to sympathize with an agent.

Yet Smith observes that our being accustomed to "gaiety, levity, and sprightly freedom" in the military character can lead us to misjudge that character in conditions of "long peace." "We laugh at the grave and careful faces" of "the captain of a city guard." But since this person does not regularly face danger, it is appropriate for him to be "commonly as sober, careful, and penurious an animal as the rest of his fellow-citizens" (V.2.7). This kind of mistake does not socially sanction the murder of an innocent. But it does socially sanction a form of cruelty. We can correct this mistake only by stepping outside of custom and applying the sentiments of the WIS to it. In doing so, we make a correction that complements the one in the infanticide case. As the ancient Greeks customarily make a mistaken judgment based upon implausible beliefs—"far-fetched considerations of utility" that are perhaps given an air of plausibility to them by forms of partiality—Smith's fellow Scots customarily make a mistaken judgment based upon partiality that generates poor understanding. They fail to consider fully the city guard's situation and thus fail to see that it indeed calls for exactly the character that he possesses because it differs from that of other military professionals. Perhaps the sight of the military uniform alone triggers their custom-based expectations, upon which they make a mistaken evaluation. This kind of mistake is an instance of a more general danger. Since judgments based on custom follow from commonality in our past experience, they can sometimes be too general. Thus, we must never forget that "the propriety of a person's behavior, depends not upon its suitableness to any one circumstance of his situation, but to all the circumstances, which, when we bring his case home to ourselves, we feel, should naturally call upon his attention" (V.2.5). In order to judge with respect to all these circumstances, we must consider the agent's situation more individually than we are directed to by custom alone.[79] To do this is to employ a conception of the WIS that is distinct from our accustomed perspective and thus perpetually ready to criticize it.

As we have seen, Smith believes that custom-based mistakes can occur at the level of general character type encouraged by a kind of society. He also makes this point regarding societies of the same, "civilized" kind. He observes:

> That degree of politeness, which would be highly esteemed, perhaps would be thought effeminate adulation, in Russia, would be regarded as rudeness and barbarism at the court of France. That degree or order and frugality, which, in a Polish nobleman, would be considered as excessive parsimony, would be regarded as extravagance in a citizen of Amsterdam.

These differences are not about whether a quality generally falls into the category of "blamable or praise-worthy" but about which "particular degree of each quality" is the "blamable or praise-worthy" one (V.2.7). Since Smith does not claim that savage and civilized societies do not at all recognize versions of the virtues they each de-emphasize, he must interpret their differences in similar way. However, he clearly believes that these differences of degree are greater than those between Russia and France, as well as those between Poland and Holland. Smith does not explain why the latter differences *generally* track what is respectively appropriate to the Russian, French, Polish, and Dutch circumstances, but he clearly believes that they do. He must believe that they do because the WIS takes their different circumstances into account when attempting to sympathize with the members of these societies. Smith also believes that just as it leads savage and civilized societies in general to overemphasize their characteristic virtues, custom leads these particular civilized societies to overemphasize their characteristic virtues. For example, "the rustic hospitality that is in fashion among the Poles encroaches, perhaps, a little upon oeconomy and good order; and the frugality that is esteemed in Holland, upon generosity and good-fellowship." But as in the case with savage and civilized overemphases, these overemphases are "at worst" minor "perversions" (V.2.13). Nevertheless, though only minor excesses in one direction, these general mistakes that custom fosters regarding the "style of character and behavior" typical of an entire society are mistakes nonetheless (V.2.12). Again, such mistakes can only be corrected by stepping outside of custom and applying the sentiments of the WIS to it.

Thus, despite his emphasis on the coincidence between custom and morality, Smith ultimately believes that we should not make moral judgments from the perspective of custom. His view that we should make moral judgments from the perspective of the WIS, not just from custom, carves out an important role for the second kind of WIS-based correction. In response, one might ask why Smith spends so much time arguing that custom generally does not pervert our moral sentiments. One reason might be to defend the wisdom of nature by showing that two natural principles, that behind the psychology of custom and that behind the moral sentiments, do not pull against each other, at least not that much; we return to Smith's tendency to espouse such views in Section 2 of Chapter 7. Another reason might be to foster in his readers a degree of respect for custom, even though he believes that they should be ready to criticize it.

Smith's respect for custom comes through most explicitly in his discussion of political innovation. He describes the ideal reformer as someone who

> will accommodate, as well as he can, his public arrangements to the confirmed habits and prejudices of the people; and will remedy as well as he can, the inconveniencies which may flow from the want of those regulations which the people are averse to submit to. When he cannot establish the right, he will not disdain to ameliorate the wrong; but like Solon, when he cannot establish the best system of laws, he will endeavour to establish the best that the people can bear.

Here Smith assigns purely instrumental normative weight to custom. We should respect custom when enacting political reforms because the only alternative when "reason and persuasion" have failed to "conquer the rooted prejudices of the people" is "force" and "great violence," which are morally unacceptable (VI.ii.2.16). We see a similar sort of practical point about the need to respect custom in Smith's account of the "eminent artist" who introduces deviations from it:

> As the dress of an agreeable man of high rank recommends itself, and how peculiar and fantastical soever, comes soon to be admired and imitated; so the excellencies of an eminent master recommend his peculiarities, and his manner becomes the fashionable style in the art which he practices. (V.1.7)

The difference between the two forms of influence described here is that while the power that the "man of high rank" has over our taste is not necessarily based upon our perception of his merit, the power of the "eminent master" is necessarily based upon our perception of his "excellencies." We might wonder whether Smith is saying that we first recognize the master's excellencies solely with respect to the preexistent cultural form with which we are familiar and then transfer our goodwill toward his "peculiar" innovations or that we recognize the master's excellencies in more absolute terms and then directly approve of these peculiar innovations accordingly. The former seems more likely, given the passage's place in Smith's explanation of the power custom has over our aesthetic evaluations. If this is true, then it follows that he is saying that eminent artists will only be effective in introducing changes, let alone improvements to what is customary by first demonstrating proficiency in the customary form. This proficiency wins them the goodwill necessary to overcome public hostility to what goes against custom. Thus, Smith's advice to those who want to enact changes or improvements to customary aesthetic practices is first to demonstrate proficiency in the customary forms; otherwise, your innovations will be rejected.

However, at the end of his discussion of how custom can impact aesthetic evaluation of architecture in particular, Smith appears to attribute a different, more intrinsic kind of normative weight to custom. He observes:

> When custom, however, has established particular rules of building, provided that they are not absolutely unreasonable, it is absurd to think of altering them for others which are only equally good, *or even for others which, in point of elegance and beauty, have naturally some little advantage over them.* A man would be ridiculous who should appear in public with a suit of clothes quite different from those which are commonly worn, though the new dress should in itself be ever so graceful or convenient. And there seems to be an absurdity of the same kind in ornamenting a house

> after a quite different manner from that which custom and fashion have prescribed; though the new ornaments *should in themselves be somewhat superior to the common ones.* (V.1.5; emphases added)

Surely, the references to a "ridiculous" appearance and "absurdity" are at least partly psychological descriptions of how people typically react. In this respect, Smith is saying that deviations from aesthetic custom will only be accepted by the public when they introduce forms that are obviously *much* superior to the customary ones; slight improvements, let alone lateral changes, will be mocked. However, the references to a "ridiculous" appearance and "absurdity" appear to function not only as descriptions of how people react but also as endorsements of these reactions. If so, then Smith is attributing a different kind of normative weight to custom, which implies that deviations from aesthetic custom are only *justified* when they introduce forms that are much superior to customary ones. He makes a similar point in the more morally relevant context of depicting the character of the prudent person. There, Smith criticizes "men . . . of splendid talents and virtues," like Socrates, Aristippus, Swift, Voltaire, Phillip II of Macedon, Alexander the Great, and Peter the Great, who "too often distinguished themselves by the most improper and even insolent contempt of all the ordinary decorums of life and conversations, and who have thereby set the most pernicious example." The prudent man, in contrast, "is an exact observer of decency, and respects with an almost religious scrupulosity, all the established decorums and ceremonials of society" (VI.i.10).

So it seems like we have two views here: custom has normative weight instrumentally, in that respecting it is the only way to ensure the efficacy of innovation, and custom has normative weight intrinsically. Since these views are not mutually exclusive, it could be perfectly coherent for Smith to hold them both. However, the latter view fits at least oddly with his view that when the evaluations we make from custom and the evaluations we make from the natural moral sentiments differ, the latter should trump the former. Thankfully, an alternative reading of the passages just cited is available, one that doubles as an explanation for why Smith goes to such lengths to show that custom generally lines up with the natural moral sentiments. Perhaps Smith is saying that we should respect custom for epistemic reasons. If custom generally lines up with the moral sentiments, then we can take custom to be a generally reliable indicator of the requirements of moral conduct.[80] Of course, to take custom as a generally reliable indicator is not to ascribe unquestionable moral authority to it. But it is to treat custom with a form of respect, such that we practice caution in our evaluation when we find ourselves going against it. One way to ensure that we do this is to internalize as a rule Smith's observation that deviations from custom are usually "ridiculous" or "absurd" unless they constitute serious improvements. Thus, one of the main points of TMS V appears to be that even though we should not morally evaluate solely on the basis of custom, we should treat custom with the respect that is due a generally reliable indicator of right and wrong. After all, as we saw earlier, if the moral sentiments are as strong and vigorous as Smith believes they are, then conduct that flies in the face of them will never happen consistently enough to become customary. Furthermore, he observes, "no society" in which conduct that flies in the face of our natural moral sentiments becomes customary "could subsist a moment" (VI.2.16).[81]

This interesting point about the normative authority of custom aside, however, the main goal of this section has been to argue that Smith's account of how we appeal to the WIS to correct the moral judgments upon which our group agrees covers our disagreement not just with the application of social norms but also with the social norms themselves. If this interpretation works, then Smith recognizes the possibility of ideological critique, despite his commitment to remaining close to everyday life; on this interpretation, Smith's conception of everyday life includes within it a form of moral judgment that makes such critique possible.

Allow me to make two observations to close this section that will also help close this chapter and transition us to the next three. First, notice the shift we made upon turning to TMS V from Smith's explanation of a certain kind of WIS-based correction to Smith's endorsement of this kind of WIS-based correction; a similar shift occurred when we discussed the extent to which Smith both explains and endorses the assignment of authority to custom in moral judgments. These shifts should not surprise us, for as I flagged at the outset of this chapter, Smith's full-blown account of moral judgment is both explanatory and normative: he explains and endorses the way in which we make moral judgments. Having made these shifts to a different approach to the study of morality, we are now ready to turn to Smith's treatment of the second question, that of the nature of virtue, which has explicitly to do with how we should live. The next chapter will concern Smith's history of answers to this question; as Chapter 2 did, this chapter will sketch the commitments and issues that emerge from Smith's reading of other philosophers. Chapter 6 will concern Smith's own answer to the question, which provides detail about what a life lived in keeping with the WIS looks like.

The second closing observation is that in keeping with the chapter's treatment of other features of Smith's account of moral judgment, this section's treatment of a certain kind of WIS-based correction sidesteps certain metaethical questions to which it gives rise. We saw that Smith thinks that we do make these kinds of corrections, but we did not see whether his way of understanding these corrections commits him to any particular view in moral metaphysics. We turn to this issue in Section 1 of Chapter 7. We also saw that Smith thinks we should make these kinds of corrections, but we did not see the kinds of reasons he can or does provide for why we should. We turn to this issue in Section 2 of Chapter 7.

5

Smith's Survey of Answers to the Nature of Virtue Question

In Chapter 2, we saw that Smith's survey of answers to the psychological foundation of moral judgment question went back only a little more than a century from when he himself was writing; he seemed to believe that the "abstract science of human nature" involved in asking such a question was relatively new (VII.iii.2.5). However, his survey of answers to the nature of virtue question goes back to the ancient Greeks. Thus, this survey is remarkable for its historical scope alone. Like his survey of answers to the other question, this survey is also remarkable for what it reveals about Smith's own views. Accordingly, as Chapter 2 does, this chapter treats Smith's discussion of other theories as a resource for understanding what he ultimately thinks.

The chapter consists of six sections. The first, preliminary one concerns the general concept of "virtue" in Smith's moral philosophy. The rest of the chapter works almost exclusively with TMS VII's survey of virtue theories, subjecting them to the procedure I employed in Chapter 2. While Smith himself arranges the survey in almost chronological order, this chapter will take a different tack. Smith believes that there are only four possible answers to the nature of virtue question, three of which constitute positive theories of virtue and one constitutes a denial of the reality of virtue. Although Smith saves the skeptical answer for last, we will get his discussion of it out of the way first, in Section 2.

Section 3 will lay out Smith's rationale for categorizing possible theories of virtue in the way that he does. Then, rather than proceeding through the positive answers in Smith's order, we will discuss prudence theories in Section 4 and benevolence theories in Section 5. We turn to propriety theories in Section 6; since Smith himself holds a version of this kind of theory, this section will serve as a nice transition to our consideration of his own view in the next chapter.

Section 1: The Concept of Virtue in Smith

As we saw in Chapter 1, Smith believes that answers to the virtue question have a practical impact that answers to the psychological foundation of moral judgment question do not. Students of contemporary moral philosophy will find intriguing Smith's focus specifically on virtue in the practical side of his theory. Many of these readers are used to making two big distinctions between normative moral theories, the first between theories focused on showing which character traits are required for a good life and theories focused on showing which actions are the good or, more commonly, right ones to perform, and the second between action-focused theories focused on consequences and action-focused theories focused on duties and, sometimes, on motives. These distinctions produce a division of the field into virtue theories, consequentialist theories, and deontological theories. (While the first two names are self-explanatory, the latter derives from ancient Greek word for "duty" or "obligation.") Readers familiar with both this taxonomy and Smith's theory of moral judgment might find several things surprising about the fact that Smith defends a virtue theory. One is that his theory of moral judgment seems focused on individual actions and sentiments more than on character traits.[1] Another is that his theory of moral judgment assigns roles both to rules of duty and to considerations of utility (VII.iii.3.16). A third is that he often describes the motivation that emerges from moral judgment in terms of respect for duty (e.g., III.5.1).

Students of the history of moral philosophy and students of cultural history in general will also find intriguing Smith's focus specifically on virtue in the practical side of his theory. The former kind of reader will likely have questions about how to situate Smith's attention to virtue in an intellectual context that has been interpreted as shaped by concerns about the role of character-focused talk about virtue given the rise of more action-focused talk about duties, rights, obligations, and laws. The latter kind of reader will likely have questions about how to situate Smith's attention to virtue in relation to the rise of the commercial social form that he studied, celebrated, and critiqued. While I do no more than direct readers with these historical interests to some excellent scholarship on Smith's philosophical context,[2] I draw here on some features of the TMS to speak a bit to readers with the previous, less historical one.

In the context of discussing Aristotle's virtue theory, Smith makes some comments that can help us bridge his action- and individual-sentiment-focused theory of moral judgment to his virtue-focused conception of how we should live. They do so both by extending the use of the term "virtue" to cover positive actions as well as positive traits and by sketching an account of trait-focused evaluations that Smith's account of moral judgment can easily handle. Smith tells us that "virtue may be considered either as the quality of an action, or as the quality of a person." In the former case, it refers to "the affection from which the action proceeds, whether this disposition be habitual to the person or not." In the latter case, it refers to the "customary and usual disposition of the mind." Thus, Smith continues, "from an occasional fit of generosity," one can perform a "generous action," without thereby being a "generous person" (VII.ii.1.13). Obviously, Smith's account of moral judgment can handle the first kind of evaluations because they concern affections with which the WIS can sympathize or not. Since the WIS can sympathize or not with affections that happen to have crystallized into stable dispositions, the same account can also handle the second kind.

In using the term "virtue" so broadly, Smith is not doing something totally foreign to contemporary virtue theorists, who also talk about virtuous actions. But while contemporary virtue theorists often argue that virtuous actions are defined as such *because* they are performed by people with virtuous traits, Smith does not. He takes no stance on the question of priority between virtuous trait concepts and virtuous action concepts. Instead, he makes a simple, stability-focused distinction between the evaluation of actions and the evaluation of people. The only further commitment he demonstrates here is one that is already present in his account of moral judgment: the sentiment from which an agent acts in a particular case or from which an agent habitually acts is essential to the moral status we attribute to either the action or the agent. We might want to conclude from this commitment that Smith is neither a deontologist who does not care about motives nor a consequentialist. But even this might be too quick. As I mentioned earlier and as we saw in Section 6 of Chapter 3, Smith believes that our approval of "any character or action" is impacted, in some secondary sense, by the observation that it is "agreeable to the general rules by which" the WIS' sympathies "generally act" or makes "a part of a system of behavior which tends to promote the happiness of either the individual or the society" (VII.iii.3.15). In Section 5 of the next chapter, we'll see reasons to believe that the second of these considerations is more aesthetic than moral in nature. But as we've seen in Section 3 of Chapter 3, the introduction to Chapter 4, and Section 6 of Chapter 4, Smith never explicitly distinguishes moral from aesthetic sentiments on this or any other ground. And even if we interpret him as doing so, we would still be left without the means to situate Smith's theory between the remaining three present-day categories, virtue theory, deontology for which motives are morally relevant, and deontology for which motives are morally irrelevant. The fact that he talks about "virtue" a lot is not enough to settle the matter at any fundamental level.

All this said, "virtue" does seem to function for Smith as more than just a generically positive term to describe the actions or traits that win WIS-based approval (or that follow from consideration of the general rules based on this approval or that merely accord with the general rules based on this approval or that are useful to the individual or society). Early in the TMS, Smith distinguishes between "virtue" and "mere propriety" on the grounds that the former "deserve[s] to be admired and celebrated," while the latter "simply deserve[s] to be approved of." He gives the "very low instance" of eating when we are hungry as an example of the latter; "upon ordinary occasions," this behavior is "perfectly right and proper," but it would be "absurd" to say it was virtuous. In contrast, to be virtuous, one must go beyond what is "common and ordinary" or expected (I.i.5.6–8). Accordingly, virtue is the object not just of approbation but of "admiration," which Smith defines as "approbation heightened by wonder and surprise" at seeing something "uncommon" and "unexpected" (I.i.4.3; cf. I.ii.1.12; I.iii.1.13; and HA intro-II.12, 33–47). (Smith does not further explain the psychological mechanism involved in judgments of admiration, but his idea seems to be that in making them, we notice both that the WIS would sympathize with the agent and that most other agents in similar situations do not win the WIS' sympathy to the degree that this one does.) Thus, to designate an action or character as "virtuous" is to employ an honorific, not merely a positive, concept.[3]

We might be tempted to translate this distinction into another one that is common in contemporary moral philosophy,[4] that between the obligatory, the permissible, and the supererogatory. However, this attempt to make Smith speak our language would not quite work either. If a permissible action is one that is optional in the sense that neither the performer nor the refrainer is subject to censure, then the action of eating when hungry "upon most ordinary occasions" is not, strictly speaking, permissible. In classifying such an action as "right and proper," Smith implies that if we do not perform it, we have, in some sense, made a mistake. His point is simply that we do not deserve credit for not making this mistake. This might lead us to believe that the category of "mere propriety," into which eating when hungry falls, overlaps with that of the "obligatory," while the category of "virtue" overlaps with that of the "supererogatory," the category of whatever goes above and beyond the call of the obligatory. However, while Smith often uses the concept of obligation, as well as the closely related concept of duty, he does not use it with reference to the example of eating when hungry. It follows that while he might think that *some* instances of "mere propriety" count as the fulfillment of an obligation, he does not think that this is true for all them. Moreover, as we shall see in more detail in Section 6 of the next chapter, Smith's own virtue theory identifies at least some instances of virtuousness with "duty" (VI.iii.1). It follows, then, that he does not identify the category of virtue with that of the supererogatory. Thus, it is better to think of the distinction between mere propriety and virtue as one between the "ok" and the "excellent," both very loosely understood, than one between the obligatory and the supererogatory.

There is another, broader reason not to think about the distinction between mere propriety and virtue as one between the obligatory and the supererogatory.

The latter distinction is at home in act-centered moral theories focused on the distinction between rightness and wrongness. In this network of concepts, those who act permissibly do neither right nor wrong, those who meet their obligations do right, those who do not meet their obligations do wrong, and those who perform an act of supererogation go above and beyond rightness. Many virtue theories center instead on the distinction between good and bad. In this network of concepts, the virtuous live well and the vicious live badly. To emphasize the difference between these approaches as starkly as possible: the first class of theory aims at moral rectitude, while the second class of theory aims at good living or happiness, understood in terms of living well. Now, obviously, since there are always exceptions and overlaps, the terrain cannot be carved up this cleanly. Smith's virtue theory provides us with a great example of a view that defies classification in terms of this dichotomy. As we shall see in Section 2 of Chapter 7, he takes it to be obvious that the goal of a virtue theory is to show us how to be happy; this is a broad reason for believing that the obligatory/supererogatory distinction does not map onto to Smith's mere propriety/virtue distinction. But before we take this observation to imply that Smith's virtue theory belongs in the second class, we should remember that he also makes liberal use of the concepts of duty and obligation, which fit best with theories of the first class. Moreover, just as he makes no attempt to establish a priority relationship between act- and character-evaluation, he makes no attempt to establish a priority relationship between good and right.

The upshot of these reflections is that we should not assume that in treating virtue as the fundamental concern of the practical side of his moral philosophy, Smith is doing the exact same thing that a contemporary virtue theorist or any other contemporary moral philosopher is.[5] Smith ultimately does focus the practical side of his moral theory more on traits than on actions, but only because he thinks the stability of the former makes them more deserved of attention, not because he is committed to a strong view about their conceptual priority. Smith thinks of "virtue" as an honorific term, but not because he believes that virtue is supererogatory; he just thinks it marks something better than average and is thus more worthy of note. And Smith employs concepts, like duty and obligation, and value dichotomies, like right versus wrong, more often found in action-focused moral theories than in virtue-focused ones, but not with any fully developed view about the shape of the logical space these concepts inhabit. These features of Smith's practical moral philosophy might constitute weaknesses of it. But then again, if common life does not carve things up as cleanly as some contemporary moral philosophy does and there is good reason to keep practical moral philosophy close to common life, these features of Smith's might constitute strengths. Either way, in trying to understand Smith, we must be sure not to project our views and distinctions on to him, even ones about which we might have good reason to be proud.[6]

It will be useful to keep in mind this sort of general looseness in Smith's writing on virtue as we proceed through his study of other virtue theories to his presentation of his own. Let's continue preparing for this journey by considering, first, his dismissal of skepticism about the reality of virtue and, second, his taxonomy of accounts of virtue.

But before we move on, one final observation is in order regarding Smith's distinction between mere propriety and virtue. We must be careful not to overlook the "mere." For if Smith, on the one hand, distinguishes between propriety and virtue but also, on the other, recognizes and (as we shall see) holds a propriety theory of virtue, he does something deeply confusing, if not self-contradictory. The "mere" in the distinction between mere propriety and virtue must indicate that in the context of making that distinction, Smith is employing the concept of propriety only as a recognizable positive descriptor. But when he refers to propriety theories of virtue, he is employing the concept in a more technical way. The former usage points to the difference between being and acting appropriately and being and acting excellently. The latter points to the difference between defining virtue in terms of the "suitableness of the affection from which we act to the object which excites it" and defining virtue in some other way (VII.i.1.1).

Section 2: Mandeville's Denial of the Reality of Virtue[7]

Before considering the nature of virtue, we should consider whether virtue is a real thing. According to Smith, the "system of Dr. Mandeville" denies that "there is a real and essential distinction" between virtue and vice (VI.ii .4.1, 6). More specifically, Mandeville denies the reality of this distinction by denying the reality of the virtue half of it. Even more specifically, he denies the reality of virtue not by arguing that there are no criteria for distinguishing virtue from vice in principle but by arguing that no one satisfies the criteria for virtuousness. Thus, for Mandeville, the breakdown of the distinction occurs not at the level of definition but at the level of conduct: no one is virtuous as opposed to vicious because no one is virtuous at all.

On Smith's reading, Mandeville argues for this claim in two ways. The more broadly targeted argument is that no one is virtuous because virtue requires an impossible "entire conquest" of our passions that culminates in their "entire extirpation and annihilation" (VII.ii.4.12). Smith responds to this argument by rejecting the "ascetic" definition of virtue that constitutes its "real foundation." According to Mandeville, whenever we act with anything but "complete self-denial," we act viciously. Virtue, however, does not require such "complete insensibility to the objects of the passions"; rather, it only requires restricting those passions "so far as to not hurt the individual, and neither disturb nor offend the society." Thus, Mandeville has not "entirely demolished the reality of the virtues of temperance and chastity" just by demonstrating the reality of our "love of pleasure" and "love of sex." Nor has he convicted us all of vicious "luxury, sensuality, and ostentation" just by demonstrating the reality of our "love of magnificence . . . taste for the elegant arts and improvements of human life, for whatever is agreeable in dress, furniture, or equipage, for architecture, statuary, painting, and music." To think that he has, Smith argues, is to be tricked by an "ambiguity of language." Since we tend to notice some passions most when they are "disagreeable and offensive," our primary names for them "denote [only] a vicious and offensive degree" of them. Thus, it is rhetorically easy for Mandeville to pass off all "love of pleasure" as "luxury," all "love of sex" as "lust," and all love for nice things as "ostentation" (VII.ii.4.11–12). But, of course, rhetoric and argument are not the same thing. The fact that our language might lack common expressions for non-vicious ways of loving pleasure, sex, or nice things does not mean that all ways of loving pleasure, sex, or nice things are vicious.

The narrowly targeted argument is that no one can be virtuous because virtue requires a particular motive that we do not have. Smith's exposition and response to this argument are complicated because he disagrees with Mandeville regarding which particular motive is necessary for virtue but nevertheless attacks Mandeville's argument ruling out the unnecessary motive because of what it might imply about the necessary one. However, this exposition and response are worth going through in detail because it reveals an important feature of Smith's own account of virtue. For Mandeville, virtue requires acting from a "preference for public to [one's own] private interest." But it is "impossible that [man] in his heart can ever really prefer [another's] prosperity to his own." Whenever we appear to be acting from a disinterested motive, we are really acting from a selfish one, most likely the "love of praise and commendation" or "vanity" (VII.ii.4.7). However, others will not praise us unless they believe that we are disinterested, and we will not enjoy receiving praise unless we believe that we are disinterested. Thus, the vanity behind the appearance of disinterested, virtuous action requires collective delusion.[8]

According to Smith, Mandeville is wrong in thinking that the reality of virtue rests entirely upon the reality of altruistic motives. Since Smith believes that "self-love may frequently be a virtuous motive of action," he takes the question of "whether the most generous and public-spirited action" can be, "in some sense, regarded as proceeding from self-love" to be without "any importance towards establishing the reality of virtue" (VII.ii.4.8). But even if Mandeville is wrong about which motive is necessary for the reality of virtue, if he is right that the motive ultimately behind apparently virtuous conduct is vanity, then unless vanity is the motive necessary for the reality of virtue, he still succeeds in showing that virtue is not real. Of course, Smith does not believe that vanity is the motive necessary for virtue. He believes that "the source of all those actions which are commonly accounted virtuous" is the "desire of doing of what is honourable and noble, of rendering ourselves the proper objects of esteem and approbation" (VII.ii.4.11). Here, Smith is referring to the kind of moral motive that he describes in various ways but is best expressed as desire for sympathy with the WIS. Smith must believe, then, that when self-love or any other desires are "virtuous motive[s] of action," they are so only in combination with this kind of motive, the reality of which is necessary for the reality of virtue. (We will return to this point in the next section.)

So the heart of Smith's response to this argument against the reality of virtue is that the kind of self-consciously moral motive that he takes to be essential to virtue is not reducible to vanity. As we saw in the previous chapter's discussion of Smith's "doctrine," he believes these kinds of motives involve "some reference to the sentiments of others" (VII.ii.4.10). But as the loves of pleasure, sex, and nice things do, the reference our motives have to others' sentiments often goes wrong in some way. Thus, as in the case of those loves, our language for the bad instances is much more familiar than our language for the good ones. And as it does in the case of those loves, this linguistic fluke allows Mandeville to get away with using a pejorative term for every instance of a motive that has a reference to the sentiments of others. But in thus using the term "vanity" so broadly, Smith argues, Mandeville fails to distinguish between the love of praise "at any rate," "the love of true glory," and "the love of virtue." This mistake is easy to hide, Smith observes, because the reference each love has to the sentiments of others generates a "certain remote affinity among" them (VII.ii.4.9–10).

The affinity between the love of praise at any rate, which Smith himself identifies with vanity, and the love of true glory is obvious, "as both these passions aim at acquiring esteem and approbation." The latter differs from the former insofar as it is a desire for praise that we deserve; in this regard, it consists of a combination of a desire for praise and a desire "really [to be] what is honourable and noble" (VII.ii.4.9–10). Since Mandeville thinks that we believe, albeit falsely, that we deserve the praise we pursue, he recognizes something superficially similar to the love of true glory. The difference is that for Mandeville, the desire to be worthy of praise is essentially subordinate to the desire for praise. We do not desire to be worthy of praise for its own sake at all; rather, we desire praise and see worthiness as the best way to acquire it. As a result, Mandeville cannot recognize anything even superficially similar to the desire to be honourable and noble in its purest form, detached from any desire for actual praise. This is what Smith means by the love of virtue.[9]

The affinity between the love of virtue and the love of true glory is obvious in that both involve some concern for "really being what is honourable and estimable" (VII.ii.4.10). But Smith thinks that the love of virtue is also like both the second and first loves in that it too has "some reference to the sentiments of others." However, the difference between it and them is that one can act on it and be "most indifferent about what actually are the opinions of mankind"; instead, when we act from the love of virtue, we act from concern about the "opinions" that "*ought* to be entertained of us," and actually would be "if mankind were cool and candid and consistent with themselves, and properly informed of the motives and circumstances of [our] conduct" (VII .ii.4.10; emphasis added). This kind of motive, Smith concludes, "cannot with any propriety be called vanity" (VII.ii.4.8).

One can imagine Mandeville responding at this point by granting the in-principle difference between vanity and the desire to be virtuous while denying that we ever act from anything like it. Sure, we might *believe* that we do, but this belief, like so many other self-serving beliefs we hold about ourselves, is false. Smith himself is not totally unamenable to such a view. He concedes that the love of virtue for its own sake is at least rare, for it "is the most godlike motive which human nature is even capable of conceiving" (VII.ii.4.10). And, as we saw in Section 5 of the previous chapter, he certainly worries about self-deception. But we can infer that he thinks the burden of proof is on any view that requires the degree of delusion about our own motives that Mandeville's requires. Since accounts of "our desires and affections, of our sentiments of approbation and disapprobation," are accounts "not only of the affairs of the very parish that we live in, but of our own domestic concerns," there are limits to how wrong we can be about them (VII.ii.4.14). Thus, if it seems clear to everyday reflection that we can at least sometimes act from a love of virtue for its own sake, then we probably can.

That said, since moral philosophy deals with such close-to-home matters, there are also limits to how wrong its theories can be; thus, all prevalent theories in moral philosophy, including Mandeville's, must contain "a considerable mixture of truth." (Moral theories differ in this respect from those of natural science, which, because they "give an account of the affairs of a very distant country," can "be for a long time very generally received in the world, and yet have no foundation in nature, nor any sort of resemblance to the truth" (VII.ii.4.14).) Smith does not tell us exactly what he thinks Mandeville gets right. But his arguments imply that Mandeville's views are not built upon the defense of gross falsehoods so much as upon the exaggeration of what virtue requires, the uncritical adoption of ambiguities in everyday language, and the mistaken treatment of resemblances as identities. So it seems that, for Smith, Mandeville was right to notice that virtue involves self-restraint, that some desires get fundamentally pejorative names because they are difficult to restrain, and that some motives really do resemble others, but wrong in how he reasons on the basis of these observations.

I close this section with some brief comments on Smith's response to Mandeville's most famous claim, which Smith does mention here, albeit briefly. He points out that Mandeville's "favourite conclusion" to draw from his observation that no one actually completes the "entire conquest" of passion necessary for virtue is that it is a good thing that they don't. For if they did, "it would be pernicious to society, by putting an end to all industry and commerce, and in a matter to the whole business of human life." Hence the thesis for which Mandeville remains famous: "private vices are public benefits." Our vices, Mandeville argues, drive the economy and thereby allow society to "prosper and flourish." Smith too remains famous for defending a thesis about the economic benefits to the whole that accrue when individuals freely act in pursuit of what they take to be their own interests. But we can now see that Smith's version of this position is fundamentally different from Mandeville's. Smith believes it good that nobody actually completes the "entire conquest" of their passions, but not because their resulting vice has economic benefits. For Smith, an "entire extirpation and annihilation of all our passions" would be itself vicious, or at least not virtuous. In other words, Smith believes the free individual pursuit of self-interest both can have public economic benefits and can be virtuous. But as the "can's" indicate, Smith also believes that the pursuit of self-interest can be vicious and can damage the public. Thus, Smith's anti-Mandevillian view that private virtues are public benefits does not rest upon a redefinition of all productive individual economic activity as virtuous in light of its economic productivity. In Section 5 of the next chapter, I examine in more detail Smith's attitude toward such activity.

Section 3: Smith's Taxonomy of Possible Virtue Theories

Smith divides positive accounts of virtue into three categories. This tripartite division is only partly historical. Smith does not merely derive his three categories inductively from a study of the major virtue theories on offer in Western philosophy. He also grounds the distinction between these three categories in a view about the "great division of our affections . . . into the selfish and the benevolent." Given that virtue necessarily involves having affections that are "right," broadly understood, it follows from this division that virtue is either only ascribable to those affections "which aim directly at our own private happiness," those affections "which aim directly at that of others," or to both, "when under proper government and direction" (VII.ii.intro.3). Thus, virtue must fundamentally consist in prudence, benevolence, or propriety.

There are several features of this rationale for Smith's taxonomy that are potentially misleading. First, one might take him to believe that only propriety theories involve the "government and direction" of affection. But he is explicit that on prudence theories, virtue involves "the proper government and direction of . . . selfish affections," not merely selfish affections per se (VII.ii .intro.3). He is also explicit that benevolence theories treat the foundation of virtue not merely as an affection but as a "supreme and governing" principle (VII.ii.3.2). Thus, Smith's distinction between the three categories is not between two views that identify virtue with affections and one that identifies it with a governing principle that directs all our affections. For Smith, each possible theory involves self-governance of some kind.[10] Given what we just saw in Smith's discussion of Mandeville, we should expect this. There we saw Smith claim that the reality of virtue hangs on the reality of a certain kind of self-consciously moral motive. So he must believe that any account of virtue worth taking seriously must include something at least analogous to this motive. Any internal principle that *governs* our affections supplies this analogy by subjecting the affections we feel and the conduct they motivate to some kind of justification in our own eyes.

Another source of interpretive trouble is Smith's apparent exclusion of the governing principle involved in propriety theories from the "great division of our affections." For both prudence and benevolence theorists, the governing principle is itself an affect. For the former, concern for one's own "ease of body" and "security or tranquility of mind" should internally govern (VII.ii .2.7). For the latter, "benevolence or love" should internally govern (VII.ii. 3.2). But what is the governing principle for propriety theorists? The rationale he provides for his taxonomy suggests that it is something non-affective, like reason. Indeed, as we shall see in Section 6, most of the propriety theories he discusses *do* think of reason as the governing principle. But, obviously, Smith himself does not hold this view. As we can deduce from the discussion of the previous chapter, his conception of the governing principle should be understood in terms of regard for the sentiments of the WIS. Thus, his "great division of our affections" should be between the selfish, the benevolent, and the desire for sympathy, a form of which, as we saw in Sections 3 and 4 of the previous chapter, serves as a desire for sympathy with the WIS. As we shall see in the next chapter, his own virtue theory explicitly does rest upon this threefold division of affect (VI.concl.1). However, Smith's distinction between the two main questions of moral philosophy in terms of the difference between practical and nonpractical, speculative issues implies that his rejection of the view that reason is a faculty of evaluation and motivation does not matter much for his consideration of virtue theories. So his taxonomy of virtue theories can leave open this possibility without much of problem. Furthermore, whether understood as rooted in reason or sentiment, the governing principle in propriety theories differs from those in prudence and benevolence theories in that it at least partially inherits its ends from what it governs in a way that they do not. Self-love and benevolence set ends for the rest of the self. But the governing principle in propriety theories, whether rooted in reason or affect, only sets the end of doing properly whatever the rest of the self is oriented toward doing. Thus, even the most rationalistic propriety theories only ask reason to set one end for us. In denying that reason can do even this, Smith disagrees with these theories. But it turns out that his disagreement is a pretty narrow one. This is another reason why Smith's systematic taxonomy of virtue can leave open the possibility of rationalistic propriety theories without much danger. If there is any danger here, it is that the taxonomy might be taken to rule out Smith's own view.

Questions about how the sentiment at the root of Smith's governing principle *can* govern the other sentiments must wait until our discussion of normativity in Section 2 of Chapter 7. Before we turn to Smith's discussion of prudence theories, benevolence theories, and other philosophers' versions of propriety theories, three final comments are in order regarding his taxonomy. The first has to do with how Smith deals with virtue theories that do not fit so neatly into his tripartite scheme. One possible counterexample is the "system which places virtue in obedience to the will of the Deity." He argues that there are two different versions of this view, one of which amounts to a prudence theory and the other of which amounts to a propriety theory. The version of the view that says we should obey the Deity "because he is a Being of infinite power" who can sanction us for our conduct reduces to a prudence theory. The version of the view that says we should obey the Deity because "there is a congruity or fitness that a creature should obey its creator, that a limited and perfect being should submit to one of infinite and incomprehensible perfections" reduces to a propriety theory. Another possible counterexample is Hume's view, which identifies virtue with "those qualities of the mind which are agreeable or advantageous, either to the person himself or to others." This view, Smith argues, "coincides too with that which makes it consist in propriety." As propriety theories do, this view does not center on "any one" affection but attends to all of them. Moreover, in saying that virtue requires that these affections be agreeable or useful, it really says that virtue requires these affections to be in their "proper degree," which is a prerequisite for agreeableness or utility. In fact, Smith claims, the "only difference" between this view and his own is that "it makes utility, and not sympathy or the corresponding affections of the spectator, the natural and original measure of this proper degree" (VII.ii .3.21). The combination of this claim and Smith's observation that utility to self and others coincides with the dictates of the WIS implies that he takes his disagreement with Hume to take place primarily at the speculative level, something that, as we shall see in Section 6, is also true regarding Smith's disagreement with some other propriety theorists (IV.2.3). There may be other possible counterexamples that Smith fails to consider. However, even if there are theories that Smith's simple taxonomy does not cover, it is impressive for covering the many that it does.

The second comment is that Smith does not presume that the defenders of the theories he discusses saw themselves as primarily arguing in favor of one position on his taxonomical framework against the other two. As we shall see, Smith provides admirably concise accounts of the foundational concerns and commitments that motivate each philosopher he discusses. In each case, these concerns and commitments come from outside the "well, it has got be one of these three" rationale that underlines Smith's taxonomy. Thus, the taxonomy is revisionist in that it exposes an ahistorical logic underlying the history of philosophizing about virtue in the West.

My final observation about Smith's taxonomy is that it can be used to frame all the positive theories he considers as responses to Mandeville's denial of virtue. As we saw earlier, Smith believes that there are two main components of Mandeville's position: an assumption that virtue requires ascetic self-denial and purely altruistic motivation and an argument that no one meets these requirements. The prudence theorist, the benevolence theorist, and the propriety theorist allow for the reality of virtue by responding to this argument in different ways. For the prudence theorist, virtue requires serving one's own best interests, not depriving or sacrificing oneself. Obviously, this is a criterion we can meet. For the benevolence theorist, virtue does require acting from sincere concern for others. Since such concern is real, we can meet this criterion. And since such concern is an important source of happiness, we can meet this criterion without self-denial. For the propriety theorist, virtue requires an appropriate balance of our self-directed concerns and our other-directed concerns. This criterion is meetable because we also have a conscientious concern—however understood—for achieving this balance that fits into neither category. And again, since such concern is an important source of happiness, we can meet this criterion without self-denial.

Since the prudence theory feels closest to Mandeville's view, I turn to it first.

Section 4: Prudence Theories

The ancient Greek philosopher Epicurus provides Smith with his example of a prudence theory.[11] The foundation of Epicureanism is a form of motivational hedonism that is egoistic in nature. (We should note that the view that we only desire pleasure, but not just our own, is a coherent, albeit unusual one.) Epicurus's hedonism is also materialistic, in that it bases all pleasures we desire and pains we avoid on nonmental, bodily sensations. Thus, he argues that "the pleasures and pains of the mind" are "derived" from memories regarding past bodily experiences and hopes or fears regarding future ones (VII.ii.2.3). The metaphysical implications of this view do not matter much for the present purposes, but the practical ones do.

On this view, mental pleasures and pains are more important to our happiness than bodily ones are. One reason for this is that experiences of "agonizing remembrance," "horrible dread," cheerful recollection," and "joyous anticipation" can last longer than "the sensation of the present instant." Another reason why mental pleasures and pains matter more is that they are under our control to an extent that bodily ones are not. Even "under great bodily pain," we can generate mental pleasure by remembering or anticipating better times. We can also prevent ourselves from adding to our suffering with the mental pain of anxiety about its continuance, especially if we have good reason to believe the suffering is temporary. (If we find that our suffering is unbearable and permanent, "death [is] always at hand . . . [to] put an end" to it (VII.ii.2.5)).

Also on this view, contrary to contemporary connotations of adjectives like "Epicurean" and "hedonistic," the avoidance of pain is more important than the acquisition of pleasure, whether either is bodily or mental. The main reason for this is that pain is generally more "pungent" than pleasure. Thus, bodily pleasure is "less to be desired" than bodily pain is "to be feared." And the best mental pleasure is more the inverse of mental pain than something positive in its own right. Thus, the goal is "security and tranquility," not stimulation or excitement (VII.ii.2.6–7).

Traditionally recognized virtues then get their value only from their "tendency to bring about this situation." The most general, foundational virtue is "prudence," which is valuable only because it helps us avoid the greatest pains and acquire the greatest pleasures. Any other virtue only refers to a specific aspect of prudence that is valuable for the same reason. "Temperance" is valuable only because it helps us privilege longer-term, greater pleasure and pain over shorter-term, lesser pleasure and pain; "fortitude" is valuable only because it helps us endure hardship when we either cannot avoid it or must face it for the sake of greater pleasure; and "justice" is valuable only because it helps us avoid tranquility-destroying conflict with our neighbors (VII.ii.2.8–11).

In Smith's eyes, the Epicurean account of virtue has a lot going for it. First, against Mandeville, it protects the reality of virtue by defining virtue in a way that makes it possible. Second, this view clearly does not merely identify virtue with the affection of self-love, however felt or manifested. Rather, on this view, virtue requires that self-love employ reason to govern the many desires and aversions that often drive us away from our best interest, understood hedonistically, with an emphasis on tranquility and the avoidance of pain over the acquisition of pleasure (as we shall see in Section 2 of Chapter 7, this emphasis is Smith-friendly too). Thus, while this view does not recognize the exact kind of self-consciously moral motivation that Smith has in mind, the importance it places on self-regulation allows it to meet a criterion for plausibility. Third, this view is right to identify virtuous conduct with prudent conduct. Thanks to "the wise contrivance of the Author of nature, virtue is upon all ordinary occasions, even with regard to this life, real wisdom, and the surest and readiest means of obtaining both safety and advantage" (VII.ii .2.13).

But, Smith argues, Epicurus is wrong about how we attach value to virtue. The root of the problem is Epicurus's reduction of all desires and aversions to the desire for bodily pleasure and the aversion to bodily pain. On the basis of this view, Epicurus concludes that virtue is only desirable for the sake of the bodily pleasure it helps us attain and the bodily pain it helps us avoid. Smith responds that our attraction to virtue actually serves as a counterexample to Epicurus's brand of materialistic hedonism. Smith thinks it obvious that we care *way more* about "the sentiments which [our conduct] naturally excite[s] in others" than we do "the effects which [our conduct] is likely to produce upon the body." True to his "doctrine," Smith immediately runs together here concern about what others think of us with concern about being "amiable," "respectable," and "the proper object of esteem" (VII.ii.2.12). Thus, technical questions of the sort addressed in Sections 3 and 4 of the previous chapter about the relationship between these concerns immediately arise. So do those addressed in Section 1 of the previous chapter about whether these concerns are reducible to concerns about even non-bodily pleasure and pain. But these issues aside, the gist of Smith's meaning is clear: we want to be virtuous for its own sake, understood in a way that is, in some sense, tied to concern for what others think about us but not to our concern for our own bodily pleasures and pains.

In showing that Epicurus is wrong about the value we attach to virtue, Smith has not yet shown that prudence is not the only virtue we recognize. In fact, in stressing the connection between virtue and interest, Smith backs himself into a bit of a corner. Smith concedes that since they further our interests, virtues like "temperance, magnanimity, justice, and beneficence" can be approved of "under the additional character of the highest wisdom and most real prudence." But then he claims that when we consider them "under their proper characters," we approve of these virtues directly, without tracing their connection to an agent's interest. However, Smith does not provide much argument for this second claim. If all virtue is in our interest, then why *isn't* all virtue reducible to prudence? It helps Smith that he only says that virtue is in our interest "upon all ordinary occasions"; a few lines later he also says that the "practice of virtue" is, "*in general*," in our interest (VII.ii.2.13; emphasis added). If this is so, then it is possible to be, for example, beneficent and imprudent. And if it is possible to be beneficent and imprudent, then beneficence and prudence are independent qualities. However, given what we'll see in the next chapter about the unity of Smithian virtue and the following one about the connection between Smithian virtue and happiness, it would be overall better for Smith to emphasize his observation that we have separate, mutually irreducible evaluative reactions to each virtue.

In sum, Smith argues against Epicurus that the value we attach to virtue is not reducible to concern for our own bodily pleasure and that we attach value to virtues other than prudence. By now, it might seem weird how much this section has talked about what we desire and how we value: Epicurus says that we only desire bodily pleasure and thus only attach value to prudence because it helps us attain bodily pleasure, and Smith says that we desire more than just bodily pleasure and thus attach value to prudence and to other virtues because we desire them, in some sense, intrinsically. These might be interesting psychological claims, but we are supposed to be engaged in normative inquiry. What is the relationship between these claims and any claims about how we *should* live? Toward the end of the section, Smith points out that the other ancient philosophers he most discusses in TMS VII agree with Epicurus that "virtue consist[s] in acting in the most suitable manner to obtain the primary objects of natural desire"; they, like Smith, disagree with Epicurus about what the primary objects of natural desire are and about the nature of the "excellence" in acting suitably to obtain them (VII.ii.2.15). This ancient approach to philosophizing about virtue assumes that our most basic natural desires have normative force, that we, in some sense, *should* act on them. The rub lies in explaining *why* these desires have normative force. As we shall see, Smith too seems to adopt some version of this approach; we will address Smith's version of it in Section 2 of Chapter 7. Here, however, it is worth pointing out a straightforward rationale for defending Epicurus's version, one based upon the basic requirement of moral logic that ought implies can. In arguing that we *can* only desire one thing—bodily pleasure—Epicurus can at least argue that if we *ought* to pursue anything at all, it must be this one thing, for there are no other options. Of course, on its own, this strategy offers no support for fulfilling that "if"; it could be the case that we ought not desire anything at all. Furthermore, it would need to spell out reasons for maximizing our attainment of the one thing we desire, for privileging the long term over the short term, etc. But these challenges, especially the first, seem much more meetable than the fundamental one of establishing that human beings only naturally desire one thing. *That*, it seems, is where the real trouble is for Epicurus. On the other hand, for Smith, who does not believe that human beings only naturally desire one thing, the trouble is elsewhere. In treating what is natural to us as normatively significant, he cannot simply fall back on the principle that ought implies can.[12]

Section 5: Benevolence Theories

In reducing all virtues to prudence, Smith observes, Epicurus "indulged a propensity, which is natural to all men, but which philosophers in particular are apt to cultivate with peculiar fondness, the propensity to account for all appearances from as few principles as possible" (VII.ii.2.14).[13] Defenders of benevolence theories fall prey to a similar temptation, albeit in an opposite direction. Hutcheson supplies Smith with his main example of a benevolence theory. In keeping with the observation I made earlier about Smith's sensitivity to historical context despite his commitment to an ahistorical taxonomy of virtue theories, Smith frames Hutcheson's view not as a response to Epicureanism but as a development of a theologically infused strain in anciently pedigreed, post-Reformation thought. This contextualization is both intrinsically interesting and indicative of how separable Smith takes the two main questions of moral philosophy to be. He characterizes "the system which makes virtue consist in benevolence" as "not so ancient" as the prudence or propriety theories but still of "very great antiquity" (VII.ii.3.1). This system, Smith claims, has roots in the work of Neo-Platonic philosophers who argued that since benevolence is the "sole principle of action," "the supreme and governing attribute" of the "Deity," human virtue must also consist in benevolence, as "the whole perfection and virtue of the human mind [consists] in some resemblance or participation of the divine perfections." Since this system was "much esteemed by many ancient fathers of the Christian church," it came back to prominence "after the Reformation" when it was adopted in the seventeenth century by philosophers like Cudworth (VII.ii.3.2). We were introduced to Cudworth in Section 1 of Chapter 2 as a defender of the view that reason is the fundamental psychological source of moral distinctions. When discussing that view, Smith explicitly praises "Dr. Hutcheson" for correcting it (VII.iii.2.9). But when discussing Cudworth's benevolence-based virtue theory, Smith explicitly classifies Hutcheson as a "patron" of the same system (VII.ii.3.3). However, perhaps as a nod to his fundamental disagreement with the rationalism that accompanies the Cudworthian and other versions of this virtue theory, Smith also classifies Hutcheson as "undoubtedly, beyond all comparison, the most acute, the most distinct, the most philosophical, and what is of the greatest consequence of all, the soberest and most judicious" of "all the patrons of this system, ancient or modern" (VII.ii.3.3).

Smith does not spell out a view about Hutcheson's relationship to this tradition.[14] Instead, Smith identifies four nontheological observations upon which he takes Hutcheson's view to be based. In doing so, Smith also does not spell out a view about Hutcheson's relationship to the ancient advice to live according to one's nature. But since all four of these observations point to "appearances in human nature" suggesting that "virtue consists in benevolence," we can assume that Smith took Hutcheson to be at least friendly to it (VII.ii.3.4).[15]

The first observation, which Smith himself explains via the mechanism of "double sympathy" we saw in Sections 3 and 4 of Chapter 3, is that "proper benevolence is the most graceful and agreeable of all the affections" and "appears to our natural sentiments to possess a merit superior to any other." Unlike other passions, benevolence is "not very disagreeable" when it is excessive and even somewhat "engaging" when acted upon "unaccompanied by the sense of propriety," from an apparently meritless "instinctive good-will" (VII.ii.3.4). (This last point reveals, again, that Smith believes some kind of regulative self-reflection is essential to virtue.) Second, not only "the contrary inclination" to benevolence but even the "want of sufficient attention to the happiness of our neighbor" receives an especially harsh form of disapproval, which can involve a desire to punish (VII.ii.3.3.5). Third, when we believe that an action was motivated by "benevolent affections" and find out that it was at least partly motivated by self-interest or believe that an action was motivated by self-interest and find out that it was at least partly motivated by benevolent affections, our approval always respectively diminishes or increases (VII.ii. 3.6–7). And finally, in debates about "the rectitude of conduct," we often appeal to "the public good" as a standard but never question "whether what, upon the whole, tended most to the happiness of mankind, was not also morally good" (VII.ii.3.8).[16]

On the basis of these observations, Hutcheson concludes that "virtue must consist in pure and disinterested benevolence alone," that "the greater the benevolence which was evidenced by any action, the greater the praise which must belong to it," and that since actions aiming "at the happiness of a great community" demonstrate "a more enlarged benevolence," the "most virtuous of all affections" is "the desire of the general happiness of mankind," which must "direct all our actions" if we are to be maximally virtuous (VII.ii.3.6–11). The motive of self-love is at best "merely innocent" and at worst positively vicious. Benevolent actions lose merit even when they are performed "from a regard to the pleasure of self-approbation, to the comfortable applause of our own consciences" (VII.ii.3.12–13).

Since Smith agrees with the observations upon which this position is based—in Sections 3 and 4 of the next chapter, we'll see the import of his acceptance of the second and fourth ones—he agrees that if it we could reduce all the virtues to one, benevolence would be it; thus, even for Smith, benevolence is special. However, he offers three different kinds of consideration against reducing all virtue to it.[17] The narrowest one questions the implications of the importance we put on the "welfare of society" in debates about conduct. One might expect Smith to argue that the privileged position of the public welfare in such debates actually supports a view like utilitarianism, according to which a state of affairs, like the public welfare, not a motive or trait, like benevolence, is the sole or primary source of moral value.[18] Instead, likely because he simply doesn't think anyone should take seriously a view that does not ground moral value in human motives or traits, he argues that the privileged position of the public welfare in debates about conduct implies not that a regard to the public welfare is the "sole virtuous motive" but that "in any competition, it ought to cast the balance against all over motives" (VII.ii.3.17). The idea seems to be that when we introduce into a debate considerations of public welfare, which are demanded by proper benevolence, we play a moral trump card against other considerations. The demands of benevolence have this authority because it wins stronger approval than any other motive, as it wins sympathy with itself and generates sympathy with the gratitude it prompts. We see another, inverse source of authority if we stress Smith's aforementioned observation that the "want of sufficient attention to the happiness of our neighbor" can win antipathy with itself and generate sympathy with the resentment it prompts (VII.ii.3.3.5).

Even though Smith is treating considerations of public welfare as morally authoritative not in their own right, as a utilitarian would, but only insofar as they follow from the demands of benevolence, as Hutcheson does, we can generate counterexamples to this attribution of authority by adjusting a standard objection to utilitarianism. The standard objection to utilitarianism invites us to consider the moral intuitions we have in response to cases in which an action that promotes the public welfare overall damages the welfare of a few individuals. The Smithian version of this objection would invite us to consider the moral intuitions we have in response to cases in which a proper-benevolence-motivated action promotes the public welfare and thus prompts much gratitude overall also damages the welfare and thus prompts the resentment of a few individuals. This objection is not just an external one. As we shall see in Section 3 of the next chapter, Smith himself explicitly prioritizes justice, the virtue of not prompting proper resentment, over beneficence, the virtue of promoting proper gratitude. We can generate an answer on Smith's behalf, though, by observing how much is built into "proper." For benevolence, gratitude, and resentment to be proper, they must all be approved of by the WIS. To render his attribution of supreme authority to benevolence consistent with our intuitions and with his own prioritization of justice, Smith could argue that the WIS would not deem "proper" benevolence that sacrifices an important minority interest for the sake of a less important majority one; nor would the WIS deem "proper" any gratitude felt in response to such improper benevolence. Smith could also argue the WIS would deem "proper" benevolence that sacrifices an unimportant minority interest for the sake of an important majority one but would not deem "proper" any resentment this might prompt. Obviously, the devil is in the details regarding what interests we take to be "important," as well as what we take to be most relevant ratios of minority to majority interests. But Smith is under no obligation to pretend that difficult moral decisions are easy; if anything, his commitment to common moral experience imposes an obligation upon him to emphasize the difficulty of difficult moral decisions. Thus, in saying that proper benevolence "ought to cast the balance against all other motives," Smith is not committed to recommending motivation-sensitive versions of utilitarian sacrifices. He is merely committed to treating proper benevolence as the "most graceful and agreeable of all the affections," and thus actions which clearly manifest it as the best ones (VII.ii.3.4). Determining which ones clearly do is an altogether different matter.

Smith also responds more broadly to the benevolence theory that it gets wrong the moral attitude we have particularly toward a "regard to our own private happiness and interest." On "many occasions," self-regard yields "very laudable principles of action." For example, "habits of oeconomy, industry, discretions, attention, and application of thought" in pursuit of one's own interest are "very praise-worthy qualities, which deserve the esteem and approbation of every body" (VII.ii.3.16). An even stronger example is regard for one's own self-approval, which is considered "in the common judgments of mankind" as "the sole motive which deserves the appellation of virtuous." As I pointed out in Section 1 of the previous chapter, Smith appears unsure in this passage whether to classify this motive as a "selfish" one. Given what we saw in Sections 3, 4, and 5 of the previous chapter, his hesitancy likely has something to do with his unique "doctrine" of how self-approval works; in fact, if we read him as endorsing the "common judgments of mankind" regarding virtuous motives, this very passage implicitly runs together the love of self-approval and the love of sympathy with the WIS (VII.ii.3.13). However, even if the Smithian love of self-approval is something more like the latter kind of motive than how it might usually be understood, it still serves as a counterexample to the claim that we only approve of actions motivated by benevolence.

Smith's broadest response to the benevolence-based virtue theory is that it gets wrong the moral attitudes we have toward a whole host of qualities that are not all necessarily concerned with self-interest. While it gets right "the peculiar excellency of the supreme virtue of beneficence," it has the "contrary defect, of not sufficiently explaining from whence arises our approbation of the inferior virtues of [not only] prudence [but also], vigilance, circumspection, temperance, constancy, firmness" (VII.ii.3.15). This claim is not merely rooted in Smith's observations of common life. He also invites us to consider what it must mean for imperfect beings like us to live well. It might be a conceptual truth that if an "independent and all-perfect Being, who stands in need of nothing external, and whose happiness is complete in himself" acts at all, it must be from benevolence. Since ought implies can, virtue for a being like this one must consist in benevolence. The "existence" of human beings, on the other hand, "requires so many things external" to them that they must "often act from many other motives." Thus, if virtue also consisted solely in benevolence for us, our survival would often require us to act in ways that render virtue impossible. Since Smith is committed to the view that virtue is possible for us—he puts the point here in terms of "the condition of human nature" not being "peculiarly hard"—he concludes that human virtue must consist in achievable excellence with respect to *all* of our different sentiments, not just our benevolent ones (VII.ii.3.18). In other words, he concludes that virtue consists in propriety.

Section 6: Propriety Theories

Most of Smith's discussion of propriety theories concerns the work of the ancient philosophers Plato, Aristotle, and Zeno, who founded the Stoic school. But at the end of the chapter, he does make some brief comments about "modern systems" of this kind. These comments are instructive for apparently revealing what he believes sets his own view apart from all his predecessors. The modern rationalists Samuel Clarke and William Wollaston, as well as the modern proto-sentimentalist Lord Shaftesbury, offer propriety theories. However:

> None of those systems either give, or even pretend to give, any precise or distinct measure by which this fitness or propriety of affection can be ascertained or judged of. That precise and distinct measure can be found nowhere but in the sympathetic feelings of the impartial and well-informed spectator. (VII.ii.1.49)

Referring as it does to how we "measure" and "judg[e] of" propriety, this objection invites us to think of the second main question of moral philosophy. In Section 3, I interpreted in just this way the version of this objection that Smith levels at Hume. My main reason for doing so was Smith's insistence that utility to self and others coincides with the dictates of the WIS (IV.2.3). Since Smith observes that "the description of virtue, besides, which is either given, or at least meant and intended to be given" by thinkers like Clarke, Wollaston, and Shaftesbury "is no doubt quite just, so far as it goes," there is reason to interpret this objection as applied to them in the same way. However, Smith also claims that modern propriety theorists make the mistake of overlooking an important kind of moral status, "for though propriety is an essential ingredient in every virtuous action, it is not always the sole ingredient." More specifically, they do not "account either easily or satisfactorily for that superior degree of esteem" and "superior degree of detestation" involved in judgments of merit (VII.ii.1.50). There are at least two reasons for seeing this mistake as a purely speculative, second-question one. It concerns the workings of a certain kind of moral judgment. And it concerns an additional "ingredient" in virtue that, as we saw in Section 4 of Chapter 3, ultimately is a special form of propriety; as a result, it does not flag the need to recognize a distinct answer to the first question centering on the recognition of both propriety and merit. However, there are also at least two reasons for seeing this mistake as a practical, first-question one: it concerns how virtues are ranked in a way that must impact the deliberation of the virtuous agent, and it occurs in the middle of Smith's treatment of positive answers to the first question. Thus, if the modern propriety theorists make this mistake *because* of their failure to see that "the precise and distinct measure [of propriety in all its forms] can be found nowhere but in the sympathetic feelings of the impartial and well-informed spectator," then there is reason to believe that this failure *does* concern the first question (VII.ii.1.49).

Smith does not say whether he believes that this failure is what led modern propriety theorists to overlook the category of merit; that he accuses Hume of failing in the same way but does not accuse him of missing the fact that some virtues deserve reward and some vices deserve punishment suggests that Smith might not see such a connection (cf. EPM 5.17/SBN 219). Thus, it seems that we do not have a reason to consider this failure to be a practical, first-question one on the grounds that it *necessarily* generates practical, first-question mistakes. This result matters for our understanding of Smith's attitude toward the propriety theorists on which he spends the most time, Plato, Aristotle, and Zeno and the Stoics. Since none of them hold the WIS account of propriety measurement that Smith does, we can assume that he sees them as failing in precisely the same way that the modern propriety theorists do. Furthermore, given that all propriety theories claim that virtue consists "in the proper government and direction of all our affections," the most fundamental way for Smith to distinguish his own propriety theory from their propriety theories is by distinguishing between his and their accounts of what does the governing and directing (VII.ii.intro.1). But if this distinction does not have any robustly practical consequences, then it has more to do with the second question than the first. And if Smith also does not recognize in Plato, Aristotle, and Zeno and the Stoics any analogue to the potentially practical mistake of overlooking the category of merit, regardless of its source, then he does not really disagree with them about the nature of virtue, despite disagreeing with them about the nature of self-regulation.

As we shall presently see in more detail, Smith disagrees with Plato and Aristotle regarding the principle of self-regulation but also believes that they are generally right about the nature of virtue. Plato's account, Smith observes, "coincides in every respect with what we have said above concerning the propriety of conduct" (VII.ii.1.11). And Aristotle's account "corresponds too pretty exactly with what has been said above concerning the propriety and impropriety of conduct" (VII.ii.1.12). But as we shall also presently see in more detail, though he similarly disagrees with Zeno and the Stoic school he founded regarding the principle of self-regulation, Smith also believes that they are wrong about the nature of virtue; he concludes that "the plan and system which Nature has sketched out for our conduct seems to be altogether different from that of Stoical philosophy" that Zeno founded (VII.ii.1.43). Moreover, Smith believes that in the case of Zeno and the Stoic tradition, the two mistakes are related; they offer the wrong account of how we should live *because* they offer the wrong account of the psychological faculty ultimately responsible for moral judgments.

This potentially confusing tapestry of attitudes generates two interpretive questions. If all three views are wrong in not explaining self-regulation in terms of the WIS, why does this mistake only impact one of their accounts of virtue? And in showing how this mistake does impact that account of virtue, has Smith gone back on his distinction between the two main questions of moral philosophy in terms of practical import? This section of TMS VII is supposed to be about different accounts of how we should live, not different accounts of the psychological faculty ultimately responsible for moral evaluation. But if his criticism of Zeno and the Stoics on virtue is also a criticism of Zeno and the Stoics on moral judgment, Smith might have violated his own claim that the two issues are essentially distinct.

Let's start grappling with these two questions—that of why the accounts of self-regulation in Plato and Aristotle do not impact their virtue theories while the account of self-regulation in Stoicism does impact its virtue theory and that of how this latter relation fits with Smith's distinction between the two main questions of moral philosophy—by getting clear on what Smith agrees and disagrees with in each of the three accounts. We start with the agreements. In discussing these, we follow the order of Smith's text: first Plato, then Aristotle, and then Zeno.

Plato's view, as Smith points out, rests upon a tripartite conception of the soul. For Plato, "the soul is considered as something like a little state or republic" that is governed by the "judging faculty." The job of this "ruling principle," which Smith remarks is "very properly called reason," is to govern its "natural subjects," the "different passions and appetites," some of which are "irascible" or honor-focused and some of which are "concupiscible" or pleasure-focused (VII.ii.1.1–4). (In the context of presenting his own virtue theory, Smith adopts a similar distinction from "the best of the ancient moralists" that distinguishes between passions that "drive" us and which are hard "to restrain even for a single moment" and passions that "seduce" us and which are "easy to restrain for a single moment, or even for a short period of time," but plague us with "continual and almost incessant solicitations." His examples for the former category are "fear and anger"; his examples for the latter are "the love of ease, of pleasure, [and] of applause" (VI.iii.2–3).) The governing principle operates by telling us "what are the proper means for attaining any end, but also what ends are fit to be pursued, and what degree of relative value we ought to put upon each." In doing so, it does not extinguish the irascible or concupiscible passions so much as help them best do their natural work; the former are for defending us "against injuries," asserting our "rank and dignity," making us "aim at what is noble and honourable," and helping us "distinguish those who act in the same manner," while the latter are for providing "the support and necessities of the body" (VII.ii.1.3–5). Plato provides a list of particular virtues that corresponds to how well each of these three different parts of the soul is doing its job. But he also recognizes a master virtue, which he calls "justice," that is only possessed by agents for whom all of these parts of the soul are doing their jobs. This "took place," Smith writes, "when reason directed and passion obeyed, and when each passion performed its proper duty, and exerted itself towards its proper object easily and without reluctance, and with that degree of force and energy, which was suitable to the value of what it pursued" (VII .ii.1.9).

On Aristotle's view, Smith observes, virtue "consists in the habit of mediocrity according to right reason," which serves as the analogue to Plato's "ruling principle." For Aristotle, the function of this principle is to help us set our feelings and actions at a virtuous "middle [point] between two opposite vices, of which the one offends from being too much, the other from being too little affected by a particular species of objects" (VII.ii.1.12). Aristotle's list of particular virtues, then, corresponds to all the different ways in which one can feel and act correctly, excessively, or deficiently. The main difference that Smith sees between Plato and Aristotle lies in the latter's emphasis on cultivating "the *habit* of this moderation" (VII.ii.1.13; emphasis added). Plato, Smith claims, seems to have thought of virtue as "a species of science," according to which "just sentiments and reasonable judgments concerning what was fit to be done or avoided, were alone sufficient to constitute the most perfect virtue." On this view, if we make "plain and evident judgments" about such matters, we do not need to worry about ungoverned passion leading us astray. Aristotle disagreed, believing that since "no conviction of the understanding was capable of getting the better of inveterate habits," virtue must arise "not from knowledge but from action" that fosters settled practical habits (VII.ii.1.14). We might be surprised that Smith does not weigh in on this debate. We might also be surprised that he does not weigh in specifically on the side of Aristotle. This debate is at least partly about whether weakness of will is a coherent notion (I turn to another feature of the debate shortly); on Smith's telling, Plato's view is that it is impossible not to do the good once one knows what it is, while Aristotle's view is that it is possible to know what the good is but not do it. As we saw in Section 5 of the last chapter, Smith believes that we adhere to general moral rules in order to "chec[k] the impetuosity of [our] passion" when they threaten to steer us wrongly. Yet although Smith believes, in Aristotelian fashion, that when we are wrongly steered, we are "secretly conscious" that we are breaking a moral rule, he also believes that "at the time of acting," we are "no doubt, less sensible of the impropriety of [our] own conduct than afterwards, when [our] passion [is] gratified and palled" (III.4.12). By thus recognizing that the passions alter our moral opinions at the moment of action, Smith actually brings his view closer to Plato's than it first appears.[19]

I mentioned previously that Smith more or less agrees with the accounts of virtue he sees in Plato and Aristotle. This agreement must be about something general, as their lists of virtue do not coincide perfectly with each other or, as we will see in the next chapter, Smith's. Smith expresses his agreement with Plato right after summing up his "every faculty doing its job" conception of virtuousness. And Smith expresses his agreement with Aristotle right after summing up his "mean between two extremes" conception of virtuousness. So Smith's agreement with both must reflect what these two views have in common. One obvious feature they share is a notion of feeling and desiring *correctly*, as opposed to a notion of not feeling and desiring at all or even of feeling and desiring generally less than is usual. Another obvious feature they share is a conception of the self as naturally structured by a hierarchy, with some evaluative faculty at top, regulating the rest of it. I'll return to this point in Section 2 of Chapter 7. For now, we can say that Smith agrees with Plato and Aristotle regarding the general idea that we are virtuous when the faculty that is naturally supposed to be in charge ensures that we feel, desire, and act correctly.

However, though he does not say so in this section, Smith does not agree with Plato's and Aristotle's identification of the governing faculty with reason. Though Smith appears to agree that Plato's "judging faculty . . . is very properly called, reason," we know from the combination of Smith's discussion of Plato's view and his own discussion of moral rationalism that he ultimately does not. "Under this appellation," Smith observes, Plato "not only comprehended that faculty by which we judge of truth and falsehood, but that by which we judge of the propriety of desires and affections" (VII.ii.1.2). As we saw in Section 1 of Chapter 2, his attack on Cudworth's rationalism indicates that Smith does not think the same faculty can do both these jobs. In contrast with his discussion of Plato, Smith says almost nothing about Aristotle's conception of "right reason" as the faculty that determines which habits are the virtuous ones. Indeed, the way in which he contrasts Aristotle and Plato on the importance of habit suggests that he takes Aristotle to be assigning a fundamentally different practical role to reason from the one Plato does. On Smith's telling, Plato thinks we develop virtue primarily by forming true beliefs which intrinsically motivate, while Aristotle thinks we develop virtue primarily by cultivating certain habits through the repetition of certain actions. Reason's main role in the latter story seems to be that of picking out the standard "according" to which the right habits are determined (VII.ii.1.12). Smith does not indicate whether he interprets the Aristotelian process of picking out this standard as a matter of forming true beliefs which intrinsically motivate, albeit more weakly and less reliably than on Plato's story, or in some other way. Apparently, Smith agrees with Aristotle's thinking about the *content* of this standard; for Smith, the standards of propriety for different kinds of passions "must lie, it is evident, in a certain mediocrity" (I.ii.intro.1).[20] However, since Smith is clear that the sympathy of the WIS picks out the "mediocre" way to feel and act but never attributes this view to Aristotle, it is safe to conclude that regardless of how he interprets Aristotle, Smith disagrees with Aristotle's understanding of the process by which we pick out the standard for right habits.[21] Therefore, even if Smith agrees with Plato that virtue obtains when each component of the soul does its natural job and with Aristotle that virtue consists in hitting a mean between two extremes, Smith disagrees with both when they claim that reason is the ruling principle. We will return to this point after working through Smith's treatment of Zeno and the Stoic tradition.

Before turning to Zeno and the Stoic tradition, however, we should consider whether I have overstated Smith's disagreement with Plato and Aristotle regarding the ruling faculty. In his attack on moral rationalism, Smith does say that the general rules that reason induces from our particular sentiment-based moral judgments help us "regulate the greater part of our moral judgments" (VII.iii.2.5). He also says that according to both "philosophy" and "common sense," the sense of duty, which is what "regard to those general rules of conduct . . . is properly called," "should be the ruling and governing . . . principle of our conduct," even if not the "sole" principle (III.6.1; III.5.1). Thus, even though, as I pointed out in Section 5 of the previous chapter, these rules must inherit their motivational force from the sentiments upon which they are based, in assigning them a regulative, ruling, and governing role, Smith could be bringing his position closer at least to the *letter* of the Platonic and Aristotelian law. However, as we shall see in Sections 3 and 6 of the next chapter, this is only true in a limited sense. He argues that the reason-induced rules regarding the dictates of all the virtues other than justice are too "loose and inaccurate" for us to "regulate our conduct entirely by regard to them" (III.6.9). But he also argues that the rules regarding the dictates of justice are so "accurate" that we *should* regulate our conduct by regard to them and *not* by consulting our context-sensitive, WIS-based conscience (III.6.10). So it seems that neither regard to reason-induced rules nor regard to the sentiments of the WIS can be our ruling and governing principle across the board. But if so, we are stuck with alternating ruling and governing principles, with nothing ruling and governing over them. To avoid this conclusion, I propose that we stress the fact that all moral rules, even those of justice, are ultimately rooted in the sentiments of the WIS. Thus, the WIS is the only ruling and governing principle but one that, in the case of justice, delegates authority to the rules that are based on its own most "accurate" rulings. So if Smith's account of the ruling and governing principle agrees with the letter of the Platonic and Aristotelian law, it does so only with respect to a very limited domain and only even then at a secondary level.

Like Plato and Aristotle, Zeno and the rest of the Stoics[22] argue that virtue consists generally in living in accordance with our nature, under our "ruling principles" (VII.ii.1.23). The general identification of virtue with living in accordance with human nature, as we saw Smith observe, is a point of agreement between these three philosophers and Epicurus (VII.ii.2.15). However, as we also saw Smith observe, unlike Epicurus, these three philosophers identified more than one natural desire and saw virtue as valuable not only for its conduciveness to satisfying that one natural desire. They believe that we have several different kinds of desires, which are in their natural, virtuous state only when governed by the part of the soul that has authority over the rest of it. They also believe that insofar as being in this state is itself good and desirable, virtue does "deserve to be pursued for its own sake" and is "itself one of the ultimate objects of natural appetite" (VII.ii.2.17).

According to the Stoic version of this view, to live according to our nature is to perfect ourselves as the kind of thing that we are. We bring the "different parts of [our] nature" into the "best and most perfect state of which they are capable" by "choosing and rejecting all different objects and circumstances according as they were by nature rendered more or less the objects of choice or rejection" and of "bestowing upon every object the precise degree of attention it deserves, according to the place which it held in this natural scale of things." Thus, since "health, strength, agility, and ease of body, as well as the external conveniences which could promote these" are necessary for overall self-perfection, they are "fit to be chosen," and since some of these goods are more necessary than others, some are fitter than others. "So far," Smith observes, "the

Stoical idea of propriety and virtue is not very different from that of Aristotle" (VII .ii.1.15–17). Since Smith mainly agrees with both Aristotle and Plato on virtue and since this agreement relation seems transitive, we might add that this Stoical idea of propriety and virtue is also not very different from Plato's and Smith's own.

Presumably, Smith believes that at least *one* of the next few aspects of Stoicism that he introduces signals movement away from Aristotle's, Plato's, and his own view. However, Smith does not explicitly tell us *which* of the next few aspects that he introduces is the precise point of departure. He observes that on the Stoic account, nature does not limit our focus to ourselves, for we are not naturally "separate and detached from all other things." So the Stoics believe that to perfect ourselves as the kind of thing that we are is not to perfect ourselves as isolated individuals because we are *not* isolated individuals; rather, we are essentially "part[s] of a whole" (VII.ii.1.18–19) In general, this sounds like something that Plato, Aristotle, and Smith also believe: Plato has the enlightened philosopher reenter the cave, Aristotle defines man as a political animal, and Smith believes that moral self-consciousness is impossible from an asocial perspective. The break starts to occur, it seems, with the Stoic conception of the whole of which we are parts.

For the Stoics, nature teaches us to pursue "the prosperity" not only "of our family, of our relations, of our friends, [and] of our country" but also "of mankind, and of the universe in general." In doing so, nature also teaches us that the prosperity of the many is always preferable to the prosperity of the few, especially when the many in question is "all" people. As a result, "wherever our prosperity was inconsistent with that, either of the whole, or of any considerable part of the whole, it ought, even in our own choice to yield to what was so vastly preferable" (VII.ii.1.15–19). The Stoics then combine this conception of human beings as components of the entire universe with the belief that "all the events in this world were conducted by the providence of a wise, powerful, and good God." This should assure us, they argued, that "whatever happened tended to the prosperity and perfection of the whole," which, as we have just seen, we should value most. So if things are going badly for us as individuals, while it is natural for us to *try* to improve our situations, if we cannot actually do so, "we ought to rest satisfied that the order and perfection of the universe have required that we should in the mean time continue" in them (VII.ii.1

.18). In fact, since nature demands that we prefer the prosperity of the whole to our own, we should *celebrate*, not merely resign ourselves to unchangeable bad situations.

It is certainly not *obvious* that Plato and Aristotle define the moral circle this widely or recommend resignation to fate on the basis of belief in a "wise, powerful, and good God." But these are potentially contentious matters of interpretation that I would like to sidestep. (We will, however, eventually deal with them in Smith's case, in Section 4 of Chapter 6.) We can legitimately do so because the objections Smith goes on to level explicitly at Stoicism are directed not at the width of the Stoic circle or at Stoic theology but at the nature of the Stoic evaluative perspective and the particular moral commitments to which it gives rise. Stoicism demands that one evaluate by entering "into the sentiments of that divine Being and [consider oneself] as an atom, a particle, of an immense and infinite system, which must and ought to be disposed of according to the conveniency of the whole" (VII.ii.1.20). It follows that to virtuous Stoics, "all the events of human life must be in a great measure indifferent." Their passions have been "brought under perfect subjection to the ruling principles of [their] nature" such that they care only about two things: (a) "the contemplation of the happiness and perfection of the great system of the universe"; and (b) "acting properly in the affairs of this great republic whatever little part that [divine] wisdom has assigned [them]." The latter, practical concern with acting properly is totally divorced from concern with "success or disappointment" in our "endeavours." Again, it is natural for us to prefer success but "our sole anxiety" should be about "the order, the grace, the beauty" of our conduct, not the prosperity or adversity that results (VII.ii.1.21–3).

One of Smith's five main objections to this picture is that it ultimately reduces "the great business and occupation of our lives" to nothing but the "sublime contemplation" of the "benevolent wisdom" that directs the universe (VII.ii .1.46). In telling us to enter "into the sentiments of that divine Being" and thereby employ its perspective as the one from which we evaluate everything, the Stoics necessarily tell us to live an essentially passive life (VII.ii.1.20). Sure, contemplation of "that benevolent wisdom which directs all the events of human life . . . for the good of the whole" is useful for consolation when things go badly. But in making "the events which interest us the most" involve "that little department in which we ourselves have some little management and direction," nature reveals that we are made for practice, not contemplation (VII.ii.1.45–6).

This objection assumes that even if we successfully adopt it, the divine perspective is one from which we can do nothing but contemplate. One reason for believing that we cannot act from the divine perspective is that we cannot know how our decisions will impact the universe as a whole. But suppose that the Stoics showed that we can, at least sometimes, know exactly what the universe demands that we do, even if we did not know exactly how this action would impact the universe as whole. It would follow, then, that the call to think in terms of the divine perspective is not necessarily a call to abandon all practical life for passive contemplation. However, it remains a call to act with "perfect apathy" toward anything but performing the duty dictated to us by the universe (VII.ii.1.46). Smith objects to this outcome on two fronts. The first—which constitutes the second overall objection on our list—is that virtue does not involve a total lack of concern about the consequences of our conduct.

There is at least one definite Smithian reason why virtue cannot involve concern for the propriety of one's conduct without involving concern for the consequences of one's conduct. This reason is implicit in the basic structure of Smith's moral psychology. For Smith, to be motivated to act in general is to desire something. Obviously, some of the things we desire and thus act to promote are states of affairs, such as an improvement in someone else's welfare. Thus, to act to promote someone else's welfare necessarily involves caring about their welfare, i.e., the consequence of the action. Of course, the Stoic response is that the virtuous agent does not act in this way; rather, the virtuous agent always acts not from a concern for some state of affairs or outcome but from a concern with the propriety of his own action. But for Smith, the desire to act appropriately is the desire to act from sentiments that win the sympathy of the WIS. In this respect, Smithian agents acting from a desire to act appropriately are always *also* acting from a desire to do something else; the former desire is simply a reflective addition to the latter one.[23] Thus, when we act from a desire to act appropriately when we act to improve someone else's welfare, we also act from a desire to improve someone's welfare, which has its target a consequence of our conduct.[24]

There is also one *possible* Smithian reason why virtue cannot involve concern for the propriety of one's conduct without involving concern for the consequences of one's conduct. This possible reason derives from Smith's observation that even "unintended and unforeseen" consequences of actions impact our judgments of the virtue of agents; thus, insofar as the virtuous agent cares about being virtuous and virtuousness is impacted by even these kinds of consequences, the virtuous agent will care about them (II.iii.intro.4). Smith makes this observation at the end of his account of judgments of merit. As we saw in Section 4 of Chapter 3, these judgments involve determining whether we would feel gratitude or resentment upon being the recipient of an agent's action. We also saw that gratitude, resentment, and sympathy therewith depend upon perception of the agent's motive. Gratitude and sympathy therewith require not just appreciating a benefit but also approval of the motive that caused the benefit. Resentment and sympathy therewith require not just a harm but also disapproval of the motive that caused the harm. In fact, our reactions to motives are *more* important than our reactions to consequences are to gratitude, resentment, sympathy therewith, and, thus, merit. The ultimate "objects" of gratitude and resentment are not benefits and harms per se but the "character and conduct" of an agent that causes them or merely "intends" or "tends to" cause them (II.iii.intro.2; II.i.intro.2). So upon realizing this, we formulate the "equitable maxim" that "all praise or blame, all approbation or disapprobation, of any kind, which can justly be bestowed upon any action, must ultimately belong . . . to the intention or affection of the heart" behind it. Actual benefits and harms should only play the evidentiary role of revealing the intentions that cause them. And since their ability to play this already limited role is itself limited by the fact that they can "depend, not upon the agent, but upon fortune," we must be careful to distinguish between the benefits and harms that reveal a morally relevant intention and those that do not. Thus, no matter "how different soever the accidental, the unintended and unforeseen consequences of different actions . . . if the intentions or affections from which they arose were" the same, "the merit or demerit of the actions is still the same" (II.iii.intro.2–6).

So far, so Stoic, more or less. The problem, however, is that the equitable maxim rests upon a correction we don't always make. Despite not playing a foundational role in triggering gratitude and resentment, actual benefits and harms can play *some* role; this is the only way to explain how we can feel some version of gratitude and resentment even toward "inanimated" objects (II.iii.1.1). Thus, we sometimes violate the equitable maxim when someone has "failed in producing either the good or the evil which he intended" or when someone has caused "either great good or great evil" from motives that were either not properly beneficent or not improperly malevolent (II.iii. 1.7). In the former cases, we deem people less beneficent or unjust than they deserve; in the latter cases, we deem people more beneficent or unjust than they deserve.

However, still so far, so Stoic, more or less. If Smith is merely diagnosing an "irregularity of sentiment, which every body feels, which scare any body is sufficiently aware of, and which nobody is willing to acknowledge," he is not necessarily disagreeing with the Stoic insistence that we should act with focus on the propriety of our conduct, not on its consequences (II.iii.intr o.6). Yet Smith *seems* to go on to provide a qualified, nuanced excuse for, if not endorsement of, this irregularity. In Section 2 of Chapter 7, I address his complicated position. What matters for now is recognizing that *if* this position assigns to virtuous agents some concern for the consequences of their actions, it expresses disagreement with the Stoics.

The second objection to the Stoic call for apathy toward anything but performing the duty dictated to us by the universe—which constitutes the third objection on our overall list—has to do with the one possible exception to this call. The sole concern of Stoic virtuous agents other than the propriety of their conduct is for "the greatest possible happiness of all rational and sensible beings." This is not the robust other-directed concern we typically have in mind when considering certain social feelings. Rather, it is a very general, contemplative affect. Moreover, it is not an affect that involves anything we could describe as concern or, to use Smith's term, "anxiety," for there is no point in really worrying about what only "the great Superintendent of the universe" can control and will assuredly guarantee. But, Smith argues, virtuous agents care for others in a way that goes beyond contemplative appreciation of "the greatest possible happiness of all rational and sensible beings" that God ensures (VII.ii.1.21).[25] More specifically, Smith believes that virtuous agents care much about particular people for their own sake, without necessarily reflecting upon how their well-being contributes to the overall good.

Thus, Smith believes that the Stoics get wrong the moral importance of concern for other people. In TMS III, Smith makes a distinction between the operation of conscience when "the happiness or misery of others depends in any respect upon our conduct" and the operation of conscience when "the happiness or misery of others . . . in no respect depends upon our conduct." In the former kinds of cases, which we discussed in Section 5 of the previous chapter, the WIS makes us "feel the truth of that great stoical maxim, that for one man to deprive another unjustly of any thing, or unjustly promote his own advantage by the loss or disadvantage of another, is . . . contrary to nature." The "most vulgar education" and "even the ordinary commerce of the world" teach us to restrain our "active principles" in this way. The latter kinds of cases, on the other hand, involve the "hardest of all the lessons of morality." These are cases in which our "passive feelings" do not directly impact anyone else by prompting action but can still be improper or, as Smith says here, subject to "inequalities." According to what Smith says in these passages, the Stoics try to teach us this difficult lesson by recommending that we "diminish" our sensibility "to our own" interests by trying to "feel for ourselves as we naturally feel for others" (III.3.5–8). Strictly speaking, this version of the Stoic view differs from the one we have been discussing in that feeling for oneself as one naturally feels for others is not the same thing as feeling for oneself as the "Superintendent" of the universe feels. Even if we grant that the "others" Smith has in mind here are total strangers—he goes on to describe the recommendation as one that we view ourselves "in the light in which any other citizen of the world would view us"—it seems likely that they would feel differently about our predicament than a god with the perfection of the whole universe in mind would (III.3.10). But even if the Stoic view considered here is softer than the one Smith considers in his history of virtue theories, Smith believes it still pushes us a considerable way toward apathy.

Smith concedes that with respect to "misfortunes which affect ourselves immediately and directly," there are "very few cases in which we can approach too near to the stoical apathy and indifference" (III.3.16). Given how our sympathetic tendencies work, we never offend by appearing too indifferent toward our own bodily pain (III.3.17) or financial misfortune (III.3.18). (A possible exception is the "undeserved loss of reputation," especially in young people. We might believe that older people indifferent to this kind of personal calamity are so out of life-tested confidence in their own merit. But since younger people "neither can nor ought to have any such confidence," we do expect them to care about such a thing (III.3.19).) However, Smith vehemently disagrees with the Stoic advice regarding our reactions to misfortunes that "affect us only indirectly, by affecting . . . some other persons who are particularly dear to us; such as our parents, our children, our brothers and sisters, our intimate friends" (III.3.12).

Smith contrasts the Stoic advice regarding how to best regulate our passive feelings involving other people with that of the "whining and melancholy moralists" who encourage us to "increase our sensibility to the interests of others" by trying to "feel for [them] as we naturally feel for ourselves." Smith points out that these moralists are often inconsistent in scolding us for "our happiness, while so many of our brethren are in misery" but never objecting that "we have too little fellow-feeling with the joy of success." He also argues that in demanding that we constantly focus upon "the many wretches that are at every instant laboring under all sorts of calamities," the moralists demand a form of "commiseration" that is merely "artificial" and "affected." Furthermore, he argues, even if real commiseration were attainable, it would be "perfectly useless" insofar as it extends to those "out of the sphere of our activity" (III.3.8–10). But just as these moralists make the mistake of demanding that we feel too much for too many others, the Stoics make the mistake of demanding that we feel too little for at least some others (we revisit the question of how many in the next paragraph). In some cases, our other-concerned emotions are just as likely to "fall short" of propriety as they "go very much beyond" it. If our own parents or children are in distress and we care no more than we would if anyone else's parents or children are in distress, we are failing as children or parents; "such unnatural indifference, far from exciting our applause, would incur our highest disapprobation." Sure, some "domestic affections" lean more toward excess than deficiency and thus more often need restraint than encouragement; this is why, for example, we might hear advice directed at moderating our "parental tenderness." But other domestic affections lean more toward deficiency than excess and thus more need encouragement than restraint; this is why, for example, the "Decalogue" commands us to "honour our fathers and mothers" but makes no mention "of the love of our children." And even when we do excessively feel the affections that tend toward excess, we are at worst "blameable" but never detestable. In contrast, while we "easily pardon" the excess, the defect is "peculiarly odious." Thus, "the stoical apathy is, in such cases, never agreeable." Instead, virtue involves cultivating the "moderated sensibility to the misfortunes of others, which does not disqualify us for the performance of any duty" (III.3.13–15).

The very general language of "others" in the last quotation suggests that rather than encouraging us to focus solely on "our parents, our children, our brothers and sisters, [and] our intimate friends," Smith is trying to split the difference between the Stoics and the whiny and melancholy moralists regarding the issue of how many people should be the object of our concern. His objection to the latter group is that they demand something that is both impossible and practically pointless. But since it surely is possible to care about people outside of our narrow circles and since this concern surely can be practically efficacious, we should expect Smith to believe that virtue involves "moderate sensibility" to a wider scope of people than it might first appear. We deal with the question of just how wide in Section 4 of the next chapter. Here, though, we can conclude very generally that Smith takes some form of benevolence to be a virtue that the Stoics get wrong.

Despite believing that the Stoics are closer to correct regarding apathy toward ourselves than they are regarding apathy toward others,[26] Smith also objects to features of the attitude that they encourage us to adopt toward ourselves; this is the fourth objection on our overall list. As we saw previously, one of the main reasons why the Stoics believe that nature demands we care more about whether our conduct is proper than about whether it is successful is that the former is under our control in a way that the latter is not. So on this view, if we live according to nature, the propriety of our "sentiment[s] and conduct" and the "glory and . . . happiness" that it "constitutes" become as "perfectly secure, and beyond the reach of fortune" as is possible. But if it turns out that our lives contain, "without any probable hope of amendment, more circumstances contrary to nature than agreeable to it," the most important of which being circumstances that prevent us from fulfilling our duty, we should consider ourselves "called upon" by the "awful and benevolent voice of that divine Being" that governs the universe to end them (VII.ii.1.23–6). Smith clearly objects to the claim that "voluntary death" is even "upon some occasions" positively called for by nature (VII.ii.1.28). But his analysis of this issue is subtler than it might first appear.

He starts by entertaining the possibility that nature can call for such an action in some situations. Most ancient European philosophers, like most of Smith's contemporaries, argued that virtue is the best policy, no matter "how untoward soever things might be without." But since "all the principal sects of ancient philosophers" flourished in warlike times that often made things very untoward without, their versions of these arguments often culminated in the claim that if one's "situation became at any time too hard for [one's] constancy to support," death, in which there "neither was nor could be any evil," was always "at hand" as a "remedy." The Stoics were not alone in this respect; Smith points out that while they "insisted upon" this doctrine more than other ancient European sects did, it was "common to them all, even to the peaceable and indolent Epicureans" (as we saw in Section 4). Nor, Smith points out, were these ancient European sects alone in this respect; in defending this doctrine, they "prepared a death-song" in the same way as the "American savage," who also lives in constant danger, does (VII.ii.1.28–30; cf. VII.ii.2.5). Thus, it seems that there are some circumstances in which a doctrine of virtuous suicide is a natural extension of the common view that virtue is the best way to defend oneself against bad fortune.

However, Smith continues by observing that suicide itself "never seems to have been very common among the Greeks" (VII.ii.1.31). Nor has Smith "remembered to have either read or hear of any American savage, who, [even] upon being taken prisoner by some hostile tribe, put himself to death" (VII.ii .i.34). Suicide "appears to have been much more prevalent among the proud Romans." But since it was "fashionable" among them, it seems to have been motivated "rather from vanity and ostentation . . . that from what would appear, even to a sober and judicious Stoic, any proper or necessary reason" (VII.ii.1.32–3). As we saw in Section 6 of the previous chapter, Smith means something very specific by "fashion." In general, the term describes the process by which our natural sentiments are altered by our customary observation of what people of high social rank do (V.1.3; V.2.3). So in this context, Smith is saying that most of the Romans who actually committed suicide did not do so because they thought themselves called upon by nature but because they wanted to be like their society's trendsetters.

The upshot of these reflections on actual practice is that if very few people, even among those who explicitly claimed that nature sometimes demanded suicide, actually killed themselves and if most of the ones who did kill themselves did so not because they thought nature demanded it but because they were vain, then we should be skeptical that the doctrine that nature sometimes demands suicide accurately reports what nature demands. With strikingly medicalized language, Smith concedes that while there is "a species of melancholy (a disease to which human nature, among its other calamities, is unhappily subject) which seems to be accompanied with, what one may call, an irresistible appetite for self-destruction," "no natural principle, no regard to the approbation of the supposed impartial spectator, to the judgment of the man within the breast, seems to call upon us to escape from [distress] by destroying ourselves." On Smith's view, people who do kill themselves are either weak or, as he, thankfully, seems to think more likely, sick. Such people are neither virtuous nor vicious; they "are the proper objects, not of censure, but of commiseration." Thus, the doctrine that suicide can be "an object of applause and approbation, seems to be altogether a refinement of philosophy" (VII.ii.1.34).[27] To the extent that it is neither a perverse celebration of illness nor a mere rationalization of fashion-conscious vanity, it follows from theoretical commitments that themselves follow not from what observation of nature tells us.

The fifth objection to Stoicism both points to another instance of such over-refinement and explains further what Smith means by the charge. The Stoics instruct us to evaluate things from the perspective of the "great Superintendent of the universe." But from that perspective, everything that happens is equally part of "that great chain which he had predestined from all eternity" from "universal and boundless benevolence." Thus, everything a human agent does according to this being's "orders" is equally "perfect" and everything the human agent does against this being's "orders" is equally "faulty." Overlooking the problem of how the latter kind of conduct is even possible, Smith objects that this denial of moral differences of degree is "absurd" because it flies directly in the face of our natural moral sentiments, which do recognize such differences. Smith claims that the Stoics who accept this denial, if any actually did, likely followed Chrysippus. (Smith cites Seneca and Cicero as examples of Stoic writers who did not accept this doctrine.[28]) The reason he cites for this claim is that Chrysippus was "a mere dialectical pedant" who "may have been the first who reduced [his] doctrines into a scholastic or technical system of artificial definitions, divisions, and subdivisions, one of the most effectual expedients, perhaps, for extinguishing whatever degree of good sense there may be in any moral or metaphysical doctrine" (VI.ii.1.41–2).

We can trace all five of these objections to the same basic disagreement: Smith believes that virtuous agents self-regulate by entering into the sentiments of the WIS, while the Stoics believe that virtuous agents self-regulate by entering into the sentiments of the "divine Being" that governs the universe (VII.ii.1.20). While the Stoic principle of self-governance encourages contemplation and resignation, the Smithian principle of self-governance encourages activity in the world; while the Stoic principle of self-governance encourages exclusive focus on the propriety of one's conduct, the Smithian principle of self-governance also requires concern for the outcomes of one's conduct; while the Stoic principle of self-governance encourages apathy, the Smithian principle of self-governance demands appropriate, not "too vehement" feelings, especially regarding other people (VII.ii.1.44); while the Stoic principle of self-governance sometimes demands suicide, the Smithian principle of self-governance never does; and while the Stoic principle of self-governance recognizes no degrees of virtue or vice in holding up or violating the divine plan, the Smithian principle of self-governance makes many fine-grained moral distinctions.

As we saw earlier, Smith also disagrees with Plato and Aristotle regarding the faculty by which virtuous agents regulate themselves. But as we also saw earlier, Smith's overall attitude toward Plato, Aristotle, and the Stoics generates two questions. Why does Smith's disagreement with Plato and Aristotle about self-regulation not manifest itself in disagreement about how to live, while Smith's disagreement with the Stoics about self-regulation does manifest itself disagreement about how to live? And does the latter relation cohere with Smith's claim that questions about the nature of approbation, which seem to be questions about our governing evaluative faculties, have no practical implications?

We can answer both questions at once. The answer to the first question is that Smith's disagreement with the Stoics about how evaluation should work has intrinsically to do with first-order evaluative content in a way that his disagreement with Plato and Aristotle does not. This is why—in answer to the second question—the Stoic view of evaluation Smith presents has practical implications; this view itself makes substantive evaluative commitments. Smith can disagree with Plato and Aristotle's view that the faculty by which we make evaluations and regulate ourselves is reason while agreeing with their general view on the nature of virtue because these two topics come apart from each other in just the way that Smith thinks the two main questions of moral philosophy do. In disagreeing with the Stoic view that we should make evaluations and regulate ourselves by entering "into the sentiments of the divine Being," Smith is not disagreeing with an answer to second main question of moral philosophy in the same way that he is regarding Plato and Aristotle (VII.ii.1.20). In fact, if we read this language of "entering into the sentiments" literally, Smith *agrees* with what he takes the Stoic answer to the second question to be. Of course, we probably shouldn't read this language literally. The point is just that in taking a position like this on the nature of the evaluative perspective, the Stoics are not taking a position on the faculty that evaluates so much as on the nature of the virtue itself. They are saying that virtue involves evaluating things from the perspective of the universe, which is much different from saying that virtue involves evaluating things via reason or via sentiment or via some other human faculty.

One implication of this interpretation is that Smith himself is saying something evaluatively substantive in disagreeing with the Stoics about the perspective from which we make evaluations. In doing so, he does not contradict his claim that the question about the psychological foundation of moral judgment has no practical implications. As we saw across Chapters 3 and 4, he thinks that moral judgment is *founded* upon sympathy per se, even though it ultimately requires sympathy with the WIS. Thus, there is no problem if the latter claim has practical implications. But how exactly do these practical implications differ from those of the Stoic view of the evaluative perspective? There is no reason to believe that the perspective of the governor of the universe that the Stoics tell us to adopt is not well-informed and impartial. So what is the difference between this perspective and that of the WIS? We could try to answer this question by making sharp distinctions between degrees or even kinds of well-informedness and impartiality possessed by each perspective. Or we could just cut to the chase: the Stoic evaluative perspective is that of a deity and Smith's evaluative perspective is that of a qualified human being. Smith's WIS is not the "Superintendent of the universe" (VII.ii.1.23) but an imaginary person with all relevant information a human being could have and without any relevant bias. Surely, Smith believes it is difficult to evaluate, act, and feel from this perspective. But it is not impossible.[29] Thus, one aspect of Smith's most fundamental worry about the Stoic evaluative perspective is that it is impossible to adopt. In this regard, his attitude toward the Stoics resembles his attitude toward the assumptions upon which Mandeville bases his moral skepticism and his attitude toward the benevolence-based account of virtue.

Another aspect of Smith's most fundamental worry about the Stoic evaluative perspective is that it generates moral verdicts that are too far out of line with our everyday intuitions. We have seen this concern manifest itself in Smith's labelling of the Stoic doctrine of proper suicide as a "refinement of philosophy" (VII.ii.1.34), in Smith's suggestion that the Stoic denial of degrees of propriety and impropriety is rooted in obsession with establishing a "scholastic or technical system of artificial definitions, divisions, and subdivisions" (VII .ii.1.41), and in Smith's similar suggestion that the Stoic doctrine of apathy regarding our feelings toward others is rooted in "abstruse syllogisms and quibbling dialectic" (III.3.21). Such a concern is also implicit in Smith's reactions to the Stoic de-emphasis on outcomes of conduct and prioritization of contemplation over action. But in addition to manifesting itself in these particular ways, this concern cuts right to the core of the Stoic project. This project is to ground how we should live in what human nature demands of us. Of course, our main evidence for what nature demands of us comes from our particular moral views regarding how we should conduct ourselves. So when Smith argues that the Stoic theory get these views wrong, he is saying not only that the theory fails in the general way that all theories can fail when they do not account for certain particulars but also, more specifically, that the theory fails to account for the most basic things for which it must account. Thus, he can conclude that the Stoic view is not just mistaken here and there; rather, it is systematically wrong. In Smith's words: "the plan and system which Nature has sketched out for our conduct, seems to be altogether different from that of the Stoical philosophy" (VII.ii.1.43).

At this point, we are ready to develop and press Smith's claim that human nature dictates self-regulation via the sentiments of the WIS. The next chapter does the former, while the second section of Chapter 7 does the latter.

6

Smith's Own Answer to the Nature of Virtue Question and Full-Blown Account of Virtue

We have just seen that Smith takes the nature of virtue to consist in propriety, i.e., in having and acting from affections, including both "selfish and . . . benevolent" ones, "under [the] proper government and direction" of the sentiments of the WIS. However, we have only glimpsed the general schema that grounds and structures Smith's own propriety theory of virtue. As we have seen across Chapters 3 and 4, Smith believes that the internal principle of governance itself must be rooted in a non-egoistic and non-altruistic sentiment. Thus, his own schema cannot be cleanly located within a traditional taxonomy that only recognizes "the great division of our affections . . . into the selfish and the benevolent," with reason as a possible governing principle (VII.ii.intro.4). Part of the job of this chapter, then, is to present in full the framework specific to Smith's virtue theory. In completing this job, the present chapter's discussion of Smith's own answer to the nature of virtue question runs parallel to the discussion in Chapter 3 of Smith's own answer to the psychological foundation of moral judgment question. However, presenting the general framework of Smith's virtue theory is not the same thing as presenting his full-blown account of virtue, which includes descriptions of the particular categories of virtue that emerge from the framework. Thus, this chapter has the additional job of presenting this full-blown account. In completing this job, it also runs parallel to the discussion in Chapter 4 of Smith's full-blown account of moral judgment.

One reason for combining these two jobs in one chapter is that the first one can be completed quickly. I do this in the first section. Most of the rest of the chapter is dedicated to the second job, which Smith completes in TMS VI, the entirety of which he added to the sixth edition of the TMS. Since this was the most substantive change to the sixth edition and the last major piece of new writing Smith published in his lifetime, many scholars have tried to determine what prompted it. One prominent view is that Smith became worried about the moral impact of the commercial society he celebrated in the *Wealth of Nations*.[1] Such hypotheses are plausible, though obviously difficult to confirm, absent an explicit statement of intent. Minimally, we can be sure that by adding TMS VI, Smith improves his moral theory by providing a fully worked out answer to his first main question of moral philosophy. Without Part VI, one would have to glean such an answer from short chapters and comments scattered through the text.[2]

Another reason for combining these two jobs in one chapter is that it is not clear that Smith's nature of virtue question does not directly implicate both of them, or at least not as clear as it is that Smith's psychological foundation of moral judgment question does not directly implicate the job of providing a full-blown account of moral judgment. Not much beyond how to articulate precisely the organizational strategy of this book hangs on either of these claims. But even though Smith's division of possible answers to his virtue question operates at a more general level than that from which one might discuss particular virtues, there seem to be good reasons for thinking that such a discussion is essential to answering the question. As Smith's treatment of each possible answer showed, it is probably impossible to provide a general framework for virtue without also employing particular examples of virtues. Furthermore, it is easier to see the practical importance of each possible answer when these answers are taken to include depictions of particular virtues, in addition to general frameworks. The second section of the chapter develops Smith's general view on how this connection to practice works.

Doing so introduces a distinction Smith makes between ethics and natural jurisprudence. Since this distinction sheds light not only on what Smith takes himself to be doing in TMS VI but also on why, in TMS VI, he only dedicates a paragraph to justice, we break from the order of the text by turning to that specific virtue first. The third section of the chapter explains why justice gets so little space in Smith's official discussion of virtue, along with how this feature of Smith's moral theory situates it in relation to Hume's. In seeing what makes justice special for Smith, we shall also see a major organizing principle of the vast, unfinished intellectual project of which TMS was only supposed to be a part. Thus, Section 3 also lays out the structure of this proposed project. Additionally, we consider there the potential impact of this structure both on Smith's political philosophy and on his understanding of justice as a virtue. The fourth section covers justice's partner in other-directedness, beneficence. In discussing Smith's account of this virtue, we will have opportunity to revisit questions bracketed in Section 6 of the previous chapter about how wide Smith takes the moral community to be and about how he thinks we should handle conflicts in how our social affections direct us. The fifth section covers the first virtue Smith discusses in TMS VI, prudence. It also comments on Smith's attitude toward the acquisition of wealth, a topic sure to be of special interest to readers coming to this book with either text-based knowledge or cultural awareness of the *Wealth of Nations*. The sixth section covers self-command. Smithian self-command is a special virtue in that it seems to involve the kind of self-governance via regard to the sentiments of the WIS that we flagged in Section 2 of the previous chapter as crucial to Smith's conception of the virtuous agent. Thus, the sixth section also covers the relationship between this virtue and the other three and, in doing so, tries to answer an interpretive question to which this relationship gives rise, that of whether Smith is committed to a thesis about the unity of virtue.

Section 1: Smith's General Schema of Virtue

The introductory and concluding sections of Part VI best lay out the general schema that structures Smith's account of virtue.[3] The introduction consists only of the observation that "when we consider the character of any individual," we do so in two ways: "as it may affect his own happiness" and "as it may affect that of other people" (VI.intro.1). By making this distinction in terms of evaluations of character, Smith demonstrates that while he uses the term "virtue" for both actions and traits, his answer to the nature of virtue question is mainly concerned with the latter. The distinction itself carries over from the one between self- and other-directed affections that, as we saw in Section 2 of the previous chapter, Smith uses to organize his survey of other virtue theories. The concluding section of TMS VI adds a third component to this distinction. While one category of virtue is rooted in "concern for our own happiness" and another is rooted in "concern for that of other people," a third category of virtue is rooted in our "regard either to what are, or to what ought to be, or to what upon a certain occasions would be, the sentiments of other people," or, more succinctly, "regard to the sentiments of the supposed impartial spectator." These three categories of affection—self-directed, other-directed, and mutual-sympathy-directed—give rise to four kinds of virtue: prudence (from our "selfish affections"), justice and beneficence (from our "benevolent affections"), and self-command (from our "regard to the sentiments of the supposed impartial spectator") (VI.concl.1).

This fourfold scheme presents us with at least two interpretative complications. The easier of the two to address concerns the status of the other positive traits to which Smith refers both within his discussions of prudence, justice, beneficence, and self-command and in a variety of other contexts; for example, in the paragraph just cited, he refers to "industry" and "frugality." Since there is no reason not to classify these traits as virtues and since Smith sometimes uses locutions like the "virtue*s* . . . of self-command," it is best to think of the additional traits as particular manifestations of the more general, officially recognized virtues of prudence, justice, beneficence, and self-command; obviously, on this suggestion, industry and frugality are particular virtues that are both aspects of the more general virtue of prudence (VI.concl .2; emphasis added).

The second complication concerns the relationship between self-command and the other three virtues. As we saw in Section 2 of the previous chapter, Smith believes that some kind of self-governance is necessary for virtue. And as we saw across that chapter and the one previous to it, Smith's principle of self-governance is precisely the regard for the sentiments of the WIS that typifies self-command. Thus, it seems that self-command is not just one of the four main virtues but a prerequisite for the other three. However, Smith sometimes suggests that while it is in practice difficult, it is in principle possible to have the other virtues without having self-command, which is necessary

> both to enforce and to direct the practice of all those virtues; and no man during, either the whole of his life, or that of any considerable part of it, ever trod steadily and uniformly in the paths of prudence, of justice, or of proper beneficence, whose conduct was not principally directed by a regard to the sentiments of the supposed impartial spectator, of the great inmate of the breast, the great judge and arbiter of conduct. (VI.concl.1)

We can square the view that the other virtues are in principle possible minus self-regulation via the WIS with the view that virtue in general requires some kind of self-regulation by treating the basic self- and other-directed affections underlying the other virtues as possible principles of governance, much in the same way that Hutcheson's and Epicurus's theories do. Respect for the WIS, then, would serve as a sort of meta-principle of internal governance[4] that is capable of governing the other ones but is not intrinsically necessary to their work. But is this what Smith thinks? Does he think it is in principle possible to have the other virtues without self-command? Does he think it is in principle possible to have self-command without the other virtues? Since we can only grapple with these questions after we have gone through his account of each virtue, we return to it at the end of the chapter. However, before going through his account of each virtue, we should consider Smith's view on the practical impact of such accounts.

Section 2: The Practical Impact of Answers to the Nature of Virtue Question

In the previous chapter, I did not comment on Smith's title for his chapter on Mandeville's skepticism about virtue, "Of Licentious Systems" (VII.ii.4).

The title fits, Smith believes, because unlike the other theories he discusses, Mandeville's theory does not have "the general tendency" of encouraging "the best and most laudable habits of the human mind" (VII.ii.4.5). Though perhaps Mandeville's theory "never gave occasion to more vice that what would have been without it, [it] at least taught that vice, which arose from other causes, to appear with more effrontery, and to avow the corruption of its motives with a profligate audaciousness which had never been heard of before" (VII.ii.4 .13). Smith's point is that while Mandeville's denial of the reality of virtue and emphasis on the social benefits of vice do not make anyone more vicious, they do make those who already are vicious more open about it. Presumably, Smith thinks that this openness is offensive and thus counterbalances whatever good there might be in vice being revealed. But he does not seem to think that Mandeville's view has any other negative impact on practice. Since Smith is acutely aware that shame is a powerful motivator, it is notable that he does not express worry that Mandeville's view can have a negative practical impact by making us feel less of it (e.g., III.2.9). Smith must think that Mandeville's view will not make the truly vicious feel less shame, as they are shameless already. But what about those who are actively trying to be more virtuous and less vicious? What happens if Mandeville convinces these people not only that there is no reason to feel shame for their vice but also that their effort to be virtuous is pointless because virtue is in principle impossible? The affects involved in these efforts are likely somewhat resistant to changes in beliefs, but it seems implausible that a person convinced her goal is in principle impossible to achieve would not desire it less. And if this happens, she will either remain at her current moral state or slide further toward viciousness. The former outcome would be consistent with what Smith says in that it only provides evidence of Mandeville's system stopping people from getting better. But the latter outcome would contradict what Smith says by providing evidence of Mandeville's system making people worse.

That Smith does not seem to take this last possibility seriously (though, as I argue in Section 2 of Chapter 7, he does respond in some way to the discouragement that might arise upon realizing that while in principle possible, virtue is *really hard* to achieve) is indicative of an ambivalence regarding *how much* practical impact that accounts of virtue can have. Tellingly, Smith uses extremely cautious language when he sums up the practical impact of each of the three positive accounts of virtue. "It may be true," Smith concedes, that "some of them . . . tend, in some measure, to break the balance of the affections, and to give the mind a particular bias to some principles of actions, beyond the proportion that is due to them" (VI.ii.2.1). Thus, Smith worries that the Stoics are generally better on "the great, the awful, and the respectable virtues, the virtues of self-government and self-command; fortitude, magnanimity upon fortune, [and] the contempt of all outward accidents" than they are on "the soft, the amiable, and the gentle virtues, all the virtues of indulgent humanity." In contrast, Smith worries that the "benevolent system" neglects the former kind of virtues, as well as the virtues having to do with "our own interest," for the sake of the latter. And Smith worries that while encouraging "the habits of caution, vigilance, sobriety, and judicious moderation," the "system" that "makes virtue consist in prudence only" degrades "equally both the amiable and respectable virtues" (VII.ii.4.2–4). But all three theories have a "general tendency" to make people better, though in unbalanced ways, "*if it was possible, by precept and exhortation*" alone to do so (VII.ii.4.5; emphasis added).

But despite his wariness of overstating the extent to which accounts of virtue can impact practice, Smith provides at least a sketch of *how* such accounts do so, to whatever extent that they do. For all the virtues but one, the virtue theorist can only "characterize [in general] the sentiments of the heart, upon which each particular virtue is founded" and "describe, in a general manner, what is the ordinary way of acting to which each virtue would prompt us." Thus, for these virtues, the philosopher only "present[s] us with agreeable and lively pictures of manners." However, these pictures can impact how we feel and act when "by the vivacity of their descriptions they inflame our natural love of virtue and increase our abhorrence of vice" (VII.iv.6); thus, they can "animate us to what is generous and noble" and "soften us to what is gentle and humane" (VII.iv.33). Furthermore, these pictures can impact our practice indirectly, by improving our moral judgment: "by the justness as well as delicacy of their observation they may often help both to correct and to ascertain our natural sentiments with regard to the propriety of conduct"; and "by suggesting many nice and delicate attentions, form us to a more exact justness of behavior, than what, without such instruction, we should have been apt to think of" (VII.iv.6).[5]

Smith's name for practical moral philosophy that treats virtue in this way is "Ethics" (VII.iv.6). He contrasts ethics with another legitimate kind of practical moral philosophy, "natural jurisprudence," which covers the only remaining virtue, justice. According to Smith, natural jurisprudence produces a different kind of content from what ethics does and impacts practice in a different kind of way from how ethics does. While the philosopher doing ethics produces depictions of different character types that can impact practice in the ways just described, the philosopher doing natural jurisprudence produces "a theory of the general principles which ought to run through and be the foundation of the laws of all nations" and can impact practice by providing standards against which to evaluate positive laws (VII.iv.37). (Lest we think that Smith is much more optimistic about the practical efficacy of natural jurisprudence than about ethics, we should note the list he provides of factors that can foster unjust positive law doubles as a list of factors that can impede the implementation of just ones: "the constitution of the state, that is, the interest of the government," "the interest of particular orders of men who tyrannize the government," "the rudeness and barbarism of the people," and "the unfortunate constitution of . . . courts of judicature" (VII.iv.36).)

So Smith believes that accounts of virtue can impact practice in two main ways; 1) by providing depictions of character that can inspire our feelings and conduct and can sharpen our moral judgment; and 2) by providing principles of just law that can help us morally improve our existent legal codes. While the first way in which a virtue theory can impact practice seems pretty familiar—we all know what role models are—the second seems flat-out odd, for it involves turning from virtue to something much different, law. As I have already mentioned, Smith believes that consideration of the virtue of justice alone invites this consideration of law. In the next section, we turn to Smith's reasons for believing this.

Section 3: Justice

Again and again, we have seen Smith argue against a philosophical position by insisting that it strays too far from some feature of common experience.

However, he takes his own account of justice to revise how the concept is often employed. "So far as I know," he tells us, the word "justice" has "several different meanings." In one sense of the word, "we are said not to do justice to our neighbor unless we conceive for him all that love, respect, and esteem" that are due to him. In another sense of the word, which is even "more extensive" than the previous one, "what is called justice means the same thing with exact and perfect propriety of conduct and behavior." Plato has this last sense in mind when he uses the term to stand for "the perfection of every sort of virtue." Smith, however, favors a third, much more limited sense, according to which "we are said to do justice to our neighbor when we abstain from doing him any positive harm, and do not directly hurt him, either in his person, or in his estate, or in his reputation" (VII.ii.1.10). In favoring the third sense of "justice," Smith is not merely asking us to recognize a new, technical usage. Rather, he is asking us to stop using the term in the first two ways. He believes that the first one picks out a totally different virtue with its own name, beneficence.[6] And he believes that confusion caused by the second one generates works on morality that "are generally as useless as they are commonly tiresome" (VII.iv.34). Attention to Smith's reasons for these revisions of common usage will reveal why he believes that justice is a subject for natural jurisprudence, not ethics, as well as why he rejects the kind of moral philosophy done in the aforementioned useless, tiresome works.

Let's begin with the relationship between the first sense of justice and the third. Smith's distinction between beneficence—covered by the first sense—and justice proper—covered by the third—is simple. Both are rooted in our "benevolent affections" (VI.concl.1) and thus have to do with how our characters "affect the happiness of other people" (VI.ii.intro.1). But while beneficence is the virtue of properly benefiting others, justice is the virtue of properly not hurting them. Justice, then, is "upon most occasions, but a negative virtue, and only hinders us from hurting our neighbor"; thus, "we may fulfill all the rules of justice by sitting still and doing nothing" (II.ii.1.9). So one reason why justice is not best handled by ethics is that there is not much to depict about just action, as it is fundamentally *in*action.[7] Thus, in the single paragraph Smith dedicates to justice in TMS VI, he writes:

> A sacred and religious regard not to hurt or disturb in any respect the happiness of our neighbor, even in those cases where no law can properly protect him, constitutes the character of the perfectly innocent and just man; a character which, when carried to a certain delicacy of attention, is always highly respectable and even venerable for its own sake, and can scarce ever fail to be accompanied with many other virtues, with great feeling for other people, with great humanity and great benevolence. It is a character sufficiently understood, and requires no further explanation. (VI .ii.intro.2)

Recall, however, that the ethicist depicts not only "the ordinary way of acting to which each virtue would prompt us" but also "the sentiment of heart, upon which each particular virtue is founded" (VII.iv.4–5). So even if the actions or inactions prompted by justice are simple enough to resist morally illuminative depiction, the sentiment underlying justice might not be. Even in the just-quoted passage, which casts aside the character trait of justice as requiring "no further explanation," Smith observes that this character "admits of a certain delicacy of attention" that "can scarce ever fail to be accompanied with many other virtues, with great feeling for other people, with great humanity and great benevolence." The fact that other virtues and sentiments usually accompany justice and the sentiments behind it does not necessarily imply that there is anything interesting to say about these sentiments, but the fact that they admit of being carried to a certain "delicacy of attention" suggests that there is.

After laying out his WIS theory of the development and operation of conscience and his account of the general moral rules that we induce from the particular mandates of conscience, Smith provides a positive account of the sentiments behind justice. He does so as part of an investigation into how much the "regard to those general rules of conduct . . . [which] is properly called a sense of duty" should motivate our conduct (III.5.1). He concludes that while in some cases "actions ought to arise chiefly or entirely from a sense of duty," in other cases "some other sentiment or affection ought to concur [with it], and have a principal influence" (III.6.2). Smith points to two sets of "circumstances" that determine this difference: "the precision and exactness, or the looseness and inaccuracy of the general rules" which the sense of duty regards, and "the natural agreeableness or deformity of the sentiments or affections which would prompt us to any action independent of all regard to general rules" (III.6.2). His discussion of the former set of circumstances provides a positive account of the sentiment behind just conduct.

Smith believes that the rules "which determine what are the offices of prudence, of charity, of generosity, of gratitude, of friendship"—i.e., all the virtues other than justice—are imprecise. The "best general rules" we can get for prudence are the "common proverbial maxims" rooted in "universal experience." It goes without saying that such rules are vague. We might think that rules of gratitude, such as the one "that as soon as we can we should make a return of equal, and if possible of superior value to the services we have received," are highly precise. But "the most superficial examination" reveals that even this rule is subject to "ten thousand exceptions":

> If your benefactor attended you in your sickness, ought you to attend him in his? Or can you fulfil the obligation of gratitude, by making a return of a different kind? If you ought to attend him, how long ought you attend him? The same time which he attended you, or longer, and how much longer? If your friend lent you money in your distress, ought you to lend him money in his? How much ought you to lend him? When ought you to lend him? Now, or to-morrow, or next month? And for how long a time? It is evident, that no general rule can be laid down, by which a precise answer can, in all cases, be given to any of these questions. The difference between his character and yours, between his circumstances and yours, may be such, that you may be perfectly grateful, and justly refuse to lend him a halfpenny: and, on the contrary, you may be willing to lend, or even to give him ten times the sum which he lent you, and yet justly be accused of the blackest ingratitude, and of not having fulfilled the hundredth part of the obligation you lie under. (III.6.9)

Such imprecision becomes even more obvious when we consider that even if we leave prudence aside, the demands of other-directed virtues like gratitude, charity, generosity, and friendship at least sometimes seem to pull against each other. Justice, on the other hand, generates strict rules that, as we'll soon see, always have priority. Recall that for Smith, justice is "upon most occasions, but a negative virtue, and only hinders us from hurting our neighbor" (II.ii.1.9). Thus, most rules of justice will simply spell out ways to avoid harming people. But even when justice demands positive action—it is only negative "upon *most* occasions"—it still generates precise rules, such as the following:

> If I owe a man ten pounds, justice requires that I should precisely pay him ten pounds, either at the time agreed upon, or when he demands it. What I ought to perform, how much I ought to perform, when and where I ought to perform it, the whole nature and circumstances of the action prescribed, are all of them fixt and determined.

Just as there is only one way not to harm someone in a certain way (Smith lists theft and adultery as examples here—earlier we saw him speak more generally in terms of injury to person, estate, or reputation), there is only one way to repay a debt (III.6.10). You simply don't harm someone in that way, and you simply repay the debt. Thus, while "the general rules of almost all the virtues . . . are in many respects loose and inaccurate, admit of many exceptions, and require . . . many modifications," "the rules of justice are accurate in the highest degree, and admit of no exceptions or modifications"; in this regard, "the rules of justice may be compared to the rules of grammar; the rules of the other virtues, to the rules which critics lay down for the attainment of what is sublime and elegant in composition" (III.6.9–11).

Bracketing for the time being the question of why exactly Smith believes the rules of justice are so precise, let's consider the general relationship between such precision and motivation. One obvious reason why Smith believes that the practice of virtues other than justice is best "directed by a certain idea of propriety, by a certain taste for a particular tenor of conduct, [rather] than by any regard to a precise maxim or rule" is there are no such precise maxims or rules (III.6.9). We already saw him make this point explicitly with respect to gratitude. He also makes this point explicitly with respect to the ways in which different forms of beneficence—which are what the positively other-directed virtues he lists seem to be—can seem to conflict; it is "altogether impossible," he observes, to "determine by any precise rules" what beneficence requires in such instances (VI.ii.1.22). However, since we do have *some* rules for these virtues, such as the aforementioned "common proverbial maxims of prudence" and rules of gratitude, it is important to note the moral mistake in acting mainly from "a very strict and literal adherence to them." Smith understandably observes that it would be "the most absurd and ridiculous pedantry" to attempt "in all circumstances" to act primarily from regard to such rules (III.6.9). But there is more to say about the WIS' disapproval of such motivation. It is easy to see how, for example, action from strict, literal application of the aforementioned rule of gratitude can be morally insufficient; imagine waiting until a friend experienced a similar tragedy—which may never even happen—to express gratitude in response to the support she offered during yours. And even if action mainly from strict, literal application of any of these rules gets things right on the conduct side, it might be done in the wrong way, without morally important motives that the WIS expects us to have.

Part of the reason why Smith believes that the practice of justice, on the other hand, should be directed by respect for precise rules of justice is that there *are* precise rules of justice, such as the one mentioned earlier. Of course, the fact that we can act mainly from regard to such rules does not mean that we should. Thus, there must be moral reasons why "the actions of this virtue are never so properly performed, as when the chief motive for performing them is a reverential and religious regard to those general rules which require them" (II.6.10). In order to grasp these reasons, we should consider how general rules function in deliberation. Recall that for Smith, we form the "general maxims of morality" via "induction" from the "great variety of particular cases [of] what pleases or displeases our moral faculties" (VI.iii.2.6). We then employ these rules as shortcuts in deliberation that prevent us from momentarily rationalizing conduct that we know, deep down, is wrong. But even though these rules gain authority and motivational force for us "when they have been fixed in our minds by habitual reflection," they inherit this authority and motivational force from the more fundamental authority and motivational force of our consciences, which we follow out of our desire for mutual sympathy with the WIS (III.4.12). This picture leaves open the possibility of cases in which our consciences, which are more context-sensitive than the rules but less so than our momentary impulses, overturn the verdicts of at least some of the rules. The main job of the rules, then, is to make us suspect ourselves of rationalizing when we entertain the possibility that we are dealing with an exception.[8] But it remains possible that after this second-guessing, conscience reveals that we *are* indeed dealing with an exception and thus that we should not act in the way that the rule prescribes. When it does so, conscience guides us by considering "the end and foundation of the rule, more than the rule itself." Obviously, when the rules are inherently imprecise, as they are regarding all the virtues but justice, this appeal to their spirit should happen all the time. So "in the practice of the other virtues, our conduct should rather be directed by a certain idea of propriety, by a certain taste for a particular tenor of conduct" that we see as called for after consideration of the "end and foundation" of the rules they generate. But Smith worries that the moment we begin questioning whether the spirit of a rule of justice applies to our present situation, we begin to "chicane" with our consciences. For example, we might falsely tell ourselves that since the point of these rules is "to hinder us from hurting our neighbor," we can justly break them in this particular case because "this particular violation could do no hurt"; if we become good enough at providing ourselves with such a "pretext of reason," we can license our performance of any kind of injustice (III.6.9–10). Appeals to conscience in such cases are inevitably dishonest because we know that any appeal to the conscience upon which the precise rules of justice are based should bring us right back to the precise rules of justice themselves; thus, we only ever make such an appeal because we are looking for a way to justify what we know, deep down, is injustice. Smith's idea seems to be that it is morally dangerous to be motivated to perform a justice-relevant action from any other consideration than regard to a rule of justice because any additional motive can always trigger rationalizing deliberation.[9]

Thus, Smith believes that justice should be motivated mainly by a regard to its precise rules because the presence of other motives is not only unnecessary but morally dangerous in that it increases the possibility of our doing the wrong thing if not then, then at future times. So the WIS approves acting justly mainly from respect for the rules of justice because such a motive is the most trustworthy guarantee of just conduct. But does the WIS also expect us to act from this motive because it is more directly or intrinsically appropriate?[10] This is a difficult question. The answer seems to be "yes," but it is hard to see exactly why. For the WIS to see motivation by regard to the rules of justice as intrinsically appropriate, he would have to sympathize with this motivation.

We have already seen that the WIS would always be motivated by such a regard because he knows that the alternative introduces the danger of rationalization. But perhaps the WIS is also always motivated by such a regard because such a regard rests upon the desire to make one's sentiments line up with the WIS' sentiments, which, as the self-approving bearer of those sentiments, the WIS also has. However, this would not explain why in matters of justice, the WIS is *solely* motivated by a regard to the rules governing them.

Another possible reason why the just agent should be motivated by respect for the rules of justice emerges from Smith's discussion of the other set of "circumstances" that determines the extent to which conduct should be motivated by a sense of duty, that of "the natural agreeableness or deformity of the sentiments or affections which would prompt us to any action independent of all regard to general rules" (III.6.2). Recall from Section 3 of Chapter 3 that the agreeableness or disagreeableness of a sentiment determines our—and thus the WIS'—propensity to sympathize with it. Partly because "benevolent and social affections" are agreeable, we are prone to sympathizing with them; as we saw in Section 4 of Chapter 3, we are also prone to sympathizing them via "redoubled sympathy" (III.6.4). Thus, the WIS prefers benevolent and social actions done from these affections to benevolent and social actions done from a sense of duty, even if both get things right. Since, as we also saw in Section 4 of Chapter 3, selfish passions inhabit "a sort of middle place" with regard to our sympathetic tendencies, we are sometimes prone to sympathizing with them and sometimes not. Thus, the WIS sometimes prefers self-interested actions done from these passions to self-interested actions done from a sense of duty. (More specifically, Smith observes that while "in all common, little, and ordinary cases," we should act from regard to general rules, in cases involving "the more extraordinary and important objects of self-interest," we should act "with some degree of earnestness for their own sake"; the idea is that it is petty to get worked up about small matters but "mean-spirited" to not care much about big opportunities (III.6.4–7).[11]) And since "malevolent and unsocial passions" are disagreeable and, as we saw too in Section 4 of Chapter 3, causes of "divided sympathy," we are averse to sympathizing with them. Thus, the WIS would prefer that they never motivate action. However, the WIS also recognizes that an action they cause can sometimes be warranted. The only example Smith recognizes of such an action is punishment (cf. VI.ii.intro.2). Thus, the WIS believes that when punishment is warranted, it should be conducted solely from a sense of duty that "considers only the general rule, which determines what vengeance is due for each particular offence" (III.6.5).

The plausible intuition here is that while we should willingly act socially, from actual goodwill, we should punish others reluctantly, from a sense of obligation. This observation might present another way to understand why the WIS would think that the sense of duty is the intrinsically most appropriate motive for just actions, but only if the virtue of justice itself prompts us to punish. Smith does not say that it does. But that his view implies this is not ruled out by the fact that punishment is a positive action. Sure, justice is the fundamentally negative virtue of not harming others. Yet as we just saw, justice also demands some actions, such as repaying debts. So justice could also demand the positive action of punishing a wrongdoer. Moreover, just as repaying a debt can be construed as a way of not harming the creditor, the possibility of which is generated by the underlying agreement, punishing a wrongdoer can be construed as a way of not harming a victim, whose resentment demands a structurally similar "return [of] evil for evil that has been done" (II.i.1.4). So there are reasons to believe that punishment is an act prompted by the virtue of justice, though one that should only be done from a sense of duty. If this is correct, we at least have an explanation for why *one* kind of act of justice should always be done solely from a regard to the rules of justice. However, it would remain the case that the main reason Smith offers for why other kinds of acts of justice should be so motivated is only that this best guarantees just action.

Thus far we have seen reason to believe that there is more to say about the conduct and, especially, the sentiments of the just character than Smith lets on in TMS VI. While justice is fundamentally a negative virtue, it does sometimes call for positive action, such as the repayment of a debt or—maybe—the punishment of a wrongdoer.[12] The sentiment behind this positive action is a regard to the rules of justice. And lest we believe that this sense of duty is only enacted in these specified cases of positive just action, we should remember that the inaction at the foundation of justice often requires self-restraint. Thus, we can say that the just character is a person who performs some actions and does not perform others and who has a strong sense of duty, understood as respect for the rules of justice, which are induced from the particular verdicts of the WIS. Still, we can say more than this. This person must either never have positively malicious motives or only have ones weak enough to be trumped by the sense of duty. And that's not all, as the self-restraint involved in negative justice is rarely even of positively malicious motives. Injustice more commonly arises from "excessive and extravagant" self-preference that leads us to "justle, or throw down" someone with whom we are competing for a good or that leads us to sacrifice another person's interests in order to "prevent our own ruin" or even "small misfortune." As I pointed out in Section 4 of Chapter 3, this means that Smithian agents can act demeritoriously and thus unjustly not only when they actively try to hurt others but also when they do not sufficiently consider others' interests (cf. VII.ii.3.5). Smith even claims that there are forms of reckless action or "gross negligence," such as throwing "a large stone over a wall into a public street without giving warning to those who might be passing by, and without regarding where it was likely to fall," that constitute "real injustice" (II.iii.2.8). Thus, the just character has another feature besides a strong sense of duty and absent or weak malicious motives. In keeping with justice's status as a negative virtue that is distinct from beneficence, this additional feature is not so much increased positive care for others as it is decreased care for ourselves in relation to them (cf. I.i.5.5; III.3.8–20). There is also more to say about this relative decrease of self-love. The just character's realization that to the WIS, "he is but one of the multitude in no respect better than any other in it" indicates more than just the mere absence of self-love excessive enough to make him appear "the whole world to himself" (II.ii.2.1). It also indicates the development of a positive, for lack of a better word, mindset regarding the relative importance of one's own interests in comparison with others, albeit a positive mindset that manifests itself in action negatively, via self-restraint. This mindset is what Smith seems to have in mind as subject to being "carried to a certain delicacy of attention" (VI.intro.2).[13]

If there is this much to say about the conduct and sentiments of the just character, then why not treat it as a subject for ethics, the science in which Smith is clearly engaged in TMS VI? I think the best way to interpret Smith on this point is by de-emphasizing his view that the virtue of justice is inappropriate for ethics while emphasizing his view that it is simply better handled by another science. Smith does in fact hold the former view, as he remarks that the just character is one "sufficiently understood, and requires [none of the] further explanation" ethics would provide. But as we have seen, it is not the case that there is nothing to say about the just character, even if there is perhaps less to say about this character than about those implicated by the other virtues; after all, its practice remains fundamentally negative and rule-governed, and the sentiments involved in it remain definable mainly in terms of what is necessary to act from respect for these rules. The more important reason why justice gets short shrift in TMS VI, then, is that it is really "the subject of a particular science . . . that of natural jurisprudence," which is different from the one with which TMS VI is concerned.

Since Smith believed that natural jurisprudence "is of all sciences by far the most important, but hitherto, perhaps the least cultivated," we should frame our discussion of why justice is so perfectly suited for it with a brief overview of his account of its historical development (VI.ii.intro.2). Smith believes that in the study of ethics, we would do well to follow "ancient moralists," like Aristotle and Cicero. As we saw in the previous section's description of ethics, they sought "to characterize the sentiment of the heart upon which each particular virtue is founded" and "to describe . . . the ordinary way of acting to which each virtue would prompt us." These characterizations and descriptions are necessarily general. Since "it is impossible . . . to express all the variations which each sentiment either does or ought to undergo, according to every possible variation of circumstances," it is equally impossible to express all the variations of conduct produced by these sentiments; the best one can do is to provide a general account of "the alterations which they occasion in the countenance, in the air and external behavior, the resolutions they suggest, [and] the actions they prompt." As we also saw in the previous section, Smith believes these sorts of accounts of virtuous sentiments and conduct can have a positive impact on our conduct and moral judgment via mainly non-argumentative means. In offering "vivac[ious] descriptions," they can "inflame our natural love of virtue, and increase our abhorrence of vice." And in providing, to the extent possible for the subject matter, "[just] as well as [delicate] . . . observations," they can "help both to correct and to ascertain our natural sentiments with regard to the propriety of conduct" (VII.iv.1–6).

In studying ethics alone, however, the ancient moralists overlooked the domain of morality that admits of more precision. "Cicero and Aristotle," for example, mistakenly "treat of justice in the same general manner in which they treat of all the other virtues" (VII.iv.37). True progress was only made by "those who in this and in the preceding century have treated of what is called natural jurisprudence" (VII.iv.7). (Having seen that Smith wants us to revise how we think and talk about justice, we should not be surprised that he believes that the proper science of it is relatively new.) This advancement culminated in the work of Hugo Grotius whose "treatise of the laws of war and peace, with all its imperfections, is perhaps at this day the most complete work that has yet been given on this subject" (VII.iv.37). Obviously, as we saw in the previous section, works in natural jurisprudence can have just as significant a practical impact as can works of ethics. Just as the latter can transform individual characters, the former can transform bodies of positive law.

The progress from the study of ethics alone to the study of ethics and natural jurisprudence was not, however, completely smooth. Along the way, thinkers of "the middle and later ages of the Christian church" (VII.iv.7) developed a third kind of science, that of "casuistry," which, Smith argues, "ought to be rejected altogether" (VII.iv.34). Unlike the ancient moralists but like the philosophers of natural jurisprudence, the casuists "endeavor to lay down exact and precise rules." Also like the philosophers of natural jurisprudence, they rightly focused their attention "chiefly" on justice. But, Smith argues, the casuists thought about justice in the wrong way. More specifically, they thought about justice in a way that blended together the third with the second, broadest sense of justice identified earlier that covers "the direction of every circumstance of behavior." Rather than trying to prescribe rules for conduct that is undeserved of "external punishment," they tried to "prescribe rules for the conduct of a good man," who acts with "exact and scrupulous delicacy" and thus is "entitled to considerable praise" (VII.iv.8).

To highlight the difference between these two approaches, Smith uses the "trite example" of a promise made to "a highwayman" upon "fear of death." According to natural jurisprudence, since the highwayman's extortion of the promise was already a crime deserved of punishment, there is no way that he or a judge acting on his behalf would "be entitled to use force to constrain the other person to perform." However, the casuist wants to find a rule telling us what the all-things-considered best action would be. Sure, we do not deserve punishment if we break the promise. But it also seems that we should have some regard to our "own dignity and honour" and "reverence [for] the law of truth." According to "the common sentiments of mankind . . . some regard" is due to such promises, but "it is impossible to determine how much, by any general rule that will apply to all cases without exception." How willing was the promiser? How much money was promised? Does the promiser have dependents? How did the highwayman treat the promiser? Would keeping this promise interfere with the promiser's other, "more sacred" duties, "such as regard to the public interest," which are *themselves* impossible to formulate via general rules? Smith's point is that the moral relevance of all these circumstances to the question of how to act with "exact propriety" in such a situation render it impossible to achieve the casuist aim of answering it with precise general rules (VII.iv.7–12).

The casuists went on to cover "many other parts of Christian and moral duty" (VII.iv.16). In addition to what Smith recognizes as "the rules of justice," which cover "how far we ought to respect the life and property of our neighbor [and] the duty of restitution," the casuists dealt with the "laws of chastity and modesty, and wherein consisted what, in their language, are called the sins of concupiscence; the rules of veracity, and the obligation of oaths, promises, and contracts of all kinds" (VII.iv.32). Sometimes, violations of rules regarding sexual conduct and truth-telling positively injure people and thus count as violations of the Smithian rules of justice. Via natural psychological mechanisms, these violations produce shame and "remorse," which is "made up of shame from the sense of impropriety of past conduct; of grief for the effects of it; of pity for those who suffer by it; and of dread and terror of punishment from the consciousness of the justly provoked resentment of all rational creatures" (II.ii.2.3). But even the violations of these rules that do not injure anyone, Smith claims, prompt "shame" and "contrition." (Smith does not really explain why shame and contrition follow in these cases. He says that such actions violate a "pretty plain rule," but it is not clear what this has to do with shame and contrition. Perhaps Smith thinks that if a rule is clear enough and socially established enough, the experience of violating it resembles the shame- and contrition-causing experience of violating the rules of justice (VII.iv.21–2).) Shame and contrition led agents to confess all their violations of these rules to clergyman, once "the custom of auricular confession, [was] introduced by the Roman Catholic superstition, in times of barbarism and ignorance." This practice generated the first "books of casuistry," which were collections of "what are called cases of conscience, nice and delicate situations in which it is hard to determine the whereabouts the propriety of conduct may lie" (VII.iv.16–17). But in focusing not solely on what we are obligated to do to avoid deserving punishment but on what we should do full-stop, even if only in certain domains, these books "attempted, to no purpose, to direct by precise rules what it belongs to feeling and sentiment only to judge of":

> How is it possible to ascertain by rules the exact point at which, in every case, a delicate sense of justice begins to run into a frivolous and weak scrupulosity of conscience? When it is that secrecy and reserve begin to grow into dissimulation? How far an agreeable irony may be carried, and at what precise point it begins to degenerate into a detestable lie? What is the highest pitch of freedom and ease of behavior which can be regarded as graceful and becoming, and when it is that it first begins to run into a negligent and thoughtless licentiousness? With regard to all such matters, what would hold good in any one case would scarce do exactly in any other, and what constitutes the propriety and happiness of behavior varies in every case with the smallest variety of situation.

These books, "therefore, are generally as useless as they are commonly tiresome." There is little chance that the cases they discuss will be sufficiently similar to whatever particular dilemma we are facing. And their "dry and disagreeable," legalistic "style" makes them unable to "animate us to what is generous or noble" or "soften us to what is gentle and humane." If they have any practical impact, it will be the negative one of teaching "us to chicane with our own consciences" with "vain subtilties" and "evasive refinements" (VII .iv.33). (Interestingly, Smith believes that while appeal to rules can prevent rationalization, appeal to rules can also enable it.)

The result, then, is that ethics and natural jurisprudence are the only "two useful parts of [practically oriented] moral philosophy" (VII.iv.34). As we saw in the previous section, practitioners of natural jurisprudence aim to produce "a theory of the general principles which ought to run through and be the foundation of the laws of all nations" (VII.iv.37). What does Smith take to be the connection between this project and the virtue of justice? The key to this connection lies in main differences between justice and the other virtues. As we have seen, the rules regarding justice are more precise than the rules regarding the other virtues. And as we have seen, unlike the vices corresponding to the other virtues, those corresponding to injustice are worthy of punishment. It is obvious why these two features of the virtue of justice help transform the study of it into the study of law. The precision of the rules of justice lends itself to concretization in legal codes. And the worthiness of punishment that is the consequence of injustice morally justifies the legal enforcement of the virtue; moreover, as Smith points out, punishment is better handled by political institutions than by individuals because "confusion . . . would attend upon every man's doing justice to himself" (VII.iv.36–7).[14] But why does Smith believe that the rules of justice are so precise? And why does he believe that injustice is worthy of punishment?

The second question is easier to answer than the first one. Since justice is the fundamentally negative virtue of properly not harming people, injustice is the fundamentally negative vice of improperly harming people. More specifically, injustice involves "actions of a hurtful tendency, which proceed from improper motives," including, as we saw earlier, not only malice but also selfishness or carelessness that is excessive enough to blind or numb us to the impact of our conduct on others (II.ii.i.2). Such conduct from such motives produces resentment which, as we saw in the discussion of judgments of merit in Chapter 3, Section 4, is the sentiment that "most immediately and directly prompts us to punish" (II.i.1.2). In approving of the resentment that injustice provokes, then, the WIS approves of the punishment of the unjust agent (even though the WIS would ultimately prefer that this punishment not be done from resentment). Thus, injustice essentially warrants punishment in a way that other vices, which do not produce resentment and a desire to punish, do not. Since failures of beneficence, for example, "excite dislike and disapprobation" or even "hatred," but not resentment and a desire to punish, the WIS would not approve of punishing them (II.ii.1.3–4).

Smith does not explicitly answer the first question. Rather than telling us why the rules of justice are so precise, he provides an example of a precise one—that regarding repayment of a debt—from which he expects us to generalize. Since Smithian moral rules are all derived from particular instances of WIS sympathy, they must somehow inherit their precision or looseness from these instances. Thus, there must be something especially precision-friendly about the sympathy with resentment upon which the rules of justice are based. Resentment has several features that are possible sources of precision. Since resentment is usually a response to some kind of pain, one possibility is that sympathy focused on this pain is somehow more precise than sympathy focused on pleasure. Smith does believe that there are important differences between sympathy with pain and sympathy with pleasure.[15] One difference is that "our propensity to sympathy with joy is much stronger than our propensity to sympathy with sorrow." Another is that sympathy with joy "approaches much more nearly to the vivacity of what is naturally felt by the persons principally concerned" than does sympathy with sorrow (I.iii.1.5). The reason for the first difference is "it is agreeable to sympathize with joy," but "painful to go along with grief." The reason for the second difference is that the "ordinary [emotional] state of mankind" is much closer to the naturally limited heights of joy than to the naturally limitless depths of sorrow; thus, the unavoidable affective gap between sympathizer and agent is always potentially narrower in the former case (I.iii.1.8–9). The second difference seems to render sympathy with pain *less* precise than sympathy with pleasure in the sense of more accurately capturing what the agent actually feels. However, Smith continues that these differences notwithstanding, sympathy with sorrow is both "in some sense, more universal" and "generally a more lively and distinct perception" than is sympathy with joy. The reason for the former is that our sympathy with pain is degreed, while our sympathy with pleasure is "complete" or nothing; thus, we sympathize with pain at least to some extent more often than we do with pleasure (I.iii.1.1–2). The reason for the latter is that "pain . . . whether of mind or body, is a more pungent sensation than pleasure"; thus, even though sympathy with pleasure more closely mirrors an agent's actual feelings than does sympathy with pain, sympathy with pain is generally more intense because pain itself is generally more intense (I.iii.1.3; cf. I.iii.1.8; III.2.13; III.2.16; and VII.ii.2.6). Sympathy with pain, then, is especially frequent and notable. Thus, the rules of justice based in part upon this sympathy with pain might get their precision not from the fact that this sympathy is especially accurate but from the fact that it happens often and obviously.

This interpretation has several shortcomings. One is that the frequency and notability with which we sympathize with pain seems better suited to account for why we *care* so much about rules of justice than for why these rules are so precise. Another is that in stressing sympathy with the pain caused by injustice, this interpretation potentially overlooks the injustice of attempted but unsuccessful harm or even inconsequential gross negligence; surely, we could broaden our conception of the pain or harm caused by injustice so as to include that caused solely by the attitude demonstrated by the agent, but more would have to be said to explain this point. A third shortcoming of this interpretation is that while it might account for the difference of precision between rules based on sympathy with pleasure and rules based on sympathy with pain, it does not account for the difference of precision between rules based on sympathy with some kind of pain and rules based on sympathy with other kinds of pain. Smith is clear that the "mere want of beneficence" can be painful by "disappoint[ing] us of the good which might reasonably be expected" (II.ii.1.3). Yet he is also clear, as we have seen, that the rules of beneficence are imprecise. So there must be something about sympathy with this kind of pain that is not conducive to precision, but something about sympathy with the kind of pain involved in injustice that is conducive to precision. Obviously, general differences between sympathy with pleasure and sympathy with pain cannot explain this.

These last two shortcomings suggest an alternative source of precision for the rules of justice, one rooted in a more specific feature of the sympathy with resentment upon which they are based. Recall that for Smith, when we experience resentment,

> what chiefly enrages us against the man who injures or insults us, is the little account which he seems to make of us, the unreasonable preference which

> he gives to himself above us, that absurd self-love, by which he seems to imagine, that other people may be sacrificed at any time, to his conveniency or his humour. (II.iii.1.5)

Here Smith observes that the ultimate target of resentment is the offender's disrespectfulness, sense of superiority, or something articulable along these lines, rather than pain or harm understood in a general enough way to make them separable from these attitudes. (Though as I just hinted, there might be good reasons to classify being subject to these kinds of attitude as a kind of harm.) By focusing on sympathy with the resenter's disapproval of this attitude, we can see why the rules of justice would cover attempted but unsuccessful harm and even inconsequential gross negligence, as both involve this attitude. We can also see why the rules of justice do not cover conduct that disappoints expectations of benevolence, as such conduct does not include this attitude. Tellingly, rules based upon such disappointment come closest in precision to those of justice when they involve ingratitude—Smith observes that of all the duties "which the beneficent virtues prescribe to us," those of gratitude generate "the most accurate" general rules—which demonstrates something close to this attitude (III.6.9). The attitude we adopt toward others when we accept their positive services ungratefully is strikingly similar to the attitude we adopt toward others when we sacrifice their interests to advance our own. Both attitudes seem to involve seeing others as beneath us in some way; the difference is that in ungratefulness, this attitude manifests itself in our reaction to what others have done, while in injustice, this attitude manifests itself in our action toward them.

Thus, at least given what Smith's rules of justice cover, it seems that sympathy with the resenter's objection to the offender's disrespectfulness or sense of superiority is a more likely foundation for them than is sympathy with the resenter's pain, generally understood. (Sympathy with the resenter's desire to punish the offender is another promising candidate, but since it is consequent to our objection to the offender's attitude, it likely only helps at a secondary level.) But we have not yet seen how this kind of sympathy generates precision. The precision of the rules of justice consists in their being relatively unconditional. They are only relatively unconditional in that they still can "admit of . . . exceptions and modifications"; they do not have to take absolute forms like "always do this" and "never do that." These exceptions and modifications just must be able to "be ascertained as accurately as the rules themselves, and . . . generally . . . flow from the very same principles with them" (III.6.10). In other words, the precise rules of justice can contain built-in qualifications, but these must be obvious and must not make the rules unwieldy. This means, then, that the sympathy upon which such rules are based must itself be distinctive and consistent across contexts, even if it undergoes some minor modifications here and there. If this sympathy is with the experience of being disrespected or degraded, then this experience must be cross-contextually distinctive and stable enough to ground either rules like "always do this" and "never do that" or versions of such rules with a few obvious qualifications attached.

Obviously, there are reasons to be skeptical that there is such an experience.[16] However, we can make three points in Smith's defense. The first is that Smith's distinction between ethics and natural jurisprudence only requires that the rules of justice be *more* precise than the rules derived from the other virtues; the former are "accurate in the *highest degree*," he tells us (III.6.10). This difference could still be real even if there is reason to believe that the supposed sources of precision in the rules of justice do not allow for precision in some more absolute sense. And after all, the notion that it is easier to spell out precise rules for avoiding things that are bad for everyone than it is to spell out precise rules for promoting things that are good for everyone does seem intuitive.[17]

Here is the second point to be made in Smith's defense. It seems likely that if there is a cross-contextually distinctive, consistent experience with which the WIS sympathizes and thereby generates the precise rules of justice, this experience must be describable only in the thinnest terms and thus generate only the most formal rules. Maybe there is a universally distinct and stable experience of being disrespected that can take an infinite variety of context-sensitive forms. Any rules derived from such an experience will be so general as to appear practically useless. A rule like "don't disrespect or degrade people" does not tell us much about what to do or not do.[18] Smith clearly has something at least a bit more specific in mind. We saw that he cites a rule of justice against breaking contracts. He also believes that justice rules out murder, theft (II.ii.

2.2), and the damage of someone's good "reputation" (II.ii.1.9). Furthermore, he believes that these rules can be ranked in order of importance in terms of the strength of resentment the WIS would feel in response to their violation. For example, since death "excites the highest degree of resentment," it is "the greatest evil which one man can inflict upon another"; thus, murder is "the most atrocious of all crimes which affect individuals only." And since the loss of "that which we are possessed of" involves more suffering and prompts more resentment than the disappointment "of what we have only the expectation," "theft and robbery are greater crimes . . . than breach of contract" (II.ii.2.2).[19] Maybe these specific rules and their ranking do rest on universal experiences. But it seems unlikely, especially since given the obvious context-sensitivity of practices regarding property and reputation. Nevertheless, we could maintain the spirit of Smith's project by thinking of them as the ways in which the underlying, unchanging rules of justice manifest themselves within a context, given its history and cultural background. In going this road, we could still think of those highly formal, unchanging rules of justice as potentially useful critical tools for evaluating specific positive laws, though perhaps only from within the specific contexts in which the positive laws arise.[20]

Here is the third point to be made in Smith's defense. It is not obvious that Smith's success in the supposed science of natural jurisprudence depends entirely upon his ability to explain fully why the rules of justice are more precise than the rules derived from the other virtues. We could evaluate his "general principles" for evaluating "systems of positive law" in the same way we often evaluate normative theories, by seeing if they spit out the verdicts that best align with our considered intuitions (VII.iv.36). It is for a reason like this, I believe, that even though he never explains the precision of the rules of justice in the TMS, Smith feels comfortable ending the book by promising to write "another discourse" that will present his natural jurisprudence (VII.iv.37). (That he feels the need to engage in such a project should come as no surprise. As we have already seen, he believes that there are many "imperfections" in the currently best attempt at natural jurisprudence; he also believes that, in general, "the greatest part of authors whose profess design was to treat of jurisprudence" sometimes failed to keep their projects free from any casuistry (VI.iv.15).)

Smith plans for this other discourse "to give an account of the general principles of law and government, and of the different revolutions that they have undergone in the different ages and periods of society, not only in what concerns justice, but in what concerns police, revenue, and arms, and whatever else is the object of law" (VII.iv.36–7). In a two paragraph preface Smith added to the sixth edition of the TMS, he tells us that between 1759, when that proposal was first published, and 1790, when the sixth edition was published, he was only able to complete the "police, revenue, and arms, and whatever else is the object of law" portion of the project.[21] This was done in the *Wealth of Nations*. He did not live to complete the part of the project concerning "justice" proper.[22] He apparently had made significant progress, but all of it was burned at his request upon his death. Thankfully, as mentioned in the introduction, we have access to two sets of student notes from his lectures on the subject. These notes have been the subject of some excellent scholarship, most notably Haakonssen's *The Science of a Legislator*. It would be foolhardy to attempt even a sketch of Smith's full-blown theory of natural jurisprudence here. However, two crucial components of it get grounded in the TMS, and a third gets at least touched upon. All three, then, warrant some of our attention.

The first is its spectatorial theory of rights. Smith's natural jurisprudence turns on a theory of natural rights that are rooted in the WIS' sympathy with resentment.[23] In sympathizing with resentment, the WIS recognizes a natural right "antecedent to the institution of civil government" that each "individual . . . [has] both to defend himself from injuries, and to exact a certain degree of punishment for those which have been done to him" (II.ii.1.7).

The second component of Smith's natural jurisprudence that gets grounded in the TMS is its theory of punishment. As we have seen, Smith believes that punishment is justified when the WIS would sympathize with resentment that prompts it. We can derive from this view more detail regarding the features of justified punishment by considering the ends proposed by the resentment that wins sympathy from the WIS. Smith tells us that resentment "prompts us to beat off the mischief which is attempted to be done to us" (II.ii.1.4). Thus, in sympathizing with resentment, the WIS justifies punishment for the sake of defense against injury. Smith also believes that resentment makes us want a person who has injured us to "grieve for that particular wrong," so that he is "made to repent and be sorry for this very action" (II.i.1.6). Thus, in sympathizing with resentment, the WIS justifies punishment for the sake of retribution. Building on what the language of "repent" suggests, Smith later observes that "frequently the principal end proposed in our revenge" is "to bring [its object] back to a more just sense of what is due to other people," to make its object "sensible, that the person whom he injured did not deserve to be treated" so badly (II.iii.1.5). Thus, in sympathizing with resentment, the WIS justifies punishment for the sake of rehabilitation.

Smith also *seems* to think that through the action it prompts us to take toward its object, resentment aims at making "others, through fear of the like punishment . . . terrified from being guilty of the like offense" (II.i.1.6). He makes a claim like this at least twice (cf. II.ii.1.4). But in both instances, the combination of the locution he uses to express this claim and the context in which he does so makes it unclear whether he is saying that resenters aim at setting an example or whether by fulfilling their resentment, resenters happen to end up setting an example. The locution I have in mind is a "that" clause, which could operate as a "such that" clause when he says that resentment demands the offender "must be made to repent and be sorry for this very action, *that others, through fear of the like punishment, may be terrified from being guilty of the like offense*"; the contexts I have in mind are that of pointing either to the tendency that resentment has to "produce all the political ends of punishment" or "to the purpose for which nature has given us" resentment (II.i.1.6; emphasis added; II.ii.1.4).[24] One might wonder why it matters whether Smith justifies punishment on grounds of deterrence at least partly via the WIS' sympathy with resentment or solely via some other means. The issue is that if the latter is the case, we seem to end up with an interpretive puzzle.

Most likely with Hume in mind,[25] Smith points out that if we notice that "no social intercourse can take place among men who do not generally abstain from injuring one another," we might think that "the consideration of this necessity . . . was the ground upon which we approved of the enforcement of the laws of justice." On this account, we approve of punishment not because we realize that the WIS sympathizes with the resentment that prompts it but because we realize that it has social utility for both incapacitating an offender and, more importantly for the present discussion, deterring future offenders: by punishment, "the disturber of public peace is removed out of the world, and others are terrified by his fate from imitating his example" (II.ii.3.6). Smith concedes to this account that we do sometimes appeal to the utility of punishment as a secondary consideration, as when we need to steel our resolve in the face of the "pity" that even justified punishment triggers or when we need to shut up the "young and licentious" when they, usually insincerely, ridicule "the most sacred rules of morality" (II.ii.3.7–8). But no matter how obvious "the necessity of justice to the existence of society" might be, not everyone has noticed it. Yet everyone does "abhor fraud, perfidy, and injustice, and delight to see them punished" (II.ii.3.9). Thus, these reactions cannot be rooted in reflections upon social utility. Furthermore, it is "obvious" that we approve of the "punishment of crimes committed against individuals" not out of "regard to the preservation of society" but out of "a concern for that very individual who has been injured"; in suggesting otherwise, the account that appeals to the utility of punishment gets things backwards (II.ii.3.10). However—and here is where the puzzle arises—there are some cases in which "we both punish and approve of punishment, merely from a view to the general interest of society." Smith gives the example of a "centinel . . . who falls asleep upon his watch, [and] suffers death by the laws of war, because such carelessness might endanger the whole army." This punishment is "just and proper" because "nothing can be more just than that the many should be preferred to the one . . . when the preservation of an individual is inconsistent with the safety of the multitude." But the punishment "always appears to be excessively severe" because we do not actually resent the sentinel, at least not in the way we do a "murderer or parricide." Smith concludes that our reactions to these two kinds of cases must be founded upon "very different sentiments" (II.ii.3.11). And if this is so, then, contrary to Smith's argument against Hume, not all punishment is justified via the WIS' sympathy with resentment. Punishment, especially for the sake of deterrence, as the sentinel's punishment appears to be, can also be justified by considerations of social utility.

It is possible that Smith's views of the psychological source of judgments of justice comes apart from his views on what justifies these judgments. Perhaps

Smith believes that judgments of justice have their origins in sympathy with resentment but are justified by considerations that include utility. If so, the sentinel case presents no problem. But in the context of this very discussion of punishment, he argues that our hatred of injustice is justified by its "intrinsic hatefulness and detestableness" (II.ii.3.8). Obviously, there are questions about the meaning and metaethical implications of these comments; we grapple with them in Section 1 of the next chapter. But regardless of the answers to those questions, these comments give us at least prima facie reason to doubt that Smith takes our judgments of justice to be justified by utility. Another option is to insist that in these passages Smith is not trying to justify our judgments about justice at all. On this suggestion, Smith is at most reporting how we think that these judgments are justified. But his report is that we generally think they are justified by the sympathy of the WIS, not by considerations of utility. So even on this new suggestion, the exception of the sentinel case remains a problem, albeit one about how our justifications for judgments of punishment work rather than one about what justifies these judgments per se.

Since the sentinel case goes back on Smith's view that justice is fundamentally grounded—in whatever sense—in the WIS' sympathy with resentment, we must figure out how to make sense of it. If the appeal to social utility grounds the justice of punishing the sentinel, then it appears that not all judgments of justice are grounded in the WIS' sympathy with resentment. Before we react to this possibility with a shoulder shrug on the grounds that Smith has already revealed himself to be a pluralist about punishment, we must recall that that pluralism resides on a different level from the one currently under consideration. All those different ways of justifying punishment are united in that all of them follow from the resentment with which the WIS sympathizes. The pluralism currently under consideration posits a totally different additional ground, albeit one that does have secondary moral status. We might be able to avoid this result, however, if we read some of the passages cited earlier as implying that a wish to deter *is* built into resentment. If, in punishing, resenters also aim at deterrence, then, appearances to the contrary, some weak form of resentment *can* play a role in the punishment of the sentinel. Clearly, this interpretation is somewhat revisionist, in that it points to different degrees of resentment while Smith points to "very different sentiments" to explain the difference between how we feel about the sentinel's punishment and how we feel about the parricide's punishment (II.ii.3.11). But it is not totally unfounded in the text. As we saw earlier, Smith *does* list deterrence alongside the less controversially intrinsic aims of resentment; perhaps I was overreading the "that" clauses as "such that" clauses.

The biggest problem for the suggestion that a desire to deter potential offenders is built into resentment is less one of interpretation than one of principle. Regardless of what Smith thinks, this suggestion seems to ask too much of resentment. It seems plausible that resentment involves goals like self-defense and vengeance. Given the Smithian desire for mutual sympathy, it also seems plausible that resentment involves a goal like rehabilitation. But it seems like a stretch to say that when I resent you for the injury you have done me and thus want to punish you, I am intrinsically aiming to set an example for others. Having this aim seems to require a level of reflection and forethought inessential to the experience of resenting. Thus, the ambiguity of the "that" clauses might reflect Smith's realization that he cannot explain how we can ground punishment in the utility of deterrence and in sympathy with resentment at the same time.[26]

Another suggestion, which is even more revisionist, would be to push back on Smith's claim that the WIS would not feel resentment toward the sleeping sentinel.[27] The sentinel's "carelessness" can easily be construed as a lack of appreciation of the importance of the interests of other people that we saw earlier is the primary target of resentment. In falling asleep at his post, the sentinel seems even worse in this regard than the grossly negligent person who commits a "real injustice" by throwing a "large stone over a wall into a public street" and thereby demonstrates that he "evidently wants that sense of what is due to his fellow-creatures which is the basis of justice" (II.iii.2.8). In having to overcome the psychological force of orders, training, and the military culture of discipline, the sentinel's thoughtlessness seems much stronger and deeply rooted than that of even the grossly negligent man.[28]

The third component of Smith's natural jurisprudence that gets at least touched upon in the TMS is his view on the scope of the law. We might think that Smith's conception of justice leads him to hold a minimalist conception of the law's reach. According to this view, failures of justice alone are covered by the law because failures of justice alone are punishable; even serious failures of beneficence, such as those involving "parental affection," "filial affection," brotherly affection," and the most basic and easily enacted "compassion" for other human beings, do not fall under the purview of the law because they are not punishable offenses (II.ii.1.7). But Smith does not hold this view. He believes that "the civil magistrate is entrusted with the power not only of preserving the public peace by restraining injustice, *but of promoting the prosperity of the commonwealth by establishing good discipline, and by discouraging every sort of vice and impropriety*." Thus, the law "may prescribe rules . . . which not only prohibit mutual injuries among fellow-citizens, but *command mutual good offices to a certain degree*"; once these rules are written into law, violations of them become legitimately punishable (II.ii.1.8, emphases added).

Importantly, Smith does not defend these laws by reconceptualizing failures to fulfill the good offices they command in terms of injury, even though this would be easy enough to do with his examples of parental and filial affection. He is clear that the law can legitimately compel the performance of least some good offices *qua* good offices. However, given his view that "beneficence . . . is less essential to the existence of society than justice" because it is possible for society to "subsist" with the former but not the latter, we might think that this additional, positive responsibility of the sovereign is sort of a bonus to which we can appeal for distinguishing good legal codes from great ones (II.ii.3.3). But he observes that laws that "neglect it altogether [expose] the commonwealth to many gross disorders and shocking enormities" (II.ii.1.8). Thus, to fulfill this positive responsibility is not merely to apply icing to a cake, despite what Smith's comparison of justice to a building's "foundation" and beneficence to the "ornament which embellishes" it might suggest (II.ii.3.4). Of course, we must be careful not to swing too far in the other direction, as these architectural metaphors do seem to convey a ranking of importance.[29] Furthermore, Smith believes that in commanding good offices, a "law-giver" fulfills a duty that requires "the greatest delicacy and reserve to execute with propriety and judgment"; mistakes on this front can be "destructive of all liberty, security, and justice" (II.ii.1.8). Thus, Smith is inhabiting a space somewhere between a view that restricts the scope of the law only to the prevention of and recompense for harm and a view that expands the scope of the law to the enforced cultivation of full positive virtue.[30]

In this section, we have seen that while Smithian justice is a virtue involving distinctive conduct and, more importantly, distinctive sentiments (or what I referred to as a "mindset"), there are reasons why Smith believes it is best studied as a matter of law or "natural jurisprudence" than of personal morality or "ethics." We have also seen some of most foundational aspects of natural jurisprudence that emerge from the TMS. In the next three sections, we turn to Smith's science of ethics proper, which he undertakes mainly in his TMS VI study of the virtues other than justice. We begin with beneficence, the positive counterpart to the negative virtue of justice.

Section 4: Beneficence

Just as Smith's conception of justice is rooted in his account of negative judgments of merit, his account of beneficence is rooted in his account of positive judgments of merit. We make a positive judgment of merit when we realize that the WIS sympathizes with gratitude that would be felt by the recipients of an action that is "of a beneficent tendency" and done "from proper motives." Since gratitude involves a desire to reward, the WIS' approval of an agent from sympathy with a patient's gratitude also involves deeming the agent worthy of reward. Thus, among the virtues, beneficence "seems alone to deserve reward" (II.ii.1.1). As we saw in the previous section, the other side of this point is that failures of beneficence do not deserve punishment. So for Smith, part of the reason why justice at least seems to be a more important virtue than beneficence is that the failure to be just, unlike the failure to be beneficent, does deserve punishment. But we should not conclude from this that for him, beneficence is a sort of bonus to which we can appeal in distinguishing good lives from great ones. As we saw earlier, Smith believes that when a legal code neglects to manifest, encourage, or even enforce some degree of beneficence, "it exposes the commonwealth to many gross disorders and enormities" (II.ii.1 .18). The results are similarly serious when an individual fails to be beneficent. Smith is clear that people who lack this virtue, even if they are just, are not living a good life. Sure, failures of justice deserve punishment while failures of beneficence (in the absence of the aforementioned laws) only deserve reactions like blame and perhaps corrective "advice and persuasion" (II.ii.1.7). But despite not involving physical force, the negative social consequences of failures of beneficence are significant:

> As every man doth, so shall it be done to him, and retaliation seems to be the great law which is dictated to us by Nature. Beneficence and generosity we think due to the generous and beneficent. Those whose hearts never open to the feelings of humanity, should, we think, be shut out in the same manner, from the affections of all their fellow-creatures, and be allowed to live in the midst of society, as in a great desert where there is nobody to care for them, or to inquire after them. The violator of the laws of justice ought to be made to feel himself that evil which he has done to another; and since no regard to the sufferings of his brethren is capable of restraining him, he ought to be over-awed by the fear of his own. The man who is barely innocent, who only observes the laws of justice with regard to others, and merely abstains from hurting his neighbours, can merit only that his neighbours in their turn should respect his innocence, and that the same laws should be religiously observed with regard to him. (II.ii.1.10)

These are not the words of a moral philosopher who saw beneficence as merely optional.[31] Life in a "great [social] desert" sounds awful regardless of whether we agree with Smith about the existence of our deep desire for mutual sympathy. His observation that "the greater exertions" of beneficence "appear to deserve the highest reward" does suggest that beneficence is in some sense supererogatory (II.ii.1.9). But we should not overlook the import of the language of "greater exertions." One can coherently think both that heroic beneficence deserves a hero's reward and that failures of beneficence do not (in the absence of the aforementioned laws) deserve punishment, while also thinking that there is space between failure and heroism for levels of beneficence that are, if not obligatory, expected and thus *really bad*, though not punishable, not to reach. We should keep this in mind as we transition from Smith's account of justice to his account of beneficence.

In keeping with his characterization of the science of ethics, Smith uses his account of beneficence to sketch in an attractive way the beneficent character. But he also explicitly frames the account in terms of two more specific goals. The first is "to explain the foundation of that order which nature seems to have traced out for the distribution of our good offices, or for the direction and employment of our very limited powers of beneficence: first, towards individuals, and secondly towards society" (VI.ii.intro.2). The second goal is to show that "the same unerring wisdom . . . which regulates every other part of her conduct, directs, in this respect too, the order of her recommendations; which are always stronger or weaker in proportion as our beneficence is more or less necessary, or can be more or less useful" (VI.ii.intr o.3). The first goal has two aspects, one explanatory and one normative. The explanatory aspect involves providing accounts of the development and scope of our other-directed affections. The normative aspect involves establishing how we should distribute our good offices and direct and employ our powers of beneficence by revealing what is natural to us.[32] The second goal does not have multiple internal features, but it does invite us to consider what purpose it serves. One reason why Smith wants to show that nature orients our other-directed affections in the most efficacious way possible might be to support an argument for the existence of a certain kind of designer.[33] On its own, however, this aim would be peripheral to the practical function of TMS VI. Smith could also be pointing to an additional source of normativity to compensate for any worries we might have about the intrinsic normativity of nature. Yet while worries about *why* we should act or be a certain way can come up in the midst of practice, TMS VI still seems like an odd place for this motivation to be prominent. As a practically oriented work of ethics, TMS VI is more concerned with *what* we should be and do than with why. Nevertheless, I shall argue, the second goal is practically important for the beneficent person, but less because it provides an additional ground for the normativity of the beneficence than because it makes a point that has a role in the beneficent person's deliberation.

Let's turn to the explanatory aspects of the first goal. As we have seen, Smith organizes his account of beneficence partly in terms of a distinction between affections toward individuals and affection toward groups. With respect to individuals, we are "first and principally recommended to [our] own care." However, the virtue of prudence, not beneficence concerns self-care. Beneficence has to do with "care" of and "attention" to other individuals (VI.i.1.1). For Smith, there are several different categories of individuals about whom we care and to whom we attend: people who have some "connection with ourselves," people who have certain "personal qualities," people who have done "past services" for us, and people "who are distinguished by their extraordinary situation[:] the greatly fortunate and the greatly unfortunate, the rich and the powerful, the poor and the wretched" (VI.ii.1.20). For Smith, each category demands a different explanation for why we feel affection toward its members. (Clearly, people for whom we care can belong to more than one group; for example, a person with a connection to us can also have done us a service. When this happens, the different sources of affection get compounded together (VI.ii.1.21).)

Smith argues that "habitual sympathy" makes us care for people simply for "their connection with ourselves" (VI.ii.1.20). When we spend a lot of time around people, we become "habituated to sympathize with them" (VI.ii.1.2). This "habitual sympathy" either is or gives rise to "concern in [their] happiness or misery" and "desire to promote the one, and to prevent the other." As we saw in Section 1 of Chapter 3, Smith is sketchy on the relationship between sympathy and concern for others. The idea here seems to be that in repeatedly taking on other people's perspectives, we come to care about them by virtue of coming to care about what they care about, which presumably at least sometimes includes themselves (VI.ii.1.7). Smith employs this mechanism to explain our affection toward both family members and some nonfamilial friends. In treating the latter kind of affection as the product of habit, Smith is probably not saying anything very provocative. It seems obvious that "the necessity or conveniency of mutual accommodation, very frequently produces a friendship" between "colleagues in office, partners in trade," and "neighbours" (VI.ii.1.15–16). But in explaining familial affection primarily via habitual sympathy, Smith is saying something interesting. He does cite one factor independent of the habitual sympathy mechanism that exacerbates our tendency to sympathize with some family members: we have a stronger tendency to sympathize with and thus care for children than we do older people (VI.ii.1.3). But even in the case of affection for our own children, habitual sympathy, as opposed to the "force of blood" or any other "supposed physical connection," does most of the work (VI.ii.1.11; VI.ii.1.14). As Smith himself observes, the fundamental importance of habitual sympathy for all familial affections implies that these affections are contingent upon our living arrangements. Thus, since people living in "pastoral countries . . . where the authority of law is not alone sufficient to give perfect security to every member of the state," often must associate in big, multi-generational groups "for their common defense," their familial affections are often wide in scope. On the other hand, people "living in commercial countries, where the authority of law is always perfectly sufficient to protect the meanest man in the state" live in small groups consisting of fewer generations, their familial affections tend to be narrower. (Smith amusingly denies that people in commercial countries who are fond of bringing up their distant "illustrious relations" constitute an exception; that this practice derives from "the most frivolous and childish vanities," not "any thing which resembles affection," is clear from the fact that these people always reject any "more humble, though, perhaps, much nearer kinsman" (VI.ii .1.12–13)). It follows from Smith's psychology of familial affection that these are only two examples from an endless list of possible variations to the very notion of family.

The next kind of other-directed concern develops in response to our perception of someone's "personal qualities." Some of these foundations for affection are trivial, such as a "slight similarity of character, altogether unconnected with good conduct, . . . taste, perhaps, for the same studies, the same amusements, the same diversions . . . , [and] agreement in some singular principles or opinion, not commonly adopted." The most significant personal quality to ground affection is virtue, for which we feel "esteem and approbation" (VI.ii.1.18). While affections with these sources track our perception of some quality of their objects, affections rooted in habitual sympathy track only our history with their objects. To grasp the point of Smith's distinction, consider the difference between caring for someone because you think there is something worthwhile about that person and caring for someone simply because you have known that person forever. (Again, Smith's distinction allows for instances of overlap; he just believes that such instances involve distinct sources of care.)

The third source of other-directed affection for individuals is not totally foldable into the second one but is highly sensitive to it. Smith observes that we feel affection toward people who have done us "past services" because "every man [is] the peculiar object of kindness to the persons to whom he himself has been kind" (VI.ii.1.18). As we saw in Section 4 of Chapter 3, gratitude usually requires belief that a positive personal quality motivated our benefactor's service. However, Smith's treatment of past service alone as a distinct source of other-directed concern implies that he recognizes a form of gratitude that does not involve this recognition (cf. II.i.3.2).

The fourth source of other-directed affection for individuals does not bear this close a relationship to that involving perception of merit. We feel affection toward "those who are distinguished by their extraordinary situation; the greatly fortunate and the greatly unfortunate; the rich and the powerful; the poor and the wretched" because of some quirks in our sympathetic tendencies (VI.ii.1.20). As we saw in Section 3 of Chapter 3 and we will see in more detail in the next section, if envy does not get in the way, we tend to sympathize with others' joy more than we do their misery, but if their misery is great enough, we almost always sympathize with it. So as long we don't envy them, we sympathize with the joy of those on the top. And as long as it is great enough, we sympathize with the misery of those on the bottom. As a result, we feel affection for the rich and for the poor simply because they are so.

Smith turns next to explain the development of our affection for groups or, in his language, "societies." Since he obviously wants to use this section to say something about both special interest and party politics, his two main examples of groups for which we feel affection are particular "orders and societies, each of which has its own particular powers, privileges, and immunities" (VI.ii.2.7) and "the state or sovereignty in which we have been born and educated, and under the protection of which we continue to live." But the explanation he employs for these examples can also cover many different conceivable group attachments. The explanation builds affection for a group out of affection for the individuals therein. We feel affection toward our "state or sovereignty," for example, because "not only we ourselves, but all the objects of our kindest affections . . . are commonly comprehended within it; and their prosperity and safety depend in some measure upon its prosperity and safety"; thus, our country is "by nature . . . endeared to us, not only by all our selfish, but by all our private benevolent affections" (VI.ii.2.2).

It is not clear whether Smith thinks of the resulting affection for the group as something distinct from affection for the individuals therein. In arguing that the love of country "seems not to be derived from the love of mankind," he claims that "we do not love our country merely as part of the great society of mankind: we love it for its own sake, and independently of any such consideration" (VI.ii.2.4). In keeping with what we have seen, this claim suggests that the love of country is constructed bottom-up, from the love of the people in it, as opposed to top-down, from the "love of mankind." But the claim that we love our country "for its own sake" also suggests that despite its development from our love for the people in it, our love of country is essentially intrinsic and thus distinct from our love for the people in it. He eventually says that "the love of our country" ordinarily involves "two different principles; first, a certain respect and reverence for that constitution or form of government which is actually established; and secondly, an earnest desire to render the condition of our fellow-citizens as safe, respectable, and happy as we can" (VI.ii.2.11). The first "principle" is an example of the intrinsic "love of system . . . of order, of art, and contrivance" that we will also further discuss in the next section (IV.1.11). Perhaps this aesthetic attraction to the form of government implemented by our country is Smith's interpretation of what it means to love a country intrinsically and thus distinctly from the individuals therein. Given that Smith's most detailed explanations of other-directed affection concern individuals, it is hard to see how he could recognize affection for a group that is not reducible to basic affection for or sympathy with the people who make it up, perhaps combined with an aesthetic attraction to the system of rules that govern it.[34]

As interpretively appealing as it might be to read Smith's understanding of affection for a group in this deflationary, reductive way, the option potentially leaves us with a poor understanding of why he bothers treating affection for a group as a distinct category. My suggestion is that we interpret Smith's conception of non-aesthetic affection for a group as affection for individuals on the basis of their membership in that group, as opposed to affection for individuals on the basis of personal connection, personal qualities, past services, extreme wealth, or extreme poverty. I suggest we make a similar choice when faced with Smith's claim that "our good-will . . . may embrace the immensity of the universe." Smith does not mean that we have an intrinsic love for the universe. Rather, he is talking about affection for individuals on the basis of their membership in the widest, most inclusive possible group: "we cannot form the idea of any innocent and sensible being, whose happiness we should not desire, or to whose misery, when distinctly brought home to the imagination, we should not have some degree of aversion" (VI.ii.3.1). Since Smith does point out that our concern for all innocent and sensible beings can lead us to think of the universe as a "great society . . . of which God himself is the immediate administrator and director," this concern can mirror the love of country in being combined with aesthetic attraction to God's system of administration and direction (VI.ii.3.3). But there does not seem to be any room in Smith's psychology for intrinsic affection for the universe itself, understood as a category distinct from affection for individuals therein, aesthetic attraction to the system governing it, or the combination of the two.[35] Of course, the remaining challenge is to explain why the group-membership of individuals generates affection for those individuals. But it seems that Smith can do this by grounding that affection in affection based on habit, personal qualities, past services, extreme wealth, and/or extreme poverty, but directed by mechanisms like the aforementioned reflections on "prosperity and safety." Since this strategy likely will not work to explain affections for individuals on the basis of their membership in the group of "sensible beings," it is important that Smith can also apply the mechanism of habitual sympathy to explain this kind of affection in the same way as he does care for someone *qua* family member or habitual friend; the difference in strength of care would just be a function of the difference in width (understood in terms of how many sentiments are involved), intensity (understood in terms of how closely the sentiments that are involved match up), and frequency of sympathy.

Beneficence, then, is the virtue that has to do with how we feel and act upon these different kinds of other-directed affections. More specifically, since it is a virtue, beneficence involves feeling and acting *excellently* regarding these affections. Unfortunately, Smith's normative views on beneficence are sprinkled in haphazardly among his explanatory accounts of the different kinds of other-directed affections. A distinction that likely applies to any account of the virtue of beneficence should help us organize our discussion of these views. It seems that accounts of this virtue should: (a) demonstrate which beneficent affections are best to cultivate in the first place; and (b) demonstrate the best way to act upon the various beneficent affections we do have. I would venture to guess that the later topic is more recognizable than the former, for it addresses the obvious questions that arise when our "different beneficent affections happen to draw different ways" (VI.ii.1.22).[36] Smith, however, does deal with the former.

He does so in some brief off-hand remarks for which we can fill in some contextual rationale. He makes these remarks where he does and only where he does because this context concerns the personal relationships the cultivation of which is most sensitive to decision. He does not make these remarks in the context of discussing other-directed affections for groups because they are born out of other-directed affections for individuals; thus, any recommendation to develop the former affections will boil down to a recommendation to develop the latter. He also does not make these remarks in the context of discussing other-directed affections for individuals based on gratitude, respect for the rich and powerful, and compassion for the poor and weak because these affections do not really ground relationships. Instead, he makes these remarks to compare relationships based on personal connection with relationships based on personal qualities. Smith expresses concern about the fact that the habitual sympathy mechanism that makes us care about the people with whom we spend a lot of time also makes us similar to them. In this respect, habitual sympathy underlies our "natural disposition to accommodate and to assimilate, as much as we can, our own sentiments, principles, and feelings, to those which we see fixed and rooted in the person whom we are obliged to live and converse a great deal with." Smith worries about this disposition because it "is the cause of the contagious effects" not only of "good" but also of "bad character" (VI .ii.1.17). We might add that even if the people closest to us are not bad influences, there seems to something lacking if all that we can say about why we care so much for them is that we are used to them. Thus, attachments based on personal qualities seem to be the best candidates for attachments we should actively seek.

But not all attachments based on personal qualities are created equally:

> The hasty, fond, and foolish intimacies of young people, founded, commonly, upon some slight similarity of character, altogether unconnected with good conduct, upon a taste, perhaps, for the same studies, the same amusements, the same diversions, or upon their agreement in some singular principle or opinion, not commonly adopted; those intimacies which a freak begins, and which a freak puts an end to, how agreeable soever they may appear while they last, can by no means deserve the sacred and venerable name of friendship.

We might add that since attachments based on these qualities can involve vice, they can also expose us to risk of bad influence. Thus, Smith recommends that we cultivate attachments with virtuous people, on the basis of their virtue. In surrounding us with good influences, such attachments will improve our characters. They will also be as "regular and orderly" and as "permanent and secure" as virtue itself is. And the relatively impersonal affections involved in them "need not be confined to a single person, but may safely embrace all the wise and virtuous" (VI.ii.1.18).

We might think that in elevating relationships based on virtue over relationships based on "hasty, fond, and foolish intimacies," Smith overlooks the importance of simply enjoying a companion's company. We might also think that in elevating relationships based on virtue over relationships based on personal connection, Smith overlooks the importance of shared history with someone. We must remember, though, that since the people for whom care can fall into more than one of Smith's categories, so can our relationships with them. Smith's argument treats these different kinds of relationships in isolation from each other; hence the phrase in the blocked quote, "altogether unconnected with good conduct." His point seems to be that a life filled with relationships based on habit alone or fun alone, "altogether unconnected" with any appreciation of the other person's good character, is impoverished. However, Smith does not imply that we should *end* non-virtue-based relationships, unless they are bad influences upon us. If they are not, Smith's advice would be to supplement these relationships with new, better ones (although time constraints might warrant replacement instead of supplementation) or to deepen these relationships by finding and appreciating the merit in the people with whom we share them. We might want Smith to add that a life filled with relationships based on virtue alone is also impoverished, perhaps to a lesser extent than the life filled with relationships based on habit and fun alone. But there is no reason why he could not accept this view. I suspect that his emphasis is so heavily pro-virtue because he does not take seriously the possibility of such a life. Being social creatures, we always simply find ourselves with habit-based relationships. And being pleasure-loving creatures, it is hard to imagine us not having mainly fun-based ones too. Thus, Smith sees himself as being in the position of having to recommend the most important component of good relationships to people who might not realize its importance, not in the position of having to recommend the necessary but less important components of good relationships to people who already obviously do realize their importance.

So the beneficent person is someone who, like all people, has relationships on the basis of habit but who also, not necessarily like all people, looks to cultivate relationships on the basis of virtue, not only fun. This view seems sensible enough, but Smith makes an incredibly confusing claim in the context of expressing it. He claims that affections based on the perception of virtue arise "not from a constrained sympathy, not from a sympathy which has been assumed and rendered habitual for the sake of conveniency and accommodation; but from a natural sympathy, from an involuntary feeling that the persons to whom we attach ourselves are the natural and proper objects of esteem and approbation." The claim is problematic for several reasons. The first is the principled one that habitual sympathy is itself a natural process. Second, the claim appears to contradict Smith's explicit characterization of familial affection based upon habitual sympathy as "natural" and implicit characterization of nonfamilial, habitual-sympathy-based affection, which he describes as "not unlike that which takes place among those who are born to live in the same family," as the same (VI.ii.1.14–15). Smith must mean, then, that habitual sympathy is natural in a different sense from the sympathetic approval of perceived virtue. According to what he says here, one difference is that habitual sympathy rests upon a strategic choice. We happen to find people in our lives, and we decide that the best way to get along with them is by taking on their perspectives as much as possible. The result is that we feel affection for family members, people in our neighborhoods, colleagues, etc., just because they are always around. When Smith calls these ties "natural" in earlier passages, he is pointing to the fact that most of us, most of the time make the choice that generates them; "natural" in those contexts just means something like "expected." On the other hand, when he says that virtue-based affections and relationships are "natural" in a different sense, he must mean that they follow from our natures without this volition. (Note that this must also be the case regarding the affections and relationships that follow from non-virtuous personal qualities.)

Ironically, despite involving choice at some level, many purely habit-based relationships start developing in our youth and thus present themselves to us as unchosen givens (VI.ii.1.8–9).[37] This is all the more reason why Smith does not emphasize what they contribute. Since these relationships are brute facts of existence for anyone old enough to understand advice from a philosopher, it would be asinine for that philosopher to instruct anyone to cultivate them. (It does make sense, however, to advise parents how to cultivate these relationships with their children. Accordingly, Smith advises parents not to send their children to live away from home for schooling (VI.ii.1.10).) Also ironically, even if we do not have a choice in reacting positively to the perception of virtue, we do have a choice in seeking out the experience of this reaction; we can, for example, decide to associate with people we suspect to be virtuous or decide to look for virtue in the people with whom we already associate. This is all the more reason why Smith emphasizes what virtue-based friendships contribute to our lives.

Since Smith classifies the virtuous person, who is the object of our involuntary "natural sympathy," as "the natural and proper object of sympathy," Smith must also mean that virtue-based affections and relationships are "natural" in the ancient, normatively laden sense, such that in cultivating them we are fulfilling our nature in a way that we are not in cultivating affections and relationships on the basis of habit. (It is unclear where the fun-based affections and relationships stand in this regard.) For now, we can just take this as further evidence that Smith takes virtue-based affections and relationships as the best ones to cultivate. We'll revisit the normative sense of nature in Section 2 of the next chapter.

The fact that Smith does not say anything more about which beneficent affections to cultivate might seem to support my speculation that this issue comes up less often in moral philosophy than that of how best to act upon the beneficent affections we have. However, Smith does not say all that much more about more common concerns regarding how we should balance the demands of our other-directed affections based on personal connection, personal qualities, past services, respect for wealth and power, compassion for poverty and weakness, fellow group-membership, fellow national citizenship, and fellow membership in the category of "sensible being." And the two things he does say seem to be tension with each other.

Unsurprisingly, Smith believes that there are no "precise rules" to tell us what to do when our "different beneficent affections happen to draw in different directions." He gives as examples the conflicts that could arise when the demands of "friendship" conflict with the demands of "gratitude" and the conflicts that could arise when the "strongest of our natural affections" conflict with "the safety of those superiors upon whose safety often depends that of the whole society." (Given the example he eventually uses and bracketing the aforementioned complications with classifying such affections as "natural," he probably has love for one's own child in mind when he uses the former phrase.) Such cases involve "different shades and gradations of circumstance, character, and situation" and "differences and distinctions which, though not imperceptible, are, by their nicety and delicacy, often altogether undefinable." When this happens, there are "no casuistic rules" to help us. We must turn to the judgment of the WIS: "if we place ourselves completely in his situation, if we really view ourselves with his eyes, and as he views us, and listen with diligent and reverential attention to what he suggests to us, his voice will never deceive us." Smith provides as an example our presumably WIS-shaped reaction to the respective conduct of a mother and a father in the Voltaire play, "The Orphan of China." We "admire the magnanimity" of the father, "who is willing to sacrifice the life of his own child, in order to preserve that of the only feeble remnant of the ancient sovereigns and masters," but we "not only pardon, but love the maternal tenderness" that leads her to save the child, at great risk to her husband and herself (VI.ii.1.22). If these are both acts of beneficence, the first concerns the interests of a kingdom while the second concerns the interests of one child. In saying that the WIS approves of both, Smith is saying two interesting things. One is that because of differences in their "circumstances, characters, and situation," the father and the mother are not similarly situated and thus face different moral demands. Another is that it is not obvious that beneficence always prioritizes the interests of a group for which we care—the kingdom—over the interests of an individual for whom we care—the child.

Later, however, Smith claims:

> The wise and virtuous man is at all times willing that his own private interest should be sacrificed to the public interest of his own particular order or society. He is at all times willing, too, that the interest of this order or society should be sacrificed to the greater interest of the state or sovereignty, of which it is only a subordinate part. He should, therefore, be equally willing that all those inferior interests should be sacrificed to the greater interest of the universe, to the interest of that great society of all sensible and intelligent beings, of which God himself is the immediate administrator and director. (VI.ii.3.3)

The apparent contradiction is obvious. A tidy way to resolve it is by emphasizing gender. The mother who favors the child over the kingdom is a woman, and the person who always prioritizes the interests of wider circles over narrow circles and individuals is a man. This solution might feel too quick, but we should recall a passage in which Smith applauds Brutus's sacrifice of a son for the sake of Rome *just after* Smith makes a gendered distinction between two virtues that fall under the heading of beneficence—"generosity," the virtue "of a man" and "humanity . . . the virtue of woman"—*precisely* on the grounds that the former involves "sacrifice" while the latter does not (IV.2.10–11). But even if we conclude that Smith avoids contradicting himself by leaving open the possibility that the wise and virtuous *woman* would act the same way that the *mother* does in the example from Voltaire, the attitude of the wise and virtuous man still presents a problem. This figure seems to apply a pretty strict rule in a way that at least fits badly with Smith's claim that only nuanced judgment can tell us how to proceed when the demands of beneficence conflict. We might want to write off the claim that the interests of wider circles always take precedence over the interests of narrower ones, with the interests of the widest possible circle always taking precedence over all, as a rhetorical flourish regarding an unattainable ideal. But Smith goes on to point out that the prioritization of the whole over the part does not seem to be "in any respect beyond the reach of human nature"; many soldiers, for example, "cheerfully sacrifice their own little systems to the prosperity of a greater system" (VI.ii.3.4).

The question, then, is whether beneficent choices in cases of conflicting other-directed affections are a matter of WIS-guided, context-sensitive judgment or a matter of doing this kind of rule-guided utilitarian math. In grappling with this question, we must remember that the overarching job of the chapters on beneficence is to describe "in a general manner" what the beneficent person is like (VII.iv.2). Thus, we should pay careful attention to Smith's characterization of the virtuous man as "willing" to make sacrifices of narrower for wider interests. In saying this, Smith expresses the view that beneficent people are perpetually ready to make such sacrifices. But being ready to make these sacrifices is not the same thing as regularly deliberating with them in mind. So does Smith believe that the beneficent person regularly deliberates in this way?

Smith's reasons for answering "no" are simple: we usually don't know what will benefit people in our wider circles as well as we do what will benefit people in our narrower ones (VI.ii.1.1–2), and even if we did know what will benefit people in our wider circles, we usually will not be able to cause these benefits. Thus, he does not think there is much reason for the beneficent person to worry about the circle of all "sensible beings." He points out that "our effectual good offices can very seldom be extended to any wider society than that of our own country" (VI.ii.3.1). He is explicit that we should only think about the circle of the universe either for the sake of consolation in the face of unavoidable tragedies or for the sake of enjoying "sublime . . . objects of contemplation" in a manner consistent with the fulfillment of even the "smallest active [duties]" of our "more humble department"; this is true, Smith believes, even for someone with as wide a reach as the emperor of Rome (VI.ii.3.5–6).

Smith also does not think most beneficent people should worry too much about the circle of their own nations. Recall that for Smith, love of country usually involves both concern for our fellow citizens and attraction to our political system for its systematicity itself. He argues that those who find themselves in a position to enact political change should emphasize the former over the latter. The figure who reverses this order of priority becomes a "man of system" who tolerates no derivation from his "ideal plan of government." In doing so, this figure demonstrates a form of "arrogance" by "erecting his own judgment into the supreme standard of right and wrong." The reformer "whose public spirit is prompted altogether by humanity and benevolence," on the other hand, "endeavor[s] to establish" not what he takes to be the best system but the "best the people can bear," given their disagreements with him (VI.ii.2.16–17). Among the many interesting points that Smith is making here, including that it is irrational to care more for the fittingness of means to ends than for the ends (again, more on this in the next section), is that it is hard to know what is best for a circle as wide as that of one's country. Furthermore, few people will ever be in a position to impact their countries in this way. Smith's choice of other examples of beneficent people impacting the interests of their countries also makes this clear. The example from the Voltaire play deals with the sort of palace intrigue that will be experienced by only the tiniest minority of human beings. Smith does also provide a more generally applicable military example, which involves beneficent sacrifice of one's own and even of one's family's interest for the sake of one's country's interests (VI .ii.3.4). But even though many people find themselves faced with this kind of choice, not enough do and do so often enough to warrant making deliberation about how one can further the interests of one's country central to general descriptions of the beneficent character. Thus, it remains the case that, in general, the beneficent person Smith is trying to depict deliberates mainly via WIS-guided, context-sensitive judgment, not via utilitarian calculations about how to best help massive groups of people. This person is willing and ready to make sacrifices of narrower for wider interests, but will not regularly be in position to do so, let alone regularly know how to do so while in this position.

However, since they have limitless goodwill, beneficent people might find themselves thinking that they *should* be deliberating with the interests of the widest possible circles in mind. These people need to be reminded about the limitations of their knowledge and efficacy but in a way that speaks to their limitless goodwill. This is the practical job of Smith's insistence on showing that the "order which nature seems to have traced out for the distribution of our good offices, or for the direction and employment of our very limited powers of beneficence" is "always stronger or weaker in proportion as our beneficence is more or less necessary" (VI.ii.intro.3; cf. VI.ii.2.1). The upshot of this claim is that it is a good thing, even from the perspective of what Smith's calls our "universal benevolence,"[38] that we might be more attached to people in our local circles because we can best know how to help these people and can best enact this knowledge (VI.ii.1.1–2). In realizing this, beneficent people give their strongest, localized other-directed affections a baseline authority, to be overturned only when they are sure that the knowledge and efficacy problems are definitively overcome. Well-grounded skepticism about how often these problems can be overcome will prevent the beneficent person from constantly deliberating with overcoming them in mind. But, as Smith says, the beneficent person will be "willing" to act accordingly when the evidence obviously trumps this skepticism.[39]

This interpretation of how Smithian beneficent people weigh their various other-directed affections in deliberation implies that these deliberations will look very different under different circumstances of knowledge and efficacy. Obviously, we are much more capable of knowing and impacting a wide range of people's interests than were people in Smith's time. Thus, on my reading of Smith, the virtue of beneficence demands more wide-scope thinking and action of us than it did of Smith's contemporaries. I do not think Smith provides much in the way of resources for thinking about how exactly to weigh the demands of our local ties against the demands of humanity as whole, once knowledge- and efficacy-based limitations on our ability to fulfill the latter are removed or lessened; his confidence in the persistence of these limitations likely prevented him from doing so. If we follow the letter of what he says about the willingness of the wise and virtuous man, then, other things being equal, the latter demands should *always* win out when knowledge and efficacy are not issues. Whether Smith agrees with this, we agree with this, or the WIS agrees with this are all open questions. But even if we conclude that given present-day circumstances regarding the scope of our knowledge and efficacy, the virtue of beneficence always demands that we prioritize the interests of the widest possible whole, we must remember that beneficence is not the only virtue. Thus, even in ideal conditions of knowledge and efficacy, Smith's ideal person would not necessarily be the maximally altruistic saint.

Section 5: Prudence

Just as beneficence and justice have their foundation in concern for the happiness of other people, prudence has its foundation in "concern for our own happiness" (VI.concl.3). And just as he does in his discussion of beneficence, Smith begins his discussion of prudence by explaining the psychology of the concern upon which it is based. The first thing that both our nature and our caretakers teach us to look after is "the preservation and healthful state of the body." We next learn that to meet our bodily wants and needs, we must attend to our "external fortune." But though wealth is thus "originally recommended to us" only as means for acquiring and maintaining bodily goods, we also come to value it as a means to "win the respect of our equals." Indeed, since "the necessities and conveniencies of the body . . . are always very easily supplied" and since the desire for respect "is, perhaps, the strongest of all our desires," we come to value wealth *mainly* because it secures us respect. For the sake of satisfying our desire for respect, we also learn to attend to "our character and conduct." Thus, since prudence is the virtue of self-concern and since "the objects upon which [our] comfort and happiness in this life" depend most are our "health," our "fortune," and our "rank and reputation," they collectively constitute the "proper business" of prudence (VI.i.1.1–5).

There are two especially striking features of this psychology of self-concern. The first is its narrow conception of happiness. On the one hand, in making our happiness depend so much upon what other people think of us, this conception fits well with Smith's deeply social conception of human nature. But on the other hand, in neglecting to say anything about how the happiness of those for whom we care impacts our own happiness, this conception fits poorly with Smith's deeply social conception of human nature, especially as it manifests itself in the discussion of beneficence we just went through. However, we can resolve this tension by distinguishing between that which is required for one's own happiness and the virtue of pursuing one's own happiness. Smith can coherently hold both that the happiness of those for whom we care is required for our own happiness and that the virtue of pursuing our own happiness does not involve intentionally trying to ensure the happiness of these people. Rather, the virtue of intentionally trying to ensure the happiness of these people is the one we just discussed, beneficence, the practice of which will, given our social nature, make us happy. Sure, we could intentionally try to ensure the happiness of these people out of concern for our own interests. But since, as it seems, the WIS would prefer that we do so from other motives, it is not clear that we would even be practicing a virtue if we act this way.

There will be more to say in the next section about the relationship between the different Smithian virtues. The second striking feature of Smith's psychology of self-concern, both in general and with respect to his identity as the founder of modern economics, is the connection it draws between wealth and social status. Why does Smith believe that wealth secures social status? At the heart of the explanation is an observation we saw in Section 3 of this chapter and in Section 3 of Chapter 3 that "mankind are disposed to sympathize more entirely with our joy than with our sorrow" (I.iii.2.1). Smith expects this observation to feel counterintuitive because, as we have also seen, "our sympathy with sorrow" is usually much more common and noticeable than our "sympathy with joy" (I.iii.1.1). Smith points to several causes of this difference: sympathy with sorrow is "in some sense, more universal" because it occurs in degrees, while sympathy with joy is an all-or-nothing affair; since pain is generally "a more pungent sensation than pleasure," sympathy with pain is "generally more lively and distinct" than sympathy with pleasure; and since we often find ourselves wanting to get rid of sympathy with sorrow but wanting to cultivate sympathy with joy, especially when we notice that envy has prevented it, our "propensity" to sympathize with sorrow appears stronger than our propensity to sympathize with joy (I.iii.1.2–5). Nevertheless, Smith provides several reasons for thinking that we are actually more prone to sympathize with joy than sorrow: since sympathy with joy is pleasing, it simply makes sense to think that we are more prone to it than we are to sympathy with sorrow, which is painful; the best explanation for why we are "more ashamed to weep than to laugh before company" is that we realize that sorrow puts too high a demand on our company's ability to sympathize with us; and "our sorrow at a funeral" or "when we condole with our friends" is often "affected," while "our mirth at a christening or marriage" or when we "congratulate our friends" is always genuine "and without any affectation" (I.iii.1.9–12). (As we've seen too, Smith also provides several reasons for thinking that when we sympathize with joy, our sympathetic feeling approximates the agent's feeling more closely than does our sympathetic sorrow: since the affective baseline from which "the greater part of men" start is much closer to the highest peaks of happiness than it is the lowest pits of despair, it is easier, via our imaginations, to elevate ourselves to the former than drop ourselves to the latter; the best explanation for why we "pardon" grief that is too excessive for us to go along with but "have no such indulgence for the intemperance of joy" is that we realize that there is a "wider interval" between agents and spectators in the former case than in the latter case; and the best explanation for why we feel "admiration" for agents undergoing "dreadful calamities" who actually do bring their sentiments into "perfect correspondence" with our own is that we know how big the gap between their and our sentiments otherwise would be (I.iii.1.6–8; I.iii.1.13).)

This stronger tendency to sympathize with joy than with sorrow, Smith continues, makes a rich person "the object of attention and approbation" and a poor person either "disapproved of" or simply "overlooked." While Smith expresses awareness here that being noticed or ignored differs from being approved of or disapproved of, he leaves it to us to do the disentangling work. The relationships seem to be temporal in nature: people attend to us when they anticipate sympathizing with and thus approving of us once they imagine themselves into our situation, and people ignore us when they anticipate not sympathizing with us and thus disapproving of us once they imagine themselves into our situation. But regardless of how these relationships work, Smith's main point is that both the former experiences are great while both the latter experiences are terrible:

> The rich man glories in his riches, because he feels that the naturally draw upon him the attention of the world, and that mankind are disposed to go

> along with him in all those agreeable emotions with which the advantages of his situation so readily inspire him. . . . The poor man, on the contrary, is ashamed of his poverty. He feels that it either places him out of the sight of mankind, or, that if they take any notice of him, they have, however, scarce any fellow-feeling with the misery and distress which he suffers. He is mortified upon both accounts; for those to be overlooked, and to be disapproved of, are things entirely different, yet as obscurity covers us from the daylight of honour and approbation, to feel that we are taken no notice of, necessarily damps the most agreeable hope, and disappoints the most ardent desire, of human nature.

Thus, in pursuing wealth for the sake of status, we are really pursuing wealth for the sake of others' attention and sympathy, which are what convey status to wealth. The attention and sympathy received by the rich man secure his social status by conveying to him a form of sentimental power: "In a great assembly [the rich man] is the person upon whom all direct their eyes; it is upon him that their passions seem to wait with expectation, in order to receive that movement and direction which he shall impress upon them" (I.iii.2.1; cf. I.iii.3.7). The attenders and sympathizers convey this status to the rich man out of their totally unreflective disposition to sympathize with his joy, not from any "private expectation of benefit" from him or "regard to the utility of submission" to him (I.iii.2.3).

This explanation for why wealth secures social status is incomplete in at least two ways. Each of these gaps has to do with features of Smith's views about our tendency to sympathize with joy. The first has to do with envy. Smith believes that spectators only sympathize with joy when envy does not get in the way; thus, he argues that we are more likely to win sympathy when we move "gradually to greatness" than when we experience a "sudden [positive] revolution of fortune" because incremental advances are less likely to trigger envy in others (I.ii.5.1). So Smith must explain why widespread envy does not prevent spectators from attending to, sympathizing with, and ultimately lionizing the wealthy. Smith's initial discussion of envy in his chapter on sympathy with selfish passions is rife with references to preexistent social class; the situation he imagines is one in which an "upstart" triggers the envy of his "best friends" by suddenly jumping into the class of their "superior[s]" and becoming the "equal" of these people (I.ii.5.1). And in another place, he defines envy as "that passion which views with malignant dislike the superiority of those who are really entitled to all the superiority they possess"; to the envious person, however, the "superior" person does not deserve this rank (VI.iii.16). Thus, Smith seems to think of envy as a passion that involves seeing its object as a social equal who has been undeservedly elevated above oneself. If so, envy would not be triggered in cases in which we see someone as already above us.[40] Of course, if the spectators in Smith's explanation of why wealth secures social status *already* see wealthy people as above them, then that explanation becomes less powerful, as it no longer explains how we come to see the wealthy as above us in the first place. But the explanation does not thereby fail, as Smith seems to be assuming a situation in which there already are standing social ranks, not one that is one step removed from total social equality; his examples of the "rich and the great" tend to be hereditary monarchs and aristocrats, not self-made types. Rather, the explanation just covers a feature of the psychology inherent to such a situation, not the full psychology of its origins. Admittedly, Smith does provide at least one example of envy that seems to be consciously upward-looking; he observes that we tend to overstate the quality of "illustrious characters" our nations have "produced in former times" than we do those produced in the present, "for against those of our own times envy may sometimes prejudice us a little" (VI.ii.2.2). But perhaps the hesitation of Smith's language in making this observation indicates that he takes consciously upward-looking envy to be an exception to how the passion usually works.

The second gap in Smith's explanation for why wealth secures social status has more to do with the wealthy person's joy than the spectator's sympathy therewith. Smith argues that we pursue wealth past the point of necessity because of our "vanity." We want "to be observed, to be attended to, to be taken notice of with sympathy, complacency, and approbation" (I.iii.2.1). This attention and sympathy, then, must be the main source of the joy we take in being wealthy. But people give us this attention and sympathy because they perceive our joy. So do they give us attention and sympathy because we receive attention and sympathy? If the expression "famous for being famous" makes any sense, an affirmative answer to this question would not be that odd. Still, at some level, there must be something other than just being the object of attention and sympathy that makes people think of the "condition of the great" as "almost the abstract idea of a perfect and happy state" and thus give their attention and sympathy to it (I.iii.2.2). In order words, we must think there is something good about being rich beyond just the attention and sympathy it attracts.

To fill this gap, we must turn to Smith's account of why we like nice things for their own sake, not just for the sake of the attention and sympathy that having them wins us. Smith treats this issue as an aesthetic one. He observes that we find a beautiful "house" to be so in part because of the "regularity" of its organization; we would intrinsically dislike seeing "correspondent windows of different forms, or the door not placed exactly in the middle of the building" (IV.1.1). As we saw in Section 6 of Chapter 4, he elsewhere points to some other positive aesthetic qualities, such as "certain colours," "smooth[ness,]" "variety," and "connected variety" (V.1.9). However, Smith thinks that the main reason why we like nice things is that they tend to be useful for something. But why are we attracted to utility? As Smith points out, Hume argued that the "utility of any object . . . pleases the master by perpetually suggesting to him the pleasure or conveniency which it is fitted to promote. Every time he looks at it, he is put in mind of this pleasure; and the object in this manner becomes a source of perpetual satisfaction and enjoyment" (IV.1.2). On this explanation, spectators sympathizing with the joy of the wealthy person are sympathizing with this pleasure. However, Smith argues that "very frequently," we care more about the "happy contrivance," the "exact adjustment of the means for attaining any conveniency or pleasure . . . than that very conveniency or pleasure itself" (IV.1.3). For example, most people who walk into a room and find "the chairs all standing in the middle of it" will likely "set them all in their places with their backs to the wall." As a result, the floor becomes "free and disengaged" and the room easier to navigate. But since the effort they undertook to move the chairs is likely not going to be compensated by this increase in convenience, they were likely motivated "not so much by [it], as that arrangement of things which promotes it" (IV.1.4). Similarly, the people who obsess about the precision of watches are not always "more scrupulously punctual" than anyone else.

Thus, what "interests" them in hyper-precise time-telling machines is "not so much the attainment" of knowledge regarding exactly what time it is, "as the perfection of the machine which serves to attain it" (IV.1.5). The same goes for "lovers of [other kinds of] toys" (IV.1.6).

Our intrinsic attraction to means that are well arranged to promote ends, regardless of our concern for these ends, manifests itself not "only with regard to such [obviously] frivolous objects" but also with regard to "the most serious and important pursuits of both private and public life" (IV.1.7). The "private" pursuit Smith has in mind is that of "wealth and greatness in general" (IV.1.8). (The "public" one is the creation of "institutions which tend to promote the public welfare" (IV.1.11). We saw this kind of love of systematicity at work in the previous section.) Like the silly gadgets, the more considerable things that wealth and greatness can secure, like "palace[s]," "machines" for travel, and a "numerous retinue of servants," are appealing more because we think of them as "means of happiness" than because we think they will make us happy. However, unlike success in acquiring silly gadgets, success in acquiring these things is more "obvious" to everyone and thus a better source of attention and sympathy. Thus, wealth and the nice things it buys bring attention, sympathy, and status fundamentally because spectators are intrinsically attracted to the utility of wealth and nice things for achieving their possessor's ends, without much concern for these ends. Once wealthy people get this attention, sympathy, and status, they then get even more attention, sympathy, and status on account of the attention, sympathy, and status they already have. In other words, they come to be attended to, sympathized with, and followed because they are attended to, sympathized with, and followed—just like people who are famous for being famous.

This two-pronged psychology of wealth-pursuit is intuitive: we first pursue wealth because it can help us satisfy our wants and needs, and then we pursue wealth because having it gets us respect. The interesting things about this account are the details involved in its explanation of each prong, which we have seen, and its relationship to Smith's account of prudence, which we have not. How do both the intrinsic attraction to utility and the desire for status factor into the prudent character's pursuit of wealth?

We might think that Smith's prudent characters do not desire wealth and its trappings for their utility alone, without regard for the goods this utility helps them acquire. Smith seems to think the intrinsic attraction to utility itself is irrational. Immediately after observing that we often care "not so much [for] conveniency, as [for] that arrangement of things which promotes it," he comments, "yet it is this conveniency which ultimately recommends that arrangement, and bestows upon it the whole of its propriety and beauty" (IV.1.4). This comment seems to express a negative value judgment regarding our attraction to utility for its own sake: it is just dumb to care more about the effectiveness of a useful thing than the end it is effective for enabling. Smith also observes that success in the pursuit of this utility often produces more hassles than benefits:

> Power and riches appear then to be, what they are, enormous and operose machines contrived to produce a few trifling conveniences to the body, consisting of springs the most nice and delicate, which must be kept in order with the most anxious attention, and which in spite of all our care are ready every moment to burst into pieces, and to crush in their ruins the unfortunate possessor. (IV.1.8)

Anyone who has looked at a mansion and immediately thought "that looks like a lot to keep clean" knows what Smith is saying here. We put ourselves in the unfortunate position Smith describes precisely because we desire utility for its own sake. Our obsession with the "nice and delicate" springs of the machine leads us to forget it only produces "a few trifling conveniences." If we focused our attention only on what it takes to secure the latter, we would not find ourselves burdened with caring for the former.

Famously, Smith argues that the personal costs of the pursuit of wealth in this silly way are compensated by its social benefits. He claims,

> And it is well that nature imposes upon us in this manner. It is this deception which rouses and keeps in continual motion the industry of mankind. It is this which first prompted them to cultivate the ground, to improve all the sciences and arts, which ennoble and embellish human life; which have entirely changed the whole face of the globe, have turned the rude forests of nature into agreeable and fertile plains, and made the trackless and barren ocean a new fund of subsistence, and the great high road of communication

> to the different nations of the earth. The earth by these labours of mankind has been obliged to redouble her natural fertility to maintain a greater multitude of inhabits.

After this wildly short-sighted celebration of agricultural, industrial, and intellectual "progress," Smith makes a famously questionable claim about the distribution of surplus goods that follows from this progress and the pursuit of wealth and status that drives it:

> It is to no purpose, that the proud and unfeeling landlord views his extensive fields, and without a thought for the wants of his brethren, in imagination consumes himself the whole harvest that grows upon them. The homely and vulgar proverb, that the eye is larger than the belly, never was more fully verified than with regard to him. The capacity of his stomach bears no proportion to the immensity of his desires, and will receive no more than that of the meanest peasant. The rest he is obliged to distribute among those, who prepare, in the nicest manner, that little which he himself makes use of, among those who fit up the palace in which this little is to be consumed, among those who provide and keep in order all the different baubles and trinkets, which are employed in the oeconomy of greatness; all of whom thus derive from his luxury and caprice, that share of the necessaries of life, which they would in vain have expected from his humanity or his justice. The produce of soil maintains at all times nearly that number of inhabitants which it is capable of maintaining. The rich only select from the heap what is most precious and agreeable. They consume little more than the poor, and in spite of their natural selfishness and rapacity, though they mean only their own conveniency, though the sole end which they propose from the labours of all the thousands whom they employ, be the gratification of their own vain and insatiable desires, they divide with the poor the produce of all their improvements. They are led by an invisible hand to make nearly the same distribution of the necessaries of life, which would have been made, had the earth been divided into equal portions among all its inhabitants, and thus without intending it, without knowing it, advance the interest of the society, and afford means to the multiplication of the species.

The lesson here:

> When Providence divided the earth among a few lordly masters, it neither forgot nor abandoned those who seemed to have been left out in the partition. These last too enjoy their share of all that it produces. In what constitutes the real happiness of human life, they are in no respect inferior to those who would seem so much above them. In ease of body and peace of mind, all the different ranks of life are nearly upon a level, and the beggar who suns himself by the side of the highway, possesses that security which kings are fighting for. (IV.1.10)

Thus, despite the irrationality and self-undermining nature of the pursuit of wealth, it is apparently justified for its positive contributions to the whole.

Obviously, this passage gives us a lot to discuss, including Smith's apparent underestimation of the badness of poverty, which contradicts his own observation that the "most ardent desire of human nature" is precisely the one that poverty frustrates (I.iii.2.1).[41] But there are two other features of the passage that interest me. First, it provides a particular example of the following general pattern we see again and again in the TMS: it identifies a mistake that we naturally make and then reassures us that it is actually ok that we make this mistake. The question of whether this pattern only demonstrates a commitment to some kind of theodicy—"it is well that nature imposes upon this in this manner," thanks to "Providence"—or also reveals an interesting kind of normative argument will concern us in Section 2 of the next chapter. The feature of the passage most relevant to our present discussion is that it still does not go back on the implication that it would be better for us as individuals not to pursue wealth beyond necessity. Smith does say that we only notice the silliness of this pursuit when we are "reduced either by spleen or disease" and that we fall prey to it again as soon as we are "in better health or in better humour." But in a passage quoted earlier, he also indicates that in the former mood, "power and riches appear [to] be, *what they are*" (IV.1.8–9; emphasis added). Thus, Smith seems to think that it really is the case that the pursuit of wealth for the sake of its utility alone is irrational.

So is the prudent character subject to this irrationality or not? One suspects that the answer is "yes," if only because it is implausible that Smith would tie virtue to "spleen." In complement to this suspicion, Smith also sees the irrationality as a source of joy:

> But though this splenetic philosophy[, by which we notice the irrationality], which in times of sickness or low spirits is familiar to every man, thus entirely depreciates those great objects of human desire, when in better health and in better humour, we never fail to regard them under a more agreeable aspect. Our imagination, which in pain and sorrow seems to be confined and cooped up within our own persons, in times of ease and prosperity expands itself to every thing around us. We are then charmed with the beauty of that accommodation which reigns in the palaces and oeconomy of the great; and admire how every thing is adapted to promote their ease, to prevent their wants, to gratify their wishes, and to amuse and entertain their most frivolous desire. (IV.1.9)

One would hope, however, that prudent characters manifests this irrationality somehow better than the rest of us do. Since this irrational desire ends up being bound up with and driven by a desire for the status that wealth brings, the superiority of prudent characters likely has to do with the way in which they pursue status.

We might think that the prudent character does not desire wealth for the sake of status at all. If so, this figure's irrational desire for the utility of wealth alone will be thereby restrained. Most of what Smith says about the desire for wealth for the sake of status is negative. Success in the pursuit of wealth for the sake of status produces more headaches than it is worth:

> It is [being attended to], which notwithstanding the restraint it imposes, notwithstanding the loss of liberty with which it is attended, renders greatness the object of envy, and compensates, in the opinion of mankind, all that toil, all that anxiety, all those mortifications which must be undergone in the pursuit of it; and what is of yet more consequence, all that leisure, all that ease, all that careless security, which are forfeited for ever by the acquisition. (I.iii.2.1)

It seems clear that Smith does not himself hold this "opinion of mankind." Anyone who has thought about the true cost of celebrity understands what he is saying here. One is constantly being monitored, envied, or both. In a chapter added to the sixth edition of the TMS, Smith also worries that the connection between wealth and status is "the great and most universal cause of the corruption of our moral sentiments" (I.iii.3.1).[42] The problem is that it is easy to confuse the "respect and admiration" that goes to virtue and the "respect and admiration" that goes to "wealth and greatness" (I.iii.3.1). They are, "no doubt, different . . . and it requires no very nice discernment to distinguish the difference. But, notwithstanding this difference, those sentiments bear a very considerable resemblance to one another" because both are rooted in the experience of disinterested sympathy; thus, "inattentive observers are very apt to mistake the one for other." The similarity between these sentiments puts us in danger of taking the wrong "road." We notice that a similar kind of respect is attained "by the study of wisdom and the practice of virtue" and "by the acquisition of wealth and greatness" (I.iii.3.2). Since we want to be respected, if we are not sufficiently attentive both to the difference between these kinds of respect and to the superiority of the former to the latter, we could easily abandon the path to virtue in favor of the path to wealth and greatness.

We should note that Smith tempers these worries by observing that for "by far the greater part of mankind," these two roads "happily" coincide. Most of us are "in the middling and inferior stations of life," in which financial and social advancement requires "real and solid professional abilities, joined to prudent, just, firm, and temperate conduct." Thus, even if we sometimes chase respect for wealth, regardless of how it is acquired, instead of respect for our positive abilities, including those involved in the acquisition of wealth, we can still end up with "a considerable degree of virtue" as a by-product (I.iii.3.5). Nevertheless, "the road which leads to [fortune], and that which leads to [virtue]," even of a minimal kind, do "lie sometimes in very opposite directions." If we find ourselves in a situation like this one, a situation in which fortune can be attained "by fraud and falsehood" or even "by the perpetration of the most enormous crimes," the risk to our character is significant (I.iii.3.8).

We should expect that the prudent way of pursuing wealth will insulate us from temptation in these circumstances. We should also expect that the prudent way of pursing wealth will be conducive to virtue not only as a side effect but intrinsically. These are reasons to think, then, the prudent person does not pursue wealth with status in mind at all. As we saw earlier, we can also acquire respect from our "character and conduct" when it secures "confidence, esteem, and good-will" from others (VI.i.4). Maybe the prudent character pursues respect only via the cultivation of virtue. This figure pursues wealth, then, only for the sake of need, the pleasure of utility for its ends, and the pleasure of utility for its own sake.

The problem with this suggestion is that Smith just seems to think that, however silly, the connection between wealth and status is built into human psychology. We might want Smith to reject our tendency to make respect "depend" *at all*, let alone "*very much* upon the degree in which we possess, or are supposed to possess, those advantages" of wealth (VI.i.3; emphasis added). Smith is sensitive to our worries, but ultimately throws up his hands in the face of them:

> It is scarce agreeable to good morals, or even to good language, perhaps, to say, that mere wealth and greatness, abstracted from merit and virtue, deserve our respect. We must acknowledge, however, that they almost constantly obtain it; and that they may, therefore, be considered as, in some respects, the natural objects of it. (I.iii.3.4).

The phrase "almost constantly obtain it" encourages us to take Smith's use of the word "natural" to be value-free. When we do, Smith is merely reporting a fact about human beings, that due to a particular functioning of the sympathy mechanism explained earlier, they respect wealth for its own sake. A correlative fact to this one, then, is that human beings desire wealth for the sake of this respect. Thus, like everyone else does, the prudent character likely has this desire. Obviously, this matters greatly to the present discussion. As we have seen, Smith also intends "natural" to have a normative sense, one which, if employed here, legitimates the connection between wealth and respect in human psychology. So it seems that no matter which sense of "natural," we stress, the prudent character ends up desiring wealth for the sake of status.

We should observe that Smith can avoid at least some of the problematic first-order implications of granting legitimacy to the connection between wealth and status in human psychology. If respect on the basis of wealth alone is legitimate, it must be reflected in the sentiments of the WIS. Presumably, sufficiently well-informed spectators would realize that when they sympathize solely on the basis of wealth, they are sympathizing with an agent for the agent's own joy in being wealthy. And, presumably, such spectators would realize that in doing so, they are only experiencing approval of the wealthy agent's appropriate joy in being wealthy. Thus, the WIS would not attribute any other qualities to the wealthy on the basis of their wealth alone. In this regard, Smith's classification of respect for wealth as natural in a normative sense is not necessarily problematic. The case is not the same, however, when he defends the "disposition to admire, and almost to worship, the rich and the powerful, and to despise, or, at least, to neglect persons of poor and mean condition" as "necessary both to establish and to maintain the distinction of ranks and order of society" (I.iii.3.1; cf. I.iii.2.3). I return to this point in Section 2 of the next chapter.

So if prudent people, like the rest of us, desire wealth for the sake of status, then they must do so in a better way. Careful attention to some of the language in the psychology of self-concern that grounds Smith's conception of prudence provides a hint for how prudent people think about the status that unavoidably factors into their desire for wealth. Smith describes the desire for status in general specifically as for "the respect of our equals," for "credit and rank among our equals" (VI.i.3–4). When Smith looks down upon the pursuit of status, however, he does not qualify the pursuit with a reference to our "equals." Instead, he most commonly describes it as motivated by a vicious kind of "ambition" (e.g., I.iii.2.1; I.iii.3.8; IV.1.7), which he later identifies as a desire for "superiority" (VII.iv.25).[43] Thus, the prudent person must pursue wealth with an eye to being respected by others as an equal, not with an eye to being worshipped by others as a superior. If Smith's man of prudence values wealth and status in this way, he will be less tempted by the kind of fortune, fame, and power that is more of a burden than it is worth and that can sometimes be bought by horrific misconduct.[44]

Again, there are problems here regarding the normative sense of "natural." Smith believes that to pursue wealth as a means to win respect as an equal, as the prudent character does, is to follow what nature "recommends" to us (VI.i.1). Obviously, he owes us some explanation as to why we should not interpret vicious ambition or the desire for superiority as similarly natural recommendation. But let's put these issues aside and focus instead on how the prudent person's pursuit of wealth for the sake of being respected as an equal manifests itself in practice. That there is a difference between the desire to be respected as an equal and the desire to be looked up to as a superior is intuitive. The normative claim that it is generally better to have the former than the latter desire is also intuitive. However, if I live in society with established social classes, my success in being respected as one person's equal likely puts me in the position of being another person's superior. In such instances, it becomes difficult to determine what I am desiring and thus whether I am prudent. Given Smith's language of seeking "the respect of *our equals*" and "credit and rank among *our equals*," maybe the best way to ensure that we are seeking equal respect and not superiority is by staying focused on the respect of the people within our own class (emphasis added). Yet it remains unclear how to distinguish the desire for the equal respect of the people in one's own class from the desire to maintain superiority over people in the class below. But insofar as the latter desire is to maintain the status one already has, it differs from vicious ambition; thus, it very well could have a place in the Smithian prudent character.

So is Smith recommending that we give up the pursuit of upward social movement? He seems to be saying that if you find yourself in a particular social class, the prudent thing to do is seek the wealth necessary to be recognized by other members of that class as an equal. Things will go badly for you if, like "the poor man's son, whom heaven in its anger has visited with ambition," you try to move up in the world (IV.1.8). If this advice bothers us, we must pinpoint exactly why. If one lives in a society that does not allow for real social mobility, then we probably think it *is* prudent to be satisfied with membership in one's own class. If so, then what bothers us is Smith's apparent complacency regarding these social conditions. But before we rest bothered by this, we should note that there is no incoherence in recommending prudent conduct against the background of social conditions to which one objects from another perspective. Obviously, this observation only helps Smith if he does protest against such conditions from another perspective. I leave it to readers with this curiosity to decide for themselves whether Smith sufficiently does so in the *Wealth of Nations*.[45] However, before they get too excited about what they will find there, such readers should remember Smith's earlier-quoted defense of social ranks on the grounds of their importance for social stability. Elsewhere, Smith even claims that social ranks best do this job when they are based on wealth rather than merit (VI.ii.i.21). He also seems to think that the rankings based on wealth that serve this purpose are usually *detached* from merit: the "easy price at which" the rich and the great who are born into their positions "may acquire public admiration" prevents them from cultivating any worthwhile qualities "much above mediocrity" (I.iii.2.4).[46] Thus, attempts to find in Smith attacks on social stratification must grapple with these defenses of hierarchy.[47]

Thus far, we have seen that the Smithian prudent character is a person who, like everyone else, pursues wealth both because it is useful for securing necessities and conveniences and because this utility is intrinsically appealing. Also like everyone else, this character also pursues wealth for the sake of the social status it provides. However, this character is special in only pursuing the level of wealth necessary for securing respect from others as an equal.[48] Like everyone else in a third way, this character tries to win respect not just for wealth but also for "good character and conduct." However—and this is a new point—prudent people are special in that they try to win respect from others more for their good character and conduct than for their wealth. This last feature of the prudent character follows from its awareness of the asymmetry between increases in suffering and increases in joy. The prudent person realizes that a "fall from a better to a worse situation" involves more suffering than a "rise from a worse to a better" one involves joy. Thus, the prudent character is generally "rather cautious than enterprising." This aversion to risk leads the prudent person to pursue a good reputation on the basis of "the solidity of his knowledge and abilities" (VI.i.6). The previous section's discussion of friendship based on virtue is relevant for understanding why a reputation based on virtue is safer than one based on wealth alone. Smith writes:

> Men of virtue only can feel that entire confidence in the conduct and behaviour of one another, which can, at all times assure them they can never offend or be offended by one another. Vice is always capricious; virtue only is regular and orderly. The attachment which is founded upon the love of

> virtue, as it is certainly, of all attachments, the most virtuous; so it is likewise the happiest, as well as the most permanent and secure. Such friendships need not be confined to a single person, but may safely embrace all the wise and the virtuous, with whom we have been long and intimately acquainted, and upon whose wisdom and virtue we can, upon that account, entirely depend. (VI.ii.1.18)

In emphasizing the essential stability of affection based on virtue, this passage recommends on prudential grounds good character and conduct. The passage does not say that respect based upon wealth is unstable, but it would be easy to generate reasons for thinking that it is so, at least by comparison.

Risk aversiveness runs through the rest of Smith's depiction of the prudent character. This generates one final issue with which we must grapple before ending this section. In valuing "security" above all, the prudent character prioritizes maintaining over acquiring goods. When the prudent man does try to acquire wealth, he does so safely, by developing "real knowledge and skill," exercising "assiduity and industry in the exercise of it," and practicing "frugality, and even some degree of parsimony, in all . . . expenses" (VI.i.6). He never sacrifices his long-term interests for a short-term gain (VI.i.11). He tries to grow his income gradually, only "through small accumulations." "If he enters into any new projects or enterprises," it is never impulsively and always with a "well concerted and well prepared" plan (VI.i.1.12). We just saw that when he tries to acquire the respect of others, he adopts the safe strategy of doing so mainly via good character and conduct. We should also note that the prudent man adopts the safest possible version of this already safe strategy, as the good character and conduct for which he wishes to be known is not of a heroic kind but of a kind that brings minimal risk. In interacting with others, the prudent man always tells the truth but "is not always frank and open," as he takes seriously the danger of saying too much (VI.i.1.8). He "is always very capable of friendship," but only of a "steady and faithful," not "ardent and passionate" kind, "to a few well-tried and well-chosen companions"; he realizes that the feelings of "jollity and gaiety" that reward "general sociality" can "might too often interfere with the regularity of his temperance, might interrupt the steadiness of his industry, or break in upon the strictness of his frugality" (VI.i.9). His "conversation" is "always perfectly inoffensive" and modest, lest he violate the "established decorums and ceremonials of society" upon which we all rely (VI.i.10). And he is in no rush to take on any extra responsibility, even for the right reasons; he will avoid the opportunity to win "the real and solid glory of performing the greatest and most magnanimous actions," if taking it puts his "secure tranquility" at risk (VI.i.13).

Smith ends this depiction by observing that prudence "never is considered as one, either of the most endearing, or the most ennobling of the virtues"; it "commands a certain cold esteem, but seems not entitled any ardent love or admiration" (VI.i.14). This observation seems to contradict Smith's general classification of "virtue" as an honorific term that picks out admirable qualities or actions. We can avoid this problem by stressing the "ardent," so that Smith is saying that prudence is admired, but not very ardently. But regardless of this minor textual problem, Smith's observation seems right. The prudent character he just described is sort of a mixed bag: careful, solid, modest, resigned, and calm, but also unambitious, boring, meek, acquiescent, and unfeeling (as we saw in Section 3, the small, gradual gains upon which this person is most focused are precisely those to be pursued dispassionately, from a sense of obligation) (III.6.7). One looking for a less judgmental depiction of a modern European character type that so disgusted Nietzsche less than a century later could do worse than starting with Smith's discussion of prudence.

So why does Smith even classify prudence as a virtue? He provides some reasons that appeal to our intuitions and some reasons that appeal to his own moral psychology. In the direction of the former, Smith asks us to consider our respective reactions to the presence and absence of prudence in two characters who are equally devoid of any other possible virtue. Obviously, "a wicked and worthless man of parts," who is prudent but otherwise vicious, is a dangerous monster. Nevertheless, there seems to be *something* admirable about this figure that is missing from "a wicked and worthless fool," who is a vicious and imprudent, bumbling criminal type (VI.i.16). We might disagree with Smith's classification of these value judgments as "moral," but even if his view involves a miscategorization of this kind, its claim about the general valences of these judgments is not implausible. Smith also explains our positive estimation of at least part of the prudent character in terms of the WIS' sympathetic tendencies.

Since the WIS is just as impartial with respect to temporal as other forms of bias, this figure approves of the prudent character's willingness to sacrifice the "ease and enjoyment of the present moment for the probable expectation of the still greater ease and enjoyment of a more distant but more lasting period of time"; to the WIS, the prudent man's "present, and what is likely to be . . . future situation, are very nearly the same" (VI.i.11). There is no reason to believe that Smith could not explain our approval of other features of prudence along similar lines, perhaps by building upon some of the observations we have seen him make regarding our tendencies to sympathize with selfish passions (I.ii.5; I.iii.1; III.6.6–7).

In and of itself, there is nothing puzzling about Smith recognizing prudence as a virtue that we do not admire as much as we do the other virtues. But Smith muddies our understanding of how he thinks about prudence when we observes that "wise and judicious conduct, when directed to greater and nobler pursuits than the care of the health, the fortune, the rank and reputation of the individual, is frequently and very properly called prudence." This "superior" form of prudence is that possessed by the "great general," the "great statesman," and the "great legislator," not the mediocre figure we just saw described. If this distinction between "superior" and "inferior" forms of prudence were one of degree, there would also be nothing puzzling about it. However, the distinction ends up being one of kind; thus, Smith is left with two fundamentally different conceptions of prudence. Smith points out that in its superior form, prudence is "combined with many greater and more splendid virtues, with valour, with extensive and strong benevolence, with a sacred regard to the rules of justice, and all these supported by a proper degree of self-command." In this context, prudence is the virtue of "wise and judicious conduct" in general, without reference to any specific ends to which it is directed. On this understanding of prudence, it becomes "superior" when it is applied to the nobler ends set by the other virtues (VI.i.15). But up to this point and given Smith's schema for organizing the four classes of virtue, prudence is not the virtue of practical wisdom in general but of practical wisdom in reference to the specific end of self-interest. This more consistently expressed view implies that inferior and superior prudence differ in kind because they involve different ends. On the former, newer view, however, inferior and superior prudence do not differ in kind because prudence in general does not involve reference to any specific end.

It seems best to treat as Smith's considered view the conception of prudence which makes it the virtue of "wise and judicious conduct" specifically regarding self-interest. But then what do we do with Smith's willingness also to refer to the general quality of practical wisdom as a form of prudence? There is reason to read this willingness as an acknowledgment of common usage that Smith respects but ultimately rejects for the purposes of theory. To my ears, the phrase "is frequently and very properly called prudence" expresses an attitude of this sort. Given what we saw in the treatment of Smith on justice in Section 3 and in Chapter 5, treatment of Smith on Plato in Section 6, it is not a stretch to read that phrase this way. Of course, the difference between those contexts and this one is that in them, it is clear what terms Smith wants to use instead of the common ones. The best we can do in this case is harken back to a quick reference Smith makes to "intellectual virtues," which flags a possible way to categorize general practical wisdom but not a name for it (I.i.4.3).

The interpretive challenge it generates aside, the passage on superior prudence is important because it provides a brief depiction of Smith's ideal character, in which all the virtues coexist. Thus far in this chapter, we have considered the Smithian virtues separately. But we should also consider how Smith believes the virtues work together. Is it even possible to have one virtue without the others? And even if so, what does it look like when someone is virtuous across the board? The next section's discussion of the special virtue of self-command will help us address such questions.

Section 6: Self-Command

Just as prudence is "originally recommended to us by our selfish . . . affections" and justice and beneficence by our "benevolent" ones, self-command is grounded in our "regard to the sentiments of other people," a form of which becomes "regard to the sentiments of the supposed impartial spectator" (VI .concl.1). Thus, just as prudence is the virtue of self-concern and justice and beneficence are the virtues of concern for others, self-command is the virtue of concern for sympathy with the WIS. Although it does so only implicitly, Smith's discussion of self-command involves a distinction between inferior and superior types. However, in contrast with his discussion of prudence, Smith distinguishes between three types of self-command, not two.[49] In additional contrast with the distinction between inferior and superior prudence, the higher forms of self-command are best understood as the exemplars of the virtue itself. And in a third contrast with his discussion of prudence, Smith's discussion of self-command distinguishes between three types of the trait only implicitly. Thus, the burden is on us to distinguish between the three types of self-command and to show that only the second two fit with Smith's fundamental conception of the virtue.

While Smith begins his treatments of beneficence and prudence by respectively explaining the benevolent and selfish affections, he does not begin his treatment of self-command by explaining our sympathy-based concern for how other people feel about us and our sentiments, as well as the development of our sympathy-based concern for how the WIS feels about us and our sentiments. One reason for this difference is that, as we saw across Chapters 3 and 4, Smith already provided this account in other parts of the TMS. However, another reason for this difference is that self-command has as much to do with the passions being commanded as it does with our motives for commanding them. By following his lead and starting with the passions being commanded, we can build an account of Smith's distinction between three types of self-command in a way that moves from lower to higher forms.

Smith employs a distinction between classes of passion that he adopts from "some of the best of the ancient moralists," among whom, as we saw in Section 6 of the previous chapter, is Plato.[50] They divide the passions that we command into two categories: those that "drive" us down a path we do not want to take and thus require "a considerable exertion of self-command to restrain even for a single moment" and those that "seduce" us into taking a path we do not want to take and thus are "easy to restrain for a single moment, or even for a short period of time," but plague us with "continual and almost incessant solicitations." The best examples of passions in the former category are "fear and anger," while the best examples of passions in the latter category are "the love of ease, of pleasure, [and] of applause." Command of the former kind of passion requires "strength and greatness of . . . exertion," while command of the latter kind of passion requires "uniformity . . . equality and unremitting steadiness of . . . exertion" (VI.iii.2–4).[51]

The lowest form of self-command over these passions that Smith recognizes is motivated "by prudential considerations of the bad consequences which might follow from their indulgence." For example, anger can be "restrained by fear" of what might happen to us if we indulge it (VI.concl.3). This kind of self-command gets some approval from appreciation of the "beauty which it derives from its utility" in helping us accomplish a variety of ends (VI.iii .4). But as we have seen throughout, approval on the basis of utility is always secondary for Smith. Since approval on the basis of sympathy with the WIS is most important, the main reason why this kind of self-command is lowest is that it does not actually bring our sentiments into line with those of the WIS. Smith is clear that when some passions are "restrained" by some other ones, such as anger can be by fear or even love of ease—imagine restraining anger from an unwillingness to exert the effort it would take to act on it—they are "not always subdued," which means they "often remain lurking in the breast with all their original fury" (VI.concl.3). This kind of command wins less approval because the WIS "can [only] readily enter into" our passions when they have been "moderated and subdued," not merely restrained (VI.concl.5).

Smith is assuming of course that purely prudential self-command—we should note already that if it turns out that all virtue, prudence included, requires a higher form of self-command, then what is being described with this phrase invokes a lower, not fully virtuous form of prudence—does not transform our passions in a way that more conscientious self-command does. More specifically, he is assuming that our passions are not transformed when we consider them from the perspective of a future version of ourselves who is dealing with the consequences of their indulgence but are transformed when we consider them from the perspective of another, impartial person:

> The man whose anger is restrained by fear, does not always lay aside his anger, but only reserves its gratification for a more safe opportunity. But the man who, in relating to some other person the injury which has been done to him, feels at once the fury of his passion cooled and becalmed

> by sympathy with the more moderate sentiments of his companion, who at once adopts those more moderate sentiments, and comes to view that injury, not in the black and atrocious colours in which he had originally beheld it, but in the much milder and fairer light in which his companion naturally views it; not only restrains, but in some measure subdues, his anger. The passion becomes really less than it was before, and less capable of exciting him to the violent and bloody revenge which at first, perhaps, he might have thought of inflicting. (VI.concl.3)

Smith points here to recognizable phenomenon. He seems to have in mind the following kind of account of the mechanisms behind it. In the case of prudential purely self-command, I have not called my passion into question so much as I have called into question the idea of acting upon it at present. In the case of more conscientious self-command, understood either in terms of consulting the WIS or some actual impartial other person, I am led to question my passion itself by the fact that I take on a perspective from which it is not felt.

While it is true that those who command their anger from fear or some other self-interested concern do not really demonstrate self-command because they are not really commanding their fear,[52] we should remind ourselves that this matters to Smith not because there is something intrinsically valuable about sovereignty over our passions for its own sake but because mutual sympathy with the WIS requires actual transformation of feeling. Smith articulates neither the theory of value nor the metaphysically robust conception of the self, according to which the self is to be distinguished from its passions, required for the self-sovereignty-focused view. Thus, the fundamental mark of virtuousness in self-command of these and other passions remains the sympathy of the WIS. The closer we bring our actual feelings to the level at which the WIS would feel them, the more virtuous we are. (Smith also sometimes writes here as if the goal is to express our feelings in a way that coincides with the level at which the WIS would feel them, rather than actually bring the feelings to this level. For example, emphasizing expression alone, Smith remarks that "the man who, in danger, in torture, upon the approach of death, preserves his tranquility unaltered, and suffers no word, no gesture to escape him which does not perfectly accord with the feelings of the most indifferent spectator, necessarily commands a very high degree of admiration" (VI.iii.5). I dealt with this ambiguity more fully in Section 3 of Chapter 3. For the sake of simplicity, I proceed here by focusing on feelings over expressions.)

Smith also believes that purely self-interested self-restraint fails to win full sympathy from the WIS because "the meanness of the motive takes away all the nobleness of the restraint" (VI.iii.10). The WIS would prefer, it seems, that we be motivated in our self-command by a desire to win his sympathy. This point about the importance of motive could use more explanation. In several other contexts, Smith attributes significant value to at least something like the self-consciously moral motive of desire for the sympathy of the WIS. As we saw in Section 2 of the previous chapter, Smith believes that "the source of all those actions which are commonly accounted virtuous" is the love of virtue, which is love of sympathy with the WIS (VII.ii.4.11). Elsewhere, he states that "no action can properly called virtuous, which is not accompanied with the sentiment of self-approbation," a sentiment that is made possible by checking oneself against the WIS (III.6.13). And in a first pass at offering a general conception of virtue, Smith distinguishes between "amiable" and "awful" virtue on the grounds that the former rests upon the act of entering into another's sentiments, while the latter rests upon the act of bringing down one's own sentiments so that others can enter into them (I.i.5.1). Later, he points out that both acts rest upon "the very same principle" because both acts are motivated by concern for sympathy with others and involve imagining being in another's shoes (III.3.34). Thus, Smith sees the desire for mutual sympathy, which, of course, becomes desire for mutual sympathy with the WIS, as the root of all virtue. But is Smith merely relying upon an intuition that actions only really have moral value when they are performed with a sense of their moral value or does he ground this view somehow? He does not do so explicitly, but the view seems to follow from the nature of mutual sympathy and the WIS' identity. In feeling the same sentiments as himself, the WIS must sympathize with and approve of his own sentiments. Sympathy with and approval of intentional attempts to cultivate these sentiments then ends up being an outgrowth of the initial self-sympathy and self-approval.

The importance of motive to self-command helps explain why Smith also claims that the more exertion required for self-command, the more virtue is involved in it (VI.iii.11; cf. VI.iii.4). He even claims, more strongly, that "to act according to the dictates of prudence, of justice, and proper beneficence seems to have no great merit where there is no temptation to the contrary" (VI.iii.11). In some of Smith's examples, the WIS "admires" exertion in Smith's technical sense of feeling "approbation heightened by wonder and surprise" in the face of the "uncommon" and "unexpected" (I.i.4.3). Thus, the WIS admires those who demonstrate an exceptional degree of self-command in exceptionally trying situations, such as those presented by "war" and by interaction with one's "most mortal enemies" (VI.iii.8–9). But Smith also must think that the WIS is impressed by strong exertions of self-command even when they are not rare. It is not obvious that the "unremitting steadiness of those gentler exertions of self-command" in the face of universal and ever-present seductions of pleasure and ease are as rare as the heroic command of intense fear in the face of death or of powerful anger in response to personal injury, but, "though much less dazzling," the former are "not always less pleasing" to the WIS than the latter (VI.iii.13). And even if these steady exertions are as rare as the stronger but more temporary ones, Smith's discussion of both kinds is shot through with notable respect for strong-willedness itself that seems insufficiently explained by its rarity alone. When admiration-triggering rarity cannot do the job, the best explanation for why exertion matters to the WIS is that it demonstrates the strength of the virtuous motives, the most important of which is the desire for sympathy with the WIS. If the previous paragraph's suggestion of a ground in Smith's moral psychology for the WIS' sympathy with and approval of this motive works, then we also get a ground for the claim that the WIS values exertion in self-command. To the extent that stronger instances of this motive get stronger sympathy and approval and to the extent that exertion tracks strength of motivation, the WIS will more strongly sympathize with and approve of WIS-motivated self-command that involves more exertion.

Thus, self-command motivated "by the sense of propriety, by regard to the sentiments of the supposed impartial spectator," both differs from and is better than prudential self-restraint because it brings our sentiments in line with those of the WIS and because the WIS appreciates the desire to sympathize with the WIS, especially when it manifests itself in strong exertion (VI.concl .2). We should note at least one counterintuitive implication of this view.

Maximal virtue and approval from the WIS require that we practice self-command motivated by regard for the WIS. Self-command that is motivated in that way will not just restrain but alter our passions such that the WIS can enter into them. Moreover, the WIS approves of the desire to command our passions for the sake of achieving sympathy with the WIS. Thus, the WIS especially approves of WIS-motivated self-command that involves strong exertion because it indicates strong desire to achieve sympathy with the WIS. But if we succeed in this exertion, if we actually modify our passions so that we habitually feel them at the level that the WIS would feel them, we no longer have to exert ourselves for the sake of hitting this level. And if we no longer have to exert ourselves in this way, we no longer win much approval from the WIS. So it seems that as we get more virtuous, we win less approval from the WIS.[53]

One way for Smith to avoid this result is by insisting that we never reach a point at which WIS-motivated self-command no longer requires exertion. In a long discussion of the right degree of self-esteem, Smith points out that in evaluating himself, "the wise and virtuous man directs his principal attention" to "the idea of exact propriety and perfection," not to "that degree of approximation to this idea which is commonly attained in the world." Thus, this figure

> endeavours as well as he can, to assimilate his own character to this archetype of perfection. But he imitates the work of a divine artist, which can never be equaled. He feels the imperfect success of all his best endeavours, and sees, with grief and affliction, in how many different features the mortal copy falls short of the immortal original. He remembers, with concern and humiliation, how often, from want of attention, from want of judgment, from want of temper, he as, in both words and actions, both in conduct and conversation, violated the exact rules of perfect propriety; and has so far departed from that model, according to which he wished to fashion his own character and conduct. (VI.iii.25)

If this is as good as the wise and virtuous man can do, then the rest of us shouldn't worry about becoming so virtuous that we no longer win approval from the WIS because we no longer must exert ourselves in the struggle to be virtuous. Still, at the level of ideals, the problem remains. Regardless of whether we actually achieve it, there seems to be something incoherent about pursuing a goal—getting our sentiments to line up with those of the WIS (cf. III.3.25)—the actual achievement of which would undercut our reason for pursuing it—to win approval from the WIS. Since the WIS' approval rests upon sympathy, this undercutting would only be partial. The WIS would still approve of us if we succeeded in our attempt to cultivate sentiments with which he sympathizes; thus, the achievement of our goal would coincide to this extent with our reason for pursuing it. But if we take Smith at his word, the WIS would approve of us *more*, at least over time, not if we failed miserably but if we failed only to the extent necessary to guarantee the need for continued exertion. The best possible strategy for us would be to exert ourselves heavily in bringing our passions only temporarily to a level into which the WIS can enter but with no stable changes. Needless to say, it would be strange to undertake the cultivation of virtue in this way.

Another, more satisfying option for Smith would be to stress that while strength of exertion in the face of competing motives can be a good indicator of strength of motive, it is not a necessary condition of having strong motives in the sense most relevant to the WIS' sympathy and approval. According to this response, we start developing self-command by exerting ourselves from a strong desire to win the sympathy of the WIS. As we get more virtuous, our sentiments stabilize at a level closer to those of the WIS. Thus, we need to exert ourselves less in getting our sentiments to this level. But as our sentiments stabilize in this way, our motivation to win sympathy from the WIS does not suddenly get weaker. If anything, its stability indicates an increase in strength, though of a kind that does not manifest itself in exertion because there is less against which to exert it. As a result, we end up with a strong, settled motivational disposition to win the sympathy of WIS that we do not need to exert at all once we have succeeded in getting our sentiments to line up with those of the WIS. On this view, the WIS would still give us maximal approval and sympathy, despite our lack of exertion, because we still have a strong motivational disposition to win the sympathy of the WIS.[54]

We should also note that Smith spends about fourth-fifths of the TMS VI chapter on self-command trying to show that cultivating WIS-motivated self-command is in our interest.[55] He describes this project as that of defending the

> general rule, that the passions which the spectator is most disposed to sympathize with, and in which, upon that account, the point of propriety may be said to stand high, are those of which the immediate feeling or sensation is more or less agreeable to the person principally concerned: and that, on the contrary, the passion which the spectator is least disposed to sympathize with, and in which, upon that account, the point of propriety may be said to stand low, are those of which the immediate feeling or sensation is more or less disagreeable, or even painful, to the person principally concerned. (VI.iii.15)

Thus, as we saw in Section 3 of Chapter 3, the WIS generally favors the "affections which tend to unite men in society," which are agreeable to experience, and disfavors the "affections which drive men from one another," which are disagreeable to experience (VI.iii.15–16). As we also saw in Section 3 of Chapter 3, the WIS has a comparatively neutral disposition to self-regarding passions, like our "sensibility to personal danger and distress," our "sensibility to the pleasures, to the amusements and enjoyments of human life," and our "self-estimation" (VI.iii.17–22). Both excesses and deficiencies are possible in all cases of self-regarding passions, but the WIS is generally most worried about excess in the first and deficiency in the second. In obvious ways, these concerns line up with what is most agreeable to the agent. Since positive self-esteem feels good to us but often offends others, we might think that the WIS worries more about excess than deficiency regarding the third. If so, this would be an instance in which the WIS' concerns do not line up with what is most agreeable to agent. But, Smith argues across fifteen pages of a twenty-five page chapter, the WIS is equally worried about excess and deficiency in self-estimation, both of which are ultimately bad for agents themselves; thus, "that degree of self-estimation . . . which contributes most to the happiness of the person himself, seems likewise most agreeable to the impartial spectator" (VI.III.50). In Section 2 of the next chapter, we will revisit Smith's view on the coincidence of virtue and self-interest.

Thus far in this section, we have seen that Smith must recognize at least two forms of self-command, one motivated by self-interest and one motivated by regard to the sentiments of the WIS. We have also seen that the former is better described as self-restraint than self-command. Now we shall see that Smith also needs a distinction between two different varieties of self-command motivated by regard to the sentiments of the WIS. Smith observes that since "the virtues of prudence, justice, and beneficence, have no tendency to produce any but the most agreeable effects," the WIS approves of them on account of their propriety and on account of "their utility, either to the person who exercises them, or to other persons" (VI.concl.6). The "virtues of self-command," on the other hand, have "effects [that] may be sometimes agreeable, and sometimes disagreeable." Yet self-command "still appears to be a great and respectable quality even" when it is "employed . . . in the cause . . . of . . . injustice" (VI.concl.7). History is filled with examples of "excessively dangerous" and damaging people who have "been often much admired by many people of not contemptible judgment," whether for their "great warlike exploit" or their "intrepid valour . . . in times of great public disorder" (VI.iii.8, 12). We might think that these are examples of people who command their passions from purely interested considerations, to help them achieve whatever "pernicious purpose" they might have (VI.iii .12). However, Smith believes that in at least some of these cases, "the greatness and steadiness of the exertion" of self-command, which has a "splendid and dazzling quality," is motived by a "strong sense of propriety," not interest alone. "The effects" of their actions, whether on others or themselves, Smith laments, "are often but too little regarded" (VI.concl.7).

Smith's apparent willingness to recognize that self-command can be motivated "by the sense of propriety, by regard to the sentiments of the supposed impartial spectator" but still be employed in the cause of injustice means that he should also recognize a form of self-command that is so motivated but cannot be employed in the cause of injustice, since, after all, injustice is something of which the WIS does not approve. In the former case, the turn to the WIS must be extremely narrowly focused. For example, in trying to command my fear of death in the face of embarking upon a dangerous, unjustified expansionist military operation, I might employ my WIS-based sense of the propriety in tamping down my fear, without any regard to the consequences thereof nor, for that matter, to the impropriety of the motives that are driving me toward the action that is making me afraid in the first place. However, I might also consider the WIS' perspective on my situation construed more broadly, so as to include these factors. Thus, Smith needs a distinction not just between self-interest-motivated and WIS-motivated self-command but also between what we can call "narrow" and "broad" WIS-motivated self-command. Clearly, the notion of narrow WIS-motivated self-command is in tension with both the "W" and the "I" in the acronym. But this tension is acceptable so long it allows for the normative superiority of broader—or better informed and more impartial—WIS-motivated self-command and so long as the notion of narrow WIS-motivated self-command involved in it helps makes sense of Smith's belief that self-command can be motivated by regard to the WIS, who cares about both utility and justice, and still be generally damaging and unjust. I suggest that this tension is resolvable only if we allow for motivation involving impoverished conceptions of the WIS. Narrow WIS-motivated self-command amounts to self-command motivated by desire for the sympathy of a spectator that is more well-informed and impartial than I presently am but not *that* well-informed and/or not *that* impartial.

The distinction between narrow and broad WIS-motivated self-command fails to capture another kind of case in which we can employ our WIS-based sense of propriety and still get things wrong. Suppose that in the just-described circumstances, I do consider both the consequences of the action enabled by my command of fear and the propriety of the motives that are driving me toward the action that is making me afraid in the first place. And suppose that after doing this, I falsely believe that, according to the WIS, the consequences of the action enabled by my command of fear are not bad and that the motives from which I act are just, perhaps because the people I intend to harm deserve it.[56] The possibility of this kind of case introduces a need for a distinction between inaccurate and accurate WIS-motivated self-command, which can obviously overlap with the distinction between narrow and broad. Thus, there are technically more than three conceptions of self-command at work in Smith's thought. However, as long as we recognize the possibility of such subdivisions, we can safely capture the main point by staying focused on the following three: self-interested, WIS-motivated but lesser (for involving narrow and/or inaccurate conception), and WIS-motivated but higher (for involving broad and accurate conception).

Let's focus now on developing Smith's understanding of the highest form of self-command, the kind motivated by the WIS who sees things broadly and accurately. (I will have this in mind when I refer without further qualification to self-command or the WIS from here on out.) It seems that if we possess this virtue, we necessarily possess the other virtues too. Since the sentiments of the WIS pick out prudence, justice, and beneficence as virtues, self-regulation by these sentiments will lead to possession of those virtues. Thus, to have self-command is to have those other virtues. But can we have those other virtues without having self-command?

Smith opens the section on self-command by leaning toward a negative answer to this question:

> The man who acts according to the rules of perfect prudence, of strict justice, and of proper benevolence, may be said to be perfectly virtuous. But the most perfect knowledge of these rules will not enable him to act in this manner: his own passions are very apt to mislead him; sometimes to drive him and sometimes to seduce him to violate all the rules which he himself, in all his sober and cool hours, approves of. The most perfect knowledge, if it is not supported by the most perfect self-command, will not always enable him to do his duty. (VI.iii.1)

The passage contains elements that I flagged in Section 1 of the previous chapter as potentially confusing to ears trained like ours: it focuses on duty and rules even though it constitutes part of the presentation of a virtue theory. The rules talk is additionally confusing for the reason that it fits oddly both with Smith's view that rules play an essential role in justice alone and with his immediately preceding discussion of prudence and beneficence as involving much more than tendencies to follow rules. But the gist of the passage is clear: the virtue of self-command is required to ensure our consistent practice of the other virtues. However, if this is the only reason why self-command is necessary for the consistent practice of the other virtues, then it is only practically impossible to have the other virtues without self-command. In principle, however, this passage leaves open the possibility one can have the other virtues without self-command. If anything, it positively claims, in its first line, that one can, in principle, have the other virtues without self-command.

The problem with allowing for this possibility, though, is that doing so clashes with Smith's oft-mentioned insistence that guidance by a sense of propriety is a necessary condition for virtue. If it is in principle possible to be prudent, beneficent, and just without self-command, then it is possible to be prudent, beneficent, and just simply because one happens to have and act upon self- and other-directed feelings of which the WIS would approve. But as we have seen, Smith is clear that virtue requires not just having and acting from proper feelings but also having and acting from proper feelings along with the knowledge that they are proper and desire that they be so. Beneficence is the only virtue for which this additional component might not be necessary, but even it falls short of virtue without that component:

> There is something pleasing even in mere instinctive good-will which goes on to do good offices without once reflecting whether by this conduct it is the proper object either of blame or approbation. It is not so with the other passions. The moment they are deserted, the moment they are unaccompanied by the sense of propriety, they cease to be agreeable. (VII.ii.3.4)

There is at most "something pleasing" about even effective beneficence unaccompanied and guided by a sense of propriety. Without reflection upon propriety, the other virtues do not even get to this level.

This observation comes from Smith's discussion of Hutcheson's virtue theory. But Smith also makes the same point in his exposition of his own. As we saw earlier, beneficence is grounded in other-directed concerns that can sometimes pull us in opposing directions. The only way to negotiate these conflicts and thus manifest the virtue, Smith points out, is by consulting "the man within the breast, the supposed impartial spectator, the great judge and arbiter of our conduct" (VI.ii.1.22). As we also saw earlier, to the extent that justice is a virtue, it essentially involves conscious guidance by rules grounded in the sentiments of the WIS. Even prudence, insofar as it involves the attempt to secure a positive reputation for one's "good character and conduct," requires reflection upon propriety (VI.i.4). Moreover, when the prudent character is narrowly focused on increasing his own fortune, he must turn to the WIS for help:

> In the steadiness of his industry and frugality, in his steadily sacrificing the ease and enjoyment of the present moment for the probable expectation of the still greater ease and enjoyment of a more distant but more lasting period of time, the prudent man is always both *supported* and rewarded by the entire approbation of the impartial spectator, and of the representative of the impartial spectator, the man within the breast. The impartial spectator does not feel himself worn out by the present labour of those whose conduct he surveys; nor does he feel himself solicited by the importunate calls of their present appetites. To him their present, and what is likely to be their future situation, are very nearly the same: he sees them nearly at the same distance, and is affected by them very nearly in the same manner. He know, however, that to the persons principally concerned, they are very far from being the same, and that they naturally affected *them* in a very different manner. He cannot therefore but approve, and even applaud, that *proper exertion of self-command*, which enables them to act as if their present and their future situation affected them nearly in the same manner in which they affect him. (VI.i.11; all emphases added except for "them")

Even the morally lowly, unheroic but still virtuous activity of working to improve one's lot in life for the long run requires WIS-motivated self-command. Additionally, Smith explicitly says elsewhere that "the union" of "self-command" with "superior reason and understanding" constitute the "virtue of prudence" (IV.2.6).[57]

It follows, then, that we not only cannot have self-command without the other virtues but also cannot have the other virtues without self-command. Since these two claims together imply that we also cannot have some of the non-self-command virtues without others, it seems that Smith is committed to a strong thesis of the unity of the virtues. There may be reasons to reject the view that one cannot have some virtues without all of them, but Smith has a response at least to the objection that the view is too out-of-touch with common experience. We have all, the objection runs, met people who are prudent but not beneficent, beneficent but imprudent, just but not beneficent, and so on; maybe *some* virtues are natural pairs[58]—prudence requires justice, it seems—but one can grant this without granting that virtuousness is a totally all-or-nothing affair. This objection is powerful and should be taken seriously, especially given Smith's own commitment to keeping his theory in close contact with everyday experience. However, I think he can respond to it by allowing for degrees of virtuousness. Sure, the person who is prudent but not beneficent, beneficent but imprudent, or just but not beneficent might possess the virtues they do *to an extent*. But if one possesses these individual virtues *fully*, one also possesses the other virtues.[59] This claim might still be false, but not because it is wildly counterintuitive. And we must remember that for Smith, "virtue," *especially* in the full sense to which I refer here, "is excellence, something uncommonly great and beautiful, which rises far about what is vulgar and ordinary" (I.i.5.6).

What about the view that virtue requires guidance by a sense of propriety? On this view, if I just so happen to have and act upon proper self- and other-directed feelings but never think about and thus do not care about the fact that they are so, I am technically not virtuous. I do not think that Smith is committed to the stronger claim that I am thereby positively vicious, but leave that possibility aside. Why think that virtue depends upon such thoughts and concerns? On a virtue theory with teleological commitments about what a fully human life requires, such thoughts and concerns could be simply be built into what virtuousness means; on a view like this one, virtue requires knowing what one is doing and why because this is essential to specifically human excellence. Smith very well could hold a version of such a view. (We return to this issue in Section 2 of next chapter.) But even if he does, it would be nice to find a reason for attaching such fundamental importance to moral reflectiveness that is external to such commitments. We could say that such reflectiveness is practically important to ensure that our sentiments and conduct remain proper, but we are looking here for a more principled reason. One begins coming into focus if we consider that virtue involves making value judgments. When I am prudent, my desires and actions line up with my judgments about what is best for me. When I am just, my desires and actions line up with my judgments about what is noninjurious and fair to others. When I am beneficent, my desires and actions line up with my judgments about what is best for others, as well as my judgments about the relative moral weight of my various attachments. It is hard to see how, not just practically but in principle, one could be virtuous without making these judgments, and it is hard to see how, no just practically but in principle, one could make these judgments without consulting the WIS or something analogous to it.

Using TMS VI as its primary source, this chapter has attempted to sketch and critically engage with Smith's virtue theory. At first glance, the theory might appear simple. But as we saw, interesting questions, complications, and implications arise at almost every turn. Consideration of justice revealed what Smith took to be an entirely different "science" from that of ethics. Consideration of beneficence revealed Smith's nuanced practical treatment of questions regarding the width of the moral point of view. Consideration of prudence directed us to Smith's similarly nuanced understanding of what drives and how best to value wealth-acquisition. Consideration of self-command revealed that Smith is committed to the unity of virtue. And in the case of each virtue, we saw and attempted to resolve tensions in Smith's views.

In the next chapter, we turn to some of the big-ticket philosophical issues that have been lurking in the background, namely that of Smith's metaethics and that of his account of normativity.

7

Smith's Metaethics and Account of Normativity

This book has been structured by Smith's distinction between what he sees as the two main questions of moral philosophy, that of the psychological foundation of moral judgment and that of the nature of virtue. In the introduction, I suggested that we interpret this distinction as akin to the more general one contemporary philosophers make between metaethics and normative ethics, if only because in pointing out that the psychological foundation of moral judgment question lacks the practical impact of the nature of virtue question, Smith explicitly anticipates the contemporary practice of classifying questions *about* ethics as non-normative and ethical questions as normative. Initially, I made this suggestion only for the sake of familiarizing contemporary readers with the contours of Smith's project in the TMS. Now, however, I would like to employ the parallel more substantively so as to open up two new lines of inquiry. The first concerns the implications of Smith's answer to the psychological foundation of moral judgment question for how we might situate his views in some metaethical categories we recognize today regarding the nature of moral judgment and the metaphysical status of the objects of moral judgment. The second bears a different relationship to its counterpart in Smith's theory than the first does in that it is not directly concerned with the content of Smith's normative ethics. Rather, the second line of inquiry concerns the higher-order question of the nature of the normativity in Smith's moral theory; how might Smith answer the question of *why* we should orient our sentiments and conduct by the sentiments of the WIS?

The chapter is divided into two sections, one for each line of inquiry. Since, as we shall see, Smith himself does not directly or fully pursue these lines, each section defends only tentative conclusions derived from things Smith says or positions he holds.

Section 1: Smith's Metaethics

As I pointed out in the introduction, the key to understanding the notion of metaethics lies in understanding what it means to deal with questions that are *about* ethics. Ethical questions are about how we should live. Metaethical questions, in contrast, are about what we are even doing when we ask and act upon the answers to ethical ones. Since there are many different kinds of questions of this kind to ask, it helps to organize our investigation of Smith's metaethics with a broad distinction between metaethical questions regarding what is going on in us and metaethical questions regarding what is going on in the world.[1] There are also many questions to ask under each of these headings, but it seems that with respect to Smith's moral philosophy, two stand out as most worth asking: (a) when we make a moral judgment, what kind of mental state are we expressing? and (b) what is the nature of the objects of these judgment? As Smith's answer to the psychological foundation of moral judgment question seems to address the former, let's start with it.

As we saw across Chapters 2 and 3, Smith answers the question by defending a "[system] which [makes] sentiment the principle of approbation," as opposed to a "[system] which [makes] reason the principle of approbation" (VII.iii.3; VII.iii.2). (Since, as we also saw in Chapter 2, Smith's third option, that of "systems which deduce the principle of approbation from self-love," is plausibly situated in the former category, we can leave it to one side (VII.iii.1)). Smith argues that the rationalist view, according to which we "derived [the] notion [of moral distinctions] from reason, which pointed out the difference between right and wrong in the same manner in which it did that between truth and falsehood," cannot account for the facts that the consideration of right conduct "constantly pleases," the consideration of wrong conduct "constantly displeases," and the consideration of both motivate us respectively toward and away from themselves. Thus, he concludes that even though we can and do use reason to generalize from our "first perceptions of right and wrong" and even though we can and do use reason to gather factual information relevant to these first perceptions,[2] the first perceptions themselves must be "the object . . . of immediate sense and feeling" (VII.iii.5–8). Within this category of sentiment-based answers, Smith defends a view according to which we make moral judgments not by a newly recognized, special moral "sentiment of a peculiar nature . . . distinct from every other" or "a particular power of perception," like a newly recognized, special moral sense, but by the already recognized psychological "power" of "sympathy," which, as we saw in Sections 3 and 4 of Chapter 4, gets fine-tuned by reference to the WIS (VII.iii.3.2–3). As we saw in Section 3 of Chapter 2, Smith's main idea is that neither the special moral sense view nor the special moral sentiment view does a good enough job explaining moral experience to justify recognizing the new features of human psychology they demand.

For many contemporary metaethicists, moral judgments either express beliefs or they do not. If they do express beliefs, they are capable of being true or false; if they do not express beliefs, they are not capable of being true or false.[3] The former position is called "cognitivism," while the latter position is called "non-cognitivism." Since Smith argues against the rationalists that we do not make moral distinctions in the same way in which we use reason to distinguish between truth and falsity, he seems to fall squarely into the non-cognitivist camp; if moral judgments express beliefs that, by definition, are capable of being true or false, there seems to be no reason why they would not be discoverable or producible by reason in the way Smith rejects.

Yet we should not conclude too quickly that Smith is a non-cognitivist. Recall that on Smith's full-blown account, moral judgment involves consulting the sentiments of the WIS. Thus, it is possible that when I judge you—we'll stay focused on other-directed moral judgment while accepting Smith's assumption that whatever we see here must also apply to self-directed moral judgment (III.1.2; Letter 40, 49)—I am expressing my belief about whether the WIS sympathizes with you. If so, then Smith's view is straightforwardly cognitivist.

However, this is probably not how Smithian moral judgment works, all things considered. The WIS is best understood as a corrective for evaluations we naturally make on the basis of our attempts at sympathizing. As we saw in Section 2 of Chapter 2, if we observe concord between our sentiments and an agent's, we feel a pleasure "in which the sentiment of approbation properly consists"; if we observe discord, we feel a pain in which the sentiment of disapprobation properly consists (I.iii.1.9, note). Since approbation and disapprobation involve sentiments in this way, *corrected* approbation and disapprobation must involve sentiments too. Thus, whatever account we provide of the psychological details of our invocation of the WIS, this account must maintain the sentimental character of approbation and disapprobation. Furthermore, as I suggested in Section 3 of Chapter 4, it seems most likely that we invoke the WIS to correct our evaluations of others as part of our more general self-correction, such that when we evaluate others well, we directly employ our own sentiments, though after they have been corrected in self-reflection. But even if this is incorrect, and we invoke the WIS directly as a third party whenever we evaluate another person, such that we sympathize with the WIS who is attempting to sympathize with this other person, our approval or disapproval bottoms out in a sentiment. We might worry that Smith's recognition of "conditional sympathy" based upon how we know we *would* feel under different circumstances might push against what I am saying here (I.i.3.4). (See Section 2 of Chapter 4.) Perhaps we correct our moral evaluations by considering how we *would* feel if we were actually trying to sympathize with an agent on the basis of our own corrected feelings or through an attempt to sympathize with the WIS who is trying to sympathize with the agent; in either case, it seems, we judge without sentiment. However, even this kind of account assumes that evaluation, even corrected evaluation, ultimately requires sentiment. We would never evaluate on the basis of how we would feel under other conditions if we never experienced a feeling under those conditions. Furthermore, Smith's attack on moral rationalism implies that he would not think that unfeeling expressions of beliefs about what the WIS feels or what we would feel would be able to motivate us in the way that moral evaluations do. Thus, the possibility remains that Smith is a non-cognitivist.

This possibility appears to weaken, however, when we consider the nature of the sentiments involved in Smithian moral judgment. As we saw in Section 2 of Chapter 2, Smithian sentiments either contain or naturally come accompanied by not only ideas of their objects but also—more importantly—considerations that act for us as reasons justifying the sentiments. Since approval of such sentiments requires sharing them, approval also requires recognizing the same considerations that act as reasons justifying them, such that when you get angry at someone for attacking you and I sympathize with and approve of your anger, I share your view that being thus attacked is a reason to get angry in the way you did. If these considerations acting as reasons are themselves beliefs, then we have reason to think that Smith is a cognitivist, albeit one who holds that the beliefs expressed by moral judgments are bound up with affects in a way that prevents them from being discovered or generated purely by reason alone;[4] on such a view, moral judgments are necessarily both felt and believed.

Unfortunately, it is impossible to settle decisively the question of whether for Smith, the considerations acting as reasons for our sentiments are themselves beliefs, however intuitive it might be to think of them this way. Let's turn now to our second metaethical question, that of what is going on in the world, metaphysically speaking, when we make moral judgments. What exactly are these judgments tracking? Perhaps grappling with this question can shine some additional light on our first one.

Smith provides even fewer resources for addressing the second question than he does for the first. In Section 1 of Chapter 2 and in Section 2 of Chapter 5, we saw him agree with the rationalists that moral distinctions are "natural" and both "real and essential" (VII.iii.2.2; VII.ii.4.1). But with this language, Smith only conveys the view that morality is not something that people consciously invented whole cloth; beyond that, it implies little about its metaphysical status. However, Smith does make two sets of comments that at least speak to this issue. Unfortunately, though, these sets of comments suggest different views. Smith makes one set in the process of pointing out the special authority of our moral faculties:

> Every sense is supreme over its own objects. There is no appeal from the eye with regard to the beauty of colours, nor from the ear with regard to the harmony of sounds, nor from the taste with regard to the agreeableness of flavours. Each of those sense judges in the last resort of its own objects.

> Whatever gratifies the taste is sweet, whatever pleases the eye is beautiful, whatever soothes the ear is harmonious. *The very essence of each of those qualities consists in its being fitted to please the sense to which it is addressed.* It belongs to our moral faculties, in the same manner to determine when the ear ought to be soothed, when the eye ought to be indulged, when the taste ought to be gratified, when and how far every other principle of our nature ought either to be indulged or restrained. *What is agreeable to our moral faculties, is fit, and right, and proper to be done; the contrary wrong, unfit, and improper.* The sentiments which they approve of, are graceful and becoming: the contrary, ungraceful and unbecoming. *The very words, right, wrong, fit, improper, graceful, unbecoming, mean only what please or displeases those faculties.* (III.5.5; emphases added)

Let's put to one side the point about the authority of our moral faculties, which, employing other parts of this same passage, we address in the next section. Instead, let's focus on the analogy the passage makes between, on the one hand, the beauty of colors, the harmony of sounds, and the agreeableness of flavors, and, on the other, the positive and negative moral status of the sentiments which are the targets of moral judgment. Just as the "very essence" of the former qualities "consists in [their] being fitted to please the sense to which [they are] addressed," the very essence of the latter qualities, Smith implies, consists in their being fitted to "please or [displease]" our moral faculties. This analogy suggests that, in today's language, "moral properties" like virtuousness are in some sense dependent upon the mind perceiving them; our very concepts of these properties, as the last sentence in the passage indicates, reflect this.

If Smith's analogy were between the perception of moral properties and the perception of colors, sounds, and tastes, we could be immediately confident that it expresses the view that moral properties are, in today's language, response-dependent, meaning that they are the dual product of our perceptions and the external correlates in the world that cause them. On this view, just as smells, despite being caused by objectively existent molecules with certain physical properties, do not exist without smelling subjects with the right faculties, moral properties, despite being caused by objectively existent actions and sentiments with certain physical properties, do not exist without evaluating subjects with the right faculties (cf. ES 23–4, 40–1, 44, 47–8).[5] Smith's analogy here, though, is between the perception of moral properties and the perception of the *beauty* of colors, the *harmony* of sounds, and the *agreeableness* of flavors, not between the perception of moral properties and the perception of colors, sounds, and flavors per se. Thus, we must entertain the possibility that Smith is saying that all of these evaluative properties are mind-dependent in the sense of being pure projections from our minds onto the world. If this is the case, then the properties have no correlates in the world. However, the language Smith employs of the qualities he mentions being "fitted" to our faculties suggests something more like first view. Thus, on the whole, the passage suggests that moral properties are things in the world, albeit response-dependent things.

Yet in another passage, Smith suggests that moral properties are in the world but not dependent upon our responses. He makes these comments in the context of trying to explain why some philosophers might have thought that we make judgments of justice fundamentally because we recognize the utility of justice:

> Sometimes too we have occasion to defend the propriety of observing the general rules of justice by the consideration of their necessity to the support of society. We frequently hear the young and the licentious ridiculing the most sacred rules of morality, and professing, sometimes from the corruption, but more frequently from the vanity of their hearts, the most abominable maxims of conduct. Our indignation rouses, and we are eager to refute and expose such detestable principles. But though it is *their intrinsic hatefulness and detestableness*, which originally inflames us against them, we are unwilling to assign this as the sole reason why we condemn them, or to pretend that it is merely because we ourselves hate and detest them. The reason, we think, would not appear to be conclusive. Yet why should it not; if *we hate and detest them because they are the natural and proper objects of hatred and detestation*? But when we are asked why we should not act in such or such a manner, the very question seems to suppose that, to those who ask it, this manner of acting does not appear to be for its own sake the natural and proper object of those sentiments. We must show them, therefore, that it ought to be so for the sake of something else. Upon this

> account we generally cast about for other arguments, and the consideration which first occurs to us, is the disorder and confusion of society which would result from the universal prevalence of such practices. We seldom fail, therefore, to insist upon this topic. (II.ii.3.8; emphases added)

Again, let's bracket the general point the passage in making, part of which we revisit in the next section, about normative argument choice and rhetorical efficacy. Instead, let's focus on the italicized parts, which suggest, at first glance anyways, that our sentiments respond to moral qualities that exist totally independently of them. We hate and detest vices because they possess the qualities of "intrinsic hatefulness and detestableness," which appear to be conceivable independent from our reactions to them.[6] On this view, in being the "natural and proper objects of hatred and detestation," vices are not essentially fitted to generate reactions in us so much as our reactions are essentially fitted to detect them.

It is possible that Smith is merely making an observation about the phenomenology of moral judgment that is totally consistent with the response-dependent account of moral properties we saw earlier. In contemporary language, just as color judgments purport to be about a property in the world, albeit one that ends up being response-dependent, moral judgments purport to be about a property in the world, albeit one that ends up being response-dependent. So Smith could just be committed to the view that our moral judgments of response-dependent properties present themselves as being of things in world; whether these things are response-dependent things or not is a separate issue. One problem with this reading, however, is that Smith does not think that judgments of paradigmatically response-dependent properties like color, sound, and taste have any such purport; in his language, colors, sounds, and tastes "are not naturally perceived as external and independent substances; or even as qualities of such substances; but as mere affections of the organ, and what can exist nowhere but in the organ" (ES 25). So if the passage reports Smith's view that moral judgments *do* have such purport,[7] it must also report his view that the experience they involve is more like that of some experiences of touch, which indicate something "altogether external to, and independent of my hand" (ES 3).[8] When taken this way, the passage implies that moral properties have the same response-independent metaphysical status as the property of "solidity" does (ES 8).

So what do we do here? We could try to interpret the first passage in a way that makes it more friendly to the second. We can do this by emphasizing its main point. The passage draws the following analogy between the moral faculties and those of seeing, hearing, and tasting: just as "the eye," "the ear," and "the taste" are each "judges in the last resort" in matters of beauty, harmony, and sweetness, the moral faculties "in the same manner . . . determine when the ear ought to be soothed, when the eye ought to be indulged, when the taste ought to be gratified, when and how far every other principle of our nature ought either to be indulged or restrained." Since Smith's point in drawing this analogy has to do with authority to judge and not the "very essence" of the qualities being judged, it is legitimate to treat in a totally deflationary way the metaphysically suggestive language emphasized earlier. But why prioritize our initial reading of the second passage? Why not read it in a way that makes it consistent with the first one? We can do this by emphasizing its main point. In reminding us of instances in which we appeal to social utility as a reason to care about justice when it is challenged, the passage reminds us that it is really hard to argue for the value of things we value intrinsically by appealing to their intrinsic value. If sincere, the people demanding such an argument reveal that they do not just see the intrinsic value that we do; thus, we appeal to "something else," like the "support of society," that shows that the intrinsically valuable thing is also instrumentally valuable. When taken in this context, the language I emphasized has less to do with the metaphysics of value than with our experience of certain conversations about value. If so, we might still have to deal with the potential inconsistency between saying that moral experience purports response-independent properties that are not actually response-independent while touch experience purports response-independent properties that are actually response-independent. But this problem does not seem insurmountable, given how much ontologically weirder the notion of moral properties being response-independent is than the notion of solidity being response-independent.[9]

Since there do not seem to be conclusive reasons for favoring either interpretation, I suggest we focus on what they have in common. The view that makes moral properties response-dependent and the view that makes moral properties response-independent both recognize that moral properties are *in some sense*, in the world. While Smith's attack on Mandeville already implied that no one consciously made them up whole cloth, now we can also conclude that no one unconsciously made them up whole cloth, perhaps via some projective psychological mechanism. Thus, when Smith criticizes modern propriety theories of virtue for not providing "any precise or distinct measure by which . . . fitness or propriety of affection can be ascertained or judged of," we should take him at his word, which implies that "fitness or propriety of affection" is a thing that is, *in some sense*, there to be ascertained or judged (VII.ii.1.49).[10] And—to return to our first question—if it is there, *in some sense*, to be ascertained or judged, then there is additional reason to think that our ascertainments or judgments of it involve beliefs.

Section 2: Smith's Account of Normativity

The most fundamental normative position in Smith's moral philosophy is that we should make judgments and act from regard to the sentiments of the WIS. But does Smith offer an answer to the question of *why* we should privilege the WIS? Smith does not address this question in any sustained way, but we can generate some Smithian answers to it by considering some comments he makes and some aspects of the overall theory he presents. Since, in general, what counts as an acceptable answer to a question like this one will depend on what motivates the asking of it, I organize the investigation via some distinctions between different kinds of askers with different kinds of concerns.

First are the people who do not feel the pull of morality at all. They wonder why they should bother with the WIS, even though everyone else says they should. Smith addresses these kinds of askers in a passage we discussed in the previous section. He assumes that they have either not finished morally developing—"the young"—or have matured but in a way that leaves their attachment to morality weak or nonexistent—"the licentious." "We frequently hear" such people "ridiculing the most sacred rules of morality, and professing . . . the most abominable maxims of conduct." We should be able to respond by simply pointing out the "intrinsic hatefulness and detestableness" of this immoralism. But perhaps because it shakes us a bit and thus leads us to consider momentarily whether we object merely "because we ourselves hate and detest" it, though mainly because a willingness to ask sincerely "the very question" of "why we should not act in such or such a manner" demonstrates some real insensitivity to "intrinsic hatefulness and detestableness," we respond by citing the "necessity" of "the general rules of justice . . . to the support of society" (II.ii.3.8).

By conceding that we cannot respond by simply pointing to the "intrinsic hatefulness and detestableness" of immoral maxims of conduct, Smith reiterates a basic feature of his moral psychology. Even if moral properties are in some sense real, he is committed to the view that we only perceive them through sentiments that our askers, if sincere, clearly do not experience. Such people will not be satisfied if we respond to their concerns by pointing to moral properties that they do not even perceive, let alone find compelling. In responding in the way he does, Smith assumes that these askers see "the support of society" as conducive to their own interests, as the insensitivity to morality that they display is surely accompanied by insensitivity to the interests and needs of others (VII.iii.1.1–2). Obviously, this kind of response has limits. At best, it shows these askers that they have interest-based reason to encourage morality in everyone else while merely pretending to be moral to the extent necessary for neither discouraging them nor feeling their wrath. (Smith plausibly believes that given how the world works, habitual "knavery" will be detected. But he also acknowledges the possibility that a "particular knavery . . . may escape censure, or even [be met] with applause" (III.5.8).) However, for some of our askers, this response could have a more significant effect. For young people still developing, the response could install a temporary placeholder for conscience that also removes an obstacle from its development. At least such young people will start listening to the moral lessons they are taught, albeit for reasons that are initially of the wrong kind. Over time, these people could start cultivating the right kinds of attitudes in moral matters (cf. VI.iii.46). The response can also lead licentious adults who have not lost "all sense of propriety" to wonder whether they are right that vice is "the way of the world" and thus the best policy to adopt. Once shaken from that belief, perhaps their sense of propriety can gain strength, so that their respect for morality grows (V.2.2). But for the people with no present or potential attachment to morality, the limits of this response are severe.

The fact that Smith offers such a limited response to these askers is revealing in at least two ways. First, it highlights his doubts about their sincerity. He observes that they ask the question "sometimes from the corruption, but more frequently from the vanity of their hearts" (II.ii.3.8). Most of them, he believes, want to show everyone how clever and unconventional they are, but don't genuinely doubt the importance of morality with a seriousness typical of real corruption. Still, as it seems he should, Smith ultimately does recognize the possibility of such corruption. That he does not really respond to it suggests—this is the second point to make—that he does not believe one *can* respond to it. It seems that for Smith, the normative force of morality is in some sense contingent upon people already having certain concerns. On this view, to use Karsten Stueber's words, "there is no transcendental cure for psychopathy" (2017: 201).[11]

We shall see further that this last view is in possible tension with another thing Smith says that has implications for the normativity of morality. Now let's consider potentially less familiar askers of our question, those who feel the pull of morality to an at least normal degree but worry about the legitimacy of their moral faculties. Like Cartesian doubters who want to ensure the trustworthiness of their intellectual faculties, these people want to ensure the trustworthiness of their moral ones. Here we see a deeper use of the demand Smith makes in response to Hutcheson that a moral theory be able to explain how we can morally approve of moral judgment. As we saw in Section 3 of Chapter 2, Smith has mainly in the mind the ability to morally judge instances of good or bad moral judgment. But we can easily broaden his point to cover moral judgment of moral judgment as a whole. Smith could appeal to this ability to assure our askers that their moral judgment is morally legitimate because it approves of itself. Much like the Cartesian escape, this one is circular in that it appeals to moral judgment to morally legitimate moral judgment. But the circularity seems unproblematic in that it is unavoidable.[12] How else could we morally approve of our moral judgment without employing that moral judgment itself? Again, even if Smith is some kind of realist about moral properties, he is committed to the view that the moral sentiments are necessary for perceiving these moral properties. Thus, without employing these moral sentiments, there would be no way to tell whether we are accurately perceiving the properties. It is not like we can step outside the faculties of moral perception to see if they are accurately perceiving properties that only they allow us to perceive in the first place. Applying them to themselves is the best we can do.[13]

Potentially even less familiar askers of our question are people who feel the pull of morality to an at least normal degree but who are discouraged by the difficulty of living up to its demands. With lament, these people are considering giving up the project or at least some aspect of the project. As we saw in Section 2 of Chapter 5, Smith responds to Mandeville in a way that cuts off the possibility of giving up on the goal of becoming virtuous for the reason that it is in principle unachievable. But as we will now see, Smith also says some things that are possibly best interpreted as responses to at least some of those who might be discouraged by how hard the project of becoming virtuous is.

The realization that we are naturally prone to certain feelings that seem to function primarily as obstacles to the cultivation of virtue could be a particularly discouraging source of difficulty. As we saw in Section 5 of the previous chapter, the combination of our tendency to sympathize with joy and approve upon sympathizing leads us to confuse our "respect and admiration" of "wealth and greatness" for their own sakes with the "respect and admiration" of virtue (I.iii.3.1). This mistake can be morally dangerous, as when it leads us to take the wrong "road" or follow the wrong "models" in life or when it leads us "to neglect persons of poor and mean condition" (I.iii.3.1–2; I.ii.3.7–8). Thus, this is a mistake we should expect the virtuous person not to make. Smith does believe that virtuous people *can* avoid it, as "it requires no very nice discernment to distinguish the difference" between respect for virtue and respect for wealth and greatness. But he also believes that the mistake is extremely hard to avoid, so much so that "mere wealth and greatness . . . almost *constantly* obtain" our respect for their own sake (I.iii.3.3–4; emphasis added). So it is easy to foresee discouragement in the face of this propensity, especially when one lives in a society that actively encourages it,[14] becoming strong enough to motivate giving up or at least becoming less interested in the project of rooting it out of oneself.

Now, we might think that what Smith says in response to worries about this common moral mistake would exacerbate such discouragement. He observes that our tendency to respect wealth and greatness for their own sakes grounds a "distinction of ranks" that is conducive to the "order of society" (I.iii.2.3; cf. I.iii.3.1; VI.ii.1.20; VII.iii.30). While we might quibble with Smith's assumption that social ranks are necessary for social stability,[15] we should also notice the more general point he is making, which is that an aspect of human psychology that we do not endorse can be socially useful. Insofar as this point could be taken to provide positive reasons for abandoning the project of avoiding the mistake in question, it could exacerbate the discouragement with which we are concerned. But this point will only do so if it implies that things will be generally better if we fail in our project of avoiding the mistake. However, this does not seem to be what Smith means. He is more interested in revealing a bright side to failure than he is a dark side to success. The main reason why he thinks it better that "the distinction of ranks, the peace and order of society . . . rest . . . upon the plain and palpable difference of birth and fortune, than upon the invisible and often uncertain difference of wisdom and virtue" is that "the great mob of mankind can well enough perceive the former," while "it is with difficulty that . . . [even] the wise and virtuous can sometimes distinguish the latter" (VI.ii.2.10). Smith is not implying here that wisdom and virtue in both leaders and the led come at the expense of "peace and order." Things would surely be better overall if we succeeded in becoming wise and virtuous, for we would then grant authority to wisdom and virtue.[16] But the kind of failure about which our asker might be concerned is at least one that is conducive to social stability. Such an observation, it seems, can take the pressure off, maybe to the point of reintroducing fun to the project of cultivating virtue in oneself and others.

I see a similar kind of response to a similar kind of moral discouragement in Smith's discussion of the role of luck in moral assessment. As we saw in Section 6 of Chapter 5, Smith believes that we all pledge allegiance to the "equitable maxim" that "all praise or blame, all approbation or disapprobation, of any kind, which can justly be bestowed upon any action, must ultimately belong . . . to the intention or affection of the heart" behind it; thus, we claim that no matter "how different soever the accidental, the unintended and unforeseen consequences of different actions . . . if the intentions or affections from which they arose were" the same, "the merit or demerit of the actions is . . . the same." Yet even though we believe that this rule "ought entirely to regulate our evaluations," it does not (II.iii.intro.4–6). We sometimes violate the equitable maxim when someone has "failed in producing either the good or the evil which he intended." We also sometimes violate the equitable maxim when someone has caused "either great good or great evil" from motives that were either not properly beneficent or not improperly malevolent (II.iii .1.7). In the former cases, we deem people less beneficent or unjust than they deserve; in the latter cases, we deem people more beneficent or unjust than they deserve.

To support his claim that we suffer from this "irregularity of sentiment," Smith invites us to consider our reaction to several examples (II.iii.intro.6). For the first category of "irregularity," that which appears when good or bad motives respectively do not generate good or bad consequences, he provides examples of pairs of actions between which intention is constant but consequence varies. Among the positive examples is the contrast between a case in which a person tries to help someone else get a job but faultlessly fails and a case in which a person tries, from the exact same intention, to help someone else get a job but, due to better luck, succeeds; among the negative examples is the contrast between a case in which a person intentionally tries to murder someone and succeeds and a case in which a person tries to murder someone from the exact same intention but, due to luck, fails (II.iii.2.2; II.iii.2.4–5). Smith expects us to react to the first people in each pair with respectively stronger admiration and detestation than to the second ones; he also expects us to anticipate feeling respectively more pride and shame upon finding ourselves in the positions of the first people than upon finding ourselves in the positions of the second ones. For the second category of "irregularity," that which appears when morally neutral motives generate good or bad consequences, he provides examples of actions to which we have a positive or negative reaction that outruns what the agent deserves. His positive example is that of our grateful reaction to and pride upon being the messenger of good news; his negative examples include the "apology" or "atonement" both spectators and agents deem necessary when totally blameless negligence, such as a lack of "excessive care" that we might otherwise condemn as "timid weakness," results in "some damage to another" (II.iii.2.6; II.iii.2.10).

It seems that Smith takes this irregularity to be a mistake. With regard to when our reaction to good consequences impacts our evaluation of good motives, he remarks that we are "unjust" (II.iii.2.2). With regard to when our reaction to bad consequences impacts our evaluation of bad motives, he remarks that it is incorrect to distinguish between cases in which the "real demerit . . . is undoubtedly the same" (II.iii.2.4). With regard to when our reaction to good consequences impacts our evaluation of neutral motives, he points to the illusion of "look[ing] upon" someone as the "[author] . . . of our good . . . fortune, and regard[ing] [him] in some measure as if [he] had really brought about the events" (II.iii.2.6). With regard to when our reaction to bad consequences impacts our evaluation of neutral motives, he remarks that our resentment is "most unjust" (II.iii.3.4; cf. II.iii.2.10). We can ground Smith's attitude systematically by pointing out that the moral judgments we make as the result of the irregularity are ones that the WIS would not make. Such judgments are often poorly informed in that they involve false beliefs about motive and/or are biased in that they follow from a perspective narrowed by our reaction to benefits and harms alone. Thus, our corrected sentiments, the sentiments of the WIS, lie behind the equitable maxim, while our actual, often uncorrected sentiments lie behind the irregularity that leads us to stray from the equitable maxim.

Yet Smith also says that the irregularity "is felt, in some measure, even by the impartial spectator" (II.iii.2.2). After describing the reaction of the non-truly-negligent person who accidentally hurts someone, Smith asks, "why should he make an apology more than any other person? Why should he, since he was equally innocent with any other bystander, be thus singled out from among all mankind, to make up for the bad fortune of another?" (II.iii.2.10). But Smith immediately answers these rhetorical questions by pointing out that the task of compensating the person accidentally hurt "would surely never be imposed upon [the agent], did not even the impartial spectator feel some indulgence for what may be regarded as the unjust resentment of that other" (II.iii.2.10;

cf. II.iii.2.2). But if the WIS thus applies the equitable maxim irregularly, then the irregularity of our application of it does *not* constitute a mistake. We arrive at the equitable maxim in the same way we arrive at the other general rules regarding morality: via induction from the sentiments of the WIS. And we can arrive at legitimate exceptions to the equitable maxim in the same way we arrive at legitimate exceptions to the other general rules regarding morality: via consultation of the sentiments that ground and thus are prior to it. If, as Smith now seems to think, these sentiments sometimes call for exceptions to the equitable maxim, then it is not only permissible but mandatory that we abide by them.

Smith goes on to insist that the irregularity is also generally useful. Recall that there are four kinds of cases impacted by the irregularity: when bad or good intentions respectively fail to generate good or bad consequences and when neutral intentions generate bad or good consequences. The irregularity regarding bad intentions is useful because it prevents "sentiments, thoughts, [and] intentions" alone from becoming "the objects of punishment" and thus "every court of judicature" from becoming "a real inquisition" (II.iii.3.2). The irregularity regarding good intentions is useful because it ensures that we will not "be satisfied with indolent benevolence, nor fancy [ourselves] the friend of mankind, because in [our] heart [we merely wish] well to the prosperity of the world" (II.iii.3.3). The irregularity regarding neutral intentions is useful because it leads us "to reverence the happiness of [our] brethren," such that "the happiness of every innocent man is . . . rendered holy, consecrated, and hedged round against" even accidental harm by anyone else (II.iii.3.4).

So Smith appears to justify the irregularity in two ways. First, the irregularity is justified because even the WIS is subject to it. Second, the irregularity is justified because it is generally useful.[17] Bracketing for the moment the second justification, we should note that the first one alone dissolves the present kind of worry by revealing that we are not actually making a mistake. But while it is standard to read Smith as offering at least the first kind of justification,[18] I am not sure it is right to do so. Without forcing things, at least some of the just-mentioned references to the "impartial spectator" can be read as references to any old bystander who happens to be impartial only in the extremely localized sense of being a relatively disinterested third party, not a more ideal figure who scrutinizes all moral judgments. Closer attention to context suggests that Smith uses the phrase here only to indicate that both people directly involved in a moral situation and bystanders—"impartial spectators" in the mundane sense—are subject to the irregularity. The first example follows the sentence, "Nor is this irregularity of sentiment felt only by those who are immediately affected by the consequences of the action" (II.iii.2.2). We see the same pattern in Smith's comparison of consequence-impacted reactions to different degrees of negligence, albeit minus the "impartial": "the consideration" of our different reactions "may satisfy us how much the indignation, *even of the spectator*, is apt to be animated by the actual consequences of the action" (II.iii.2.8; emphasis added). Moreover, the reference to the reaction of the "impartial spectator" to the person who causes accidental harm only after acting without needlessly extreme caution can be read as simply explaining why "the person himself, who by an accident" for which we would not otherwise blame him "has involuntarily hurt another, seems to have some sense of his own ill-desert"; the answer is that he takes on the reactions of the people around him—again, "impartial spectators" in the mundane sense—despite knowing better than they that he did nothing of which the real WIS would disapprove (II.iii.2.10). Furthermore, as others have noticed, Smith ends his discussion of the irregularity by pointing out that if we happen to find ourselves on the losing end of it, the "consolation" for either our unrecognized "innocence" or "reward" for unrecognized "virtue" is the judgment of the WIS, which recognizes "that just and equitable maxim, That those events which did not depend upon our conduct, ought not to diminish the esteem that is due to us." A person in this position

> strives to regard himself, not in the light in which he at present appears, but in that in which he ought to appear, in which he would have appeared had his generous designs been crowned with success, and in which he would still appear, notwithstanding their miscarriage, if the sentiments of mankind were either altogether candid and equitable, or even perfectly consistent with themselves. (II.iii.3.6)

Granted, Smith does not explicitly mention well-informedness or impartiality here, but the notion of turning to a corrected imaginary spectator is unmistakably the same in this passage as it is in the more explicit references to the WIS. Notably, developing the theory that grounds these explicit references is the very next thing Smith does in the text.[19]

To develop this interpretation fully, I would have to provide an account of the substantive difference between the casually referenced impartial spectator and the technically referenced WIS. Perhaps this could be done by stressing the latter's ability to filter out the impact of consequences on his moral sentiments via his knowledge of intent and sensitivity to the difference between his reaction to an outcome and his reaction to an intent; sufficiently strong interpretations of the "W" and the "I," it seems, could cover both. I would also have to formulate a systematic account of Smith's different uses of the phrase, lumping some into the category of "casual" and some into the category of "technical." I do not attempt this here, though I believe that the distinction I make in Section 6 of the previous chapter between narrow and broad, as well as accurate and inaccurate, conceptions of the WIS could help. Thus, I am only stressing the possibility that Smith does not believe that the WIS is subject to the irregularity. I do so in order to highlight how the second apparent justification of the irregularity might function as a response to our worrier.

If Smith does not believe that the WIS is subject to the irregularity, he must believe that we should try remove it from ourselves.[20] But if Smith believes this, then why does he insist upon the utility of the irregularity? If he believes that the WIS is not subject to and thus disapproves of the irregularity, it would be odd for him to argue that the irregularity is justified anyways. And it would be incoherent for him to recommend that we keep trying to fix a problem while hoping that we fail. However, closer attention to the nature of Smith's insistence upon the utility of the irregularity reveals that it can serve the purpose of speaking to a similar kind of moral discouragement, in a similar way, as does his insistence upon the utility of our tendency to mistake wealth and status for virtue.

Most of Smith's discussion of the utility of the irregularity stresses the bright side of our failure to correct more than the dark side of correction. Consider his discussion of cases in which good intentions fail to generate good consequences. As we saw earlier, the irregularity in these cases is useful because it reminds us that we must actually do stuff for people, not just wish them well, to count as a "friend of mankind" (II.iii.3.3). But he does not provide any reason to believe that we could not keep appreciating this point after correcting the irregularity. Consider his discussion of cases in which neutral intentions accidentally generate bad consequences. (Interestingly, he does not discuss cases in which neutral intentions accidentally generate good consequences.) As we saw previously, the irregularity in these cases encourages us "to reverence the happiness of [our] brethren" (II.iii.3.4). But again, he does not provide any reason to believe that we could not keep appreciating this point after correcting the irregularity. (Furthermore, in pointing out that when we hurt someone from neutral conduct, we take ourselves to be "piacular, though not guilty," he explicitly invokes what appears to be a distinction between the nonmoral and the moral that we would employ upon correcting the irregularity (II.iii.3.4).[21])

The only kinds of cases in which Smith appears to stress the dark side of correction over the bright side of failure to correct involve bad intentions that fail to generate bad consequences. But even here, his focus is fairly narrow. To fix the irregularity in these cases is to resent equally bad intentions that do not generate harmful actions at all, bad intentions that generate harmful actions that fail, and bad intentions that generate harmful actions that succeed. If only by not mentioning it, Smith does not seem to see a dark side in breaking down the distinction between the latter two kinds of cases, such that we would, for example, judge attempted but unsuccessful murder as harshly as we do attempted and successful murder (cf. the qualification "where no crime has been committed" at II.iii.3.3). But as we saw earlier, he believes that there is serious danger in not keeping the first category distinct from the second two; to collapse this distinction is to risk becoming endlessly suspicious in a way that would disastrously bleed into our law courts. However, Smith believes that this danger is the result of our human limitations:

> Actions, therefore, which either produce good or evil, or attempt to produce it, and thereby put us in the immediate fear of it, are by the Author of nature rendered the only proper and approved objects of human punishment and resentment. Sentiments, designs, affections, though it is from these

> that according to cool reason human actions derive their whole merit or demerit, are placed by the great Judge of hearts beyond the limits of every human jurisdiction, and are reserved for the cognizance of his own unerring tribunal. That necessary rule of justice, therefore, that man in this life are liable to punishment for their actions only, not for their designs and intentions is founded upon this salutary and useful irregularity in human sentiments concerning merit or demerit, which at first sight appears so absurd and unaccountable. But every part of nature, when attentively surveyed, equally demonstrate the providential care of its Author, and we may admire the wisdom and goodness of God even in the weakness and folly of man. (II.iii.3.2)

In stressing the dark side of correction in these cases and thereby insisting that we limit our attempts to correct regarding them, Smith is asking us to appreciate our built-in epistemic "weakness." Ultimately, then, he is stressing the bright side of our inevitable failure to correct, not the dark side of success in correction.

Again, I could be wrong to suggest that Smith believes that the WIS is not subject to the irregularity. But—in indirect support for my suggestions—if Smith believes that the WIS is subject to and thereby justifies the irregularity, then the meaning of his pervasive stress on the bright side of failing to correct it over the dark side of succeeding becomes unclear. However, if Smith believes that the WIS is not subject to the irregularity and thus that we should try to correct it, then this stress serves the purpose of preventing the kind of discouragement I mentioned earlier that we might feel in the face of realizing that correction is extremely difficult. Again, Smith would be doing something borderline incoherent if, in pointing out the upsides of our limitations, he was recommending that we continue trying to become virtuous while hoping that we fail. But on my reading, he is not doing this. Rather, he is recommending that we continue trying to be virtuous to the extent that we can be while not becoming discouraged when we realize some of the challenges we face.

My claim that Smith appeals in these two ways to the bright side of failures in order to cut off moral discouragement is consistent with one general role he ascribes to religion in moral life. Since God is responsible for these bright sides, appeal to them for reassurance is an appeal to God (VI.ii.1.20; II.iii.2.2). Smith believes that when we are falsely condemned by others, our "only effectual consolation . . . lies in an appeal" to a god who knows the truth (III.2.33).[22] He also believes that "we naturally appeal" to a god that will make things right in the next world when we notice the mismatch between our moral estimation of what people deserve and what they typically get (III.5.9–10). And he believes that "conviction" that "all the inhabitants of the universe, the meanest as well as the greatest, are under the immediate care and protection of that great, benevolent, and all-wise Being, who directs all the movements of nature" is crucial for the support of our "universal benevolence" (VI.ii.3.2).[23] In all these cases, Smith points to belief in God as a source of moral encouragement.

Smith also recommends certain morally infused religious beliefs as morally salutary in another way when he responds to other, more recognizable askers of our question.[24] These people feel the pull of moral demands to an at least normal degree but also feel the pull of other demands, such as those of self-interest. These people want to know why the moral demands should win out when they appear to conflict with other ones. The response that Smith most explicitly offers to this question trades on a point he might have adopted from Butler.[25] In a passage we have already partly investigated, Smith explains:

> Upon whatever we suppose that our moral faculties are founded, whether upon a certain modification of reason, upon an original instinct, called a moral sense, or upon some other principle of our nature, it cannot be doubted, that they were given us for the direction of our conduct in this life. They carry along with them the most evident badges of this authority, which denote that they were set up within us to be the supreme arbiters of all our actions, to superintend all our senses, passions, and appetites, and to judge how far each of them was either to be intended or restrained. Our moral faculties are by no means, as some have pretended, upon a level in this respect with the other faculties and appetites of our nature, endowed with no more right to restrain these last, than those are to restrain them. No other faculty or principle of action judges of any other. Love does not judge of resentment, nor resentment of love. Those two passions may be opposite to one another, but cannot, with any propriety, be said to approve

> or disapprove of one another. But it is the peculiar office of those faculties now under our consideration to judge, to bestow censure and applause upon all the other principles of our nature. Every sense is supreme over its own objects. There is no appeal from the eye with regard to the beauty of colours, nor from the ear with regard to the harmony of sounds, nor from the taste with regard to the agreeableness of flavours. Each of those senses judges in the last resort of its own objects. . . . It belongs to our moral faculties, in the same manner to determine when the ear ought to be gratified, when they eye ought to be indulged, when the taste ought to be gratified, when and how far every other principle of our nature ought either to be indulged or restrained. (III.5.5)

The experience to which Smith appeals here is that of seeing all our "senses, passions, and appetites" as beholden to our moral faculties for permission to be enacted. Deliberation about whether to act on resentment does not invite deliberation about whether the action is consistent with (nonmoral) love, and deliberation about whether to act on love does not invite deliberation about whether the action is consistent with (nonmoral) resentment. But the deliberation to act on either *does* invite deliberation about whether the action is consistent with morality. Importantly, Smith takes this experience to reveal that our moral faculties are not just strong but "authoritative." In the text leading up to this passage, Smith seems to be circling around making a distinction between power and authority. In distinguishing between the court of public opinion and that of conscience, Smith acknowledges both the "power and [the] jurisdiction" such tribunals can have (III.2.31). He also acknowledges both features, albeit with different language, when he goes on to investigate the "influence and authority" of conscience (III.3.1). But he does not clarify the difference between them until we get here. While the "power" and "influence" side of the distinction invoke conscience's ability to govern, the "jurisdiction" and "authority" side invoke conscience's "right" to govern our evaluations and conduct. By appealing to this legitimacy, Smith can respond to our askers, who presumably feel or have felt a strong desirous pull against that of morality, that they should obey conscience, no matter how strong that pull against it is in the moment.

But what grounds this authority of conscience? Some of the language in the passage and in some of its context suggests that the authority comes wholly from our "lawful superior," the "Author of nature." The passage refers to what our moral faculties were "given us for," to what "they were set up within us to be," and to the "right" with which they were "endowed." In the next paragraph, Smith concludes from their apparently inherited authority that our moral faculties were "plainly intended" by the "Deity" to be the "governing principles of human nature" and serve as "viceregents" in his stead. It follows, he continues, that the "rules which they prescribe are to be regarded as the commands and laws of the Deity" (III.5.6–7). Certain religious beliefs, then, are salutary for grounding an answer to our askers that is rooted in an appeal to the divinely backed authority of conscience. These beliefs are also, Smith continues, salutary for supplying "additional" motivation to be moral (III.5.13).

However, before we commit to this interpretation of what grounds the authority of conscience for Smith, we should also notice the language in this passage and its context that suggests that conscience has intrinsic natural authority. In the passage, Smith points out that "it *belongs to* our moral faculties" to rule our other ones (emphasis added). And the passage is part of a more general account of how the idea of god is "first impressed" upon us by our natural moral sentiments and then "confirmed" by philosophical reflection upon, among other things, the natural authority of our moral faculties (III.5.3). But in order for the natural authority of our moral faculties to *confirm* the idea that the god who made them wants us to be moral, they must first present themselves as authoritative independent of god.[26] If Smith thinks of the experience of authority as evidence of authority, which would be in line with the trust he puts in everyday moral experience, his view is that conscience has its own natural authority that is not dependent upon but is perhaps buttressed by the authority of its maker. His response to our askers, then, becomes to point to the natural authority of conscience and to recommend belief in god as a backer for belief in this authority and for its motivating power.[27]

In appealing to the intrinsic natural authority of conscience, Smith is employing a normative conception of human nature, according to which we should live in line with what our nature dictates. As we have to some extent seen, Smith uses the term "nature" and its variants in at least two importantly different ways. He sometimes uses the term with these two different meanings in the same sentence, as when he comments, "man naturally desires, not only to be loved, but to be lovely; or to be that thing which is the natural and proper object of love" (III.2.1). The first use appears to make a factual claim about a desire that is a component of the human frame, while the second use appears to make a value-laden claim about what should be loved. We see a similar equivocation within the same stretch of paragraphs in which Smith employs a normative conception of nature against that employed by the Stoics; just after he concludes that "Nature" has "prescribed" and "sketched out" a particular "plan and system . . . for our conduct" that differs from what the Stoics think it has, he observes that "Nature" has established the "necessary connection . . . between causes and effects" that results in human psychology being the way it is (VII.ii.1.43–7). If we read Smith's point about the authority of conscience in terms of his normative conception of human nature, he ends up with the view that the better we get at respecting the authority of conscience, the better a job we do at fulfilling our nature as the things we are and the better a life we live as these things. Sometimes Smith describes the process of getting better in this way at living naturally in terms of achieving "the perfection of human nature" (I.i.5.5).[28]

To interpret, let alone evaluate Smith's normative appeal to human nature is a huge task. Since he says nothing to develop what he has in mind, we would have to explore the anciently pedigreed views from which he seems to have adopted the strategy and project certain elements of those onto his theory. Also, this appeal fits awkwardly with my insistence that for Smith, the normative force of morality is contingent upon our having certain concerns. If the normative force of morality is derived from the fact that we are human, then it is hard to see how it could remain contingent. Thus, there are at least two reasons to look in Smith for another response to our askers, though one that remains broadly consistent with his observation about the experience of the authority of our moral faculties.

There is a family of views in recent scholarship either on Smith or inspired by Smith that attempt to ground the normativity of morality in features of everyday social interaction that are either practically or in principle unavoidable. (Given my just-mentioned view about the contingency of moral demands in Smith, I obviously prefer versions of this strategy that do the former.) The general idea common among these views is, roughly, that by engaging in social practices like negotiations for mutual sympathy, we implicitly commit ourselves to norms regarding how people are to be treated and respected, which we would contradict were we to ignore the call of conscience in order to satisfy our apparent self-interest.[29] Thus, we should abide by our consciences on pain of self-contradiction. We might think that this appeal to a straightforwardly rational norm to motivate moral conduct contradicts Smith's attack on moral rationalism. But recall that he specifically attacks the view that we make moral distinctions in the same way that we determine the difference between "truth and falsehood" (VI.iii.2.5). In this way, he rejects the notion that what is often called "theoretical reason" has motivational power. Yet he leaves open the possibility of recognizing a distinct form of "practical reason" that is intrinsically governed by norms like consistency and coherence and that very well can motivate.[30] Thus, he could offer as an answer to our askers some version of "because you'll contradict yourself if you don't abide by your conscience"; doing so would certainly fit well with the explicit references he makes to consistency as a quality of a qualified moral judge (VII.ii.4.10; II.iii.3.6).

I do not intend to argue with this approach either, especially since I have provided the barest sketch of it in general and have said nothing at all about the differences between the views of its adherents. However, I would like to sketch a third style of Smithian response to our askers. This response starts from Smith's tendency to connect virtue and happiness. Smith draws such a connection in two broadly different ways. The first, less directly relevant of the two works through the benefit that virtue has on the whole. As we have seen several times, although Smith believes that conscious considerations of overall utility do not play a fundamental role in our making and enacting WIS-based moral judgments, he believes that our making and enacting these judgments does in fact best promote overall utility. He demonstrates this belief both with respect to WIS-governed virtue in general (IV.2.1) and with respect to each class of virtue. The justice dictated by the WIS is so necessary to society that it "cannot subsist" without it. And though it is less essential to the existence of society than justice is, beneficence is essential to a society that "flourishes and is happy" (II.ii.3.1–4); the WIS-guided distribution of beneficence too is best for the whole (VI.ii.intro.3; VI.ii.2.4). While lesser versions of self-command can win approval despite enabling conduct that is damaging to the public, this is not true of the WIS-guided version (VI.concl.7). And as readers of the *Wealth of Nations* know, Smith believes that prudent rather than reckless pursuit of self-interest is also best for the whole (cf. IV.2.1).[31] Since we are parts of the whole that the practice of these virtues benefits, we also benefit as individuals. Thus, these observations imply that being virtuous is conducive to being happy.

Smith also believes that virtue is in the direct interest of virtuous individuals, not just virtuous individuals parts of the whole. As we saw in Section 5 of the previous chapter, Smith believes that the path dictated by the WIS is the path to prudential success (I.iii.3.5–8; VI.i; VII.ii.2.13). (I mentioned above that Smith does acknowledge the possibility of "particular knavery" being in our interest (III.5.8). However, he also seems to think that this is true only for those without a conscience at all, not our askers (I.ii.3.8).) As we saw in Section 4 of the previous chapter, friendships based upon virtue and thus mutual respect for the WIS are "the happiest, as well as the most permanent and secure" (VI .ii.1.18). And as we saw in Section 6 of the previous chapter, even when the WIS dictates difficult exercises of self-command, the compensating "reward" of pleasing self-approbation is "in proportion to the degree of self-command which is necessary to conquer our natural sensibility" for the sake of "good behavior under misfortune" (III.3.27). In general, "the degree" of "every . . . emotion, passion, and habit . . . that is most agreeable to the impartial spectator is likewise most agreeable to the person himself" (VI.iii.53).[32]

Smith makes several other comments that either imply or explicitly reference a direct link between virtue and the virtuous person's happiness (e.g., I.ii.3.7; I.ii.4.1; I.ii.5.2; I.iii.1.7; III.1.6; III.2.9). To be clear, he does not seem to think that virtue alone is sufficient for happiness. In remarking that little "can be added to the happiness of the man who is in health, who is out of debt, and has a clear conscience," Smith acknowledges the importance of two factors that are at least potentially unrelated to one's virtue (I.iii.1.7); elsewhere, he acknowledges the importance of "personal liberty" (III.3.32); and he also acknowledges the possibility of an "extreme" and "exquisite sensibility" that renders hardship inconsistent "with internal tranquility and happiness," even when it is dealt with virtuously (VI.iii.19). However, he does seem to think virtue is necessary for happiness. Thus, if we want to be happy, we must respect the authority of the WIS.[33]

But can we say anything more about the necessary contribution to happiness made by respect for the authority of the WIS? Smith's explicit definition of happiness as consisting "in tranquility and enjoyment" helps here. Of the two components, tranquility is foundational, for "without [it] there can be no enjoyment; and where there is perfect tranquility there is scare any thing which is not capable of amusing" (III.3.30).[34] Tranquility also seems most connected to virtue in Smith's thinking, as he sometimes explicitly stresses the connection between vice and the opposite of tranquility (e.g., I.iii.3.8). So it seems likely that respect for the authority of the WIS specifically enables us to achieve tranquility. We see a similar relationship by comparing Smith's conception of the WIS-ruled self with the Platonic view we saw him examine in Section 6 of Chapter 5. On that view, respect for the authoritative faculty generates internal harmony, peace, and seamless cooperation among the various components of the self, while disrespect for the authoritative faculty generates internal disharmony, war, and strife (VII.ii.1.8–11). Thus, to the extent that we can read Plato's view as a model for Smith's (though minus the natural teleology that I am presently bracketing)—recall Smith's observation that Plato's account of "the nature of virtue, or of that temper of mind which is the proper object of praise and approbation . . . coincides in every respect" with his own—we can conclude that respect and disrespect for the WIS yield similar internal states (VII.ii.1.11).

So the third style of Smithian response to the question of why we should follow conscience when we seem pulled against it by momentary considerations of interest is at least partly that our interest is actually best served by respecting conscience because doing so allows us to maintain a state of internal peace, harmony, and—to use a term that Smith also uses, though sometimes in a seemingly narrower sense than I am—integrity[35] that is necessary for our happiness (cf. III.5.9; V.2.3; VI.iii.43; VII.iv.8). Smith is not the first philosopher to see virtue as necessary for happiness either in general or in this specific way; he adopts the former view as uncritically from the ancients as he does the view that virtue is natural,[36] and as we just saw, he himself reminds us that

Plato holds the latter. But the way in which Smith's moral psychology explains the appeal of the inner state maintained by virtue makes his version of the traditional position unique.

As we saw across Chapters 3, 4, and 6, the respect we have for the sentiments of the WIS is a particular product of our general desire for mutual sympathy. The nature of the WIS is such that desire for mutual sympathy with him is desire for maximal sentimental concord among all human perspectives for its own sake. This identification follows from the fact that the WIS inhabits the one position anyone can adopt; as a "man in general," the WIS perspective is what remains when we filter out any personal idiosyncrasies that prevent our sentiments from aligning (III.2.31, note r). Obviously, in inhabiting this position or in aspiring to inhabit this position—an important addition—we put ourselves out of sentimental concord with those people who do not. However, in putting ourselves in sentimental concord with these people, we necessarily put a cap on the number of people with whom we can experience sentimental concord. In putting ourselves in sentimental concord with the WIS, we remove this cap and thereby open up the possibility of sentimental concord with anyone. In this respect, then, desire for mutual sympathy with the WIS is desire for this kind of maximally widespread concord with others. Perhaps more importantly, desire for mutual sympathy with the WIS is also a desire for maximal internal concord (or peace, harmony, integrity, etc.). Obviously, our selfish drives can conflict with our social drives. And drives of each category can also conflict among themselves. But by bringing all of these drives in line with the sentiments of the WIS, we bring them into the same kind of harmony we seek in our relationships with other people.[37]

Here we see another way in which Smith's view is traditional. As I mentioned in Section 5 of Chapter 4, in aligning ourselves with the WIS, we experience something much like whatever his rationalist opponents had in mind by recommending that we align ourselves with reason. In both cases, we end up feeling and acting in ways that are essentially public, in that anyone could endorse them. Thus, if I am right to see the Smithian desire for internal peace, harmony, and integrity as the desire for mutual sympathy with the WIS turned inwards, then Smith's view ends up resembling Plato's not only with respect to their shared recommendation of inner peace, harmony, and integrity but also with respect to the way they understand what causes this harmony. For Smith it is an affect, not reason. But it is certainly a reason-like affect.

In ultimately rooting the happiness for which abidance by the sentiments of the WIS is necessary in a desire, the third style of response is limited. It will only apply to those who have the relevant desire to the required degree. Smith is pretty confident about the size of this group. He remarks that "nothing pleases us more than to observe in other men a fellow-feeling with all the emotions of our own breast; nor are we ever so shocked by the appearance of the contrary" (I.i.2.1). He also remarks that "the most ardent desire . . . of human nature" is to win sympathy and thus approval from others (I.iii.2.1; cf. I.ii.4.1; I.ii.5.1). And he explicitly clams that we care most about mutual sympathy with the WIS: he remarks that to "act so as that the impartial spectator may enter into the principles of [our] conduct" is "of all things" that which we have "the greatest desire to do" (II.ii.2.1). He also remarks that "the sentiments of moral approbation and disapprobation," which occur when we consult the sentiments of the WIS, "are founded on the strongest and most vigorous passions of human nature," i.e., the desire to be in sympathy with the WIS (V.2.1). Still, the fact remains that what Smith says here might not apply to everyone.

This limitation, however, is an interpretive strength. As we saw toward the beginning of this section, Smith does not seem to have much to say to the sincere moral skeptic. Thus, it is fitting that the third possible Smithian response maintains the contingency of the authority of moral demands by grounding them in a desire that most of us just happen to have. One might worry that it does so at the expense of overlooking Smith's appeal to the natural intrinsic authority of conscience. As I pointed out more recently, this appeal fits awkwardly with his apparent belief in the contingency of the authority of moral demands. The whole point of appealing to the authority of conscience, it seems, is to insulate its normative force from an agent's contingent concerns. However, if we read Smith's appeal to the authority of conscience merely as a phenomenological description of the experience of having a conscience, this tension dissolves. Taken this way, it becomes an appeal to something that Smith believes our askers already recognize but have momentarily forgotten rather than a call for them to recognize something that they never did; these askers just need to be reminded that they already see conscience as authoritative in a way that reflections upon their momentarily apparent interest are not. This kind of appeal is clearly consistent with the third response's emphasis on the contingency of the authority of moral demands. Now we see that the third response is also limited in that it only applies to those who experience conscience as authoritative enough not to be totally silenced by other concerns. People who do not might even be able to satisfy a desire for inner peace, harmony, and integrity, maybe even one rooted in some form of the desire for mutual sympathy turned inwards, by allowing another part of themselves to silence conscience's protestations on the way to the throne.[38]

This third style of response—which, in sum, is that abiding by the sentiments of the WIS is necessary for happiness because doing so satisfies a fundamental desire—is a broad complement to the previous two. More specifically, it complements the first in speaking to what seems most practically important about living in accordance with human nature, whatever that means. On normative conceptions of human nature like Smith's, to live naturally is to live the best, happiest life possible for us, given what we are. That Smith might also want to classify "best" and "happiest" as "natural" is philosophically interesting but not practically relevant to the askers of our question; for them, "best" and "happiest" is good enough. The third style of response also complements the second in that it provides a sentimental explanation for any concern we might have for being internally consistent. Even if Smith does believe that we are beholden to certain norms of practical reasoning, that he also has the resources to provide a sentiment-based account of our concern for them is worth observing, especially since this would demonstrate the unique explanatory power of the "Hinge" upon which Smith's "system" turns, the desire for mutual sympathy (Letter 36).

However, I also see prima facie reason to prioritize responses of the third kind over responses of both the second and the first, at least with respect to the project of capturing Smith's own view. The advantage over responses of the second kind has mainly to do with the connection Smith frequently makes between virtue and happiness. The idea that the ultimate reason he offers for being virtuous is not fundamentally about happiness seems strange to me. The first kind of response maintains this connection and is intuitive for that reason. But as I've also pointed out, this kind of response fits awkwardly with Smith's apparent commitment to the contingency of moral authority. This, I think, gives us prima facie reason to favor the third kind of response over the first kind as well. (This reasoning would also apply to versions of the second kind that make moral authority necessary.) At this point, I leave it to the reader to decide whether these apparent reasons hold up to scrutiny.[39]

8

Conclusion

So what is Smith's theory of moral sentiments a theory of? We've seen that it is partly a theory of both moral judgment and good moral judgment, according to which a form of our desire to be in mutual sympathy with others becomes a desire to be in mutual sympathy with an especially qualified other, the WIS. We've also seen that it is partly a theory of virtue, loosely understood, according to which a good character is one in which a sentiment-based respect for the sentiments of the WIS governs our self-directed desires, our other-directed desires, and our non-WIS-based desires for mutual sympathy. And we've seen that these theories likely involve the view that moral judgments involve beliefs about moral properties that are, in some sense, really in the world, as well as the view that virtue is worth cultivating at least because it is necessary for happiness, understood at least as requiring a form of internal peace, harmony, and integrity that most of us already desire.

In covering all this terrain, Smith's TMS is a remarkable achievement. Perhaps the most remarkable aspect of the TMS, however, has little directly to do with theory. Very few books in the history of Western philosophy are as jam-packed with nuanced and engaging descriptions of human experience as the TMS is.[1] With a few exceptions, I have not done justice to this aspect of the work. This is the case for at least two good reasons. The first is that Smith's wonderful phenomenologies are beautiful enough that they could only be ruined by exposition and clear enough that they stand in no need of commentary. The second is that my aims have been primarily to explicate, interpret, and assess the arguments that Smith employs these phenomenologies to express and support. Yet I feel compelled to close by urging the reader to pay careful attention to these phenomenologies. I do so partly because they are so beautiful and clear. But I do so mainly as a final act of critical commentary, albeit one of a crude variety. As a general rule, anyone capable of writing the way Smith does about human life surely has something to teach us about how we do and should live it. Consider this a reason for taking seriously every theoretical position he defends.

Notes

Chapter 1

1 Up until two years before Smith received the fellowship, it was a requirement that recipients be considering ordination. See Gordon Graham, "Adam Smith and Religion," in *Adam Smith: His Life, Thought, and Legacy*, ed. Ryan Patrick Hanley (Princeton: Princeton University Press, 2016), 307.

2 Dugald Stewart, "Account of the Life and Writings of Adam Smith, LL.D.," ed. I. S. Ross, in *Essays on Philosophical Subjects*, ed. W. P. D. Wightman and J. C. Bryce (Indianapolis: Liberty Fund, 1982), 306–7.

3 Obviously, this account of Smith's life is very brief. There are several full biographies available. The most recent ones are Ian Simpson Ross, *The Life of Adam Smith* (Oxford: Oxford University Press, 1995); James Buchan, *The Authentic Adam Smith: His Life and Ideas* (New York: W. W. Norton, 2006); and Nicholas Philipson, *Adam Smith: An Enlightened Life* (New Haven: Yale University Press, 2010). Also see Dennis C. Rasmussen, *The Infidel and the Professor: David Hume, Adam Smith, and the Friendship that Shaped Modern Thought* (Princeton: Princeton University Press, 2017). For an excellent, concise discussion of the history of Smith biography, see James Buchan, "The Biography of Adam Smith," in *Adam Smith: His Life, Thought, and Legacy*, ed. Ryan Patrick Hanley (Princeton: Princeton University Press, 2016), 3–16.

4 Stewart, "Account," 329–30.

5 Philipson, *Adam Smith: An Enlightened Life*, 131.

6 Throughout, I cite letter numbers from *Correspondence of Adam Smith*, ed. E. C. Mosssner and I. S. Ross (Indianapolis: Liberty Fund, 1987).

7 Philipson, *Adam Smith: An Enlightened Life*, 257–8.

8 Ibid., 136.

9 This is a central thesis of his *Adam Smith*.

10 I cite here and hereafter paragraph numbers from *The Theory of Moral Sentiments*, ed. D. D. Raphael and A. L. Macfie (Indianapolis: Liberty Fund, 1982). The book frequently cites this text. Thus, I omit "TMS" from the citations for the sake of brevity.

11 Knud Haakonssen points out that by "police," Smith means "administrative regulations which deal with the 'cheapness of commodities, public security, and cleanliness.'" See *The Science of a Legislator: The Natural Jurisprudence of David Hume and Adam Smith* (Cambridge: Cambridge University Press, 1981), 95. The embedded quotation is from the second set of student notes on Smith's lectures of jurisprudence (LJ.b.5). See *Lectures on Jurisprudence*, ed. R. L. Meek, D. D. Raphael, and P. G. Stein (Indianapolis: Liberty Fund, 1982). (Here and hereafter, LJ, cited with "a" or "b" to pick out the relevant set of notes, along with paragraph numbers.) In other words, "police" conveys something like particular institutional policies, as opposed to foundational principles of governance.

12 See previous note.

13 Charles L. Griswold, *Adam Smith and the Virtues of Enlightenment* (Cambridge: Cambridge University Press, 1998), 32. Cf. Eric Schliesser, *Adam Smith: Systematic Philosopher and Public Thinker* (Oxford: Oxford University Press, 2017), 12–15.

14 *Lectures on Rhetoric and Belles Lettres*, ed. J. C. Bryce (Indianapolis: Liberty Fund, 1985). (Hereafter, LRBL, cited with "i" or "ii" to pick out the relevant set of notes, along with paragraph numbers, and sometimes with a "v" that the editor employs to flag revisions to the original text.)

15 These are all available in *Essays on Philosophical Subjects*, ed. W. P. D. Wightman and J. C. Bryce (Indianapolis: Liberty Fund, 1982).

16 For example, Griswold, *Adam Smith and the Virtues of Enlightenment*.

17 For example, Ryan Patrick Hanley, *Adam Smith and the Character of Virtue* (Cambridge: Cambridge University Press, 2009); Fonna Forman-Barzilai, *Adam Smith and the Circles of Sympathy: Cosmopolitanism and Moral Theory* (Cambridge: Cambridge University Press, 2010); Jack Russell Weinstein, *Adam Smith's Pluralism: Rationality, Education, and the Moral Sentiments* (New Haven: Yale University Press, 2013); and Samuel Fleischacker, *Being Me Being You: Adam Smith and Empathy* (Chicago: University of Chicago Press, 2019).

18 For example, see Haakonssen, ibid.; and Fleischacker, *On Adam Smith's* Wealth of Nations*: A Philosophical Companion* (Princeton: Princeton University Press, 2004).

19 For example, see James R. Otteson, *Adam Smith's Marketplace of Life* (Cambridge: Cambridge University Press: 2002); and Schliesser, *Adam Smith: Systematic Philosopher*.

20 For example, see Haakonssen, ibid.; Fleischacker, *A Third Concept of Liberty: Judgment and Freedom in Kant and Adam Smith* (Princeton: Princeton University Press, 1999); Dennis C. Rasmussen, *The Problems and Promise of Commercial Society: Adam Smith's Response to Rousseau* (USA: Pennsylvania State University Press, 2008); and Griswold, *Jean-Jacques Rousseau and Adam Smith: A Philosophical Encounter* (London: Routledge, 2017).

21 Hanley, *Our Great Purpose: Adam Smith on Living a Better Life* (Princeton: Princeton University Press, 2019).

22 Otteson's *Adam Smith's Marketplace of Life* comes close to what I have in mind, but it differs from the present project in articulating and defending an interpretation of the TMS as proposing a "model . . . to account for the growth and development of human institutions" in general (2002: 1). T. D. Campbell's *Adam Smith's Science of Morals* (Oxford: Routledge, 2010) comes close to what I have in mind too, but it reads the TMS as a work of sociology and psychology, while the present book does not. It might be helpful to think of the present book as a sort of parallel to Fleischacker's *On Adam Smith's* Wealth of Nations. But insofar as part of that book's main point is that the WN must be read against the background of the TMS, it is necessarily about both and is thus more ambitious in scope than the present project.

23 With the former audience in mind, I do most—but not all—of my engagement with scholarship on Smith in the notes.

24 For a presently unparalleled example of the latter kind of project, see Vivienne Brown, *Adam Smith's Discourse: Canonicity, Commerce and Conscience* (New York: Routledge, 1994).

25 Griswold has stressed that the sudden opening to the TMS reflects its attempt "to embed ethical theorizing properly in our ordinary moral understanding" (1999: 44). If this is right, my organizational plan risks obscuring a deep feature of the TMS. However, for the reasons being laid out here, I believe this risk is worth taking. For more on Smith's apparent commitment to theorizing about moral life from within moral life, see Section 2 of Chapter 2.

26 For further discussion of the importance of TMS VII for understanding Smith's moral theory, as well as a research agenda for situating Smith in the history of philosophy, see Michael Biziou, "Adam Smith and the History of Philosophy," in *Adam Smith: His Life, Thought, and Legacy*, 422–42.

27 Throughout the text, I treat the concepts of "ethics" and "morality" as synonymous. The question of the precise relationship between these two concepts is a big one. For a good place to start investigating it, see Julia Annas, "Ancient Ethics and Modern Morality," *Philosophical Perspectives*, 6, Ethics (1992): 119–36.

28 Cf. Jesse Prinz, "Neoclassical Sentimentalism," *in Ethical Sentimentalism: New Perspectives*, ed. Remy Debes and Karsten R. Stueber (Cambridge: Cambridge University Press, 2017), 32–51.

29 In Section 1 of Chapter 5 and Section 1 of Chapter 7, respectively.

Chapter 2

1 In doing so, I demonstrate agreement with Joseph Duke Filonowicz regarding the most straightforward way to think about the logical relationship between the views Smith discusses. See *Fellow-Feeling and the Moral Life* (Cambridge: Cambridge University Press, 2008), 25–31, 55–9.

2 Partly on the basis of Smith's reported observation in his lectures of rhetoric that we "naturally [have] a greater curiosity to examine the causes and relations of those things which pass without us, than of those which pass within us" (LRBL ii.v.19), Haakonssen suggests a Smithian explanation for the relative lateness of this development (1981: 80).

3 Of course, thoroughly grappling with the former sorts of questions would require deep investigation into the work and context of each thinker he discusses; thus, the list of works one could consult that do this is vast. To grapple with the latter sorts of questions would also be a massive undertaking. But there are a few obvious places to start. For a treatment of the concept of the "human sciences" in Smith's context, albeit one focused mainly on political economy as an example, see Margaret Schabas, "Philosophy of the Human Sciences," in *The Routledge Companion to Eighteenth Century Philosophy*, ed. Aaron Garrett (New York: Routledge, 2014), 731–53. For treatments of Smith's own conception of "science" in general, see Schliesser, *Adam Smith: Systematic Philosopher*, 255–332; Christopher Berry, "Smith and Science," in *The Cambridge Companion to Adam Smith*, ed. Knud Haakonssen (Cambridge: Cambridge University Press, 2006), 112–35; and Fleischacker, *On Adam Smith's* Wealth of Nations, 31–6.

4 E.g., see Thomas Hobbes, *Leviathan*, ed. Edwin Curley (Indianapolis: Hackett, 1994), 87, 99, 144–5, 218–19.

5 As the editors of the TMS point out in a footnote to this passage, Smith's explication of Cudworth's argument is a bit off (he also cites the wrong chapter of Book I of Cudworth's *A Treatise Concerning Eternal and Immutable Morality*). Cudworth's argument focuses on showing that when we do think ourselves obliged to obey the command of a "civil power" or even God, it is because we think the "civil power" or God and their commands have a moral authority we recognize as prior to the power to enforce commands. (See *A Treatise Concerning Eternal and Immutable Morality*, ed. Sarah Hutton [Cambridge: Cambridge University Press, 1996], 18–21.) But as the editors of the TMS also point out, the discrepancy between Smith's account and Cudworth's actual argument is inconsequential for Smith's present purposes. Smith represents the spirit of the argument well enough.

6 Smith cites Hutcheson's *An Inquiry Concerning the Original of Our Ideas of Virtue or Moral Good*. Smith might have in mind passages like those at *An Inquiry into the Original of Our Ideas of Beauty and Virtue in Two Treatises*, ed. Wolfgang Leidhold (Indianapolis: Liberty Fund, 2004), 133–4, 140. But there are fuller versions of these kinds of arguments at *An Essay on the Nature and Conduct of the Passions and Affections, with Illustrations on the Moral Sense*, ed. Aaron Garrett (Indianapolis: Liberty Fund, 2002), 137–44, 173-81. Cf. Otteson, *Adam Smith's Marketplace*, 51.

7 As we shall see in Section 3 of Chapter 6, reason's performance of this job is especially crucial with respect to one particular kind of affect-rooted moral judgment.

8 For an overview of the connections between various forms of moral rationalism and moral realism in the early modern period, see Debes, "Moral Rationalism and Moral

Realism," in *Routledge Companion to 18th Century Philosophy*, ed. Aaron Garrett (New York: Routledge, 2014), 500–34.

9 For an overview of the multifaceted eighteenth-century debate regarding this issue, see David Fate Norton and Manfred Kuehn, "The Foundations of Morality," *The Cambridge History of Eighteenth-Century Philosophy*, Vol. II, ed. Knud Haakonssen (Cambridge: Cambridge University Press, 2006), 939–87.

10 There is so much discussion of the kind of position I suggest here that it is hard to know where to direct readers of this book who are looking to pursue it further. A good place to start, both because it is intrinsically clear and because it deals with a thinker from Smith's context, is Kenneth Winkler, "Hutcheson's Alleged Realism," *Journal of the History of Philosophy* 23, no. 2 (1985): 179–94. (This paper is part of a larger exchange with Norton initially catalyzed by his discussion of Hutcheson in *David Hume: Common-Sense Moralist, Sceptical Metaphysician* [Princeton: Princeton University Press, 1982], 55–93. In recommending Winkler's paper, I take no stance on the issue of how to interpret Hutcheson.)

11 This was in spite of the fact that, as Christian Maurer points out, Hobbes himself rarely ever used the expression "self-love." See *Self-Love, Egoism, and the Selfish Hypothesis* (Edinburgh: Edinburgh University Press, 2019), 17.

12 For an overview of this kind of view's place in Smith's intellectual culture, see Forman-Barzilai, *Adam Smith and the Circles of Sympathy*, 37–45.

13 Maurer argues that in Smith's context, five distinct conceptions of "self-love" were at play. Here, Smith seems to be using the one Maurer identifies as "self-love as egoistic desire, or egoistic self-love." See Maurer, 1–31.

14 Even the obvious point becomes interesting when we consider both the depth and the scope of the commitment it expresses. Several scholars have observed how Smith's wider inquiry into all of social, political, and economic life is shaped by his dedication to theorizing as closely as possible to ordinary life. This is a pervasive theme in Griswold, *Adam Smith and the Virtues of Enlightenment*; see especially 40–75 and 355–76. For a discussion of Smith's "contextual" conception of knowledge, see Haakonssen, *The Science of a Legislator*, 79–82. For a discussion of Smith's "particularist" epistemology, see Fleischacker *On Adam Smith's* Wealth of Nations, 27–44. For a discussion of the different relations to "common sense" born by Smith's study of natural philosophy and his study of moral philosophy, see Schliesser, *Adam Smith: Systematic Philosopher*, 272–4.

15 Griswold argues that this methodological commitment generates a fundamental difference between Smith and Rousseau on the issue of the extent to which such critique is possible. See *Jean-Jacques Rousseau and Adam* Smith, esp. 74–88 and 150–87. Also see Fleischacker, "Smith and Cultural Relativism," published as "Smith und die Kulturrelativismus," in *Adam Smith als Moralphilosoph*, ed. Christel Fricke and Hans-Peter Schuett, (Berlin: Walter de Gruyter, 2005), 100–27. Thanks to Fleischacker for providing access to the English-language version of this paper.

16 Maurer tell us that by the late eighteenth century, "the claim that all facets of sociability should be analysed as ultimately self-interested" was no longer taken seriously in Scotland (though, interestingly, it was "generally accepted" as true in England). Thus, Scottish discussions of sociability tended to focus on "its mechanisms, its development, and its workings and consequences," as Smith does. See Maurer, *Self-love, Egoism and the Selfish Hypothesis*, 171–2; full discussion runs from 171 to 212. In support of Maurer's claim about Scottish attitudes to egoism, there does seem to be a pattern of decreasing concern with this issue from Hutcheson to Hume to Smith. For examples of Hutcheson's treatment of it, see *An Inquiry*, 101–15, 159–61; and *An Essay*, 22–9. For an example of Hume's treatment of it, see EPM App2/E 295–302. (Here and hereafter, I refer with "EPM" and paragraph numbers to *An Enquiry Concerning the Principles of Morals*, ed. Tom L. Beauchamp (Oxford: Oxford University Press, 1998.) Here and hereafter, I also refer with "E" and page numbers to *Enquiries Concerning Human Understanding and Principles of Morals*, ed., L. A. Selby-Bigge and P. H. Nidditch (Oxford: Clarendon Press, 1975).)

17 Smith might be reacting to the fact that Hutcheson himself sometimes blurs the line between the moral sense and the sentiment of benevolence to which it is attuned. See, for example, *An Inquiry*, 135. Cf. Filonowicz, *Fellow-Feeling and the Moral Life*, 118–19.

18 For an overview of views in the period, see Amy Schmitter, "Passions, Affections and Sentiments: Taxonomy and Terminology," in *The Oxford Handbook of British Philosophy in the Eighteenth Century*, ed. James Harris (Oxford: Oxford University Press, 2013), 197–225. For an overview that situates those views in a wider historical context, see Thomas Dixon, *From Passion to Emotions: The Creation of a Secular Psychological Category* (Cambridge: Cambridge University Press, 2003).

19 For a helpful discussion of the use of this phrase in the period, see Lukas Wolf, "The Analogy of Nature," Groningen Centre for Medieval and Early Modern Thought blog, post written 5/18/18, accessed 6/18/19. <https://www.rug.nl/filosofie/organization/departments/history/gcmemt/blog/the-analogy-of-nature>

20 It also warrants mentioning here that in a way that Hutcheson does not, both Smith and Hume assign important roles to historical development in their sympathy-based accounts of moral judgment. See Forman-Barzilai, *Adam Smith and the Circles of Sympathy*, 59; and Colin Heydt, "The Problem of Natural Religion in Smith's Moral Thought," *Journal of the History of Ideas* 78, no. 1 (2017): 73–94, 84–6.

21 In this discussion of Hutcheson, Smith cites *An Essay on the Nature of the Conduct of the Passions*. In that text, Hutcheson describes all the senses Smith lists here except that of "ridicule." See 14–15. However, Hutcheson discusses all four of Smith's examples at *Short Introduction to Moral Philosophy*, ed. Luigi Turco (Indianapolis: Liberty Fund, 2007), 27–43. As the note after next explains, the editors of the TMS provide additional reason for thinking Smith actually had the latter text in mind.

22 Hutcheson, *An Essay*, 14.

23 As the editors of the TMS point out, Smith incorrectly cites *An Essay on the Nature and Conduct of the Passions* as the place where Hutcheson makes the exact distinction between "direct and antecedent" and "reflex or subsequent" perceptions. They cite *Short Introduction*, 27. But terminology aside, the basic distinction Smith is making between perception and perception *of* a preceding perception is present throughout Hutcheson's many discussions of how the non-external senses work. This distinction is implicit, for example, in his classification of the sense of beauty as an "internal sense." See *An Inquiry*, 23–4.

24 See Hutcheson, *An Inquiry*, 121. Michael Gill situates Hutcheson's generally positive conception of human nature as part of a common project of showing, against certain strains in English Calvinism and Scottish Presbyterianism, that human nature is basically good. See *The British Moralists on Human Nature and the Birth of Secular Ethics* (Cambridge: Cambridge University Press, 2006), 135–97. This is also a major theme in Maurer's treatment of Hutcheson, though Maurer highlights the Augustinian roots of the negative view of human nature that Hutcheson wants to overturn. See *Self-Love, Egoism and the Selfish Hypothesis*, 86–116.

25 The most prominent example is Christine Korsgaard, who tries to ground the normative authority of morality in its ability to satisfy its own reflection. See *The Sources of Normativity*, ed. Onora O'Neill (Cambridge: Cambridge University Press, 1996), 49–89. Also see Geoffrey Sayre-McCord, "Sentiments and Spectators: Adam Smith's Theory of Moral Judgment," *The Adam Smith Review* 5, ed. Brown and Fleischacker (Oxford: Routledge, 2010), 124–44. Sayre-McCord sees in this point the seeds for an account of what makes moral judgments distinctive, i.e., in making them, we commit ourselves to thinking of the standards they employ as justifiable by their own lights. Sayre-McCord revisits this passage in "Hume and Smith on Sympathy, Approbation, and Moral Judgment," *Social and Political Philosophy* 30 (2013): 208–36. I revisit Sayre-McCord's thinking on it in note 12 of Chapter 7.

26 For a discussion of this issue regarding sentimentalism in general, see Debes, "Moral Sentiments," in *International Encyclopedia of Ethics*, ed. Hugh LaFollette, John Deigh, and Sarah Stroud. Vol. 8 (Malden: Wiley Blackwell, 2013).

27 Moreover, if Debes is right, then Smith's claim here undercuts his project of explaining how moral deliberation works, which requires identifying a peculiar moral sentiment. See "Recasting Scottish Sentimentalism: The Peculiarity of Moral Approval," *The Journal of Scottish Philosophy* 10, no. 1 (2012): 91–115.

28 I should note that this last point is my interpretation of the following potentially confusing lines:

> The word conscience does not immediately denote any moral faculty by which we approve or disapprove. Conscience supposes, indeed, the existence of *some such faculty*, and properly signifies our consciousness of having acted agreeably or disagreeably to its directions. When love, hatred, joy, sorrow, gratitude, resentment, with so many other passions which are all supposed to be the subjects of this principle, have made themselves considerable enough to get titles to know them by,

is it not surprising that the sovereign of them all should hitherto have been so little heeded, that, a few philosophers excepted, nobody has yet thought it worth while to bestow a name upon it? (VII.iii.3.15; emphasis added)

The emphasized phrase is confusing because it can be read as saying that while common language does not directly point to the existence of a distinctive moral faculty, it *implies* the existence of one. But if this is what Smith is saying, he severely weakens his main point, if not contradicts it. My "whatever they be" in the paragraph earlier is intended to suggest an alternative reading, according to which it is not the case that we have a distinctive moral faculty or sentiment. On this reading, Smith is only committed to there being *something* in human nature responsible for moral evaluation but not necessarily a distinctive moral faculty or sentiment.

Chapter 3

1 Some of this section is adopted from "Working out the Details of Hume and Smith on Sympathy," *Journal of the History of Philosophy* 56, no. 4 (2018): 683–96. This section also draws on "Ways of Desiring Mutual Sympathy in Adam Smith's Moral Philosophy." *British Journal for the History of Philosophy* 24, no. 4 (2016), 614–34; "Relaxing a Tension in Adam Smith's Account of Sympathy," *The Journal of Scottish Philosophy* 9, no. 2 (2011): 189–204; and the first chapter of *Sympathy, Self, and Society: Adam Smith's Response to David Hume's Moral Theory*, Boston University Doctoral Dissertation, 2010.

2 See Hanley, "The Eighteenth-Century Context of Sympathy from Spinoza to Kant," in *Sympathy: A History*, ed. Eric Schliesser (Oxford, Oxford University Press: 2015), 171–98. (The rest of the papers in that volume collectively provide a broader historical survey of the concept.) As Hanley points out, this usage of the concept was not limited to theories of social and political matters; it also extended into the natural sciences. Cf. the discussion of the anciently pedigreed medical concept of sympathy in Alexander Broadie, "Sympathy and the Impartial Spectator," *The Cambridge Companion to Adam Smith*, 158–188, 158–62.

3 The terminological switch from sympathy to empathy is natural enough for us that discussions of Hume and Smith substituting the latter for the former can be perfectly clear and accurate. See, for example, Imola Ilyes, "Empathy in Hume and Smith," in *The Routledge Handbook of Philosophy of Empathy*, ed. Heidi L. Maibom (New York: Routledge, 2017), 98–109. For an account of how Smith's conception of sympathy fits in with several currently common conceptions of empathy, see Fleischacker, *Being Me Being You*, 1–22. However, for pressure on the view that Smithian sympathy is akin to what we often mean by empathy, see Bence Nanay, "Adam Smith's concept of sympathy and contemporary interpretations," *The Adam Smith Review* 5, 137–68.

4 Here and hereafter, I refer with "T" and paragraph numbers to David Hume, *A Treatise of Human Nature*, ed. David Fate Norton and Mary J. Norton (Oxford: Oxford

University Press, 2000). Here and hereafter, I refer with "SBN" and page numbers to David Hume, *A Treatise of Human Nature*, ed. L. A. Selby-Bigge and P. H. Nidditch (Oxford: Clarendon Press, 1978).

5 Cf. Fleischacker, "David Hume and Adam Smith on Sympathy: A Contrast, Critique and Reconstruction," in *Intersubjectivity and Objectivity in Adam Smith and Edmund Husserl*, ed. Fricke and Dagfinn Føllesdal (Frankfurt: Ontos Verlag, 2012), 284–91.

6 Perhaps with hints like these in mind, Haakonssen comments, "obviously it would have been quite possible for Smith to explain the functions of imagination by means of [Humean] association. Presumably he did not do so because for his purposes it would have been an unnecessary detail in the general theory" (1981: 48).

7 Obviously, questions abound regarding how, after explicitly denying that we even have an impression of self, Hume can invoke an "idea, or rather impression of ourselves [that is] always intimately present with us" and of which we have "so lively a conception . . . that 'tis not possible to imagine, that any thing can in this particular go beyond it" (T 2.1.11.4/SBN 317; cf. T 1.4.6.1–4/SBN 251–53). The literature on the differences and relationship between the conception of self at work in Book I of the *Treatise* and that at work in Books II and III is extensive, most of it leaping off from Hume's distinction between "personal identity, as it regards our thought or imagination, and as it regards our passions or the concern we take in ourselves" (T 1.4.6.5/SBN 253). A particularly good piece with which to start exploring this literature is Jane L. McIntyre, "Personal Identity and the Passions," *Journal of the History of Philosophy* 27 (1989): 542–57. For a more recent example, see Jennifer Welchman, "Self-Love and Personal Identity," *Hume Studies* 41 (2015): 33–55.

8 One can also ask questions about what Hume thinks is so forceful about the idea/impression of self. This mystery is compounded by the fact that, in Humean sympathy, the "mind passes easily from the idea of ourselves to that of any other object related to us." Thus, the idea/impression of self involved in sympathy cannot be "the object of any passion," as it would be if Hume had in mind a form of self-concern; if this were the case, we would always remain too fixated on ourselves to sympathize with others (T 2.2.2.17/SBN 340). Hume's view seems to be that sympathy occurs when the idea of another person's passion enters into the atmosphere of our own and becomes enlivened by picking up some run-off energy from *something like* our self-concern but without requiring any particular focus on ourselves. For a discussion of Hume on sympathy that is generally sensitive to this issue, see Debes, "Has Anything Changed? Hume's Theory of Association and Sympathy after the *Treatise*" *British Journal for the History of Philosophy* 15, no. 2 (2007): 313–38, 337–8. For a discussion of Hume's account of the kind of focus on the self that is involved in sympathy, see Gerald Postema, "'Cemented with Diseased Qualities': Sympathy and Comparison in Hume's Moral Psychology," *Hume Studies* 31 (2005): 249–98. For a discussion of how the forcefulness of the idea/impression of the self in Humean sympathy can be situated within the general doctrine of "vivacity" in Hume's theory of mind, see Annette C. Baier and Anik Waldow,"A Conversation between Annette Baier and Anik Waldow about Hume's Account of Sympathy," *Hume Studies* 34 (2008): 73–6.

9 For example, see Stephen Darwall, "Empathy, Sympathy, Care," *Philosophical Studies* 89 (1998): 261–82. Robert Gordon uses "cold catching" language to describe emotional contagion in general but believes that Hume's sympathy theory involves too much cognition to qualify as a contagion view. We will see shortly why it matters that Gordon is right about this. See "Sympathy, Simulation, and the Impartial Spectator," *Ethics* 105 (1995): 727–30.

10 Schliesser complicates these standard classifications of Smith's view by arguing that causal and counterfactual reasoning play important roles in the process of Smithian sympathy. See *Adam Smith*, 107–36.

11 Cf. Ilyes, "Empathy in Hume and Smith," 100–1.

12 David Raynor, "Adam Smith and the Virtues," *The Adam Smith Review 2*, ed. Brown (Oxford: Routledge, 2006), 239–45, 240.

13 "Hume and Smith on Sympathy," 279–86.

14 Fleischacker also suggests that Smith might see Hume's account of phenomena like sympathy with nonexistent passions as "torturous" in comparison with his own more "straightforward" one (2012: 281–2).

15 Other scholars have noticed the epistemic features of Smith's sympathy theory. See Tony Pitson, "*The Theory of Moral Sentiments* and Smith's Account of Sympathy," in *New Essays on Adam Smith's Moral Philosophy*, ed. Wade L. Robison and David B. Suits (Rochester: RIT Press, 2012), 116–21; Griswold, *Adam Smith and the Virtues of Enlightenment* (Cambridge: Cambridge University Press, 1999), 76–112; "Imagination, Morals, Science, and Arts," in *The Cambridge Companion to Adam Smith*, 22–56; "Smith and Rousseau in Dialogue: Sympathy, *Pitie*, Spectatorship, and Narrative," *The Adam Smith Review* 5, 59–84; and *Jean-Jacques Rousseau and Adam Smith*, 93–149; and Olivia Bailey, "Empathy, Concern and Understanding in *The Theory of Moral Sentiments*," *The Adam Smith Review 9*, ed. Fonna Forman (Oxford: Routledge, 2017), 255–74.

16 I adopt this phrasing from Bailey, ibid.

17 Cf. Darwall, "Empathy, Sympathy, Care," upon which Fleischacker draws.

18 If Schliesser is correct about the importance of causal and counterfactual reasoning in Smithian sympathy, it becomes unclear how to categorize Smith in terms of this trichotomy. See note 10 of this chapter.

19 As with any long-standing debate, the literature concerning this one is immense. For a great overview of the debate, as well a defense of a now common hybrid view, see Shannon Spaulding, "Cognitive Empathy," in *The Routledge Handbook of Philosophy of Empathy*, ed. Heidi L. Maibom (New York: Routledge, 2017), 13–21. For a discussion of the debate in relation to Smith's interpretation, see Brown, "Intersubjectivity and Moral Judgment in *The Theory of Moral Sentiments*," in *Intersubjectivity and Objectivity*, 243–72.

20 We should note here that the epistemic elements of sympathy we are presently putting to one side can have important moral implications. In *Being Me Being You*,

Fleischacker develops a fascinating and powerful defense of the moral importance of Smithian-style sympathy that focuses in large part on what follows from the central role it assigns to grasping another's distinct perspective in the way suggested earlier.

21 For example, see Debes, "Adam Smith and the Sympathetic Imagination," in *Adam Smith: His Life, Thought, and Legacy*, 192–207, 193; Griswold, *Jean-Jacques Rousseau and Adam Smith*, 94–5; and Maurer, *Self-Love, Egoism, and the Selfish Hypothesis*, 178–9, 186–8.

22 Debes does not attribute this view to Hume either.

23 "Adam Smith's Model of Man," in *Acta Philosophica Fennica: Human Nature as the Basis of Morality and Society in Early Modern Philosophy*, eds. Juhana Lemetti and Eva Piirimae (Hakapaino Oy: Helsinki: 2007), 169–188.

24 "Hume and Imagination: Sympathy and the Other,'" *International Philosophical Quarterly* 34, no. 1 (1994): 39–57.

25 "'Cemented with Diseased Qualities': Sympathy and Comparison in Hume's Moral Psychology," *Hume Studies* 31 (2005): 249–98.

26 See "Letter to Lord Kames," *On Moral Sentiments: Contemporary Responses to Adam Smith*, ed. John Reeder (New York: Thoemmes Press, 1997), 65–8.

27 See "A Sketch of Dr Smith's Theory of Morals," *On Moral Sentiments*, 69–88.

28 The passage from Polybius that Hume cites argues in—as we shall see in Section 4—particularly Smithian fashion that people share "the resentment of their injured neighbor" by "imagining themselves in the same situation." See Book VI, chapters 4–6 of Polybius, *Histories*, trans. W. R. Paton (London: Loeb, 1922). For a discussion skeptical of the influence of Polybius on Smith, see Gloria Vivenza, *Adam Smith and the Classics: The Classical Heritage in Adam Smith's Thought* (Oxford: Oxford University Press, 2001), 44–6, 83, note 157.

29 From observations broadly similar to these, Fleischacker concludes, "the main moral advantage of Smithian empathy is not that it leads us to care about others, but that, if we do care, it improves the quality and direction of that care" (2019: 64–5). Also see Tony Pitson, "*The Theory of Moral Sentiments* and Smith's Account of Sympathy," 118–21, 127–30; and Darwall, "Empathy, Sympathy, Care." For observations more narrowly similar to the ones I am making, see Bailey, ibid.

30 The relationship between the sympathy-focused account of moral judgment in Hume's *Treatise* and the apparently not sympathy-focused one in Hume's *An Enquiry Concerning the Principles of Morals* is the subject of scholarly debate. For an example of a treatment emphasizing their commonality, see Debes, "Humanity, Sympathy, and the Puzzle of Hume's *Treatise*," *British Journal for the History of Philosophy* 15, no. 1 (2007): 27–57; and "Has Anything Changed?" For an example of a treatment highlighting their differences, see Jacqueline Taylor, *Reflecting Subjects: Passion, Sympathy, and Society in Hume's Philosophy* (Oxford: Oxford University Press, 2015), esp. 99–129.

31 See T 2.2.6-9/SBN 366-389. I propose an account of this story in "Working Out the Details of Hume and Smith on Sympathy," 688–89. However, the experience of commenting on a pre-published version of Rachel Cohon's "Disapproval and Resentment: Two Aspects of the Moral Sentiments in Hume and Adam Smith," in *Oxford Handbook of Moral Psychology*, ed. John Dorris and Manuel Vargas (Oxford: Oxford University Press, forthcoming), has led me to doubt the accuracy of this account. Also see Rico Vitz, "Sympathy and Benevolence in Hume's Moral Psychology," *Journal of the History of Philosophy* 42 (2004): 261–75.

32 For this reason, while I believe that Bailey is right to see a problem with Smithian sympathy's ability to explain concern for others, I do not think this problem is a very big one for Smith's overall moral theory. See ibid.

33 Cf. Christine M. Korsgaard, "Reflections on the Evolution of Morality," *The Amherst Lecture in Philosophy* 5 (2010), http://www.amherstlecture.org/korsgaard2010/, 9–10; and Fleischacker, "David Hume and Adam Smith on Sympathy," 274–5.

34 The editors of the TMS point out that Hobbes and Mandeville do not even discuss the phenomena Smith has in mind. They suggest that Smith might be misremembering a part of Joseph Butler's sermon on compassion. They call explicit attention to Butler's explanation for why "compassion for [others'] distress" is stronger than "delight in [their] prosperity." Butler explains that the latter is weaker because unlike people in distress, people in prosperity are not in "want [of] the assistance of another"; thus, there is no need for our delight to be strong enough to motivate action. Smith certainly uses similar language regarding "assistance," but there is little else in common between his discussion of mutual sympathy and what Butler is saying here. An especially striking difference is that Butler provides a teleological explanation for an emotional phenomenon, while Smith does not do so here. See TMS I.i.2.2, note 1; and *Fifteen Sermons and Other Writings on Ethics*, ed. David McNaughton (Oxford: Oxford University Press, 2017), 46–7.

35 Interestingly, Robert Sugden argues that contemporary rational choice theorists in economics hold a view like the one Smith attacks in that passage. See "Beyond Sympathy and Empathy: Adam's Smith's Concept of Fellow-Feeling" *Economics and Philosophy* 18 (2002): 63–87, 71–2, 79–81.

36 Cf. Sayre-McCord, "Hume and Smith," 223.

37 For discussion of Smith on the problem of tragedy in particular, see Arby Ted Siraki, "Adam Smith's Solution to the Paradox of Tragedy," *The Adam Smith Review* 5, 213–30.

38 I cite page numbers of David Hume, "Of Tragedy," in *Essays: Moral, Political, and Literary*, ed. Eugene F. Miller (Indianapolis: Liberty Fund, 1985), 216–21.

39 Fleischacker points out that the fact that Smith goes on to characterize the pleasure we take in observing our sympathy with others as a sentiment of approval implies that a visit to the hospital can be more agreeable than attendance of a ball: "imagine being at a ball where you *disapprove* of the pleasure people are having: perhaps it is being held right after a catastrophe, and you think people should not be celebrating" (2012: 302).

Also see *Being Me Being You*, 25–8. We turn to the sympathy-approval connection in the next section.

40 I cite page numbers from "A Dissertation on the Passions," *The Philosophical Works*, ed. T. H. Green and T. H. Grose, Vol. 4 (London: Scientia Verlag Aalen, 1964), 139–66. Here and hereafter, DP.

41 John Immerwahr argues that the importance of this feature of Hume's theory of the passions for his response to the tragedy problem should inform how we read his "Dissertation on the Passions." See "Hume's *Dissertation on the Passions*," *Journal of the History of Philosophy* 32 (1994): 225–40, 230–1, 233–5.

42 Cf. Broadie, "Sympathy and the Impartial Spectator," 174.

43 Indeed, his account of the "general point of view" might even assume that we seek mutual sympathy for its own sake (T 3.3.14–18/SBN 580–84; T 3.3.3.2/SBN 602–3). Hume seems to think that we start to evaluate each other in terms of how things feel from a point of view that is more "general" than the idiosyncratic ones that we more naturally inhabit because we need to solve a communication problem. He writes, "'tis impossible we cou'd ever converse together on any reasonable terms, were each of us to consider characters and persons, only as they appear from his own peculiar point of view"; thus, "the intercourse of sentiments . . . in society and conversation" leads us to treat sentiments felt from a general point of view as the standards of morality (T 3.3.1.15/SBN 581–82; T 3.3.3.2/SBN 603). To the extent that this explanation assumes that we want it to be possible for our sentiments to agree with those of others, it at least leans in the Smithian direction of implying that agreement of this kind is something that interests us for its own sake, that is, that sympathy itself interests us for its own sake. Fully defending an interpretation of this kind one would require much more discussion. For critical analysis of the communication problem to which the general point of view is a response, see Cohon, "The Common Point of View in Hume's Ethics," *Philosophy and Phenomenological Research* LVII, no. 8 (1997): 835; and Korsgaard, "The General Point of View," *Hume Studies* 25, no. 1–2 (1999): 16. For a non-Smithian interpretation of the psychology behind the solution to this problem, see J. L. Mackie, *Hume's Moral Theory* (Oxford: Routledge, 1980), 122–3; for an interpretation of this psychology that is at least partly (though not wholly) in line with the Smithian one sketched here, see Korsgaard, "The General Point of View," 24–5.

44 "Virtue, Utility, and Rules," *The Cambridge Companion to Adam Smith*, 190–1.

45 Cf. Debes, "Adam Smith and the Sympathetic Imagination," 196.

46 Cf. Campbell, ibid., 89–93. He also sees psychological and logical elements in Smith's position, but his discussion differs greatly from mine in how it interprets the nature of the sentiments involved in it. See the following.

47 *The Search after Truth*, trans. and ed. by Thomas M. Lennon and Paul J. Olscamp (Cambridge: Cambridge University Press, 1997), 399–403.

48 "History of Astronomy," *Essays on Philosophical Subjects*, ed. W. P. D. Wightman, J. C. Bryce, and I. S. Ross (Indianapolis: Liberty Fund, 1982), 31–105. Here and hereafter, "HA," cited with paragraph numbers.

49 Smith is likely echoing Hutcheson's adoption of Malebranche's doctrine here. On Hutcheson's version, to say that "all the Passions, and Affections justify themselves" is to say that "we approve of our being affected in a certain manner on certain Occasions, and condemn a Person who is otherwise affected." This quotation is from the second edition of *An Inquiry into the Original of Our Ideas of Beauty and Virtue in Two Treatises*. In later editions, Hutcheson makes the exact same point but attributes it explicitly to "Malebranch." See *An Inquiry*, 110, 221.

50 Cf. Gabriele Taylor, "Justifying the Emotions," *Mind* 84, no. 335 (1975): 390–402; and Sayre-McCord, who sees a view much like this one in Hume's theory of the passions (2013: 221). Maria Alejandra Carrasco and Christel Fricke comment that for Smith, we have a baseline trust of our own sentiments as "adequate responses." See "Adam Smith's Impartial Spectator," *Econ Journal Watch* 13, no. 2 (2016): 250.

51 If we stress a conceptual over a causal interpretation of the connection Smith sees between affect and approval, then he becomes, in current parlance, some kind of cognitivist about emotion. Others hold this interpretation. Griswold, for example, points out that "for Smith, the emotions are in some way cognitive; beliefs are part and parcel of emotions, and beliefs may be true or false, adequate or inadequate" (1999: 115; cf. 137, 240). And Martha Nussbaum has argued that Smith "refers back to the Greek Stoics" by making the "passions have a cognitive dimension—they are at least partially made up out of beliefs." See "Steerforth's Arm: Love and the Moral Point of View," *Love's Knowledge: Essays on Philosophy and Literature* (Oxford: Oxford University Press, 1990), 339. Also see *Upheavals of Thought: The Intelligence of Emotions* (Cambridge: Cambridge University Press, 2001), 34. However, because Smith does not conclusively favor the conceptual over the causal reading and because Debes has suggested strong reasons for seeing the entire contemporary debate between cognitivists and non-cognitivists about emotion as resting upon a confused conception of cognition that masks mere differences of degree, I shy away from emphasizing this terminology here. See "Neither Here Nor There: The Cognitive Nature of Emotion," *Philosophical Studies* 146, no. 1 (2009): 1–27. I realize that any problems with *this* debate should impact that about the mental states expressed by moral judgments, but the cognitivist/non-cognitivist terminology is so entrenched and so bound up with metaphysical matters there that I continue to use it. This won't really matter until Section 1 of Chapter 7.

52 Cf. Pitson, "*The Theory of Moral Sentiments* and Smith's Account of Sympathy," 126.

53 It seems that Gill would disagree. He sees the response to Hutcheson that I have identified as problematic as support for Smith's argument that Hutcheson is wrong to limit all virtue to benevolence. However, it is not clear why Smith couldn't hold that sympathy-based approval is always the same feeling but simply covers more than just benevolence. See "Moral Pluralism in Smith and His Contemporaries," *Revue Internationale de Philosophie* 68, no. 269 (2014): 282.

54 Here and hereafter, I refer with "EHU" and paragraph numbers to David Hume, *An Enquiry Concerning the Human Understanding*, ed. Tom L. Beauchamp (Oxford: Oxford University Press, 2001). I also refer with "E" and page numbers of the aforementioned, *Enquiries* (see note 16 of Chapter 2).

55 Again, if Debes is right, doing so is a crucial aspect of Smith's project. See "Recasting Scottish Sentimentalism."

56 My thinking on this point was clarified in part by the experience of commenting on a pre-published version of Cohon's "Disapproval and Resentment."

57 By identifying a special kind of "sanctioning" judgment, Debes defends the connection Smith draws between sympathizing and evaluating in "The Authority of Empathy (Or, How to Ground Sentimentalism)," *Ethical Sentimentalism*, 171–91. Cf. Darwall, ibid.

58 For a discussion of the historical context, meaning, and importance of Smith's introduction of the moral category of propriety, see Leonidas Montes, *Adam Smith in Context: A Critical Reassessment of Some Central Components of His Thought* (New York: Palgrave MacMillan, 2004), 97–129.

59 As we shall see both in the next section and in Section 3 of Chapter 6, Smith means something very specific by "just" and "unjust"; thus, I believe my bracketed modification of his language best captures his meaning in the present context.

60 For discussion of what Smith might mean by "proportion" here, see Schliesser, *Adam Smith: Systematic Philosopher*, 115–18.

61 Cf. Campbell, ibid., 88–9.

62 For critical discussion of Smith on romantic love, see Nussbaum, "Steerforth's Arm."

63 Smith also argues that our sympathy with joy more closely approaches the agent's actual feelings than does our sympathy with sorrow, though our sympathy with sorrow is ultimately more noticeable (I.iii.1.5–12). I return to this point in Sections 3 and 5 of Chapter 6, as aspects of Smith's development of it are relevant to his accounts of justice and prudence.

64 In apparent tension with what he says here, Smith later remarks that we should pursue small gains in interest more out of a sense of obligation than from strong desire, which we should reserve only for the pursuit of large gains in interest (III.6.6–7). We will return to this point after we have discussed Smith's thinking on the kind of motivation with which he is concerned in those remarks in Section 4 of Chapter 6 and while we are discussing Smith's explicitly normative theory of prudence in Section 5 of Chapter 6. For now, I only register the opinion that it is not absurd to believe that there should be this kind of mismatch between the affective character of one's pursuit of a goal and one's reaction to success in that pursuit; I find the celebration of minor victories endearing but passion in their pursuit annoying. However, that fact that I would feel ashamed of any envy I feel in the celebration of major victories, despite my approval of passion in their pursuit, suggests to me that we have all the more reason to emphasize the descriptive over the normative aspects of the present stretch of text, as I have been doing.

65 Using the example of anger, Gabriele Taylor employs an account of the structure of sentiment much like that sketched out in the previous section to explain how sentiments themselves can be indicative of moral failures or successes. See "Justifying the Emotions."

66 Cf. Griswold, *Adam Smith and the Virtues of Enlightenment*, 115–16.

67 Cf. Griswold, *Adam Smith and the Virtues of Enlightenment*, "Smith and Rousseau in dialogue," 61–71; *Jean-Jacques Rousseau and Adam Smith*, 130–5.

68 See Otteson, *Adam Smith's Marketplace of Life*, 42; Forman-Barzilai, *Adam Smith and the Circles of Sympathy*, 67–8; Fleischacker, *Being Me Being You*, 35–6.

69 See Shaver, "Virtue, Utility, and Rules," 192.

70 Fleischacker, *Being Me Being You*, 41.

71 Ibid, 34–43.

72 As we shall soon see, Smith recognizes nonstandard cases of gratitude and resentment in which we do not find all these features. For a sustained investigation of different senses of resentment in particular in Smith's moral psychology, see Alice MacLachlan, "Resentment and Moral Judgment in Smith and Butler," *The Adam Smith Review* 5, 252–78.

73 Cf. Marie Martin, "Utility and Morality: Adam Smith's Critique of Hume," *Hume Studies* 16, no. 2 (1990): 107–20, 110–1; and Shaver, "Virtue, Utility, and Rules," 201–2.

74 It is interesting question whether this is also true for nonhuman animals. For an argument that one can sympathize in Smith's sense not only with nonhuman animals but also with non-sentient nature, see Patrick R. Frierson, "Adam Smith and the Possibility of Sympathy with Nature," *Pacific Philosophical Quarterly* 87 (2006): 442–80.

75 In *Being Me Being You*, Fleischacker employs what he sees in Smith as a "new conception of humanity as consisting in the having of distinctive perspectives that are accessible to one other by empathy" to develop a distinctive approach to morality (2019: 47). If Fleischacker's project succeeds, then one could make the case that Smith is not observing a brute fact but saying something about what is *in principle* required for a being to have moral status. Cf. the conception of "affective dignity" at work in Debes, "Adam Smith on Dignity and Equality," *British Journal for the History of Philosophy* 20, no. 1 (2012): 109–40; and "The Authority of Empathy."

76 Readers familiar with Hume will recall that despite these quoted appeals to the brute factness of the experience of moral approval, he does provide an account of a special process by which what appears to be the special feeling of moral approval is felt, namely the process of imagining oneself into a less subjective point of view. As we shall see in the next chapter, Smith adds similar, though different steps to his own account of the process by which moral approval is felt. However, these details do not seem to matter much to the present debate, which focuses on the steps that take place *between* these and the experience of moral approval.

77 Of course, Smith and Hume might both be wrong in seeing a difference between the kinds of approval at issue here. See Shaver, "Virtue, Utility, and Rules," 202. For other discussions of Smith's "chest of drawers" objection, see Haakonssen, *The Science of a Legislator*, 70–1; Martin, "Utility and Morality," 109–10; and Otteson, *Adam Smith's Marketplace of Life*, 52–4.

78 Some portions of the previous few paragraphs are adopted from chapter two of *Sympathy, Self, and Society: Adam Smith's Response to David Hume's Moral Theory*, Boston University Doctoral Dissertation, 2010.

Chapter 4

1 Cf. Hanley's claim that "Smith's account of moral judgment and his theory of virtue interestingly overlap" precisely at some of the aspects of the former to be discussed in this chapter. See *Adam Smith and the Character of Virtue*, 136.

2 For discussion of the difficulty in separating the descriptive from the normative in Smith because of the difficulty in separating the descriptive from the normative in general, see Fleischacker, *Being You Being Me*, 16–22. The relationship between the descriptive and normative aspects of Smith's project, as captured by his distinction between the two questions, is a major theme in Griswold, *Adam Smith and the Virtues of Enlightenment*. See 173–78, 366–7.

3 Cf. Forman-Barzilai, *Adam Smith and the Circles of Sympathy*, 13–14.

4 For an example regarding the first, see Fleischacker, *On Adam Smith's* Wealth of Nations, 82–3. For an example regarding the second, see Debes, "Adam Smith and the Sympathetic Imagination," 201.

5 For a reading that is open to the possibility that Smith is a kind of hedonist, see Griswold, *Adam Smith and the Virtues of Enlightenment*, 125–9. Bailey raises the possibility that the desire for mutual sympathy is hedonistic. See ibid.

6 Cf. Fleischacker, ibid., 84, including note 5.

7 Cf. Maurer, *Self-Love, Egoism, and the Selfish Hypothesis*, 173–80.

8 Much of what follows from here to the discussion of Smith's theory of emotion is adopted from "Ways of Desiring Mutual Sympathy."

9 For Butler's version of this line of thought, see *Fifteen Sermons*, 12–13, 93–6. For Hutcheson's, see *Essay*, 24–7. Correspondence with Cohon has revealed to me that there might be significant differences between Butler's, Hutcheson's, and Hume's versions of the argument.

10 Cf. Bailey, ibid.

11 For a discussion of this feature of Hutcheson's account of moral motivation (in at least some texts), see John D. Bishop, "Moral Motivation and the Development of Francis Hutcheson's Philosophy," *Journal of the History of Ideas* 57, no. 2 (1996): 277–95. For a discussion of this general issue that draw a conclusion similar to the one I draw about Smith, see Gilbert Harman, "Moral Agent and Impartial Spectator," *Explaining Value and Other Essays in Moral Philosophy* (Oxford: Oxford UP, 2000), 181–95.

12 Cf. Fleischacker, ibid., 46.

13 Cf. Haakonssen, *The Science of a Legislator*, 52; and Griswold, *Adam Smith and the Virtues of Enlightenment*, 126–7.

14 Since they all offer some version of the argument against moral rationalism that it fails to account for the fact that moral judgments motivate, there is reason to apply to Hutcheson, Hume, and Smith the contemporary label of "motivational internalist" (roughly, the view that when one makes a moral judgment, one is thereby, to some extent, motivated to act). But in more explicitly identifying the mental state grounding moral judgment with the mental state grounding moral motivation, Smith's claim to this label is stronger than that of his predecessors.

15 Cf. Jesse Norman's emphasis on "dynamism" in Smith's philosophy. See *Adam Smith: Father of Economics* (New York: Basic Books, 2018).

16 Cf. Griswold, *Adam Smith and the Virtues of Enlightenment*, 125, 147, 175–6

17 For an extended account of what I have referred to here as the "perspective trading model" but which does not distinguish it from what I soon call the "autonomy model," see Otteson, *Adam Smith's Marketplace of Life*, 13–133.

18 Cf. Haakonssen, *The Science of a Legislator*, 55.

19 For a fully developed account of Smith's own substantive theory of human nature, see Schliesser, *Adam Smith: Systematic Philosopher*, 25–106. This account is notable not only for its detail but for developing and articulating a distinction between various classes of passions that captures the essential importance of social interaction to Smith's thinking about human nature.

20 See *Jean-Jacques Rousseau and Adam Smith: A Philosophical Dialogue*, 94–101. Cf. Otteson's response to Eugene Heath's argument that Smith fails to explain the emergence of morality. See *Adam Smith's Marketplace of Life*, 128–33; and Heath, "The Commerce of Sympathy: Adam Smith on the Emergence of Morals." *Journal of the History of Philosophy* 33, no. 3 (1995): 447–66.

21 In his lectures on jurisprudence, Smith is reported to have said, "it in reality serves no purpose to treat of the laws which would take place in a state of nature . . . as there is no such state existing" (LJ.b.3).

22 *Jean-Jacques Rousseau and Adam Smith: A Philosophical Dialogue*, 101–2; for more discussion, see 114–41.

23 I interpret Bailey's concerns about the epistemic and affective "egocentric primacy" in Smith's psychology to be of this nature. See ibid.

24 Thus, I agree with Otteson, *Adam Smith's Marketplace of Life*, 14. Also see Maria Pia Paganelli, "*Theory of Moral Sentiments* 1759 vs. *Theory of Moral Sentiments* 1790: A Change of Mind or a Change in Constraint?," *New Essays*, 35–44.

25 Those interested in thinking through these changes for themselves are advised to consult, first, the masterful editorial notes in D. D. Raphael and A. L. Macfie's edition of the TMS, and, second, the discussions of them that have been provided in the scholarly literature. For a summary of these notes, see Raphael, *The Impartial Spectator* (Oxford: Oxford University Press, 2007), 32–45. Contrary to my position, Forman-Barzilai argues that the revisions I have in mind here express important changes in Smith's views. See *Adam Smith*, 73–134.

26 Cf. Martin, "Utility and Morality," 115–19.

27 Cf. Griswold, *Jean Jacques Rousseau and Adam Smith*, 115–30.

28 This feature of Smith's philosophy has been frequently observed and discussed. See Griswold, *Adam Smith and the Virtues of Enlightenment*, 105; Haakonssen, *Natural Law and Moral Philosophy: From Grotius to the Scottish Enlightenment* (Cambridge, Cambridge University Press, 1996), 131; Fleischacker, *A Third Concept of Liberty*, 122; On *Adam Smith's* Wealth of Nations, 47; "True to Ourselves: Adam Smith on Self-Deceit," *The Adam Smith Review* 6, ed. Forman-Barzilai (Oxford: Routledge, 2011), 75–92; *Being Me Being You* 37–43; and Schliesser, *Adam Smith: Systematic Philosopher*, 47–8.

29 It is not standard practice to include the "W" in shorthand references to this concept in Smith. My reason for including it here is not so much for the sake of completeness. (I do not think anyone forgets the well-informedness condition. Moreover, if completeness was my concern, I should also include in the acronym candidness, coolness, consistency, etc.) I mainly include it because: (a) I find the use of an acronym immensely helpful, especially when discussing thorny matters (such as those that immediately follow), and (b) even though "I.S." is easier to *say* than "WIS" or "W.I.S.," "WIS" is easier to *read* than "IS" because "is" is such a recognizable word. My apologies if the reader finds WIS too jarring or cumbersome, but, in my opinion, it remains less so than the alternatives. Thank you to Craig Smith for urging me to reflect upon this decision.

30 For other accounts of the mechanics of invoking the WIS, see Haakonssen, *The Science of a Legislator*, 53; and Otteson, *Adam Smith's Marketplace of Morals*, 42–50.

In order to highlight the role of counterfactual reasoning therein, Schliesser spells out in detail the steps involved in Smithian sympathy-based judgments of propriety (2017: 119–20). He does not explicitly situate the WIS in these steps. However, his observation that "our social passions" become "properly moral" when they "incorporate the standards of the right sort of observer" suggests an account of WIS-infused evaluation of others much like the first one I suggested (2017: 137).

31 Cf. Fricke, "Adam Smith: The Sympathetic Process," in *The Oxford Handbook of Adam Smith*, ed. Christopher J. Berry, Maria Pia Paganelli, and Craig Smith (Oxford: Oxford University Press, 2013), 178–9, 187. Another reason to favor the former account is that it makes everyday appeals to the WIS less cognitively demanding and thus more consistent with Smith's eventual observation that we come to do so out of "habit" (III.3.2). See Millicent Churcher, "Can Empathy Be a Moral Resource? A Smithean Reply to Jesse Prinz," *Dialogue* 55 (2016): 429–47.

32 As we will see in Section 1 of Chapter 7, however, some such details matter for understanding some features of Smith's metaethics.

33 This section draws upon but alters McHugh, "Ways of Desiring Mutual Sympathy."

34 See "Equal Dignity in Adam Smith," *The Adam Smith Review* 1, ed. Brown (Oxford: Routledge, 2004), 205; and "Sympathetic Liberalism: Recent Work on Adam Smith," *Philosophy and Public Affairs* 28.2 (1999), 139–64. Cf. Fleischacker's development of an approach to morality rooted in Smithian empathy in *Being Me Being You*.

35 Drawing on Darwall, as well as the work of Griswold and Fleischacker, Debes develops the second, normative argument in "Adam Smith on Dignity and Equality." Also see "The Authority of Empathy."

36 Here and hereafter, I cite with WN and paragraph numbers from *An Inquiry into the Nature and Causes of the Wealth of Nations*, edited by R. H. Campbell, A. S. Skinner, and W. B. Todd (Indianapolis: Liberty Fund, 1981).

37 Cf. Forman's use of Foucault's notions of "surveillance" and "discipline" to interpret different aspects of Smithian sympathy. See *Adam Smith*, 63–71.

38 While I am focused mainly on the attitude adopted in the pursuit of mutual sympathy and they are focused mainly on the beneficial results of this pursuit, the distinction that Michelle A. Schwarze and John T. Scott make between "negative-sum" and "positive-sum . . . sympathetic coordination" is broadly consonant with my recognition of a spectrum like this one, at least insofar as it recognizes that Smith's psychology of mutual sympathy is complex and multifaceted. See "Mutual Sympathy and Moral Economy: Adam Smith Reviews Rousseau," *The Journal of Politics*, 81, no. 1(2019): 73. Also see Carrasco, "From Psychology to Normativity," *The Adam Smith Review* 6, 9–29.

39 One might object that insofar as my interpretation of Smithian sentiments presents them as committing us to some thought about their rectitude and insofar as my suggested interpretation of the Smithian desire of mutual sympathy posits a fundamental human concern with actually being correct in approving of these sentiments as correct, it gets things backward. Isn't it more plausible to think that we most basically view the world through totally subjective lenses and then learn from our experience with others that our sentiments and evaluations thereof can even be correct or not? Well, it depends upon what we mean by "view the world through totally subjective lenses." If what we mean by this is that we see our pre-corrected sentiments and evaluations thereof *as* subjective preferences, then the answer is by no means obviously "yes." It seems more plausible to me to think, with Smith, that we initially view our own sentiments and evaluations thereof as "standards and measures" of value and then learn from experience with others that these sentiments and evaluations thereof *actually are* often expressions of our subjective preferences, despite what we initially thought (I.i.3.1). This experience does not teach us that there is a distinction between correct and incorrect ways of feeling so much as it teaches us that we do not always and automatically feel correctly.

40 For another attempt to link the love of praiseworthiness and the love of mutual sympathy, see Otteson, *Adam Smith's Marketplace of Morals*, 89.

41 For a reading of Smith that distinguishes between "natural" and other kinds of passions, Schliesser, *Adam Smith: Systematic Philosopher*, 49–106.

42 Cf. Griswold, *Adam Smith and the Virtues of Enlightenment*, 131; and Robert Fudge, "Sympathy, Beauty, and Sentiment: Adam Smith's Aesthetic Morality," *The Journal of Scottish Philosophy* 7, no. 2 (2009): 133–46.

43 There is a common and understandable tendency to suggest that the love of praiseworthiness grows, develops, etc., *out of* the love of praise. The most developed version of a reading of this kind is Sveinung S. Siversten, "Love Redirected: On Adam Smith's Love of Praiseworthiness," *The Journal of Scottish Philosophy* 15, no. 1 (2017): 101–23. (For another explicit example, see Griswold, *Adam Smith and the Virtues of Enlightenment*, 213.) As will immediately become clear, the connection that Siversten sees between the love of mutual sympathy and both the love of praise and the love of praiseworthiness brings broadly together our readings of this aspect of Smith's moral psychology. But for some reasons that have been given and for others that will be given in the next subsection, I remain insistent that we not lose sight of Smith's belief that the love of praise and the love of praiseworthiness are fundamentally independent.

44 For the sake of simplicity, I am leaving out reference to a third relevant kind of sentiment, between the love of praise per se and the love of praiseworthiness per se: the "love of true glory," or deserved praise (VII.ii.4.10). Since this third kind of sentiment amounts to a mixture of the love of praise and the love of praiseworthiness, I think we can safely omit it from the present discussion.

45 Smith cut this passage from the sixth edition of the TMS. The only reason I can think of for this decision is that it (much like an edition 1–5 passage mentioned parenthetically earlier) *can* be read as making the concern for praise more fundamental than the concern for praiseworthiness. But since (as in the case of that other passage), this reading is not unavoidable, the passage can be treated as a valuable suggestive account of how the love of praiseworthiness leads us to a conception of a WIS.

46 Otteson helpfully observes ways in which our sympathy with everyone else undergoing this same process bolsters our commitment to its outcome. See Otteson, *Adam Smith's Marketplace of Life*, 45, 68.

47 Cf. Hanley, ibid., 138–40. Also cf. Annas's identification of a "drive to aspire" that prevents moral education from stopping at the level of rote, mechanical copying of the teacher. See *Intelligent Virtue* (Oxford: Oxford University Press, 2011).

48 I develop this point further in "Hume's General Point of View, Smith's Impartial Spectator, and the Moral Value of Interacting with Outsiders," *The Journal of Scottish Philosophy* 19, no. 1 (2021): 19–37. Cf. Fleischacker, "Hume and Smith on Sympathy," 275.

49 This section draws upon "Adam Smith's Kantian Phenomenology of Moral Motivation," *Kant and the Scottish Enlightenment*, ed. Elizabeth Robinson and Chris W. Surprenant (New York: Routledge, 2017), 286–303.

50 Cf. Harman, ibid.

51 Possible references to Hume in the immediately preceding paragraphs, which concern his account of the "general point of view" from which we feel moral sentiments, are equally complex (III.3.1-3). For a discussion relevant to these, see Jon Rick, "Hume's and Smith's Partial Sympathies and Impartial Stances," *The Journal of Scottish Philosophy* 5, no. 2 (2007): 135–58.

52 Since I do not wish to enter here into the debate about the relationship between the moral theory of the *Treatise* and the moral theory of the second *Enquiry*, let alone defend a stance on which text was more important for Smith, I treat the explicitly humanity-centered latter as primary here and merely refer secondarily to similar-sounding passages in the explicitly sympathy-centered former. Sorting out such matters requires projects distinct from the present one. See note 30 of Chapter 3.

53 This is not the only place where Smith criticizes Hume's humanity-based account of moral sentiment for inadequately accounting for moral motivation. In the midst of attacking Hume's utility- and therefore humanity-based account of moral approbation, Smith, in a move mentioned at the end of Section 1, tacitly slides from concern with the perspective of the approving spectator to concern with reflections that are "capable of supporting the agent" in the face of great temptation; once he has made this move, Smith immediately initiates a criticism of the "exquisite" but inactive and feminine—it is "the virtue of a woman," he tells us—virtue of "humanity" (IV.2.8). The issue of gender in Smith is a big one that I do not address here. See Stewart Justman, *The Autonomous Male of Adam Smith* (Norman: University of Oklahoma Press, 1996) contributions to "Symposium: Smith and Women," guest ed. Maureen Harkin, *The Adam Smith Review 7*, ed. Fonna Forman (Oxford: Routledge, 2014), 1–78; Harkin, "Adam Smith on Women," in *The Oxford Handbook of Adam*

Smith, 501-20; and Jacqueline Taylor, "Adam Smith and Feminist Ethics: Sympathy, Resentment, and Solidarity," *Adam Smith*, 354–70.

54 For a much more robust discussion of agency in Hume's moral psychology, see Kate Abramson, "Two Portraits of the Humean Moral Agent," *Pacific Philosophical Quarterly* 83, no. 4 (2002): 301–34.

55 Such a reading would be broadly in line with Harman's account of the main difference between Smith and both Hume and Hutcheson. See ibid.

56 With apparent approval, Smith also claims that "in the common judgments of mankind . . . regard to the approbation of our own minds" is not just morally relevant but "is rather looked upon as *the sole* motive which deserves the appellation of virtuous" (VII.ii.3.13; emphasis added); accordingly, Smith also explicitly states that "no action can properly be called virtuous which is not accompanied with the sentiment of self-approbation" (III.6.13). This last comment supports the aforementioned suggestion that Smith is at least criticizing Hume for not realizing the importance of conscience. It is hard to imagine Hume holding that conscious moral self-approbation is a necessary condition for virtue.

57 Thank you to Chris Pines for reminding me of the importance in this context of Smith's discussion of general moral rules. Otteson seems to read the reference to reason in the passage as a reference to the account of general rules. See *Adam Smith's Marketplace of Morals*, 73, 118.

58 Cf. Fleischacker, "True to Ourselves."

59 Note, however, that Smith is unclear here on which side of this distinction is most relevant to the case in question. If it is the latter, then it becomes unclear whether we even have a case of Smithian injustice.

60 Given the social structure of his conception of moral self-approval, his secondary point might be that he can do so while avoiding some of Hutcheson's worries about the selfishness of self-approbation.

61 Along similar lines, Hanley interprets the turn to the WIS in this passage in terms of the love of nobility understood as a form of "noble self-love." See Hanley, ibid, 147–50.

62 Cf. Carrasco, "Adam Smith's Modern Reconstruction of Practical Reason," *The Review of Metaphysics* 58 (2004): 81–116; "Hutcheson, Smith, and Utilitarianism," *The Review of Metaphysics* 64, no. 3 (2011): 541–43; and "Adam Smith: Self-Command, Practical Reason, and Deontological Insights," *British Journal for the History of Philosophy* 20.2 (2012): 391–414.

63 In "Adam Smith's Kantian Phenomenology of Moral Motivation," I suggest that Smith anticipates Kantian rationalist phenomenology in particular.

64 Cf. Forman, *Adam Smith*, which diagnoses and explores ambiguity in Smith's thinking regarding the issue of whether the second kind of correction is possible and, if so to what extent. Note that a central feature of this project is a reading of the alternations between editions of the TMS as substantive; as I indicated in Section 3, I disagree with this reading.

65 Again, drawing on Darwall's, "Empathy, Sympathy, Care," Fleischacker employs a distinction in *Being Me Being You* between "feeling *what* another might feel" and "how things feel *for* him or her" that helps articulate this notion (2019: 24).

66 I discuss this solution in more detail in McHugh, "Relaxing a Tension in Adam Smith's Account of Sympathy." Also see Brown, "The Impartial Spectator and Moral Judgment," *Econ Journal Watch* 13, no. 2 (2016): 237; and Bailey, ibid.

67 Cf. the discussion in this paragraph with the distinction between "weak" and "strong approvability" in Ben-Moshe, Nir, "An Adam Smithian Account of Moral Reasons," *European Journal of Philosophy* (2019): 1–15, 7. Ben-Moshe also discusses and attempts to solve problems similar to those to which I return here in "Making Sense of Smith on Sympathy and Approbation: Other-Oriented Sympathy as a Psychological and Normative Achievement," *British Journal for the History of Philosophy* 28, no. 4 (2020): 735–55.

68 Focusing on corrections for bias, Forman helps frame this issue with an illuminating distinction between "spatial," "affective," and "cultural" bias. It is one thing for an appeal to the WIS to help us enlarge our moral perspective beyond our (spatial) location and range of (affective) concern; it is another for an appeal to the WIS to help us transcend the (cultural) standards of our societies. See Forman-Barzilai, *Adam Smith and the Circles of Sympathy*, 137–95.

69 Fleischacker's concept of demonization can help fill out this kind of example. See *Being Me Being You*, 149–65.

70 Cf. Amartya Sen's distinction between "closed" and "open impartiality," which maps onto the distinction I make between two different kinds of correction for partiality. See "Open and Closed Impartiality," *Journal of Philosophy* 99, no. 9 (2002): 445–69.

71 For an expression of the contrary suspicion, see Fleischacker, "Smith and Cultural Relativism." Fricke seems to share my suspicion but only as a point regarding how Smith thinks his account works. See "Adam Smith: The Sympathetic Process, 192. But she ultimately seems to believe that Smith's view is only plausible with regard to the rules of justice, which we discuss in Section 3 of Chapter 6. See "Adam Smith and 'the Most Sacred Rules of Justice," *The Adam Smith Review* 6, 46–74.

72 For another interpretation of the WIS that sees it as the means by which Smithian moral judgment can transcend the norms of our group, see Hanley, ibid., 135–50.

73 For a theory that grounds morality in our sentiments in broadly Smithian fashion but that, in broadly un-Smithian fashion, argues for relativism, see Prinz, *The Emotional Construction of Morals* (Oxford: Oxford University Press, 2007).

74 Griswold highlights the aesthetic features of Smith's moral theory. See, e.g., *Adam Smith*, 67, 152, 183, and 330. Also see Fudge, ibid.

75 As Forman and Jennifer Pitts point out, we should also realize that Smith's use of the distinction is more descriptive than evaluative. See Forman-Barzilai, ibid., 244; and Pitts, *A Turn to Empire: The Rise of Imperial Liberalism in Britain and France* (Princeton: Princeton University Press, 2005), 264, note 2.

76 The *Wealth of Nations* supplements this passage with condemnation of the behavior of European colonialists (e.g., WN IV.vii.b.58–9).

77 See note 53 of this chapter.

78 Forman questions whether Smith's distinction between a general "style of manners" and particular "usages" and "actions" holds up to scrutiny. See Forman-Barzilai, ibid., 242–3.

79 Relevantly, as we saw earlier, while discussing the impact of custom on our aesthetic sentiments, Smith points out how this custom-based form of partiality can lead us to conclude, falsely, that "what takes place in [our] own age and country" is "founded upon reason and nature, not [at all] upon habit and prejudice" and thus that no alternative modes are consistent with propriety (V.1.4).

80 Cf. Fricke, "Adam Smith: The Sympathetic Process," 194.

81 Cf. Craig Smith's account of how Smith avoids "the charge of conventionalism by nesting his account of custom and fashion within a wider and more universalized account of human moral beliefs as in some sense 'natural.'" See "Adam Smith's 'Collateral' Inquiry: Fashion and Morality in *The Theory of Moral Sentiments* and *The Wealth of Nations*," *History of Political Economy* 45, no. 3 (2013): 505–22, 520.

Chapter 5

1 See Schliesser, *Adam Smith: Systematic Philosopher*, 226.

2 For the first interest, see Heydt, *Moral Philosophy in Eighteenth-Century Britain* (Cambridge: Cambridge University Press, 2018). For the second interest, see Hanley, ibid.

3 For a discussion of the tension this understanding of virtue sits in with Smith's apparent belief that ordinary life presents us with many instances of virtue, see Schliesser, ibid., 225--9.

4 As Smith himself points out, however, this distinction has a long historical pedigree (VII.iv.18).

5 Perhaps the best present-day analogue to Smith on some these fronts is the first few chapters of Annas's *Intelligent Virtue*, which aim not at developing and defending virtue ethics as a distinct approach to moral theory but at developing and defending an account of what virtues are and how they are learned.

6 For a similar view regarding the difficulty situating Smith into common contemporary categories, see Garrett, "Smith as Virtue Ethicist," 2012. <https://www.uncanonical.net /garrett/>.

7 This section draws upon McHugh, "Pursuing Sympathy without Vanity: Interpreting Smith's Critique of Rousseau through Smith's Critique of Mandeville," *Adam Smith and Rousseau: Ethics, Politics, Economics* (Edinburgh: Edinburgh University Press, 2017), 109–26.

8 For Mandeville's own account of this delusion, see "An Enquiry into the Origin of Moral Virtue," *The Fable of the Bees*, ed. F. B. Kaye, vol. 1. (Liberty Fund: Indianapolis, 1988), 41–57.

9 In interpreting the love of virtue as the love of doing and being what is honorable and noble and interpreting the love of doing and being what is honorable and noble as the love of sympathy with the WIS, I am committed to interpreting the love of virtue as the love of sympathy with the WIS, in potential contrast with what Smith says about virtue being a thing "desirable for its own sake" (VII.iii.2.8). However, what we soon see Smith say about the "affinity" between the love of virtue and the loves of both praise and deserved praise justifies this interpretation. See Section 1 of Chapter 4.

10 Cf. Hanley, ibid., 176.

11 Interestingly, Smith nods here toward a scholarly controversy regarding how much Epicurus borrowed from his predecessor Aristippus.

12 However, as Schliesser (2017: 233) succinctly shows, Smith's own commitment to satisfying the requirement that ought implies can is clear from his often misread distinction between the study of "what principles a perfect being" should follow and the study of "what principles so weak and imperfect a creature as man" should follow (II.i.5.10). We revisit this distinction in the next section.

13 Cf. Hume's comments on the "love of simplicity" (EPM App2.6/SBN 298).

14 For a discussion of the relationship between this tradition and Hutcheson, see Gill, "From Cambridge Platonism to Scottish Sentimentalism," *The Journal of Scottish Philosophy* 8, no. 1 (2010): 13–31. Notably, Gill stresses the anti-elitist strain in Hutcheson's and his rationalist predecessors' versions of the aforementioned, anti-Mandevillian view that virtue is possible. For them, virtue is possible *for everyone*, not just certain elites. As I point out in note 1 of this chapter, Schliesser argues that there is tension in Smith's account of virtue to the extent that he too holds this view.

15 Hutcheson himself was friendly to it. Perhaps his clearest defense of the view that virtue involves living in accordance with nature is in "Inaugural Lecture on the Social Nature of Man," *Francis Hutcheson: Two Texts on Human Nature*, ed. Thomas Mautner (Cambridge: Cambridge UP, 1993), 124–47.

16 Smith sources these observations in *An Inquiry*, 89–115.

17 For an interpretation that grounds this position in Smith's sympathy-based moral psychology, see Carrasco, "Hutcheson, Smith, and Utilitarianism," 536–7.

18 Darwall argues that Hume actually does bring elements of Hutcheson's moral theory one step closer to this view. See "Hume and the Invention of Utilitarianism," *Hume and Hume's Connexions*, ed. M.A. Stewart and John P. Wright (UK: Penn State, 1995), 58–82.

19 For an interpretation of this example in Smith, see Fleischacker, "True to Ourselves."

20 For discussion of the relationship between Smith and Aristotle on this point, see Vivenza, ibid., 46–50; and Hanley, "Adam Smith, Aristotle, and Virtue Ethics," *New Voices on Adam Smith*, ed. Leonidas Montes and Eric Schliesser (New York: Routledge, 2006), 17–39.

21 For a contrary reading, see Carrasco, "Adam Smith's Modern Reconstruction of Practical Reason."

22 We should note that Smith is more interested in Stoicism as a general doctrine than he is Zeno's original version of it. As Smith's specific references not only to Zeno but also to thinkers like Epictetus (VII.ii.1.19), Marcus Aurelius (VII.ii.1.37), Cleanthes (VII.ii.1.41), Chrysippus (VII.ii.1.41), Seneca (VII.ii.1.42), and Cicero (VII.ii.1 .42) demonstrate, he was well aware of the many twists, turns, and disagreements within the Stoic tradition. But we will follow his lead in treating Stoicism as a unified doctrine, commenting on internal differences only when necessary. We should also note that Smith heavily revised this stretch of text before the sixth edition of the TMS. However, Smith himself tells us in an "Advertisement" he attached to the sixth edition that in it, he has "brought together the greater part of the different passages concerning the Stoical philosophy, which, in the former Editions, had been scattered about in different parts of the work" (p. 3). Thus, most of the revisions relevant to Smith's discussion of Stoicism simply moved and reorganized passages. Of course, as Fleischacker points out, revisions of this nature can still have an important effect (2004: 112). And as Brown points out, some of these revisions downplay praise while playing up critique of Stoicism (2016: 239–40). Nevertheless, I will focus on the sixth edition while ignoring them. (Those interested in thinking through these changes for themselves are advised again to consult the editorial notes in D. D. Raphael and A. L. Macfie's edition of the TMS.)

23 There are potentially striking parallels to develop between this line of thought implicit in Smith and Hume's famous argument regarding action from duty. See T 3.2.1.2-9, 307-9/SBN 477-80.

24 In supplement to this argument, Vivenza suggests that for Smith, "indifference" to "the end result" of one's actions "cannot fail to have an effect on the quality of them." See ibid., 78.

25 Focusing specifically on Smith's discussion of the Stoic doctrine of suicide, to which I turn later, Getty Lustilla argues that Smith's criticism of Stoicism has both an epistemic and a moral side. See "Adam Smith and the Stoic Principle of Suicide," *European Journal of Philosophy* 28, no. 2 (2020): 350–63.

26 Cf. Vivenza, ibid., 59.

27 Thus, as Vivenza points out, Smith is more interested in condemning the *approval* of suicide than the act itself. See ibid., 73. Cf. Lustilla, ibid.

28 For discussion of Smith's admiration of the Stoics who "admitted that there might be a degree of proficiency in those who had not advanced to perfect virtue and happiness" (VII.ii.1.42) and a degree of deficiency in those who had not regressed to perfect vice and unhappiness, see Norbert Waszek, "Two Concepts of Morality: A Distinction of Adam Smith's Ethics and Its Stoic Origin," *Journal of the History of Ideas* 45, no. 4 (1994): 591–606.

29 Many of those writing on Smith have made a version of this point. For two recent examples, see Churcher, ibid.; and Michael L. Frazer, "Natural and Artificial Impartiality," *Econ Journal Watch* 12, no. 3 (2016): 284–97. Cf. Sayre-McCord's discussion of Hume's account of the moral point of view. See "On Why Hume's 'General Point of View' Isn't Ideal—and Shouldn't Be," *Social Philosophy & Policy* 11, no. 1 (1994): 202–28.

Chapter 6

1 The most fully developed articulation and defense of a reading in this vein is Hanley, ibid. Note that Hanley's project is less the historical one of establishing Smith's intentions than it is the intellectual one of demonstrating the function of TMS VI.

2 I intend the distinction I have been employing between a general schema for virtue and a full-blown account of virtue to respond to D. D. Raphael's perception of a hole in the TMS. He observes that prior to the addition of Part VI, the TMS presents "an elaborate, systematic theory of moral judgement, and . . . some incidental remarks about particular virtues, but nothing remotely resembling a systematic theory of the nature of virtue. In short, the book [did] not live up to the programme set for moral philosophy." However, Raphael concludes, TMS VI does not fill this gap: "The requirement that a treatise of moral philosophy should explain the nature of virtue . . . did indeed include the content of virtue, which is what we are now given; but the essential problem was to find a theory that explains that content, just as the second problem assigned to moral philosophy was to find a theory that explains moral judgement." See *The Impartial Spectator* (Oxford: Oxford University Press, 2007), 69–70. In my view, via the general schema I lay out in the first section, Smith does explain the content of virtue. As we shall see, while the seeds of this explanation are present in editions 1–5, it is completed by the sixth edition addition of TMS VI.

3 Hanley presents and defends an account of Smith's virtue theory that takes its general schema from Smith's observation that "there are no rules by the knowledge of which we can infallibly be taught to act upon all occasions with *prudence*, with just *magnanimity*, or proper *beneficence*" (III.6.11; emphases mine). Hanley argues that reading Smith this way best captures how "TMS VI forms a response to the problem

of commercial corruption" and "helps us better see the internal unity of its theory of the virtues." See ibid. 92–3. I cannot fully engage here with the original and rich reading of Smith's virtue theory that Hanley provides in making these arguments. However, I must at least register that in locating Smith's general schema for virtue in a different place, I am disagreeing with some of Hanley's reading. I will only say here that it seems odd to me to read TMS VI in a way that replaces the organizing framework it explicitly provides with one found elsewhere in the book. It also seems odd to me to do so at least partly on the basis of concerns about internal unity when, as the present section shows, the TMS VI framework does possess an internal unity, one that derives from Smith's most basic division of the affections in terms of their objects. Hanley goes on to argue that "Smith's three principal character virtues of prudence, magnanimity, and beneficence" together make up a unified account in that they are "each manifestations of a specific disposition on a continuum of self-love that extends from the low to the high." See ibid., 93. I also cannot fully engage here with the fascinating dialectical account Hanley provides of the relationship between these Smithian virtues, according to which movement from prudence to magnanimity to beneficence can be characterized as an ascent from lower to higher forms of self-love. I only express my concern that this reading elides the distinction between arguing that the more virtuous you are, the happier you will be and conceptualizing the virtues as all about—in some sense implicating their content—the agent's happiness. This worry aside, however, Hanley's general approach of reading the normative aspects of the TMS as responses to the problems of commercial corruption that are framed in terms of a reconceptualization of what is in our actual interest seems fundamentally plausible to me.

4 Cf. Haakonssen, ibid., 57; Montes, ibid., 86; and "Adam Smith: Self-interest and the Virtues," *Adam Smith*, 138–56.

5 Heydt's argument that Smith's writing on virtue helps the reader become a better moral diagnostician strikes me as best capturing the former way of improving our judgment. See "'A Delicate and Accurate Pencil': Adam Smith, Description, and Philosophy as Moral Education," *History of Philosophy Quarterly*, 25, no. 1 (2008), 57–73. Griswold's emphasis on Smith's use of the "protreptic 'we'" in part "to persuade us to view things in a certain light" strikes me as best capturing the latter way of improving our moral judgment. See ibid., 48. For discussion of moral education in Smith, see Weinstein, *Adam Smith's Pluralism*, esp. 68–81, 181–4.

6 Smith's explicit classification of what I have identified here as the first sense of "justice" as "distributive justice," as opposed to own "commutative" sense of justice, invites questions regarding the nature of his attitude toward issues like wealth inequality (VII.ii.1.10). Here I take Smith at his word in classifying Smithian justice as "commutative." In doing so, I follow, for example, Craig Smith, "Adam Smith: Left or Right?" *Political Studies* 61 (2013): 784–98. However, the reader should note Fleischacker's nuanced argument that across his *corpus*, Smith ultimately does in fact have a lot to say about distributive justice. See *On Adam Smith's* Wealth of Nations. I call more specific attention to this argument in note 29 of this chapter.

7 Thus, as many have noticed, Smith offers more of a theory of injustice than he does justice. See, for example, Nicholas Wolterstorff, "Adam Smith on Justice and Injustice," *Adam Smith: His Life, Thought, and Legacy*, 173–91.

8 Griswold observes that rules also "help focus attention on what matters ethically in this or that context" (1999: 191).

9 For another account of the role of general rules in Smithian moral deliberation, see Fleischacker, "True to Ourselves."

10 Cf. the minimalist account of the virtue of justice in particular that Julia Driver sees in Hume. On this account, the moral value of the virtue derives from the consequences of its practice and does not require the possession of an independently good motive. I'm not sure exactly how the distinction I am making fits with Driver's. On the one hand, the moral value of Smithian justice does not derive from its promotion of utility—I turn to this difference between Hume and Smith on justice later. But on the other hand, if the value of the motive to be just is solely derived from its being the best guarantor of just conduct, then this value does seem instrumental in a way that is structurally parallel to what Driver has in mind, even though Smith does not define just conduct in terms of utility. See "Minimal Virtue," *The Monist* 99, no. 2 (2016), 97–111.

11 In note 283, I address the possible tension between this observation and what we saw Smith say about sympathy with selfish passions in Section 3 of Chapter 3.

12 Fricke suggests that though Smith does not say so, his account of justice could also require the positive act of intervening on behalf of others who are victims of injustice. Obviously, work would have to be done to explain why this kind of action is not one of benevolence. But I suspect that if such a distinction is possible, it will rest upon a rationale similar to the one I employ in entertaining the possibility that justified punishment is a positive act of justice. See Fricke, ibid.

13 Others have seen a broadly similar positive account of the just character in Smith. See Griswold, *Adam Smith and the Virtues of Enlightenment*, 229; and Fleischacker, *On Adam Smith's* Wealth of Nations, 49, 147.

14 Chad Flanders stresses the importance of this point. See "Adam Smith's Jurisprudence: Resentment, Punishment, Justice," *Adam Smith: His Life, Thought, and Legacy*, 371–86.

15 Haakonssen provides an example of an account of the precision of the rules of justice that emphasizes this feature of Smith's psychology. See ibid., 84–7.

16 Arguing against the possibility of recognizing a distinctive, cross-contextual experience of harm that seems a bit more general than what I have in mind by emphasizing the experience of being disrespected, Fleischacker concludes that Smith cannot argue that justice is itself naturally precise. Rather, he can only argue that justice must be "expressed in clear, precise, and general rules" because such enforcement of rules with these features is "more conducive to liberty, and expressive

of equality, than the rule of magistrates." Such an argument would not imply "that there is a type of human experience that naturally lends itself to being promoted or prohibited by way of clear, precise, and general rules." See ibid., 166–7; cf. 153–69. One way to understand the suggestion I am presently entertaining is as pointing to such an experience, that of being treated unequally. Nevertheless, I think that Fleischacker's concerns about the experience of harm are also pressing regarding this experience.

17 Cf. Forma-Barzilai, ibid., 231–7, 250–4.

18 Cf. Fleischacker, "Smith and Cultural Relativism."

19 I am leaving out here the entire system of justice-based natural rights that we see in the student notes on Smith's lectures on jurisprudence. More on this in the following.

20 As I point out in the following, the most fully developed account of Smith's critical jurisprudence is Haakonssen, ibid. Also see Fleischacker, *On Adam Smith's* Wealth of Nations, 169–73.

21 See note 11.

22 Notice in the line just quoted that both aspects of the jurisprudence project include normative and historical elements. I take the relationship between these two elements of the jurisprudence project to mirror that between the descriptive and normative aspects of Smith's more general moral theory. For investigations of Smith's ambiguity regarding the relation between these two elements of the jurisprudential project and of the possible consequences of this ambiguity for Smith's failure to complete the project, see Griswold, *Adam Smith and the Virtues of Enlightenment*, 33–7; 256–8. Also see Flanders, ibid.

23 Cf. Haakonssen, ibid., 120.

24 Note that in the context of discussing "the purpose for which nature has given us" resentment at II.ii.1.4, Smith uses a similar "that" clause in the phrase, "that the offender may be made to repent." But in discussing repentance at II.i.1.6, while showing that resentment produces "all the political ends of punishment," Smith does not use a "that" clause regarding repentance, though he does use one regarding deterrence.

25 The differences between Hume and Smith on justice are a major aspect of Haakonssen, ibid. Also see Raphael, "Hume and Smith on Justice and Utility," *Proceedings of the Aristotelian Society* 73, no. 1 (1973): 87–104. Spencer Pack and Schliesser, "Smith's Humean Critique of Hume's Account of the Origin of Justice," *Journal of the History of Philosophy* 44, no. 1 (2006): 47–63; Michael S. Pritchard, "Taming Resentment," in *New Essays*, 151–72; Stephen Buckle, "Hume and Smith on Justice," in *The Routledge Companion to Social and Political Philosophy*, ed. Gerald Gaus and Fred D'Agostino (Routledge: New York, 2013), 92–102; and Paul Sagar, "Beyond Sympathy: Smith's Rejection of Hume's Moral Theory," *British Journal for the History of Philosophy* 25, no. 4 (2017): 681–705.

26 Haakonssen stresses Smith's classification of the sentinel's carelessness as a violation "of what is called either civil police or military discipline" (II.ii.3.11) Thus, Haakonssen concludes that the sentinel does not really violate a law of justice; rather, he violates one of the aforementioned laws regarding "police, revenue, and arms." Haakonssen argues that since such laws aim at utility, utility is the primary reason to enforce them via punishment. When this utility concerns "the survival of society as a coherent whole," as it does in military cases like that of the sentinel, it can even trump considerations of justice (1981: 120). The most obvious problem with this reading, of course, is that Smith describes the punishment of the sentinel as "just and proper" (II .ii.3.11). But, Haakonssen argues, Smith is likely using the term justice with "a wider and looser meaning" here, similarly to how he uses it in at least one other context, which allows for "necessity" to be considered "a part of justice," though not justice "properly so called" (1981: 123; LJ.b.343). Haakonssen's whole argument runs from ibid., 120–3. He levels it at least partly against Raphael, "Appendix II: The Passage on Atonement, and a Manuscript Fragment on Justice," in the TMS, pp. 394–5. Also see Raphael, "Hume and Adam Smith on Justice and Utility." If Haakonssen is right, then the present point stands that punishment for reasons of deterrence must have a fundamentally different basis from punishment rooted in sympathy with resentment. However, the parallels between Smith's observation here that "nothing can be more just than that the many should be preferred to the one . . . when the preservation of an individual is inconsistent with the safety of the multitude" (II.ii.3.11) and his description of the just man's characteristic realization that "he is but one of the multitude in no respect better than any other in it" (II.ii.2.1) should give us pause before we decide that Smith is not talking about justice in his most basic sense in the sentinel passage.

27 This possibility was raised by Julie Rooney in my fall 2014 seminar on Hume and Smith at Denison University.

28 This difference between the sentinel and the grossly negligent man matters. If the case of the sentinel ends up being just like the case of the grossly negligent man, the argument for a reading like Haakonssen's becomes stronger. Though he classifies gross negligence as "a real injustice," Smith says that "a very accurate *police* would punish" such conduct (II.iii.2.8; emphasis added).

29 Fleischacker argues that Smith actually does not prioritize the virtue of justice over the virtue of beneficence or "care" (2019: 69–70). Note that since the present point I am making about their relative importance applies to sovereign duties, it is consistent with Fleischacker's view.

30 Readers interested in locating Smith more precisely on this spectrum are advised to consult not only the lecture notes on jurisprudence but also Book V of the *Wealth of Nations*, where Smith explains how the sovereign can best fulfill its main positive duties. For an interpretation emphasizing such positive aspects of Smith's theory of governance, including those having to do with matters of distribution, see Fleischacker, *On Adam Smith's* Wealth of Nations, e.g., 138–42, 236–42, 200–26, 273–81. For criticism of this interpretation, see Douglas Den Uyl, "Critical Notice,"

The Journal of Scottish Philosophy 3, no. 2 (2005): 171–80. Also see Craig Smith, "Adam Smith: Left or Right?" *Political Studies* 61 (2013): 784–98.

31 In Hanley's words, Smith "thinks a life dedicated to justice but indifferent to beneficence is second-rate" (2009: 182).

32 A central theme of Forman, ibid., is that Smith adopts and modifies the Stoic answer to this question which is, roughly, that while "human affection weakens as it radiates outward in degrees from the self," we should "overcome" this feature of our nature by weakening our affection towards the near so as to make it match up with that toward the distant (2010: 8). As Forman stresses and as we saw in Section 1 of the previous chapter, Smith does not hold the normative aspect of this view. And as Forman stresses and we shall see here, Smith does hold the explanatory one.

33 It is important to note that Smith never explicitly offers such an argument. See Graham, ibid., 311–12; and Heydt, "The Problem of Natural Religion," 80.

34 Fleischacker makes a similar point about what is capable of moral evaluation for Smith. See *On Adam Smith's* Wealth of Nations, 56–7. Of course, if this is right, a complication arises for Smith regarding what we mean when we say that a government's policies or laws are "just."

35 Frierson argues that mainly via anthropomorphization, Smith can allow for sympathy with nature in a way that is relevant to environmental ethics. Perhaps Smith can allow for sympathy with groups by a similar mechanism. But if so, I contend, such sympathy would still be sympathy with an individual who anthropomorphically represents the group. See Frierson, ibid.

36 Cf. Griswold, ibid., 208.

37 Cf. Campbell, ibid., 56.

38 In Section 2 of the next chapter, I interpret other instances of Smith's insistence that our natural sentiments pull us in ways that ultimately are for the best as similar kinds of moral encouragement.

39 Hanley rightly stresses a feature of Smith's discussion of "universal benevolence" that I overlook here, the role of the importance of belief in god for speaking to the beneficent person's limitless good-will. (As Smith powerfully puts it, "to this universal benevolence . . . the very suspicion of a fatherless world, must be the most melancholy of reflections" (VI.ii.3.2).) See ibid., 187–9. The best way to see the relationship between this point and the one I am presently making is as complementary responses to what this goodwill demands. I also return turn to the role of god in Smith's moral theory in Section 2 of the next chapter.

40 By tying envy to perception of class, we can resolve the apparent tension between Smith's observation that a "sudden revolution of fortune" triggers sympathy-inhibiting envy (I.ii.5.1) and his observation that we expect people to pursue "extraordinary and important objects of self-interest" with passion (III.6.7). The latter refer to great successes that still keep one within the same class.

41 Appealing to later writing that Smith completed for WN and for later editions of TMS, Fleischacker argues that despite what the present passage might suggest, Smith is committed neither to the view that irrational pursuit of wealth is *necessary* for economic growth nor to the view that poverty does not really matter. See ibid., 104–18. In defending the former claim, Fleischacker engages with Griswold, ibid, 217–7; in defending the latter, he engages with Nussbaum, "'Mutilated and Deformed': Adam Smith on the Material Basis of Human Dignity," in *Cosmopolitan Tradition* (Cambridge: Belknap Press, 2019), 141–205.

42 Obviously, the addition of this chapter supports the suggestion mentioned earlier that some of Smith's other sixth edition revisions to the TMS were motivated by reservations about the commercial society he defended in WN. For a full investigation of Smith's more general attitude toward "corruption" and how it fits with other views, see Spiros Tegos, "Adam Smith: Theorist of Corruption," in *The Oxford Handbook of Adam Smith*, 353–71.

43 The qualifier "vicious" is important, for as Heath points out, Smith also "allows for a non-blameworthy ambition." See "Adam Smith and Self-Interest," in *The Oxford Handbook of Adam Smith*, 241–64, 260.

44 Fleischacker also stresses Smith's attack on vicious ambition in this context. See ibid., 104–20.

45 Although, Rasmussen shows, one can interpret the aforementioned TMS worry about the corruption of moral sentiment brought on by the worship of the wealthy as an argument against economic inequality. See "Adam Smith on What Is Wrong with Economic Inequality," *American Political Science Review* 110, no. 2 (2016): 342–52.

46 We might think that by overemphasizing this point, Smith undercuts his own view about the importance of maintaining social ranks. In following people of high rank, we follow those who possess "none of the virtues which are required" in any difficult situation (I.iii.2.5). However, Smith is not worried about this, since he believes that most governments are actually run "by men who were educated in the middle and inferior ranks of life, who have been carried forward by their own industry and abilities" (I.iii.2.5). This observation further complicates Smith's understanding of both the possibility of social mobility and the importance of maintaining strict ranks. Clearly, the middle- and lower-class men to whom Smith refers were able to jump ranks and do so in way that is conducive to social stability. Cf. note 15 of Chapter 7.

47 Cf. Raphael, *The Impartial Spectator*, 122–6.

48 Fleischacker suggests that for Smith, "some material goods may be necessary because *they signify moral status*," not just social status more superficially understood (2004: 119–20). If this is right, we have another reason not to reject out-of-hand the connection Smith sees between prudence, pursuit of wealth, and status in general. Also see Emma Rothschild and Sen, "Adam Smith's Economics," in *The Cambridge Companion to Adam Smith*, 319–65, 359–60.

49 For another reading of Smith on self-command that recognizes multiple versions, though only two, see Carrasco, "Adam Smith: Practical Reason, Self-command, and Deontological Insights."

50 Obviously, given the ancient roots of its jumping off point, Smith's account of self-command overall has echoes in ancient philosophy. For a discussion of Smithian self-command that highlights its connections to Aristotle's conception of magnanimity in particular, see Andrew J. Corsa, "Modern Greatness of Soul in Hume and Smith," *Ergo* 2, no. 2 (2015): 27–58.

51 Philippa Foot highlights the fundamentally "corrective" aspect of virtue implied here that runs through the tradition of which Smith is a part. See "Virtues and Vices," in *Virtues and Vices and Other Essays in Moral Philosophy* (Oxford: Oxford University Press, 2002), 1–18.

52 Cf. Montes, ibid.

53 For a detailed treatment of this problem in Smith, see Abramson, "Ideals of Virtue in Smith's *Theory of Moral Sentiments*," published as "Tugendideale in Smiths Theorie der moralischen Gefühle," in *Adam Smith als Moral Philosoph*, 214–50. In treating the actual alteration of our passions as indicative of full virtue in Smith, I differ with Abramson, who argues that the strong exertion involved before this happens is also indicative of full virtue in Smith; thus, she concludes, he is left with two competing ideals. Abramson's reading is well-developed and strongly textually substantiated. My view is simply that in normatively prioritizing self-command that actually alters our passions, Smith commits himself to one ideal and thereby invites us to interpret his celebration of self-command that involves strong exertion over unchanged passions as indicative that one remains an earlier stage of moral development. Thanks to Abramson for providing an English version of her paper.

54 The specter of a long-running debate between moral philosophers inspired by Plato and Aristotle, who stress the goal of inner harmony, and moral philosophers inspired by Kant, who stress the value of strength of will in service of duty, floats in the background of this discussion. For a nice overview of that debate (and an attempt to get around it via consequentialism), see Driver, *Uneasy Virtue* (Cambridge: Cambridge University Press, 2001), 45–50. In proposing the solution that I have here, I am obviously attempting to situate Smith in the former camp. See Abramson, ibid., for a detailed account of different ways to interpret Smith's version of this harmony view.

55 Cf. Montes, ibid.

56 If I command my fear from this belief about the WIS and subsequently act, I do so from what Smith calls "erroneous conscience," which he believes is only caused by "false notions of religion." This kind of falsity-based self-command actually deserves a certain lesser kind of approval; as Smith points out, the WIS will still seek to punish any crimes done from it, but "with reluctance" (III.6.12). In fact, Smith believes that acting from a regard to the sentiments of one's conception of the WIS in the face

of the temptation to do otherwise is so important to one's merit that we have more respect for a person who successfully does this on the basis of a false conception of the WIS than we would if, by succumbing to temptation, the same person coincidentally got things right (III.6.13). It remains the case, however, that the person who acts on the basis of a false conception of the WIS is in error.

57 Cf. Griswold, ibid., 206.

58 In Annas's language, some virtues "cluster" together. See ibid., 84–5.

59 Annas's reference to stages of development of the virtues is also helpful here. See ibid. 83–99.

Chapter 7

1 For an excellent overview of the contemporary metaethical landscape that is organized partly by this distinction, see Alexander Miller, *Contemporary Metaethics*, 2nd edition (Cambridge: Polity, 2013).

2 As I said in Section 1 of Chapter 2, this second point is implied more than explicitly stated.

3 For the sake of simplicity, I am leaving out of this schema quasi-realist positions that provide an account of the truth-aptness of moral judgments that do not express beliefs.

4 Cf. the readings of Hume's response to moral rationalism in Cohon, *Hume's Morality: Feeling and Fabrication* (Oxford: Oxford University Press, 2007), 63–125; and Peter Railton, "Sentimentalism and Realism in Epistemology and Ethics," in *Ethical Sentimentalism: New Perspectives*, 107–32.

5 I cite here the only writing we have from Smith on such matters, "Of the External Senses," in *Essays on Philosophical Subjects* (here and hereafter "ES" followed by paragraph numbers). This essay provides evidence that Smith held a view of this kind about colors, smells, and tastes in particular.

6 I take the word "intrinsic" in this passage as a reason against reading it as espousing a version of the contemporary view that although moral properties are response-dependent, they can be meaningfully said to *merit* our moral reactions. For the sake of simplicity, I leave this kind of view out of the discussion.

7 For an argument that the phenomenology of moral judgments does not necessarily involve such purport either, see Terry Horgan and Mark Timmons, "Sentimentalist Moral-Perceptual Experience and Realist Pretensions: A Phenomenological Inquiry," in *Ethical Sentimentalism*, 86–106.

8 Cf. Schliesser, ibid., 277–8.

9 Obviously, I have in mind Mackie's famous "argument from queerness" in mind from section nine of chapter one of *Ethics: Inventing Right and Wrong* (London: Penguin, 1977).

10 Cf. Fudge, ibid.

11 "Smithian Constructivism: Elucidating the Reality of the Normative Domain," in *Ethical Sentimentalism*, 192–209.

12 Sayre-McCord sees another potential problem here. He celebrates Smith's (and Hume's) ability to show how our moral standard can be justified by its own lights; similar to our askers, Sayre-McCord thinks that this ability is required to explain our sense that what wins the approval of our moral standard merits that approval. But he worries that unless Smith's view is properly interpreted, his standard approves of itself in a trivial sense; *of course*, the WIS approves of the WIS. Thus, Sayre-McCord argues that for Smith, the WIS approves not of itself but of our using the WIS as a standard. However, I am not sure this helps with the triviality problem. On Smith's moral psychology, the WIS approves of our using the WIS by imagining himself into our shoes when we are doing so, comparing how we are judging with how he would, and seeing that the two ways of judging correspond. But then it seems that the WIS just ends up automatically approving of the WIS again. So if there is a triviality problem here—and there may not be, if the condition both Sayre-McCord and our askers have in mind just is unproblematically easy to satisfy—then the problem has its roots in how Smith thinks that approval in general, whether corrected or not, works via the observation of mutual sympathy. See Chapter 2, Section 2, and "Hume and Smith," 231–5.

13 As I pointed out in Chapter 2, Korsgaard is the contemporary forerunner of this general way of thinking about moral normativity. See *Sources of Normativity*, 49–89. For another application of this method of "reflective endorsement" to Smith, see Fleischacker, "Adam Smith: Moral and Political Philosophy," *Stanford Encyclopedia of Philosophy*, ed. Edward N. Zalta, https://plato.stanford.edu/archives/spr2017/entries/smith-moral-political/, 2017. Note that Fleischacker employs it as a way to ground the normativity of morality absent realism about moral properties. Here, I suggest a role for the test even if Smith is some kind of realist.

14 For a thorough diagnosis of this problem, see Hanley's *Adam Smith and the Character of Virtue*. In reading Smith as responding to a worry like this one, I demonstrate a deep affinity with Hanley's project.

15 We might also quibble with the fact that Smith does not seem to think that our tendency to mistake approval of wealth and greatness for approval of actual merit is politically dangerous—and thus not generally useful—in that it could lead us to follow meritless, though rich and high-status leaders. That he describes Louis XIV as "frivolous" but nevertheless possessed of "a degree of . . . talents and virtues" that remain at least a *little* "above mediocrity" and observes that while some important "virtues are hardly ever to be met with in men who are born to . . . high stations," the real work of governing usually ends up being done by those "carried forward by their

own industry and abilities" implies that Smith did not worry about an outcome of this kind (I.iii.2.4–5). However, as an American writing after November 2016, I can assure you that he was wrong not to.

16 Cf. Schliesser's interpretation of Smith's essentially humble "wise and virtuous man" that I reference here as an essentially political figure. See *Adam Smith*, 230–33.

17 Paying careful attention to Smith's overall goals, Garrett argues that his discussion of this issue reveals his justificatory eclecticism. See "Adam Smith on Moral Luck," published as "Adam Smith uber den Zufall als moralisches Problem," in *Adam Smith als Moralphilosoph*, 160–77. Thanks to Garrett for providing access to an English version of this paper. Keith Hankins also argues that Smith intends to endorse the irregularity, not lament or apologize for it, and that the appeal to utility is part of this endorsement. Additionally, Hankins argues that Smith uses the irregularity to identify a kind of moral judgment that does not require intention and which sits unproblematically alongside the kind that does. See "Adam Smith's Intriguing Solution to the Problem of Moral Luck," *Ethics* 126 (2016): 711–46. While Flanders rejects the conclusion that Smith approves of the irregularity, he argues, that he should have noticed the morally relevant impact that the irregularity can have on our lives; issues of Smith interpretation aside, what Flanders has in mind by this impact is broadly similar to what Hankins does. See "'This Irregularity of Sentiment': Adam Smith on Moral Luck," *New Voices*, 193–218.

18 See Paul Russell, "Smith on Moral Sentiment and Moral Luck," *History of Philosophy Quarterly* 16, no. 1 (1999), 37–58; Garrett, ibid.; and Hankins, ibid.

19 As Garrett points out, Smith observes after his development of the WIS theory that "fortune . . . according as she is either favourable or adverse" impacts the estimation of "every impartial spectator" regarding the "excessive self-estimation and presumption" that leads to "ambitious and proud pursuits" (VI.iii.29–30). I find the text here similarly ambiguous, especially in light of the distinction I see in Smith between two different kinds of WIS-guided self-command. See Section 6 of the previous chapter.

20 Flanders, ibid., draws this conclusion but calls Smith to task for it. Russell, ibid., does not but stresses that Smith seems torn between justifying the irregularity and calling upon us to fix it.

21 Though see Flanders, ibid., and Hankins, ibid.

22 For an exploration of this view in Smith, see Vincent Bissonette 'The Most Cruel Misfortune': Suffering Innocents in *The Theory of Moral Sentiments*," *New Essays*, 137–50.

23 See note 39 of Chapter 6.

24 For discussion of how Smith's emphasis on the practical importance of religion distinguishes him from Hume and anticipates Kant, see Hanley, "Adam Smith on the 'Natural Principles of Religion,' *The Journal of Scottish Philosophy* 13, no. 1 (2015): 37–53. For a defense of a weaker version of this conclusion, see Heydt, ibid., 89–91.

25 See, e.g., Butler, ibid., 8–10.

26 I agree on this point with Lauren Kopajtic, "The Vicegerent of God? Adam Smith on the Authority of the Impartial Spectator," *The Journal of Scottish Philosophy* 17, no. 1 (2019): 61–78, 67.

27 Invoking Smith's intellectual context and his developmental account of conscience, Heydt presents convincing additional reasons against reading Smith as grounding the authority of conscience in God. However, Heydt admits that "there is nothing conceptually incompatible with God having designed" the process by which the Smithian conscience develops. See ibid., 82–6.

28 As we saw in Section 6 of Chapter 5, Smith also sometimes uses the term "perfect" and its variants in different ways. Just after he refers to the "perfection of human nature," he refers to the standard of the "most perfect propriety" (I.i.1.5–7). The latter use can be read as a totally unloaded, non-technical reference to ultimate achievement, while the former undoubtedly calls to mind the normative sense of human nature we are addressing now (cf. I.iii.2.9, note c; III.5.10; IV.1.5; IV.1.11; VII.ii .1.18; VII.ii.3.2; VII.iii.4.1).

29 See Fricke, ibid.; Debes, "The Authority of Empathy"; and Stueber, ibid. In my opinion, Darwall's application of his own second-personal account of moral reasons to Smith is also a view of this kind. See "Smith's Ambivalence about Honour," *The Adam Smith Review* 5, 106–23. Note that Fricke focuses on the authority of the rules of justice, not conscience; she also connects this strategy with the human nature one that is more explicitly present in Smith. Also note that Stueber is most explicit about having in mind the same kind of contingency that I do.

30 Though she has a different, more Aristotelian conception of practical reason in mind from that at work in the views I just described, Carrasco has most forcefully stressed this point about Smith. See ibid.; and "Adam Smith's Modern Reconstruction of Practical Reason."

31 Cf. Fleischacker, *On Adam Smith's* Wealth of Nations, 105, 109, 115.

32 Smith certainly appears to believe that the ultimate cause of the coincidence between following the WIS and promoting what is best for both the whole and individuals therein is god's benevolent design. See Richard A. Kleer, "Final Causes in Adam Smith's *Theory of Moral Sentiments*," *Journal of the History of Philosophy* 33, no. 2 (1995): 275–300. However, for an argument that Kleer overemphasizes this point, see Heydt, ibid., 77–80.

33 Cf. Otteson, ibid., 236.

34 For an interesting meditation on this view, see Hanley, *Our Great Purpose*, 40–3.

35 Thus, I agree with Hanley's emphasis on internal unity as a central component of Smith's conception of a life well lived. See "Adam Smith on Living a Life," *Adam Smith: His Life, Thought, and Legacy*, 123–37.

36 Cf. Vivenza, ibid., 43–4.

37 Cf. Fleischacker's account of Smithian inner conflict and inner conflict resolution in "True to Ourselves."

38 I argue elsewhere that in these respects Smith is both similar to and different from some more contemporary recommenders of authenticity. See "Rousseau and Smith on Sincerity and Authenticity," *The Rousseauian Mind*, ed. Eve Grace and Christopher Kelly (Oxford: Routledge, 2019), 130–8.

39 For a more fully developed account of the nature and authority of moral reasons in Smith that is of a piece with the account sketched here but that attempts to avoid its potentially most troubling aspect—that it makes the authority of moral demands *too* contingent—see Ben-Moshe, ibid.

Chapter 8

1 Thanks to Sam Cowling for reminding me to think about this.

Bibliography

Abramson, Kate. "Ideals of Virtue in Smith's *Theory of Moral Sentiments*." Published as "Tugendideale in Smiths Theorie der moralischen Gefühle." In *Adam Smith als Moralphilosoph*, edited by Christel Fricke and Hans-Peter Schuett, 214–50. Berlin: Walter de Gruyter, 2005.

Abramson, Kate. "Two Portraits of the Humean Moral Agent." *Pacific Philosophical Quarterly* 83, no. 4 (2002): 301–34.

Annas, Julia. "Ancient Ethics and Modern Morality." *Philosophical Perspectives* 6, Ethics (1992): 119–36.

Annas, Julia. *Intelligent Virtue*. Oxford: Oxford University Press, 2011.

Baier, Annette C. and Anik Waldow. "A Conversation between Annette Baier and Anik Waldow about Hume's Account of Sympathy." *Hume Studies* 34 (2008): 61–87.

Bailey, Olivia. "Empathy, Concern and Understanding in *The Theory of Moral Sentiments*." In *The Adam Smith Review* 9, edited by Fonna Forman, 255–74. Oxford: Routledge, 2017.

Ben-Moshe, Nir. "An Adam Smithian Account of Moral Reasons." *European Journal of Philosophy* (2019): 1–15.

Ben-Moshe, Nir. "Making Sense of Smith on Sympathy and Approbation: Other-Oriented Sympathy as a Psychological and Normative Achievement." *British Journal for the History of Philosophy* 28, no. 4 (2020): 735–55.

Berry, Christopher. "Smith and Science." In *The Cambridge Companion to Adam Smith*, edited by Knud Haakonssen, 112–35. Cambridge: Cambridge University Press, 2006.

Bishop, John D. "Moral Motivation and the Development of Francis Hutcheson's Philosophy." *Journal of the History of Ideas* 57, no. 2 (1996): 277–95.

Bissonette, Vincent. " 'The Most Cruel Misfortune': Suffering Innocents in *The Theory of Moral Sentiments*." In *New Essays on Adam Smith's Moral Philosophy*, edited by Wade L. Robison and David B. Suits, 137–50. Rochester: RIT Press, 2012.

Biziou, Michael. "Adam Smith and the History of Philosophy." In *Adam Smith: His Life, Thought, and Legacy*, edited by Ryan Patrick Hanley, 422–42. Princeton: Princeton University Press, 2016.

Broadie, Alexander. "Sympathy and the Impartial Spectator." In *The Cambridge Companion to Adam Smith*, edited by Knud Haakonssen, 158–88. Cambridge: Cambridge University Press, 2006.

Brown, Vivienne. "Intersubjectivity and moral judgment in *The Theory of Moral Sentiments*." In *Intersubjectivity and Objectivity in Adam Smith and Edmund Husserl*, edited by Fricke and Dagfinn Føllesdal, 243–72. Frankfurt: Ontos Verlag, 2012.

Brown, Vivienne. "The Impartial Spectator and Moral Judgment." *Econ Journal Watch* 13, no. 2 (2016): 232–48.

Brown, Vivienne. *Adam Smith's Discourse: Canonicity, Commerce and Conscience*. New York: Routledge, 1994.

Buchan, James. "The Biography of Adam Smith." In *Adam Smith: His Life, Thought, and Legacy*, edited by Ryan Patrick Hanley, 3–16. Princeton: Princeton University Press, 2016.

Buchan, James. *The Authentic Adam Smith: His Life and Ideas*. New York: W. W. Norton: 2006.

Buckle, Stephen. "Hume and Smith on Justice." In *The Routledge Companion to Social and Political Philosophy*, edited by Gerald Gaus and Fred D"Agostino, 92–102. Routledge: New York, 2013.

Butler, Joseph. *Fifteen Sermons and Other Writings on Ethics*, edited by David McNaughton. Oxford: Oxford University Press, 2017.

Campbell, T. D. *Adam Smith's Science of Morals*. Oxford: Routledge, 2010.

Carrasco, Maria Alejandra and Christel Fricke. "Adam Smith's Impartial Spectator." *Econ Journal Watch* 13, no. 2 (2016): 249–63.

Carrasco, Maria Alejandra. "Adam Smith: Self-Command, Practical Reason, and Deontological Insights." *British Journal for the History of Philosophy* 20, no. 2 (2012): 391–414.

Carrasco, Maria Alejandra. "Adam Smith's Modern Reconstruction of Practical Reason." *The Review of Metaphysics* 58 (2004): 81–116.

Carrasco, Maria Alejandra. "From Psychology to Normativity." In *The Adam Smith Review* 6, edited by Fonna Forman-Barzilai, 9–29. Oxford: Routledge, 2011.

Carrasco, Maria Alejandra. "Hutcheson, Smith, and Utilitarianism." *The Review of Metaphysics* 64, no. 3 (2011): 515–53.

Churcher, Millicent. "Can Empathy Be a Moral Resource? A Smithean Reply to Jesse Prinz." *Dialogue* 55 (2016): 429–47.

Cohon, Rachel. "Disapproval and Resentment: Two Aspects of the Moral Sentiments in Hume and Adam Smith." In *Oxford Handbook of Moral Psychology*, edited by John Dorris and Manuel Vargas. Oxford: Oxford University Press, forthcoming.

Cohon, Rachel. "The Common Point of View in Hume's Ethics." *Philosophy and Phenomenological Research* LVII, no. 8 (1997): 827–50.

Cohon, Rachel. *Hume's Morality: Feeling and Fabrication*. Oxford: Oxford University Press, 2007.

Corsa, Andrew J. "Modern Greatness of Soul in Hume and Smith." *Ergo* 2, no. 2 (2015): 27–58.

Cudworth, Ralph. *A Treatise Concerning Eternal and Immutable Morality*, edited by Sarah Hutton. Cambridge: Cambridge University Press, 1996.

Darwall, Stephen. "Empathy, Sympathy, Care." *Philosophical Studies* 89 (1998): 261–82.

Darwall, Stephen. "Equal Dignity in Adam Smith." In *The Adam Smith Review* 1, edited by Vivienne Brown, 200–209. Oxford: Routledge, 2004.

Darwall, Stephen. "Hume and the Invention of Utilitarianism." In *Hume and Hume's Connexions*, edited by M. A. Stewart and John P. Wright, 58–82. UK: Penn State, 1995.

Darwall, Stephen. "Sympathetic Liberalism: Recent Work on Adam Smith." *Philosophy and Public Affairs* 28, no. 2 (1999), 139–64.

Debes, Remy. "Adam Smith and the Sympathetic Imagination." *Adam Smith: His Life, Thought, and Legacy*, edited by Ryan Patrick Hanley, 192–207. Princeton: Princeton University Press, 2016.

Debes, Remy. "Adam Smith on Dignity and Equality." *British Journal for the History of Philosophy* 20, no. 1 (2012): 109–40.

Debes, Remy. "Has Anything Changed? Hume's Theory of Association and Sympathy after the *Treatise*." *British Journal for the History of Philosophy* 15, no. 2 (2007): 313–38.

Debes, Remy. "Humanity, Sympathy, and the Puzzle of Hume's *Treatise*." *British Journal for the History of Philosophy* 15, no. 1 (2007): 27–57.

Debes, Remy. "Moral Rationalism and Moral Realism." *Routledge Companion to 18th Century Philosophy*, edited by Aaron Garrett, 500–34. New York: Routledge, 2014.

Debes, Remy. "Moral Sentiments." *International Encyclopedia of Ethics*, edited by. Hugh LaFollette, John Deigh, and Sarah Stroud, vol. 8. Malden: Wiley Blackwell, 2013.

Debes, Remy. "Neither Here Nor There: The Cognitive Nature of Emotion." *Philosophical Studies* 146, no. 1 (2009): 1–27.

Debes, Remy. "Recasting Scottish Sentimentalism: The Peculiarity of Moral Approval." *The Journal of Scottish Philosophy* 10, no. 1 (2012): 91–115.

Debes, Remy. "The Authority of Empathy (Or, How to Ground Sentimentalism)." In *Ethical Sentimentalism: New Perspectives*, edited by Debes and Karsten R. Stueber, 171–91. Cambridge: Cambridge University Press, 2017.

Den Uyl, Douglas. "Critical Notice." *The Journal of Scottish Philosophy* 3, no. 2 (2005): 171–80.

Dixon, Thomas. *From Passion to Emotions: The Creation of a Secular Psychological Category*. Cambridge: Cambridge University Press, 2003.

Driver, Julia. "Minimal Virtue." *The Monist* 99, no. 2 (2016): 97–111.

Driver, Julia. *Uneasy Virtue*. Cambridge: Cambridge University Press, 2001.

Ferreira, M. Jamie. "Hume and Imagination: Sympathy and the 'Other.'" *International Philosophical Quarterly* 34, no. 1 (1994): 39–57.

Filonowicz, Joseph Duke. *Fellow-Feeling and the Moral Life*. Cambridge: Cambridge University Press, 2008.

Flanders, Chad. "'This Irregularity of Sentiment': Adam Smith on Moral Luck." In *New Voices on Adam Smith*, edited by Leonidas Montes and Eric Schliesser, 193–218. New York: Routledge, 2006.

Flanders, Chad. "Adam Smith's Jurisprudence: Resentment, Punishment, Justice." In *Adam Smith: His Life, Thought, and Legacy*, edited by Ryan Patrick Hanley, 371–86. Princeton: Princeton University Press, 2016.

Fleischacker, Samuel. "Adam Smith: Moral and Political Philosophy." *Stanford Encyclopedia of Philosophy*, edited by Edward N. Zalta, https://plato.stanford.edu/archives/spr2017/entries/smith-moral-political/. 2017.

Fleischacker, Samuel. "David Hume and Adam Smith on Sympathy: A Contrast, Critique and Reconstruction." In *Intersubjectivity and Objectivity in Adam Smith and Edmund Husserl*, edited by Fricke and Dagfinn Føllesdal, 273–312. Frankfurt: Ontos Verlag, 2012.

Fleischacker, Samuel. “Smith and Cultural Relativism.” Published as “Smith und die Kulturrelativismus.” In *Adam Smith als Moralphilosoph*, edited by Christel Fricke and Hans-Peter Schuett, 100–27. Berlin: Walter de Gruyter, 2005.

Fleischacker, Samuel. “True to Ourselves: Adam Smith on Self-Deceit.” *The Adam Smith Review* 6, edited by Fonna Forman-Barzilai, 75–92. Oxford: Routledge, 2011.

Fleischacker, Samuel. *A Third Concept of Liberty: Judgment and Freedom in Kant and Adam Smith*. Princeton: Princeton University Press, 1999.

Fleischacker, Samuel. *Being Me Being You: Adam Smith and Empathy*. Chicago: University of Chicago Press, 2019.

Fleischacker, Samuel. *On Adam Smith's Wealth of Nations: A Philosophical Companion*. Princeton: Princeton University Press, 2004.

Foot, Philippa. “Virtues and Vices.” In *Virtues and Vices and Other Essays in Moral Philosophy*, 1–18. Oxford: Oxford University Press, 2002.

Forman-Barzilai, Fonna. *Adam Smith and the Circles of Sympathy: Cosmopolitanism and Moral Theory*. Cambridge: Cambridge University Press, 2010.

Frazer, Michael L. “Natural and Artificial Impartiality.” *Econ Journal Watch* 12, no. 3 (2016): 284–97.

Fricke, Christel. “Adam Smith: The Sympathetic Process.” In *The Oxford Handbook of Adam Smith*, edited by Christopher J. Berry, Maria Pia Paganelli, and Craig Smith, 177–200. Oxford: Oxford University Press, 2013.

Frierson, Patrick R. “Adam Smith and the Possibility of Sympathy with Nature.” *Pacific Philosophical Quarterly* 87 (2006): 442–80.

Fudge, Robert. “Sympathy, Beauty, and Sentiment: Adam Smith's Aesthetic Morality.” *The Journal of Scottish Philosophy* 7, no. 2 (2009): 133–46.

Garrett Aaron. “Adam Smith on Moral Luck.” Published as “Adam Smith uber den Zufall als moralisches Problem.” In *Adam Smith als Moralphilosoph*, edited by Christel Fricke and Hans-Peter Schuett, 160–77. Berlin: Walter de Gruyter, 2005.

Garrett, Aaron. “Smith as Virtue Ethicist.” 2012. <https://www.uncanonical.net/garrett/>.

Gill, Michael. “From Cambridge Platonism to Scottish Sentimentalism.” *The Journal of Scottish Philosophy* 8, no. 1 (2010): 13–31.

Gill, Michael. “Moral Pluralism in Smith and His Contemporaries.” *Revue Internationale de Philosophie* 68, no. 269 (2014): 275–306.

Gill, Michael. *The British Moralists on Human Nature and the Birth of Secular Ethics*. Cambridge: Cambridge University Press, 2006.

Gordon, Robert. “Sympathy, Simulation, and the Impartial Spectator.” *Ethics* 105 (1995): 727–42.

Graham, Gordon. “Adam Smith and Religion.” *Adam Smith: His Life, Thought, and Legacy*, edited by Ryan Patrick Hanley, 305–20. Princeton: Princeton University Press, 2016.

Griswold, Charles L. “Imagination, Morals, Science, and Arts.” *The Cambridge Companion to Adam Smith*, edited by Knud Haakonssen, 22–56. Cambridge: Cambridge University Press, 2006.

Griswold, Charles L. “Smith and Rousseau in Dialogue: Sympathy, *Pitie*, Spectatorship, and Narrative.” *The Adam Smith Review* 5, edited by Vivienne Brown and Samuel Fleischacker, 59–84. Oxford: Routledge, 2010.

Griswold, Charles L. *Adam Smith and the Virtues of Enlightenment*. Cambridge: Cambridge University Press, 1998.

Griswold, Charles L. *Jean-Jacques Rousseau and Adam Smith: A Philosophical Encounter*. London: Routledge, 2017.

Haakonssen, Knud. "Introduction." In Adam Smith, *The Theory of Moral Sentiments*, edited by Haakonssen, vii–xxix. Cambridge: Cambridge University Press, 2012.

Haakonssen, Knud. *Natural Law and Moral Philosophy: From Grotius to the Scottish Enlightenment*. Cambridge: Cambridge University Press, 1996.

Haakonssen, Knud. *The Science of a Legislator: The Natural Jurisprudence of David Hume and Adam Smith*. Cambridge: Cambridge University Press, 1981.

Hankins, Keith. "Adam Smith's Intriguing Solution to the Problem of Moral Luck." *Ethics* 126 (2016): 711–46.

Hanley, Ryan Patrick. "Adam Smith on Living a Life." In *Adam Smith: His Life, Thought, and Legacy*, edited by Hanley, 123–37. Princeton: Princeton University Press, 2016.

Hanley, Ryan Patrick. "Adam Smith on the "Natural Principles of Religion." *The Journal of Scottish Philosophy* 13, no. 1 (2015): 37–53.

Hanley, Ryan Patrick. "Adam Smith, Aristotle, and Virtue Ethics." *New Voices on Adam Smith*, edited by Leonidas Montes and Eric Schliesser, 17–39. New York: Routledge, 2006.

Hanley, Ryan Patrick. "The Eighteenth-Century Context of Sympathy from Spinoza to Kant." In *Sympathy: A History*, edited by Eric Schliesser, 171–98. Oxford: Oxford University Press, 2015.

Hanley, Ryan Patrick. *Adam Smith and the Character of Virtue*. Cambridge: Cambridge University Press, 2009.

Hanley, Ryan Patrick. *Our Great Purpose: Adam Smith on Living a Better Life*. Princeton: Princeton University Press, 2019.

Harkin, Maureen (ed.). "Symposium: Smith and women." In *The Adam Smith Review 7*, edited by Fonna Forman, 1–78. Oxford: Routledge, 2014.

Harkin, Maureen. "Adam Smith on Women." In. *The Oxford Handbook of Adam Smith*, edited by Christopher J. Berry, Maria Pia Paganelli, and Craig Smith, 501–20. Oxford: Oxford University Press, 2013.

Harman, Gilbert. "Moral Agent and Impartial Spectator." In *Explaining Value and Other Essays in Moral Philosophy*, 181–95. Oxford: Oxford UP, 2000.

Heath, Eugene. "Adam Smith and Self-Interest." *The Oxford Handbook of Adam Smith*, edited by Christopher J. Berry, Maria Pia Paganelli, and Craig Smith, 241–64. Oxford: Oxford University Press, 2013.

Heath, Eugene. "The Commerce of Sympathy: Adam Smith on the Emergence of Morals." *Journal of the History of Philosophy* 33, no. 3 (1995): 447–66.

Heydt, Colin. "'A Delicate and Accurate Pencil': Adam Smith, Description, and Philosophy as Moral Education." *History of Philosophy Quarterly* 25, no. 1 (2008): 57–73.

Heydt, Colin. "The Problem of Natural Religion in Smith's Moral Thought." *Journal of the History of Ideas* 78, no. 1 (2017): 73–94.

Heydt, Colin. *Moral Philosophy in Eighteenth-Century Britain*. Cambridge: Cambridge University Press, 2018.

Hobbes, Thomas. *Leviathan*, edited by Edwin Curley. Indianapolis: Hackett, 1994.

Holler, Manfred. "Adam Smith's Model of Man." In *Acta Philosophica Fennica: Human Nature as the Basis of Morality and Society in Early Modern Philosophy*, edited by. Juhana Lemetti and Eva Piirimae, 169–88. Hakapaino Oy: Helsinki, 2007.

Horgan, Terry and Mark Timmons. "Sentimentalist Moral-Perceptual Experience and Realist Pretensions: A Phenomenological Inquiry." *Ethical Sentimentalism: New Perspectives*, edited by Remy Debes and Karsten R. Stueber, 86–106. Cambridge: Cambridge University Press, 2017.

Hume, David. "A Dissertation on the Passions." In *The Philosophical Works*, Vol. 4, edited by T.H. Green and T.H. Grose, 139–66. London: Scientia Verlag Aalen, 1964.

Hume, David. "Of Tragedy." In *Essays: Moral, Political, and Literary*, edited by Eugene F. Miller, 216–21. Indianapolis: Liberty Fund, 1985.

Hume, David. *A Treatise of Human Nature*, edited by David Fate Norton and Mary J. Norton. Oxford: Oxford University Press, 2000.

Hume, David. *A Treatise of Human Nature*, edited by L. A. Selby-Bigge and P. H. Nidditch. Oxford: Clarendon Press, 1978.

Hume, David. *An Enquiry Concerning the Human Understanding*, edited by Tom L. Beauchamp. Oxford: Oxford University Press, 2001.

Hume, David. *An Enquiry Concerning the Principles of Morals*, edited by Tom L. Beauchamp. Oxford: Oxford University Press, 1998.

Hume, David. *Enquiries Concerning Human Understanding and Principles of Morals*, edited by L. A. Selby-Bigge and P. H. Nidditch. Oxford: Clarendon Press, 1975.

Hutcheson, Francis. "Inaugural Lecture on the Social Nature of Man." In *Francis Hutcheson: Two Texts on Human Nature*, edited by Thomas Mautner, 124–47. Cambridge: Cambridge UP, 1993.

Hutcheson, Francis. *An Essay on the Nature and Conduct of the Passions and Affections, with Illustrations on the Moral Sense*, edited by Aaron Garrett. Indianapolis: Liberty Fund, 2002.

Hutcheson, Francis. *An Inquiry into the Original of Our Ideas of Beauty and Virtue in Two Treatises*, edited by Wolfgang Leidhold. Indianapolis: Liberty Fund, 2004.

Hutcheson, Francis. *Short Introduction to Moral Philosophy*, edited by Luigi Turco. Indianapolis: Liberty Fund, 2007.

Ilyes, Imola. "Empathy in Hume and Smith." In *The Routledge Handbook of Philosophy of Empathy*, edited by Heidi L. Maibom, 98–109. New York: Routledge, 2017.

Immerwahr, John. "Hume's *Dissertation on the Passions*." *Journal of the History of Philosophy* 32 (1994): 225–40.

Justman, Stewart. *The Autonomous Male of Adam Smith*. Norman: University of Oklahoma Press, 1996.

Kleer, Richard A. "Final Causes in Adam Smith's *Theory of Moral Sentiments*." *Journal of the History of Philosophy* 33, no. 2 (1995): 275–300.

Kopajtic, Lauren. "The Vicegerent of God? Adam Smith on the Authority of the Impartial Spectator." *The Journal of Scottish Philosophy* 17, no. 1 (2019): 61–78.

Korsgaard, Christine M. "Reflections on the Evolution of Morality." *The Amherst Lecture in Philosophy* 5 (2010), http://www.amherstlecture.org/korsgaard2010/

Korsgaard, Christine M. "The General Point of View." *Hume Studies* 25, no. 1–2 (1999): 3–41.

Korsgaard, Christine M. *The Sources of Normativity*, edited by Onora O'Neill. Cambridge: Cambridge University Press, 1996.

Lustilla, Getty. "Adam Smith and the Stoic Principle of Suicide." *European Journal of Philosophy* 28, no. 2 (2020): 350–63.

Mackie, J. L. *Ethics: Inventing Right and Wrong*. London: Penguin, 1977.

Mackie, J. L. *Hume's Moral Theory*. Oxford: Routledge, 1980.

MacLachlan, Alice. "Resentment and Moral Judgment in Smith and Butler." *The Adam Smith Review* 5, edited by Vivienne Brown and Samuel Fleischacker, 252–78. Oxford: Routledge, 2010.

Malebranche, Nicolas. *The Search after Truth*, trans. and edited by Thomas M. Lennon and Paul J. Olscamp. Cambridge: Cambridge University Press, 1997.

Mandeville, Bernard. "An Enquiry into the Origin of Moral Virtue." *The Fable of the Bees*, vol. 1, edited by F.B. Kaye, 41–57. Liberty Fund: Indianapolis, 1988.

Martin, Marie. "Utility and Morality: Adam Smith's Critique of Hume." *Hume Studies* 16, no. 2 (1990): 107–20.

Maurer, Christian. *Self-Love, Egoism, and the Selfish Hypothesis*. Edinburgh: Edinburgh University Press, 2019.

McHugh, John. "Rousseau and Smith on Sincerity and Authenticity." In *The Rousseauian Mind*, edited by Eve Grace and Christopher Kelly, 130–8. Oxford: Routledge, 2019.

McHugh, John. "Adam Smith's Kantian Phenomenology of Moral Motivation." In *Kant and the Scottish Enlightenment*, edited by Elizabeth Robinson and Chris W. Surprenant, 286–303. New York: Routledge, 2017.

McHugh, John. "Hume's General Point of View, Smith's Impartial Spectator, and the Moral Value of Interacting with Outsiders." *The Journal of Scottish Philosophy* 19, no. 1 (2021): 19–37.

McHugh, John. "Pursuing Sympathy without Vanity: Interpreting Smith's Critique of Rousseau through Smith's Critique of Mandeville." In *Adam Smith and Rousseau: Ethics, Politics, Economics*, edited by Maria Pia Paganelli, Dennis C. Rasmussen, and Craig Smith, 109–26. Edinburgh: Edinburgh University Press, 2017.

McHugh, John. "Relaxing a Tension in Adam Smith's Account of Sympathy." *The Journal of Scottish Philosophy* 9, no. 2 (2011): 189–204.

McHugh, John. "Ways of Desiring Mutual Sympathy in Adam Smith's Moral Philosophy." *British Journal for the History of Philosophy* 24, no. 4 (2016): 614–34.

McHugh, John. "Working out the Details of Hume and Smith on Sympathy." *Journal of the History of Philosophy* 56, no. 4 (2018): 683–96.

McHugh, John. *Sympathy, Self, and Society: Adam Smith's Response to David Hume's Moral Theory*. Boston University Doctoral Dissertation, 2010.

McIntyre, Jane L. "Personal Identity and the Passions." *Journal of the History of Philosophy* 27 (1989): 542–57.

Miller, Alexander. *Contemporary Metaethics*. Cambridge: Polity, 2013.

Montes, Leonidas. "Adam Smith: Self-interest and the Virtues." In *Adam Smith: His Life, Thought, and Legacy*, edited by Ryan Patrick Hanley, 138–56. Princeton: Princeton University Press, 2016.

Montes, Leonidas. *Adam Smith in Context: A Critical Reassessment of Some Central Components of His Thought*. New York: Palgrave MacMillan, 2004.

Nanay, Bence. "Adam Smith's Concept of Sympathy and Contemporary Interpretations." In *The Adam Smith Review 5*, edited by Vivienne Brown and Samuel Fleischacker, 137–68. Oxford: Routledge, 2010.

Norman, Jesse. *Adam Smith: Father of Economics*. New York: Basic Books, 2018.

Norton, David Fate and Manfred Kuehn. "The Foundations of Morality." In *The Cambridge History of Eighteenth-Century Philosophy*, Vol. II, edited by Knud Haakonssen, 939–87. Cambridge: Cambridge University Press, 2006.

Norton, David Fate. *David Hume: Common-Sense Moralist, Sceptical Metaphysican*. Princeton: Princeton University Press, 1982.

Nussbaum, Martha. "'Mutilated and Deformed': Adam Smith on the Material Basis of Human Dignity." In *Cosmopolitan Tradition*, 141–205. Cambridge: Belknap Press, 2019.

Nussbaum, Martha. "Steerforth's Arm: Love and the Moral Point of View." In *Love's Knowledge: Essays on Philosophy and Literature*, 335–64. Oxford: Oxford University Press, 1990.

Nussbaum, Martha. *Upheavals of Thought: The Intelligence of Emotions*. Cambridge: Cambridge University Press, 2001.

Otteson, James R. *Adam Smith's Marketplace of Life*. Cambridge: Cambridge University Press, 2002.

Pack, Spencer and Eric Schliesser. "Smith's Humean Critique of Hume's Account of the Origin of Justice." *Journal of the History of Philosophy* 44, no. 1 (2006): 47–63.

Paganelli, Maria Pia. "*Theory of Moral Sentiments* 1759 vs. *Theory of Moral Sentiments* 1790: A Change of Mind or a Change in Constraint?" In *New Essays on Adam Smith's Moral Philosophy*, edited by Wade L. Robison and David B. Suits, 35–44. Rochester: RIT Press, 2012.

Philipson, Nicholas. *Adam Smith: An Enlightened Life*. New Haven: Yale University Press, 2010.

Pitson, Tony. "*The Theory of Moral Sentiments* and Smith's Account of Sympathy." In *New Essays on Adam Smith's Moral Philosophy*, edited by Wade L. Robison and David B. Suits, 115–35. Rochester: RIT Press, 2012.

Pitts, Jennifer. *A Turn to Empire: The Rise of Imperial Liberalism in Britain and France*. Princeton: Princeton University Press, 2005.

Polybius. *Histories*, trans. W.R. Paton. London: Loeb, 1922.

Postema, Gerald. "'Cemented with Diseased Qualities': Sympathy and Comparison in Hume's Moral Psychology." *Hume Studies* 31 (2005): 249–98.

Prinz, Jesse. "Neoclassical Sentimentalism." In *Ethical Sentimentalism: New Perspectives*, edited by Remy Debes and Karsten R. Stueber, 32–51. Cambridge: Cambridge University Press, 2017.

Prinz, Jesse. *The Emotional Construction of Morals*. Oxford: Oxford University Press, 2007.

Pritchard, Michael S. "Taming Resentment." In *New Essays on Adam Smith's Moral Philosophy*, edited by Wade L. Robison and David B. Suits, 151–72. Rochester: RIT Press, 2012.

Railton, Peter. "Sentimentalism and Realism in Epistemology and Ethics." In *Ethical Sentimentalism: New Perspectives*, edited by Remy Debes and Karsten R. Stueber, 107–32. Cambridge: Cambridge University Press, 2017.

Raphael, D. D. "Hume and Smith on Justice and Utility." *Proceedings of the Aristotelian Society* 73, no. 1 (1973): 87–104.

Raphael, D. D. *The Impartial Spectator*. Oxford: Oxford University Press, 2007.

Raphael, D. D. "Appendix II: The Passage on Atonement, and a Manuscript Fragment on Justice." In Adam Smith, *The Theory of Moral Sentiments*, edited by A. L. Macfie and Raphael, 383–401. Indianapolis: Liberty Fund, 1982.

Raphael, D.D. *The Impartial Spectator*. Oxford: Oxford University Press, 2007.

Rasmussen, Dennis C. *The Infidel and the Professor: David Hume, Adam Smith, and the Friendship that Shaped Modern Thought*. Princeton: Princeton University Press, 2017.

Rasmussen, Dennis C. *The Problems and Promise of Commercial Society: Adam Smith's Response to Rousseau*. USA: Pennsylvania State University Press, 2008.

Rasmussen, Dennis C. "Adam Smith on What Is Wrong with Economic Inequality." *American Political Science Review* 110, no. 2 (2016): 342–52.

Raynor, David. "Adam Smith and the Virtues." *The Adam Smith Review* 2, edited by Vivienne Brown, 239–45. Oxford: Routledge, 2006.

Reid, Thomas. "A Sketch of Dr Smith's Theory of Morals." In *On Moral Sentiments: Contemporary Responses to Adam Smith*, edited by John Reeder, 69–88. New York: Thoemmes Press, 1997.

Reid, Thomas. "Letter to Lord Kames." In *On Moral Sentiments: Contemporary Responses to Adam Smith*, edited by John Reeder, 65–8. New York: Thoemmes Press, 1997.

Rick, Jon. "Hume's and Smith's Partial Sympathies and Impartial Stances." *The Journal of Scottish Philosophy* 5, no. 2 (2007): 135–58.

Ross, Ian Simpson. *The Life of Adam Smith*. Oxford: Oxford University Press, 1995.

Rothschild, Emma and Amartya Sen. "Adam Smith's Economics." In *The Cambridge Companion to Adam Smith*, edited by Knud Haakonssen, 319–65. Cambridge: Cambridge University Press, 2006.

Russell, Paul. "Smith on Moral Sentiment and Moral Luck." *History of Philosophy Quarterly* 16, no. 1 (1999): 37–58.

Sagar, Paul. "Beyond Sympathy: Smith's Rejection of Hume's Moral Theory." *British Journal for the History of Philosophy* 25, no. 4 (2017): 681–705.

Sayre-McCord, Geoffrey. "Hume and Smith on Sympathy, Approbation, and Moral Judgment." *Social and Political Philosophy* 30 (2013): 208–36.

Sayre-McCord, Geoffrey. "On Why Hume's 'General Point of View' isn't Ideal – and Shouldn't Be." *Social Philosophy & Policy* 11, no. 1 (1994): 202–28.

Sayre-McCord, Geoffrey. "Sentiments and Spectators: Adam Smith's Theory of Moral Judgment." *The Adam Smith Review* 5, edited by Vivienne Brown and Samuel Fleischacker, 124–44. Oxford: Routledge, 2010.

Schabas, Margaret. "Philosophy of the Human Sciences." In *The Routledge Companion to Eighteenth Century Philosophy*, edited by Aaron Garrett, 731–53. New York: Routledge, 2014.

Schliesser, Eric. *Adam Smith: Systematic Philosopher and Public Thinker*. Oxford: Oxford University Press, 2017.

Schmitter, Amy, "Passions, Affections and Sentiments: Taxonomy and Terminology." In *The Oxford Handbook of British Philosophy in the Eighteenth Century*, edited by James Harris, 197–225. Oxford: Oxford University Press, 2013.

Schwarze, Michelle A. and John T. Scott. "Mutual Sympathy and Moral Economy: Adam Smith Reviews Rousseau." *The Journal of Politics* 81, no. 1 (2019): 66–80.
Sen, Amartya. "Open and Closed Impartiality." *Journal of Philosophy* 99, no. 9 (2002): 445–69.
Shaver, Robert. "Virtue, Utility, and Rules." In *The Cambridge Companion to Adam Smith*, edited by Knud Haakonssen, 189–213. Cambridge: Cambridge University Press, 2006.
Siraki, Arby Ted. "Adam Smith's Solution to the Paradox of Tragedy." *The Adam Smith Review* 5, edited by Vivienne Brown and Samuel Fleischacker, 213–30. Oxford: Routledge, 2010.
Siversten, Sveinung S. "Love Redirected: On Adam Smith's Love of Praiseworthiness." *The Journal of Scottish Philosophy* 15, no. 1 (2017): 101–23.
Smith, Adam. *An Inquiry into the Nature and Causes of the Wealth of Nations*, edited by R. H. Campbell, A. S. Skinner, and W. B. Todd. Indianapolis: Liberty Fund, 1981.
Smith, Adam. *Correspondence of Adam Smith*, edited by E. C. Mosssner and I. S. Ross. Indianapolis: Liberty Fund, 1987.
Smith, Adam. "History of Astronomy." In *Essays on Philosophical Subjects*, edited by W. P. D. Wightman, J. C. Bryce, and I. S. Ross, 31–105. Indianapolis: Liberty Fund, 1982.
Smith, Adam. *Lectures on Jurisprudence*, edited by R. L. Meek, D. D. Raphael, and P. G. Stein. Indianapolis: Liberty Fund, 1982.
Smith, Adam. *Lectures on Rhetoric and Belles Lettres*, edited by J. C. Bryce. Indianapolis: Liberty Fund, 1985.
Smith, Adam. "Of the External Senses." In *Essays on Philosophical Subjects*, edited by W. P. D. Wightman, J. C. Bryce, and I. S. Ross, 135–70. Indianapolis: Liberty Fund, 1982.
Smith, Adam. *The Theory of Moral Sentiments*, edited by J. L. Macfie and D. D. Raphael. Indianapolis: Liberty Fund, 1982.
Smith, Craig. "Adam Smith's 'Collateral' Inquiry: Fashion and Morality in *The Theory of Moral Sentiments* and *The Wealth of Nations*." *History of Political Economy* 45, no.3 (2013): 505–22.
Smith, Craig. "Adam Smith: Left or Right?" *Political Studies* 61 (2013): 784–98.
Spaulding, Shannon. "Cognitive Empathy." In *The Routledge Handbook of Philosophy of Empathy*, edited by Heidi L. Maibom, 13–21. New York: Routledge, 2017.
Stewart, Dugald. "Account of the Life and Writings of Adam Smith, LL.D.," edited by I. S. Ross, in *Essays on Philosophical Subjects*, edited by W. P. D. Wightman and J. C. Bryce, 269–351. Indianapolis: Liberty Fund, 1982.
Stueber, Karsten R. "Smithian Constructivism: Elucidating the Reality of the Normative Domain." In *Ethical Sentimentalism: New Perspective*, edited by Remy Debes and Stueber, 192–209. Cambridge: Cambridge University Press, 2017.
Sugden, Robert. "Beyond Sympathy and Empathy: Adam's Smith's Concept of Fellow-Feeling." *Economics and Philosophy* 18 (2002): 63–87.
Taylor, Gabriele. "Justifying the Emotions." *Mind* 84, no. 335 (1975): 390–402.
Taylor, Jacqueline. "Adam Smith and Feminist Ethics: Sympathy, Resentment, and Solidarity." In *Adam Smith: His Life, Thought, and Legacy*, edited by Ryan Patrick Hanley, 354–70. Princeton: Princeton University Press, 2016.
Taylor, Jacqueline. *Reflecting Subjects: Passion, Sympathy, and Society in Hume's Philosophy*. Oxford: Oxford University Press, 2015.

Tegos, Spiros. "Adam Smith: Theorist of Corruption." In *The Oxford Handbook of Adam Smith*, edited by Christopher J. Berry, Maria Pia Paganelli, and Craig Smith, 353–71. Oxford: Oxford University Press, 2013.

Vitz, Rico. "Sympathy and Benevolence in Hume's Moral Psychology." *Journal of the History of Philosophy* 42 (2004): 261–75.

Vivenza, Gloria. *Adam Smith and the Classics: The Classical Heritage in Adam Smith's Thought*. Oxford: Oxford University Press, 2001.

Waszek, Norbert. "Two Concepts of Morality: A Distinction of Adam Smith's Ethics and Its Stoic Origin." *Journal of the History of Ideas* 45, no. 4 (1994): 591–606.

Weinstein, Jack Russell. *Adam Smith's Pluralism: Rationality, Education, and the Moral Sentiments*. New Haven: Yale University Press, 2013.

Welchman, Jennifer. "Self-Love and Personal Identity." *Hume Studies* 41 (2015): 33–55.

Winkler, Kenneth. "Hutcheson's Alleged Realism." *Journal of the History of Philosophy* 23, no. 2 (1985): 179–94.

Wolf, Lukas. "The Analogy of Nature." Groningen Centre for Medieval and Early Modern Thought Blog, post written 5/18/18, accessed 6/18/19. <https://www.rug.nl/filosofie/organization/departments/history/gcmemt/blog/the-analogy-of-nature>

Wolterstorff, Nicholas. In *Adam Smith: His Life, Thought, and Legacy*, edited by Ryan Patrick Hanley, 173–91. Princeton: Princeton University Press, 2016.

Index

www.ingramcontent.com/pod-product-compliance
Ingram Content Group UK Ltd.
Pitfield, Milton Keynes, MK11 3LW, UK
UKHW020906190926
475560UK00010B/301

9 781350 088573